CONRAD
IN THE
TWENTY-FIRST
CENTURY

CONRAD
IN THE
TWENTY-FIRST CENTURY

Contemporary Approaches and Perspectives

EDITED BY

**Carola M. Kaplan, Peter Mallios,
and Andrea White**

ROUTLEDGE
New York • London

Published in 2005 by
Routledge
270 Madison Avenue
New York, NY 10016
www.routledge-ny.com

Published in Great Britain by
Routledge
2 Park Square
Milton Park, Abingdon
Oxon OX1 4RN, U.K.
www.routledge.co.uk

Library of Congress Cataloging-in-Publication Data

Conrad in the twenty-first century : contemporary approaches and perspectives / edited by Carola M. Kaplan, Peter Lancelot Mallios, and Andrea White.
     p. cm.
Includes bibliographical references and index.
ISBN 0-415-97164-0 (hardcover : alk. paper) — ISBN 0-415-97165-9 (pbk. : alk. paper)
1. Conrad, Joseph, 1857-1924—Criticism and interpretation. I. Kaplan, Carola M., 1942-
II. Mallios, Peter Lancelot. III. White, Andrea, 1942-
PR6005.O4Z581154 2004
823'.912—dc22   2004015991

In Memory of Edward W. Said
(1935–2003)

Contents

Abbreviations

Citations to Conrad's writings are to *Dent's Collected Edition of the Works of Joseph Conrad*. London: Dent, 1946–55. Where the introduction or annotation of a Conrad novel in a different edition is cited in an essay, that edition appears separately in the Bibliography at the end of this volume. Where a work by Conrad is not included in the Dent edition, it is listed in the Bibliography under both Conrad's and the editor's names.

AF	*Almayer's Folly*
AG	*The Arrow of Gold*
Ch	*Chance*
In	*The Inheritors*
LE	*Last Essays*
LJ	*Lord Jim*
MS	*The Mirror of the Sea*
NLL	*Notes on Life and Letters*
NN	*The Nigger of the "Narcissus"*
No	*Nostromo*
OI	*An Outcast of the Islands*
PR	*A Personal Record*
Re	*The Rescue*
Ro	*The Rover*
SA	*The Secret Agent*
SL	*The Shadow-Line*
SS	*A Set of Six*
Su	*Suspense*
TH	*Tales of Hearsay*
TLS	*'Twixt Land and Sea*
TOT	*Typhoon and Other Tales*
TU	*Tales of Unrest*
UWE	*Under Western Eyes*
Vi	*Victory*
WT	*Within the Tides*
YOS	*Youth, a Narrative; and Two Other Stories*
Letters	*The Collected Letters of Joseph Conrad*. Eds. Frederick R. Karl and Laurence Davies. Cambridge: Cambridge University Press, 1983.

Acknowledgments

It is impossible, given the dimensions of this volume, for us to acknowledge all of the people whose presence, input, and support have contributed vitally—professionally and personally—to its making. It would be remiss of us, however, not to acknowledge a crucial debt to the remarkable scholarly communities of the Joseph Conrad Societies of the United Kingdom, Poland, France, and North America. We further deeply appreciate the efforts of certain individuals who have come through for this volume in important ways: Andrezj Busza, Sandra Fayh, Michael Israel, Sangeeta Ray, Brian Richardson, Donald Rude, Allan Simmons, Jennifer Olds, and especially John Auchard. Bill Germano, Matt Byrnie, and everyone we've dealt with at Routledge have provided valuable advice and gracious support. Finally, there are special personal debts we wish to acknowledge as well: to Bruce, Jonathan, Daniel, and Sophia Kaplan and Heidi Taylor; to Seth, Ronna, and William Mallios, Shoham Ray, and Elizabeth Dahl; and to Naomi, Molly, and Bernard White, go our appreciation and gratitude.

Introduction

CAROLA KAPLAN, PETER LANCELOT
MALLIOS, ANDREA WHITE

I.

Why read Conrad now? The question asks and answers itself almost too easily. In any given moment, one will be interested in "contemporary" implications; and in our moment—the moment of the incipient twenty-first century— Conrad's implications are so extensive and plural, so urgent and uncanny, that reading his works has already become a principal strategy of attempting to discern the terms of contemporary existence. It is not a matter of what we should do; it is a matter of what we are already doing as we do everything else.

Since at least 1902, when *Lord Jim* (1900) was adopted for the newly conceived "Modern Novels" class at Yale, Conrad has been recognized as current, with something crucial to tell contemporaries about themselves and the world they live in. In 1923, Conrad appeared on the cover of *Time* magazine; in 1963, the back dust jacket of an influential academic text, not on Conrad, read, "There is a new Conradism in the air,"[1] and at the 1970 Modern Language Association meeting, the first president of the newly formed Joseph Conrad Society of America convened the first annual panel of the society, entitled "Conrad, Our Contemporary."

But since the beginning of the twenty-first century, things have taken a peculiarly Conradian turn. In the summer of 2001, in an essay centennially reassessing *Lord Jim*, Geoffrey Galt Harpham described *Lord Jim* as a book that, though "of the nineteenth century in so many respects, seems to have skipped over the twentieth century ... to assume, perhaps, its true status and significance as a twenty-first century text, one of our own" ("Conrad's Global Homeland" 31). This was an intrepid comment with respect to the twentieth century, and a positively prescient one with respect to Conrad's place in the twenty-first. For, since that summer, witness to such curious developments as the rerelease in theaters of Francis Ford Coppola's *Apocalypse Now!* (based on *Heart of Darkness*) and the worldwide tour of a French expressionist ballet featuring "Conrad" and "Marcel Duchamp" as dueling principals,[2] the new century, young as it is, has begun to define itself through a series of key terms and events that have pointed squarely and repeatedly to Conrad, resurrecting him as something of the key modernist figure of our time.

The examples of Conrad's prevailing importance are many: the attacks of September 11, 2001, which commentators were quick to link to the images of "terrorists" and the plot to bomb the Greenwich Observatory in Conrad's *The Secret Agent* (1907); the recent U.S. war with Iraq, whose terms, trajectory, and participants, as Anthony Fothergill and Robert Hampson point out in this volume, are chillingly scripted in *Nostromo* (1904); renewed violence in the Middle East and across the world, which Daphna Erdinast-Vulcan and Edward Said in very different ways illuminate below through *Heart of Darkness* (1899); the recent resurgence of powerfully politicized deployments of mass media, which Mark Wollaeger and others identify as a crucial concern in Conrad's writings from beginning to end; and today's vexed questions of a new world order, which, as William Bonney explains, put us right back in the quandaries of "suspense" the post-World War I period held for Conrad in his final novel. Also during the past three years: V.S. Naipaul, the controversial Trinidad-born postcolonial novelist who won the Nobel Prize in literature in 2001, was introduced by the Swedish Committee as "the heir to Joseph Conrad" (qtd. in "Academy Praises," D3); South African novelist Nadine Gordimer, another Nobel laureate, wrote an introduction to Conrad's first novel, *Almayer's Folly* (1895), observing "the astonishing relevance [Conrad's] themes have to our recent past and present international preoccupations" (x); British photojournalist Marcus Bleasdale published a book—*One Hundred Years of Darkness: A Photographic Journey to the Heart of the Congo*—exposing political abuses in the Congo today by juxtaposing his own pictures with resonant passages from *Heart of Darkness*; internationally acclaimed performance artist Ping Chong began production of the multidisciplinary theater work *Blind Ness*, which explores colonialism's legacy in Africa through the inspiration of *Heart of Darkness*; American film director Martin Scorsese began to solicit funds for a film version of *Nostromo*; and distinguished Conrad scholar Zdzislaw Najder, former director of Radio Free Europe's Polish language service, delivered an address in Vancouver identifying Conrad as the first modern writer to write from beyond "provincial national egotism."

In these and other respects, the themes of global contact, dislocation, homelessness, cultural clash, lost causes, irreconcilable antagonisms, and personal and political failures of vision and compassion so central to Conrad's work have become the titles of our headlines and the stuff of our dreams and nightmares. That they are concerns of a widening number of readers and scholars is also clear from the increasingly international roster of scholars writing and speaking about Conrad's works, from a multiplicity of viewpoints and backgrounds. The recent emphasis on extrinsic theoretical approaches to literary texts has further opened up Conrad studies to a continuing relevance. The early scrutiny of the aesthetic and formal features of Conrad's fiction that claimed him as an early exemplar of British modernism could not account for certain insistent, strange qualities and concerns in the writing. Understanding the importance of restoring contexts of various sorts to literary productions has allowed these concerns to surface, so that themes of reading and misreading, of cultural encounters and misunderstandings, of the resultant dark eruptions of the irrational in the face of the unknown now are seen to be bound up with the modernist experimentalism of Conrad's work.

These contexts—in particular, the context of the imperial West and its intricate and far-reaching relationship to the colonial world, with attention to the effects of colonialism on both colonized and colonizer—have drawn the interest of new scholars from formerly colonized and silenced groups whose readings of Conrad's texts illuminate them anew. In addition, investigations of the complicated relation between Conrad and his world, as a sailor and an immigrant in twentieth-century England, have enriched our understanding of his works. Such readings have opened up these texts in ways that invite the participation of many readers who had previously not found themselves in his texts at all, and that have made visible the questions that are still ours today: How does culture define us? What role does language play in shaping our desires and beliefs about ourselves as gendered subjects? How do we live in a world without guides? How do we understand subjectivities that are alien to us? And what are the consequences of not doing so? Thus, students in and beyond our ethnically diverse urban classrooms and political subjects seeking to understand our ethnically diverse world today are more sensitive to the doubt and questioning behind Marlow's mantra that Jim is "one of us," more likely to hear the irony behind "and this also has been a place of darkness," more sensitive to the themes of loneliness and alienation, more attentive to the unsettled world of the political exile in the twentieth and twenty-first centuries.

Why read Conrad now? Because works like *Heart of Darkness* make so much writing that followed in its wake intelligible by providing the necessary context for many twentieth- and twenty-first-century African, Indian, South and North American, Australian, and Caribbean novels. Indeed, such novels as *Things Fall Apart, Season of Migration to the North, The God of Small Things, Praisesong for the Widow, The Snake Tree*—many of which are referenced in the essays that follow—might all have been written in one form or another but, without *Heart of Darkness*, they would be very different books.

II.

As this volume attests, the foregoing is merely the briefest indication of the contemporary interest, academic and otherwise, in Conrad's writings. But to say that Conrad holds great and plural interest in the contemporary moment—to say, indeed, that Conrad has become something of a fetish, celebrity, discourse, and industry *of* the contemporary moment—is not really to address the question of what conceptually is being undertaken in the effort to imagine Conrad *as contemporary*—an important issue because it is the coordinating project of this volume, and the implicit gamble waged by each of its essayists, despite their great differences of approach and perspective.

For one can be of interest in, "relevant" to, a certain historical moment without being a contemporary of that moment, just as being contemporary involves a complex and even contradictory polysemy whose multiple meanings the simple condition of timeliness alone cannot accommodate. "Contemporary," indeed, is a conflicted conceptual gesture whose twin tensions with respect to the gathering of time (*con-* together, *tempor-* time) it performs cast light on the spirit of this volume. Etymologically, the term's baseline and prior strand of definitions turn on the idea of *simultaneity*, as in the first definition presented in the *OED*: "Belonging to the same time, age, period; living, existing, or occurring together in time." Here, one is contemporary, or "a contemporary," not because one simply occupies the same context or "period" as someone or something else, but because of an active pedagogical operation that produces the historical "period" from two or more temporally or contextually distinct data points. "Contemporary" is in this sense, then, despite its own ostensible presentist biases, actually a profoundly retrospective gesture. Like Walter Benjamin's backward-facing angel (*Illuminations* 257)—like, in fact, most of the essays in *Illuminations*—it reaches outward and backward from the present into an irretrievably fading history: to ask where the present begins, when and why the past ceased, how history's implications travel (or do not), and who counts and how one counts (or does not) as "one of us." This is part of the game we play when we ask, and have been asking, how and why Conrad is "our contemporary."

But there is another strong subcurrent of the term—dating, according to *OED* 2, from 1866 (A.4.n), and sufficiently new that it is not mentioned at all in *OED 1*—that turns, in the spirit of *The Secret Agent*'s Professor, on the happy and willing obliteration of history altogether. Here, contemporary means: "Modern; ... esp. up-to-date, ultra-modern; spec. designating art of markedly avant-garde quality ... having modern characteristics" (A.4). This definition is offered in explicit opposition to the word "period," as in the historically circumscribed "period piece," and, indeed, what has happened etymologically is that "contemporary" has come to refer so exclusively to the specific openended moment of the present that it refuses to acknowledge implication by any historical period or periodizing logic at all. Indeed, here the referent is a heightened newness so absolute that it exists to the exclusion of not only history and historically calibrated time, but also to any element of the *present* implicated by either category. So, one finds Wyndham Lewis deriding "the contemporary" as "a cultural élite ... [which] has nothing to do with time, nor with age" (*Demon* 3.8.67): i.e., a fashionable pose of being maximally "up with the times," predicated on the elitist erasure of the significance of all others existing in the same moment in time, on the grounds of those others being too claimed by time. Likewise, "contemporary" in this sense—apropos of its oncepopular historical variant, "co–temporary"—generally implies the specter of the ephemeral and disposable: i.e., that the object in question has not only yet to be classified by time, but may not survive its test. Here, there is always a heightened allegiance to treating the present as part of a future that is reserved as a radically, even terrifyingly, open-ended space: as when Derrida writes that "the future ... breaks absolutely with constituted normality and can only be proclaimed, presented, as a sort of monstrosity" (qtd. in Pease 1); or when Donald Pease reports of graffiti reading: "There is no future and we are in it" (11). In the "monstrosity" of the former and the emptiness of the latter lies the terrifying and insistent anti-temporality of this kind of "contemporary"; not nostalgic in the slightest, and insisting on the absolute annihilation of one's pedagogical investments in time to move forward to a different and performatively enacted space of time.[3]

In the spirit of Adorno's phrase, "The whole is the false," this volume does not try to erase but rather to make consistent productive use of the tensions between these two irreconcilable dimensions of the "contemporary." Substantively, what connects this volume as a whole is that we explicitly asked each of the contributors to frame their discussions of Conrad—which cover very nearly the comprehensive course of his writings, and with an astonishingly diverse array of perspectives, methodologies, emphases—in relation to the question: Why read Conrad now? But at a greater conceptual remove, what organizes this volume as a *project*, its pieces situated in dialogic relation, is its self-conscious spirit of temptation and reservation, assertion and qualification, necessity and defiance, when it comes to mapping the present and future in terms of history. Put another way, this volume seizes on the rich and polymath occasion of Conrad's interest in our own moment, in light of the many possibilities of historical proximity his work presents, so as to generate narratives of contiguity and relation whose ultimate investments lie in the intellectual, institutional, pedagogical, political, and social challenges of the twenty-first-century future—which, precisely because their course is uncertain, requires a certain fundamental skepticism, implies a certain fundamental provisionality, with respect to any narrative generated. However provisionally, though, this volume's essayists use the present to explore and elaborate narratives of relation to the past in the interests of a better world in the future—all through the prism of Conrad, because of the rare, rich, and plural opportunities his work affords.

Admittedly, these are tall aspirations for a mere volume of essays on Conrad. But if it is a rare occasion to find so many prominent scholars, backed by the support and scholarship of so many exceptional others, gathered together in conversation within one volume, it will also be clear to anyone familiar with the work of Edward W. Said—who died during the production of this book, but was a galvanizing force during the writing of every essay in it—that engaging with Conrad lies at the core of a body of work that has, without exaggeration, changed the course of the world and many lives within it. Conrad is the subject of Said's first book, *Joseph Conrad and the Fiction of Autobiography* (1966); a prominent element in Said's next two major literary-critical works, *Beginnings* (1974) and *The World, the Text, and the Critic* (1982); and a crucial and oft-referenced conceptual underpinning of his numerous books on Orientalism, Palestine, and the Middle East. Further, in the work leading up to and including *Culture and Imperialism* (1994), Said changed the landscape of British and anglophone literary studies by moving Conrad and the issues of imperialism foregrounded in his writings to its center, reversing the metropolitan biases and blindness of the Western canon as previously constructed, and opening the door to global and postcolonial articulations of literary and cultural history. In this sense alone, Said's work, like the work of J. Hillis Miller in a different critical context, perfectly emblematizes this volume's contemporary spirit for, with respect to Conrad, what Said consistently does is measure the present's implication by the past in a way that offers up contingent, contrapuntal, and secular narratives whose ultimate "worldly" referents are unequivocally those of the shaping needs (of justice, of understanding, of resistance) of the future.

But there is another sense—a bit more quiet, even ostensibly disavowed—in which Said's work may be said to represent not simply the general "contemporary" spirit of this volume but the actual substance of the twenty-first-century Conrad it perceives. Here we must brush Said a bit against the grain. Although across his work Said champions Conrad for recognizing culture's role in facilitating the projects of empire (*Culture* 11; *Palestine* 77; *Reflections* 280); and although he also appreciates Conrad's keen sensitivity to the rhetoric, systematicity, contingency, and disavowed externalities of imperialist ideology (*Culture* 28–30; *World* 90–110; *Reflections* 280–81), Said is nevertheless almost always severely firm in his view that Conrad is ultimately unable to see beyond the limits of the imperial structures he deconstructs: unable to perceive as autonomous, discerning, and independent-minded human agents the various natives whose victimization his novels nonetheless indict. Even the most charitable reading of *Heart of Darkness*, hence, must acknowledge "Conrad's tragic limitation" in being unable to recognize that "a non-European 'darkness' was in fact a non-European world *resisting* imperialism so as to one day regain sovereignty and independence" (*Culture* 30); likewise, even the reader who stands in awe of *Nostromo* must concede its patronizing and debilitating "inability to imagine that Costaguana could ever have had a meaningful existence of its own" (*Reflections* 278). Conrad, it would seem, despite a comprehensive grasp of the artful dodges of imperial European psychology and ideology, is completely incapable of granting cognitive independence to, opening up channels of empathy with, and enabling the voices of Others.

Yet this is the very same Conrad Said describes in his first book, which has been linked to Said's own autobiographies (Said, *Reader* 421), as someone whose "individuality resides in a continuous exposure of his sense of himself to what is not himself" (*Fiction* 9). This is the same Conrad, indeed, whose "extraordinarily persistent sense of his own exilic marginality" and whose "provisionality that came from standing at the juncture of one world with respect to another" (*Culture* 24) seems to license not only Said's ability to articulate the world in essentially alteritous and counterpointed terms, but to articulate his own alterity as well. The first Conrad is an essentially, though by no means exclusively, *twentieth*-century Conrad. This view of Conrad recognizes his writings as an unusually interesting and fecund political *object* whose ideological stance and merits—in certain respects complicit and reactionary, in others idiosyncratic and subversive, invariably "ambiguous" and "ambivalent"—are the subject of debate. The second Conrad is an essentially *twenty-first*-century Conrad. This perspective understands Conrad as an unusually receptive and interesting political *subject*, whose vitality—*to be debated*—lies in the degree to which his texts have listened to, registered, and become an enabling voice of alterity itself, facilitating plural and useful articulations of literary and cultural history for an as yet open-ended and abysmally commenced century. The movement of Conrad from the object to the subject position, in which the subject is indigenous to the margins; the use of Conrad to conduct Hélène Cixous's famous thought experiment, *J'est l'autre*; the recovery, mapping, and invention of Conrad as a woman's writer, a lesbian writer, an African, Indian, Indonesian, Jewish, Palestinian, Native American, and U.S. writer, a hybrid writer (culturally or narratively), a "terrorist" writer, a working-class writer, an AIDS or a disabled writer, an older writer, an immigrant writer, a popular writer, a writer written out of the power structure or beyond revolution by media and politics—this is the secret Conrad of the twenty-first century that interpenetrates all the essays in this volume. This book notices the crucial elision of subject in the framing question "Why read Conrad now?"—and uses it strategically to conceive the future.

III.

As befits its concerns with the multi-inflected temporality of the "contemporary," this volume is book-ended by two of the most influential voices in Conrad criticism in particular and of literary criticism in general: J. Hillis Miller, whose challenging foreword builds on his transformatively original body of work on Conrad; and Edward W. Said, whose extensive interview, reflecting back on a lifelong engagement with Conrad, closes the volume. The body of the volume is divided into four sections that work to identify, organize, and narrate the principal dimensions of Conrad's contemporary interest. As the order of these essays suggests, the story of Conrad's intensifying and compounding claims on our attention emanates in widening concentric circles from *Heart of Darkness*, a Conrad text of unusual millennial and apocalyptic authority, to multiple other Conrad works that speak urgently to current and future global issues, literary concerns, and questions of human subjectivity.

The volume devotes the entire first section, "Millennial Conrad," to *Heart of Darkness*, because it was clear from the number and quality of proposals submitted to this volume that this novella is still the single Conrad work that carries the most pressing and varied interest today. The section begins with Geoffrey Galt Harpham's essay meditating on *identification* as a crucial animating concept not only in *Heart of Darkness* but in Conrad's unusually vital prose generally from 1897–1901. Blending considerations of social identity and aestheticized language, Harpham traces this fiction's ability to solicit intense identifications from a wide range of readers to an aesthetic of mastery predicated on Conrad's embattled and externalized sense of how identity happens. Benita Parry follows with an essay considering and theorizing the conditions of possibility of African and postcolonial rewritings of *Heart of Darkness*, arguing that the text's own self-conscious gaps have served as a sympathetic invitation to later African and postcolonial voices to rewrite it. Daphna Erdinast-Vulcan's essay offers a psycho-textual reading exploring the isomorphic relationship between Marlow and Conrad in the unconscious of the text, to reveal its desire for the father and the frightening consequences of that desire. Finally, Mark Wollaeger discusses *Heart of Darkness* in the context of recent wars in Iraq and Afghanistan, using Conrad's under-discussed essay " The Unlighted Coast" to read the novella retrospectively through the lens of Conrad's complex and ambivalent engagement with the eroding boundaries between information and propaganda, between truth and lies, that has been a concern since the early twentieth century.

The second section, "Global Conrad," presents essays that fall into two categories: one, the transmission and contemplation of Conrad beyond traditional Anglo-European boundaries; and two, the significance of Conrad's writings for political issues of global dimension. Padmini Mongia and Christopher GoGwilt begin with essays considering Conrad's work in relation to novels by contemporary Indian and Indonesian authors, respectively. Focusing on Arundhati Roy's *The God of Small Things* and Amitav Ghosh's *The Shadow Lines*, Mongia explores the fluid trope of male homosocial desire that these texts evoke from Conrad; she argues that Indian fiction ultimately offers the opportunity to transcend models of "influence" and "writing back" to Conrad that presuppose his priority, in favor of intertextual strategies that "provincialize" Conrad and the Western traditions his work has often instrumentalized. Advancing the trope of opera appreciation as a revealing connective between Conrad's Malay trilogy and the "Buru" quartet of novels by Pramoedya Ananta Toer, GoGwilt offers a new paradigm of comparative global literary study by pursuing opera as an "abysmal" trigger of both questions of aesthetic taste and crises of infinite regress with respect to the totalizing capacities of any one cultural perspective. Moving matters from cultural geography to political cartography, Robert Hampson considers the curiously composite nature of "place" in *Victory, Lord Jim*, and *Nostromo*, demonstrating that Conrad's settings are frequently collages of many different places and maps, and arguing that this "heterotopic" strategy is predicated on exposing force relations in the world and undermining monolithic attempts to map the world in the image of the capitalized West. In the volume's perhaps most "contemporary" essay, Anthony Fothergill examines issues of globalized commodity capitalism and "anarchist" violence in *Nostromo* and *A Set of Six*, with an emphasis on Conrad's consistently subtle and complex analysis of symbioses between state power and its subversive "terrorist" Other. Peter Mallios closes the section with a discussion of the text most frequently cited in the media today, *The Secret Agent,* and argues that the British press itself, in its historic politicality, its service as an instrument of social control, its various political aesthetics, and its powers of simulation, is the true secret agency of the novel.

The third section, "Conrad and Textuality," moves the question of Conrad's contemporaneity from the world to the provinces of textuality and literature proper, and presents a series of essays exploring how Conrad's literary innovations in his own day set the stage for rethinking conventional literary and textual paradigms in our own. While these essays continue the interest of the earlier sections in the possibilities and effects of political action, they focus on Conrad's textual innovations in grappling with these issues. William Bonney's "Suspended" resurrects Conrad's all but undiscussed final novel, *Suspense,* for the twenty-first century, arguing that suspense has meaning as an aesthetic strategy of deferring through existential evasion meaningful political resistance to social authority, and contending that this is in fact a central issue in much of Conrad's work. Susan Jones returns to Conrad's sea fiction with an analysis of *Typhoon* that sees postmodern and feminist implications in the novella's material circumstances of production and reception. Brian Richardson investigates the relationship between class representation in *The Nigger of the Narcissus* and the text's strikingly innovative technique of "We" narration in relation to postmodern and postcolonial narrative practices. Finally, Laurence Davies challenges, complicates, and illuminates Conrad's most central textual strategy—that of irony—investigating its power as a corrective to today's mass-mediated discourses that homogenize the complexity of twenty-first-century issues.

The fourth section, "Conrad and Subjectivity," turns the discussion of Conrad's current relevance from the political and textual to the personal, while suggesting throughout how his global and aesthetic concerns are mirrored in his examination of the human subject. This group of essays demonstrates, from various perspectives, how Conrad's complex construction of subjectivity enlisted but also transcended contemporary thinking and, in so doing, largely specified the terms in which we struggle today with this still vexatious topic. Andrea White's essay enlists recent understandings of the constructedness of identity to revisit Conrad's "autobiographical" writings, arguing that his early memoir, *The Mirror of the Sea,* contributed to the particularly English discourse of the sea while narrating a subjectivity in turn shaped and interpellated by that same discursive tradition. Jennifer Fraser's essay examines two interlocking texts, *Under Western Eyes* and "The Secret Sharer," to advance a fresh consideration, informed by a Derridean understanding of loss and mourning, of the role of unrealized grief in the Conrad canon. Finally, Carola Kaplan argues for a more complex reading of sexuality and gender in Conrad's work than has heretofore been proposed. Kaplan argues that Conrad's later works, particularly

Foreword

J. HILLIS MILLER

This book contains a dazzling series of essays about Joseph Conrad. I have read them with immense interest. They have changed my understanding of Conrad in manifold ways. They have made me see. They have also sent me back to Conrad's books with an eager desire to re-read for myself, with fresh eyes, some works I have not read for a long time, for example, *Victory* and "Typhoon." It is an honor to be allowed to have a word here at the beginning. A foreword is preliminary in the etymological sense of coming before the threshold. A foreword is a word that comes before the real words. It prepares the reader for them. It opens the door to hearing them, as from an anteroom outside the room where the concert is going on. I will try to obey the laws of this genre.

The essays in *Conrad in the Twenty-First Century* appear, at least at first, to be extremely diverse. They discuss in one way or another most of Conrad's major works, both novels and stories. Little is said about *Chance*, for some reason, nor about *The Arrow of Gold*, for which I have a soft spot, perhaps because I came to it so late. It was *Chance* that Henry James praised for manifesting what he saw as Conrad's chief characteristic and mode of excellence. Conrad, said James, was "a votary of the way to do a thing that shall make it undergo the most doing" (James 147). *Chance* exemplifies this in Marlow's "prolonged hovering flight of the subjective over the outstretched ground of the case exposed" (James 149). The critical methodologies employed in the essays in this book are quite diverse, though James's critical vocabulary is more or less foreign to them. Most of the viable present-day modes of criticism are represented here: cultural studies, postcolonial studies, feminist criticism, Freudian and Lacanian criticism, even rhetorical and deconstructive criticism. One use for this book: It is an admirable introduction to these various approaches, not through abstract description, but as examples of reading methods put concretely to work.

In spite of this diversity, however, something like an unstated consensus is present throughout, with a few exceptions. All are singing somewhat the same tune, or variations on it. All agree that the goal of literary study still today is to account for literary works, to explain them, to rationalize them, to justify them, to incorporate them within the discourse of the academic interpretative

1

community. This means, as always, that within that community certain things can be said and certain others are tacitly forbidden. To account for literary works is our task, I agree. It may, however, be a task that is to some degree impossible to accomplish. Insofar as a literary work is irreducibly idiosyncratic, singular, "wholly other," what Gerard Manley Hopkins called, in "Pied Beauty," "counter, original, spare, strange" (Hopkins 70), it may be impossible to account for it. It may be unaccountable.

Though most of Conrad's works are discussed in *Conrad in the Twenty-First Century*, an implicit assumption is that *Heart of Darkness* has special salience and needs most explaining. Most of the essays agree that placing Conrad's fictions within some external cultural, historical, biographical, or intellectual context is the best way to do this. The almost unanimous assumption is that extrinsic criticism is the way to go these days. Little use is made of what used to be called "intrinsic criticism," or "close reading," or "formalist" reading. There is little detailed attention to narrative technique, such as one finds in Jakob Lothe's *Conrad's Narrative Method*. An exception is Laurence Davies' fine essay on irony in Conrad, along with comments or analyses here and there among the other essays. Contexts invoked include the actual history of American and European imperialism in South America for *Nostromo*; the history of anarchism for *The Secret Agent*; the history of opera and of mechanical reproductions of operatic music for present-day postcolonial novels in Indonesia; the development of postcolonial African fiction, as influenced by Conrad, especially by *Heart of Darkness*; popular fiction of Conrad's time and the illustrations for Conrad's *Typhoon* as background for reading that story; the tradition of mapmaking as a feature of Western imperialism's world conquest, in a discussion of the "heterotopias" of *Lord Jim* and *Nostromo*.

Another important kind of context used in these essays is some previous body of critical theory, for example, feminist theory in the several feminist essays here, or Derrida's work on mourning in Jennifer Fraser's essay on *Under Western Eyes*. Her essay interweaves citations from Derrida's Freudian-inspired ideas about mourning with citations from Conrad, employing Derrida's work as context for interpreting Conrad's novel.

One final context is all the previous scholarship on Conrad. One essay mentions that around a hundred essays a year on Conrad get listed in the MLA Bibliography. Thinking about that boggles the mind. You could spend the rest of your life just reading secondary literature on Conrad. Most of the new essays here are by authors who have already written brilliantly and authoritatively about Conrad. In their new essays they place themselves explicitly in the context of previous work on Conrad. One oddness I noticed, however, is that different essays tend to mention different previous essays and books on Conrad. Many essays or books are cited only once, in a single one of the new essays gathered here. Each author takes what he or she needs or happens to know from previous scholarship. The essayists do not often mention one another's work.

A canon of books and essays on Conrad that everyone needs to know and to refer to does not seem to exist. Two exceptions to this are Fredric Jameson's treatment of Conrad in *The Political Unconscious* and Edward Said's discussions of Conrad in *Beginnings* and, especially, in *Culture and Imperialism*. These seem to have achieved canonical status, since so many of the essays collected here refer to them.

Readers of this book will find the climactic interview of Edward Said by Peter Mallios of special interest and distinction. Now that Said, alas, has departed from us, this will be his last word on Conrad, unless he left some unpublished essay. The interview is full of wonderful insights into Conrad's work. It also contains a moving account of Said's relation to Conrad's work over the years, as well as a scrupulous and somewhat equivocal statement of where he disagrees with Conrad:

> Oh, I have a great contempt for such policy-intellectuals. I learned that all from Conrad. That if you get involved in the machine, as he calls it in a famous letter, or, say, in something like the mine in Costaguana, there's no escape. What you must try to do is to maintain division [I suppose he means some distance, some detachment]: of corruption, of power, leading to all sorts of dark places, and from becoming part of it oneself. And also to be able to do what Conrad did aesthetically, which is to stand outside and to say: Well, yes, those things are happening. But there are always alternatives. But the big difference between Conrad and me in the end—and this is true of *Nostromo* as well as *Heart of Darkness*—is that politically for Conrad there are no real alternatives. And I disagree with that: there's always an alternative.

For both Conrad and Said there are alternatives. These can be seen by standing outside, in a detachment that, Said says, takes aesthetic distance as one of its forms, though, he implies, only one of its forms. The difference between Conrad and Said, in Said's understanding, is that Conrad does not see any purely *political* alternative to the series of cruel and futile revolutions in *Nostromo*'s Costaguana that only make submission to American imperialism more inevitable. Said, on the contrary, always believes in the possibility of a political alternative; for example, in the possibility of a political resolution to the Palestinian–Israeli conflict. Perhaps my own most important contribution to Conrad scholarship, if I may mention in passing, is to have been, many years ago now, a reader of Said's first book, the one on Conrad's short fiction, for the Harvard University Press. I recommended enthusiastically that Harvard publish it.

All the contributors to this book have accepted as their charge providing a response to the questions: "Why read Conrad now? What good is Conrad in the twenty-first century, in a time of globalization, in a time of United States' worldwide economic and military imperialism, in a time when new media are fast displacing printed literature as a primary influence on the way people think, believe, and behave?" It does not go without saying that it is a good thing nowadays to read Conrad, to teach his works, or to write about them. If

Conrad really is a "bloody racist," or an unequivocal admirer of imperialism, or a sexist fearful and disdainful of women, then one might argue plausibly that his works should be dropped from the curriculum. Each generation of readers, teachers, and critics must decide about that anew. This book takes passing judgment on Conrad now as its task. Most of the authors of these essays believe that it is their responsibility to reinterpret Conrad as part of global literature in English, not just as a canonical British writer. This is part of an important present-day shift away from British literature to world literature in English, or indeed to world literature in all languages, as the proper field for literary study. One concomitant of this is the way the essays in this book, like Said's interview, are thoroughly politicized. Sharing in Conrad's aesthetic or ironic distance, for example, is seen as valuable only if it can be imagined to lead somehow to political alternatives that might make ours a better world. It is hard not to sympathize with this earnest idealism.

This is related to another feature of these essays. Much previous scholarship on Conrad has condemned Conrad for being a racist, as in Achebe's famous "Conrad was a bloody racist" (Achebe 124); or has seen Conrad as a spokesperson for imperialism; or as a political conservative who views the class struggle with disdain; or as a nasty, paralyzed, skeptical ironist; or as an unconstructive pessimist, as in that famous letter to Cunninghame Graham describing the universe as a self-generated, self-generating machine ("It knits us in and it knits us out. It has knitted time, space, pain, death, corruption, despair, and all the illusions—and nothing matters" [Conrad, *Graham* 57]); or as a sexist, as in Marlow's remark in *Heart of Darkness* that women are out of it, or in the stereotyped personification in the same novel of the jungle as a feminine unknown that must be penetrated and dominated. The authors of the essays in this book take as their responsibility either (occasionally) to echo that condemnation or (more often) to recuperate Conrad by demonstrating that these readings of Conrad are wrong or at any rate need to be made much more complicated. *Heart of Darkness* is the focus of so many of these essays partly because it is so often read, or taught, or written about, partly because it is a crucial text in which to come to terms with these charges against Conrad. The powerful feminist essays here, for example, attempt to show that Conrad's attitude toward women was complex. A number of his female characters, Carola Kaplan's essay persuasively demonstrates, particularly in later works like *Under Western Eyes*, *Victory*, and *Nostromo*, are sympathetically presented and also presented as wiser than the men in those novels. Laurence Davies' essay on Conrad's irony ends by defending it through saying that "to be willing to hold more than one set of ideas in one's mind at the same time, and, better still, stay critically alert to all of them is not so much decadent or paralyzing (as single-minded folk would have us think) as fortifying." Quite a number of the essays confront the issue of Conrad's racism head on and more or less successfully defend Conrad from Achebe's angry charge.

The reader will want to read all these essays for himself or herself to see what I mean by saying that they are "dazzling," and to see whether my characterization of their approximate consensus is accurate. Perhaps I may now be permitted to say a word about my own reading of Conrad, as it has been renewed, reshaped, and challenged by reading *Conrad in the Twenty-First Century*. To do that, I must make several unfashionable observations or "Unzeitgemässene Betractungen," as Friedrich Nietzsche calls his essays in the title of an early book. "Untimely Meditations" would be a better translation. Nietzsche meant that his essays did not fit what people in general believed, could see, or could say. His essays were out of joint with the time, either behind the time or ahead of it. My remarks also are to some degree anachronistic, a contretemps, countertime, or counterpoint to the essays that follow. I use terms that gesture toward the musical vocabulary Said also employs.

My first untimely observation is to agree gratefully with Laurence Davies that Conrad, for better or for worse, is an ironic writer through and through. Adeptness in reading him requires a skill in reading irony, no easy accomplishment. The word "irony" recurs frequently in Conrad's self-characterizations. An example is his description of *The Secret Agent*, in the Author's Note of 1920, as based on the attempt to apply "an ironic method to a subject of that kind," "in the earnest belief that ironic treatment alone would enable me to say all that I felt I would have to say in scorn as well as in pity" (*SA* xiii). The Author's Note is itself ironic through and through, as, surely, is the subtitle: "A Simple Tale." Ha! I would differ a bit from Davies, however, in taking Friedrich Schlegel and Paul de Man as more my cues for understanding irony— Conrad's or that of any other writer—than Kierkegaard and D.C. Muecke. Schlegel, and de Man after him, make it clear that the distinction between the *alazon* and the *eiron*, the dumb guy and the smart guy ironist, is extremely tricky. They change places all the time, rather than being stable positions. No one is more the victim of irony, Schlegel said, than the person who thinks he or she has mastered it and is the smart guy. Another fundamental feature of irony is that it is a performative use of language. As de Man, somewhat surprisingly, puts it in "The Concept of Irony": "Irony also very clearly has a performative dimension. Irony consoles and it promises and it excuses. It allows us to perform all kinds of performative linguistic functions ..." (de Man 165). Davies' essay ends, in a passage I have already cited, by saying that Conrad's irony is "fortifying," rather than "decadent" or "paralyzing." "Fortifying" would be another performative effect of ironic literary language. Davies means, I suppose, that Conrad's irony fortifies the reader against being taken in by the various illusions with which his fictitious characters are bewitched. Irony, it may be, also fortifies the reader to be able to take without flinching the dismaying political and psychological insights his novels express. In addition, however, if irony has a performative as well as cognitive dimension, this means it is the pervasive irony in Conrad's discourse that gives it its power to change the reader's political beliefs and actions. This happens, for example, through a pitiless revelation, in a fictive rendition such as *Heart of Darkness* or *Nostromo*, of the evils of imperialism, colonialism, and economic exploitation of "third world" countries by those of the "first world," especially, these days, by the United States. The United States, however, was already Conrad's target in *Nostromo*, by way of the truly sinister American financier Holroyd. I see further investigation of the function, political and otherwise, of irony's performative dimension in Conrad's work as a major and timely project for the future. I am grateful to Davies for instigating me to think again about this issue.

If stressing Conrad's irony is untimely because it is not fashionable these days to put the tropological dimensions of literature in the foreground, what I am about to claim is even more untimely. All the essays in this book are unanimous in not taking seriously any "metaphysical" dimension of Conrad's work. This comes up especially, not unexpectedly, in discussions of *Heart of Darkness*. The critics here are somewhat embarrassed by this feature of *Heart of Darkness*. They either pass over it in silence or follow a long tradition going back to F.R. Leavis and others by saying it is nonsense, "moonshine," or a blight in Conrad's style, or a cover-up for his submission to ideologemes about "darkest Africa" that would justify military, religious, and economic imperialism. The latter would be necessary, as was often said, to "wean the savages from their horrid ways and civilize them," that is, to turn their countries into western-style democracies so we can get safe access to their oil, minerals, gems, etc. Once they are stable democracies, moreover, we then have them as markets so we can sell back to them manufactured products we have made from their raw materials. We can set up for them MacDonald franchises and Starbucks cafes. "The conquest of the earth, which mostly means the taking it away from those who have a different complexion or slightly flatter noses than ourselves," as Marlow observes and as his story forcefully demonstrates, "is not a pretty thing when you look into it too much" (*YOS* 50). Marlow, it should be noted, is speaking not of present-day imperialism in Africa, but of the Roman conquest of Britain, though of course what he says applies to both. That is Conrad's point. We are now, I suspect, already selling Iraqi oil back to the Iraqis, with big profits, I suppose, for Halliburton or to other American companies. Combining military occupation with economic exploitation is much more effective than trying to deal with indigenous authorities, as King Leopold and President Bush well knew and know.

I do not doubt the usefulness of Conrad's work for understanding imperialism's ideology and its actions. Nevertheless, I think an important feature of that ideology is precisely those metaphysical elements that critics of *Heart of Darkness* so scorn, or bypass in silence. One must remember that Marlow is not Conrad. He is an invented character and narrator. Conrad the author ascribes to Marlow the character/narrator a belief in, and experience of a metaphysical principle he calls the "darkness." When Marlow says, "It was the stillness of an implacable force brooding over an inscrutable intention. It looked at you with a vengeful aspect" (98), or when he says, "the silent wilderness surrounding this cleared speck on the earth struck me as something great and invincible, like evil or truth, waiting patiently for the passing away of this fantastic invasion" (76), or when he says, "All this was great, expectant, mute, while the man jabbered about himself. I wondered whether the stillness on the face of the immensity looking at us two were meant as an appeal or as a menace" (81), he means just what he says. To Marlow, in a powerful prosopopoeia, the jungle seems like an enormous threatening quasi-human personage. What Conrad thought about this is not all that easy to tell, but to make a straightforward identification of Marlow and Conrad is an elementary reading mistake.

As one essay here observes, Conrad's works tend to be parodies or variations on established narrative genres, sea stories for "Typhoon," historical novels for *Nostromo*, and so on. *Heart of Darkness*, as the title of the Francis Ford Coppola film based on the novel, *Apocalypse Now!*, recognized, is a parody of the genre of the apocalypse. "Apocalypse" means "unveiling," as does the word "revelation." *Heart of Darkness* proceeds by a series of unveilings one behind the other, as Marlow penetrates deeper and deeper into Africa. It culminates, however, not in a final unveiling of the "truth," but in a confrontation of the impossibility, as long as you are alive, of attaining that ultimate revelation. It is only Kurtz who steps over that final threshold, while Marlow has not: "True, he had made that last stride, he had stepped over the edge, while I had been permitted to draw back my hesitating foot. And perhaps in this is the whole difference; perhaps all the wisdom, and all truth, and all sincerity, are just compressed into that inappreciable moment of time in which we step over the threshold of the invisible. Perhaps!" (151). Perhaps yes. Perhaps no. There is no way to tell, since dead men, as we know, tell no tales. All the historical, personal, and psychological details of Marlow's narrative in *Heart of Darkness*, including his description of Kurtz—"His was an impenetrable darkness" (149)—are there as vehicles of the allegorical apocalypse that is the novel's dominant literary mode. That other vehicles besides the African ones could have, for Marlow, carried the same tenor, is indicated by the stress on the parallel between Africa and England. Both are, or were, dark places on the earth, or appear as such when seen from Marlow's perspective. "Metaphysical" language so permeates Marlow's discourse that no convincing way exists to explain it away.

I add that Marlow's discourse is also ironic through and through. Irony in its performative dimension is a mode of unveiling. To describe something ironically hollows it out, prepares its removal for the sake of perceiving something hidden behind it, as when Marlow says of the representatives of progress and economic exploitation at the Central Station, "They wandered here and there with their absurd long staves in their hands, like a lot of faithless pilgrims bewitched inside a rotten fence. The word 'ivory' rang in the air, was whispered, was sighed. You would think they were praying to it" (*YOS* 76). Irony is a regular feature of apocalyptic narrative. My two first untimely observations are therefore not unconnected, as the reader can see.

The third and final untimely observation builds on the first two and is an aspect of them, or they of it. Conrad's novels and stories are literary works, not works of history, cultural or ethnographical studies, autobiographies, political theory, or psychological investigations. All the authors of the essays in this book no doubt know this, but important consequences follow for the project most of them undertake, that is, the project of explaining or accounting for Conrad's work by its historical, social, and biographical contexts. "Literature," as we know it, is a peculiar and specifically Western institution with its own individual history. The modern concept of what we call "literature" begins more or less in the late Renaissance in Europe. It is a concomitant of the rise of the modern nation state, of print format's domination, and of the appearance of Western-style democracies with their, at least theoretical, freedom of speech. This is the freedom to say, write, or publish anything and not be punished for it. Literature is a peculiar exercise of the right to free speech. The author of a work that defines itself as literature and that is taken as literature by its readers and by the "authorities" (which includes college and university teachers as the "guardians of the humanistic tradition"), can always say of anything asserted in a literary work, "That was not me speaking, but an imaginary, invented character." This excuse is enshrined in modern narrative theory in the distinctions between author and narrator and between author and character. Shakespeare is not Hamlet, Lear, or Macbeth. He is the author who invented those characters. Conrad is not the narrator of *Nostromo*, nor is he Marlow. These are invented characters or ways of narrating. This does not mean that fictional works, as institutionalized in the West, are not embedded in history. They come from history and return to it as historical events that have such effects as they do have when they are read. Their relation, both before and after, to what is outside them is, however, of a specific kind. It is indirect and complex. Conrad has a precise phrase for this in *A Personal Record*. *Nostromo* is, he says, "a tale of an imaginary (but true) seaboard" (98). The word "imaginary" here is as important as the word "true." How can a collocation of words on the page be both imaginary and true? "True" must mean here something other than direct referential accuracy. Another way to put this is to say that you can encounter Costaguana nowhere but in the pages of *Nostromo*, even though it represents accurately, in a fictive transformation, South American history. Or does Conrad just mean that it is true to his own sensations? Such fidelity, Conrad says more than once, is essential to a genuine literary work. Conrad's assimilation of this peculiarly Western definition of literature is revealed not only in the influence on him of Flaubert, say, or of Polish popular literature, but also in an odd moment in *A Personal Record*. He says that when he sat down to write, almost inadvertently, the first words of his first novel, *Almayer's Folly*, he had been reading, of all things, as well as he can remember, "one of Trollope's political novels" (*PR* 73). It is a startling conjunction. Though it is difficult to imagine Conrad being influenced by Trollope's political novels, a clever critic could make out a strong case for such influence or for saying that Trollope's novels influenced Conrad's narrative technique. The image of Conrad reading Trollope is further evidence, if any were needed, that Conrad most likely defined what he was writing within conventional and traditional Western assumptions about what literature is.

Conrad came toward the end of the epoch of literature. That epoch is fast coming to an end these days through the displacement of the "imaginary" to other media, for example to cinema, television, popular music downloaded from the Internet, and computer games. A lot of what used to be called literary inventiveness goes into the concoction of the latter. It will not do to be condescending to these new media. They have immense power to influence the way people think, believe, and behave, while literature's power, once paramount, is fading. Thousands of people today, I am sure, have seen the film *Apocalypse Now!* for every one person who has read *Heart of Darkness.* If Conrad were around today he would probably be writing movie or television scripts, or programming computer games. I can imagine a game called "Costaguana," in which the players try to bring off or thwart a revolution in an imaginary South American republic, just as there is a video game as well as a film for *Lord of the Rings.* The goal of "Costaguana" would be to establish a new nation state, with a constitution, laws, institutions, industries, corporations, and so on, as we are now cooperating with those we have conquered in doing so in Afghanistan and Iraq. The fading of literature's power may be one reason that such strenuous efforts have to be made by university professors to justify the study of literature. They love literature, but they are sometimes perhaps a little embarrassed to be caught reading a work of literature "for pleasure," or "for its own sake," that is, for the sake of the entry into a purely imaginary realm, unique and different in each case, that each literary work allows.

The first Conrad work I read was *Typhoon.* I came upon the book by sheer accident, in the way such things frequently happen. I was about 13 or 14 at the time, rummaging around one day in my father's library, on the shelves in his study, trying to find something to read. My father was a Baptist minister turned educational administrator. He earned his Ph.D. for a dissertation on *The Practice of Public Prayer,* directed at Columbia by John Dewey. Most of the books in his library were in psychology, theology, or philosophy. I was looking, however, for something other than William James's *Varieties of Religious Experience* and the like, something in the way of literature, some story or other to read. The only such book I could find was "Typhoon." I opened the book and read, and then read and read, with fascinated attention. I became "lost in the book," as they say. I can still remember that I found "Typhoon" enchanting, in the literal sense. I was carried away. The words on the page exerted a magic power to take me to an imaginary place and to cause me to relive an imaginary action. It seemed to me, when I finally raised my head from the book, that I had lived through that storm, in all its fury, and had been with Captain MacWhirr, Mr. Jukes, and the rest, sharing their experience. I have just re-read the novel for the first time in a number of years. I must confess that it still has the same effect on me as it did when I was a teenager over sixty years ago. Last night I was again on the *Nan-Shan* battling a typhoon in the China sea. I claim that this kind of reading is a primordial and authentic way to be related to a literary work. All the superstructure of criticism, analysis, and commentary is erected on the foundation of such an "enchanted" reading. If such a reading were not a common response to Conrad's work, that work would not be worth talking about, in praise or in blame.

I think, by the way, that one of the essays in this book is making a dubious judgment in claiming that something goes wrong when Conrad elides what, according to that essay, should have been the climax of "Typhoon," that is, the second encounter with the typhoon after they have passed through its "eye." The narrator just says, ironically, that MacWhirr was "spared the annoyance" (*TOT* 90) of losing his ship. In my judgment it would have been anticlimactic and redundant to again go through the whole business of describing the effect of the storm on the ship and its crew. The real climax of the novel, in any case, as my present, though probably not my first, reading discloses, is the power of the storm to disturb Captain MacWhirr's almost imperturbable equanimity. He is irrationally upset not by the devastation of the ship's deck, the twisting of its railings, the caking of the whole superstructure with salt, and so on, but, in a wonderful irony, by the disarrangement of things in his cabin, his rulers, pencils, and inkstand, for instance: "The hurricane had broken in upon the orderly arrangements of his privacy. This had never happened before, and a feeling of dismay reached the very seat of his composure" (85). My second motif, I add, the metaphysical dimension, is present in "Typhoon" only in the effaced form of personifying the storm as deliberately and consciously malignant: "A furious gale attacks [a man] like a personal enemy, tries to grasp his limbs, fastens upon his mind, seeks to rout his very spirit out of him" (40).

Much more attention is paid, in this volume, to *Nostromo* than to *Typhoon*. I have been re-reading that too. I have benefited greatly from what is said about it in the following essays. I have learned especially from Robert Hampson's essay on the history of mapping and on Sulaco as a "heterotopia." Sulaco is both a place made of the uneasy transformative combination of a number of real places and a place that does not quite hang together rationally as something that, however imaginary, could be mapped. I take this as good evidence that Costaguana is an imaginary place, like the *Nan-Shan* in the typhoon. You can go to Sulaco and meet the people there only by reading the novel, not by taking a jet-plane to some country in South America. This is so despite the fact that Conrad based the geography of the novel and some of its characters on his own knowledge of Cracow in Poland, on his reading of books about Paraguay, Venezuela, Peru, Colombia, Panama, and Mexico, and on his interchanges with Cunninghame Graham about South America, which Graham had visited and about which he had written memoirs and stories. Conrad had read the latter. As Conrad wrote Graham, Costaguana is "meant for a S. Am^can state in general; thence the mixture of customs and expressions" (*Letters* 3: 175).

That Costaguana is in an extravagant way an imaginary place or a "virtual reality" is evident not only in a candid reading of the work itself in relation to its sources, but also in the peculiar things Conrad says about it in the Author's Note of 1917, and in a wonderfully funny, yet serious, passage in *A Personal Record*. The latter is an anecdote about how a neighbor, a general's daughter, interrupted him while he was writing the last part of the novel.

In the Author's Note, Conrad speaks, no doubt ironically, half-jokingly, and as he says, "figuratively," of his two years' absorption in writing *Nostromo* as his absence in that imaginary country: " . . . my sojourn on the Continent of Latin America, famed for its hospitality, lasted for about two years. On my return I found (speaking somewhat in the style of Captain Gulliver) my family all well, my wife heartily glad to learn that the fuss was all over, and our small boy considerably grown during my absence" (*No* x). What is odd about this and similar passages in the Author's Note is that Conrad speaks of the people and places of Costaguana as having a real existence, independent of his language, not as something he has invented through language, even though only he has access to this strange place and its people. He says, for example, "My principal authority for the history of Costaguana is, of course, my venerated friend, the late Don José Avellanos, Minister to the Courts of England and Spain, etc., etc., in his impartial and eloquent 'History of Fifty Years of Misrule.' True that this work was never published—the reader will discover why [the manuscript gets destroyed by the revolutionary mob]—and that I am, in fact, the only person in the world possessed of its contents" (x). Conrad of course invented Don José and all the other characters, or, perhaps it might be better to say, he "discovered" them by an effort of imagination. We can meet Don José only by reading Conrad's book.

In *A Personal Record* Conrad takes a somewhat different way of defining how Costaguana is a virtual reality:

> I had, like the prophet of old, 'wrestled with the Lord' for my creation, for the headlands of the coast, for the darkness of the Placid Gulf, the light on the snows, the clouds on the sky, and for the breath of life that had to be blown into the shapes of men and women, of Latin and Saxon, of Jew and Gentile. These are, perhaps, strong words, but it is difficult to characterize otherwise the intimacy and strain of a creative effort in which mind and will and conscience are engaged to the full, hour after hour, day after day, away from the world, and to the exclusion of all that makes life really lovable and gentle . . . (*PR* 98).

In this passage, Conrad speaks of his creation of the world of Costaguana as a counter-creation, as something that he had to wrestle with the Lord to obtain, since it is in opposition to His creation. Conrad's writing of *Nostromo* is like Jehovah's breathing life into Adam and Eve. This creation of an alternative world, complete with its own landscape and geography, takes place "away from the world," that is, away from God's creation, in a solitary creative struggle that, Conrad says, is like nothing so much as "the everlasting sombre stress of the westward winter passage round Cape Horn" (*PR* 98–99).

Just as God's creation, in the thought of certain seventeenth-century French theologians, depends absolutely on what they called "continuous creation," that is, on God's willing from moment to moment to keep the world and all the people in it in existence, since otherwise they would vanish, so Costaguana depends for its existence on the continuous exercise of Conrad's will and creative imagination. This must be kept up from minute to minute, day after day, month after month. If Conrad's effort flags, the whole shebang disappears in an instant, like a snuffed candle. This happens when the general's daughter walks in on him unawares and says, "How do you do?" Conrad stresses the quasi-material nature of *Nostromo*'s virtual world as it existed in his imagination and nowhere else. It is a matter of mountains, sea, and clouds, even of grains of sand, as well as of imaginary people. Conrad also stresses the way Costaguana is a spatio-temporal whole. It exists as a "whole world," all at once, present all together in his mind. All novels create a counter-world, separate from the real one, with its own laws, geography, and weather, but I know of no other novel that makes this so explicit as *Nostromo* does, as in the initial description of its topography in the opening chapters. The visit of the general's daughter destroys it all:

> The whole world of Costaguana (the country, you may remember, of my seaboard tale), men, women, headlands, houses, mountains, town, campo (there was not a single brick, stone, or grain of sand of its soil I had not placed in position with my own hands); all the history, geography, politics, finance; the wealth of Charles Gould's silver-mine, and the splendor of the magnificent Capataz de Cargadores, whose name, cried out in the night (Dr. Monygham heard it pass over his head—in Linda Viola's voice), dominated even after death the dark gulf containing his conquests of treasure and love—all that had come down crashing about my ears. I felt I could never pick up the pieces . . . . (*PR* 100)

We can have access to Costaguana only because Conrad wrote down his vision, whereas Conrad apparently lived there before he wrote it down. Or perhaps the act of imagining Costaguana coincided with the act of writing it down, in what might be called a performative "act of literature," a special mode of speech act. Edward Said, with his usual clairvoyance as a reader, even when what he sees goes to some degree against what he might wish to find, notices in his own way, employing the musical analogy that recurs in the interview, how *Nostromo* detaches itself from its sources:

… What Conrad is attempting in *Nostromo* is a structure of such monumental solidity that it has an integrity of its own quite without reference to the outside world. Though this is only a speculation, I think that halfway through the book it's as if Conrad loses interest in the real world of human beings and becomes fascinated with the workings of his own method and his own writing. *It* has an integrity quite of its own—the way, for example, Bach might construct a fugue around a very uninteresting subject, and by the middle of the piece you are so involved in keeping the five, or four, voices going, and understanding the relationships between them, that this becomes the most interesting thing about it. I think there is a similar impulse at work in *Nostromo*.

Said is right on the mark. Having assembled his Costaguana from the imaginative transformation of miscellaneous materials, Conrad became more and more absorbed in working out the intertwined destinies of the characters with which he had peopled his heterotopia.

What difference does it make that *Nostromo* is a virtual reality, like a Bach fugue, in which complex internal relationships are all-important, and in which the straightforward referential function of language is suspended? It does not mean we should not learn all we can about Conrad's "sources" or about what Benita Parry calls the "historical, political, and ideological materials" of Conrad's works. Robert Hampson's discussion of *Nostromo* is exemplary in doing this. Nor does it mean that we should not concern ourselves with Conrad's relevance to our globalized political and economic situation today. It is hard to read *Nostromo* and not think of the long sad history before and after Conrad wrote that novel of United States intervention in South America, or even of our present intervention, governed as it is by "material interests," in Iraq. The relation of *Nostromo* to history, politics, and ideology, however, is one version of the specific kind of such a relation that works of literature can have. In one direction, toward its origin, *Nostromo* is a transformation, in the alembic of Conrad's creative imagination, of the materials that went into it. It is a magical translation or transmogrification of those materials into something rich and strange. The sum total of the "sources" cannot predict this result, nor can they fully account for it. The small anecdote Conrad had encountered about the "original" of Nostromo (the character) is completely transcended by the complex personality and story Conrad has invented for his Capataz de Cargadores. One has to read the novel to find out about Nostromo. The same thing can be said for the novel's relation to its other "sources," including the facts of South American history, its revolutions, and its acts of nation building.

In the other direction, toward the future, *Nostromo* enters back into history not by giving us constative facts about South American history. History books are the place to find out about that. *Nostromo* reenters history, rather, by way of the performative effects it may have on readers. It does its work by getting its readers to see history differently by way of fiction, not by direct representation of history. A work of fiction "works" performatively not by way of discursive statements but, as Aristotle knew, by its action, its plot, the stories it tells. Its essential dimension is temporal sequence. The story told may possibly work to get its readers to see their own histories differently, and to behave differently as a result, to vote differently in the next election, for example. Conrad's ironic method of narration, by no means absent from *Nostromo*, aids in bringing about this performative effect. Irony, we remember, excuses, promises, and consoles.

I add one more notation: The forlornness of the characters in *Nostromo*, the way each lives imprisoned in a private ideological illusion, as a reading could show in detail, is made even more forlorn by the almost complete absence, so far as I can see, of the "metaphysical" dimension so important in *Heart of Darkness*. The characters of *Nostromo* do not even have the somber consolation of having confronted a transnatural antagonist force that obscurely governs their lives. They have brought their trouble on themselves, collectively, or have been subject to those outside economic forces that Conrad calls "material interests." All the "metaphysics of darkness" seems to have vanished from Conrad's work in the few short years between *Heart of Darkness* and *Nostromo*. Decoud is driven to suicide by "solitude," solitude total and absolute, not by a confrontation with the heart of darkness. The sad implication of *Nostromo* is that, for Conrad at that moment, only some ideological illusion or other can hold my sense of my personality together and protect me from the suicide-inducing emptiness of what Conrad calls "solitude."

I have now said my say in praise and in characterization of the admirable essays that make up this book. I have also sung, a little, my own tune in counterpoint to theirs. Now I make a somewhat awkward bow and open the door from this anteroom to the music hall proper. May you enjoy the concert.

1
Millennial Conrad:
Heart of Darkness in the Twenty-First Century

1
Beyond Mastery: The Future of Conrad's Beginnings

GEOFFREY GALT HARPHAM

I. Identification

The dedication of this book to the memory of Edward Said is, for me, particularly appropriate, for Said's relation to Conrad was not confined to academic interest; it was, rather, an obsessive relationship that lasted from youth—when he read "Youth"—to the very end of his life. As his career unfolded, taking him in so many directions, he remained imaginatively bewitched by a few Conradian images and permitted these to penetrate his sensibility, to organize his thinking on any number of subjects, including himself. His career, like his character, was, of course, singular; but in one respect I believe that he spoke for many of Conrad's most passionate readers when he described, in the remarkable interview with Peter Mallios that concludes this book, his relationship to Conrad as "totally individual." Said learned about youth from "Youth"; and, in later years, he learned about the "sense of being invaded by outside forces," the necessity of a "relentlessly open-ended, aggressively critical inquiry into the mechanisms and ... abuses of imperialism," and the attraction to "lost causes" from other books. I find myself hoping that he discovered, at the end, a sense of ultimate victory through his engagement with *Victory*. But my real point is that Conrad, the most exotic and singular of authors, was somehow able to solicit a direct and personal identification not only from the equally exotic and singular Said, but from a wide range of readers who have felt themselves not merely entertained or enlightened by his work, but in a sense represented in it.

How can Conrad be so uncannily intimate with the minds of others who share none of his experiences, none of his attributes, none of his values? How can his work provide a docking point for such a vast range of personalities, attitudes, and ideologies? How can someone as overpoweringly peculiar as Conrad speak to and for so many?

We might be tempted to explain Conrad's appeal by pointing to his vast world experience. He was undoubtedly the most traveled author in history at that time, having experienced life in his native Poland, Russia, much of Europe, Southeast Asia, South America, and Africa, not to mention twenty years at sea, before settling in England. But Conrad was not simply a tourist, accumulating an enriching store of experience. He was, from early childhood, dispossessed. After leading a failed revolution against Russian dominance of Poland, Conrad's father was sent, with his wife and four-year-old son, into exile to Vologda, 250 miles northeast of Moscow. As was the custom, they walked, with Conrad's mother barely surviving the journey. So, after beginning life in a country that, having been carved up like Lear's kingdom by three great imperial powers at the end of the eighteenth century, did not exist in a geopolitical sense, Conrad attained the age of reason in a household where daily life consisted of paternal lamentations about the death of the mother and the loss of the motherland, lamentations that ceased only with the death of Conrad's father, when the young Joseph was eleven. When Conrad abruptly decided he would go to sea, those around him were astonished, for landlocked Poland had no navy, no merchant marine, no maritime tradition; at the time, there were virtually no Poles on the oceans of the earth.

It is possible in retrospect to see that the sea, with its clear hierarchy of command, its time-honored traditions, its intense fellowship of the craft, provided Conrad with a consoling metaphor for the sense of belonging associated with a true homeland. But it was likely that, in the first and most literal instance, the sea appealed to the youth as an escape, a departure, a negation of his entire life—in other words, as an abandonment of total loss, a departure from deprivation. And so we may say that, in going to sea, Conrad was not trying to accumulate experience, to see the world in all its richness, but something far more complex: he was both compulsively replicating his initial experience of dispossession and loss, and seeking to turn that experience to good account, to turn it into a profession, an identity, a life.

Taking him to the farthest corners of the earth, Conrad's nautical career introduced him to countless others who, like himself, were uprooted or unrooted; he was repeatedly forced to discover within himself resources and capacities that would have lain dormant if he had remained at home, or what passed for home. By the time he began to write, in his thirties, Conrad understood, better than those who had remained in their own communities, that human identity was not limited to the possibilities available only in one's original circumstance. Indeed, he had proved this himself in dramatic fashion, when, in 1889, he briefly piloted a steamer called the *Roi des Belges* up the Congo River. This former colonial subject, now an employee of King Leopold, became perhaps the only person in the world who had managed, in his time, to be both a victim and an agent of imperial oppression. By the end of his voyages, Conrad was, in short, intimate to a degree we can scarcely imagine with the human capacity for adaptation, a capacity that, for most people, most of the time, is unused and even largely unsuspected.

Conrad's acquired sensitivity to the human capacity to assume different forms became the basis for both his self understanding and his understanding of human beings generally. At first, this singular understanding was couched in conventional forms. He began his first novel, *Almayer's Folly*, with an "Author's Note" that asserts "a bond between us and that humanity so far away," referring to the inhabitants of Borneo, where his tale was set. Still, the real germ of Conrad's career, as he says in an account written years later, was not just an enlightened cosmopolitanism, but something far more personal and direct, a connection he had formed with a Dutch trader he had met in Southeast Asia, Olmeijer, whom Conrad rechristened Almayer. "If I had not got to know Almayer pretty well," Conrad wrote, "it is almost certain there would never have been a line of mine in print" (*PR* 87). In fact, Conrad did not know Almayer that well at all, having visited him no more than four times in 1887. But even without, in all likelihood, any reciprocal interest on Almayer's part, Conrad somehow penetrated him imaginatively, investing him with his own concerns, his own circumstances, his own dreams. What seems to have impressed Conrad most forcibly was, as Ian Watt writes, "the vast disparity between the extravagant hopes of Almayer's inner life and the petty actualities of his achievement," a disparity, Watt adds, "which Conrad was familiar with, no doubt, in himself" (*Almayer* xxiii). The novel's only trace of this unusual attachment is in the epigraph Conrad chose: "Who of us has not had his promised land, his day of ecstasy, and his end in exile?" (*Qui de nous n'a eu sa terre de promesse, son jour d'extase, et sa fin en exil?*) These words apply only at a great stretch to a man Watt describes as "apparently a fairly successful and respected" trader, but seem to come straight from the heart of that ecstasy-prone exile, Conrad himself (xxii). Conrad did not put it this way, but the stimulation he later attributed to Almayer seems actually to have come from Conrad's experience of discovering himself, some unexpressed or even unacknowledged facet of himself, within the other man. The experience that made Conrad a writer, I am suggesting, was his discovery that he could locate himself, his own authentic essence, outside himself, in another being.

Over the next few years, Conrad found ways to incorporate this experience into his works, recording a series of peculiarly intense imaginative relationships between men, generally conducted in fraught silence across a distance. At first, he scarcely seems to know what he is doing or why he is doing it. The famous preface to *The Nigger of the "Narcissus"* continues the rather conventional cosmopolitanism of the preface to *Almayer's Folly*, with its evocation of a "bond" with distant humanity, by describing the artist's task as one of speaking to "the latent feeling of fellowship with all creation" (*NN* viii). The cliché is, however, immediately revealed as having a darker and more intimate signification, with the entire passage reading: "[The artist speaks] to the latent feeling of fellowship with all creation—to the subtle but invincible conviction of solidarity that knits the loneliness of innumerable hearts . . . which binds together all humanity." In this critical document, often taken as his artistic "credo," Conrad is clearly struggling to convert his own painful experience of profound solitude into a basis for universal kinship: we are alike, he says, in being totally alone. Indeed, it almost seems that a connection between the unvoiced term *solitude* and solidarity has, as if by a sudden inspiration, enabled him to imagine this conversion—as if the language supplies him with a thought that he needed, but was unable to formulate on his own.

Then, in the following year, 1898, Conrad begins the creative explosion that issued in *Heart of Darkness* and *Lord Jim* in rapid sequence; and here, one senses, he has at last found his subject. For in these books, he seems to discover, within stock phrases about human oneness or a fellowship with all creation, something far stranger and more unsettling: a kind of subrational or obsessive attachment in which one person apprehends in another the secret of his own identity, some deeply implicit or unrealized condition, some concealed principle of his own being. When Marlow sits in the court of inquiry, staring at the man who will become Lord Jim, he exemplifies the Conradian scenario of a solitary, disconnected character projecting a mysterious affinity between himself and another, fitting himself into the other's skin, taking the other's experience as his own. "It is not my own extremity I remember," Marlow says, recollecting Kurtz; "No! It is his extremity I seem to have lived through" (*YOS* 151).

Marlow is a man with little investment in his own identity, a man capable of surrendering himself without surrendering much, but he is Conrad's most psychologically crucial figure, for he serves *Heart of Darkness* and *Lord Jim* as a lightning rod for the kind of ambiguous, passionate, and nonreciprocal relationships that define Conrad's distinctive sensibility. The general idea Marlow "represents" is that boundaries between people are porous and transgressable—that identity is fluid and less crystallized or "mastered" than we generally think. The idea, in other words, is that identity itself—the character we present to the world and to ourselves—is a deeply unstable configuration: it could be otherwise, and in a sense *is* otherwise: we are not as distinct from each other, as integrated in ourselves, as we might like to think, or as it seems we are. It's entirely possible to locate the center of our being outside rather than inside. So, when we read Conrad and feel that he has expressed us somehow, that it describes as well as appeals to us, we replicate the experience of Marlow. In short, we find it easy to identify with Conrad's work because identification is what his work, or some of his work, is all about.

II. Adoption

The concept of identification dominated his work for only a brief period, from 1897 to 1900. After this, he wrote a number of worthy books and two extraordinary ones, *Nostromo* and *The Secret Agent*, but he never again returned to this idea, or theme, in quite the same spirit. Still, during this time, he wrote three of his very greatest works, *The Nigger of the "Narcissus," Heart of Darkness*, and *Lord Jim*. Moreover, this period also marks the moment when Conrad's language is at its most magical, its most strangely suggestive, its most distinctively "Conradian," and the intriguing question I'd like now to consider concerns the relationship between these two aspects of Conrad's art.

Almost from the very first, Conrad was accounted a "master of the English language," and this phrase has continued to affect our thinking about his remarkable linguistic achievement.[1] Like many compliments, this one seems empty, suggesting that all we need to do to understand Conrad is to admire him. But the idea of linguistic mastery, rightly understood, actually leads us into a new understanding of Conrad's particular genius. Mastery, we should note, is not precisely synonymous with ease or fluency. It refers not to untroubled dominion or uncontested control but rather to a situation where a potentially rebellious force has been contained or managed. Mastery is achieved against resistance and maintained by effort, with the mastered force constantly threatening to reverse positions with the mastering power. Such a situation is described perfectly by Conrad's friend and collaborator Ford Madox Ford, who marveled at the way Conrad "took English, as it were by the throat and, wrestling till the dawn, made it obedient to him as it had been obedient to few other men" (*Remembrance* 109). The great Polish Conrad scholar Zdzisław Najder points out that for every non-native speaker, there is a moment when the new language is "resistant like every object that is strange and newly discovered, and at the same time softly pliable because not hardened in schematic patterns of words and ideas inculcated since childhood" (*Chronicle* 116). This account accurately characterizes Conrad's relationship to English, but equally important, it confines that relationship to a moment—the very moment, I would suggest, when Conrad achieved a mastery of the language, the moment when identification was his primary theme.

Coming to English as an adult, Conrad passed through a period of awkward apprenticeship, and his accent—idiosyncratic even for a Pole—remained a lifelong marker of foreignness. Yet, he later wrote, he sensed that he was somehow destined to be an English writer, if not an English speaker, and even felt himself "adopted by the genius of the language, which directly I came out of the stammering stage made me its own so completely that its very idioms I truly believe had a direct action on my temperament and fashioned my still plastic character" (*PR* v). Most native speakers do not think of themselves as "adopted" by the language they speak, nor do they think of language in this external, quasi-human sense, as a superior being. But Conrad always regarded English as an alien medium; and besides, the concept of adoption was especially resonant for him because he had been effectively adopted on two other critical occasions. The first was by his uncle, who took responsibility for the young orphan after his parents' death, and the second was by a retired sea captain, who examined Conrad for his captain's license. This gentleman, Conrad wrote years later, was a sort of "grandfather in the craft" who made him feel "adopted" into the fellowship of the sea (*PR* 119, 118).

Conrad sometimes fixes on particular words, especially those with multiple meanings, which he explores in various contexts, the result being, on occasion, a startling disclosure of a web of odd associations in his mind. In this case, Conrad seems to respond in the first instance to the fact that adoption compensates for the lack of a given or "natural" identity by conferring an external or contingent identity that can still be effective as a principle of psychic organization. But beyond this, when Conrad says he was adopted by the English language, he seems to be exploring, and applying to himself, the fact that adoption gives one the opportunity to find one's identity in an external or non-natural field of possibilities, and forces one to produce oneself by volition and will rather than merely accepting the gifts of genetic determination. Adopted identity may be bestowed, but it requires assent, a kind of seconding of the motion, and can even be refused. Adoption entails, therefore, a certain openness, an experimental freedom, that might represent, for a creative artist, a salutary condition. The son of a failed Polish patriot, young Conrad might well have felt himself limited to few options, none promising; but adoption opened before him a space for innovation and self-invention—even, perhaps, for self-mastery—without the traumas of the Oedipal crisis: the father already dead, no further fathers need die for the son to flourish.

Conrad seems, then, to have intuited a connection between paternity and linguistic facility, and to have discovered a punning way to express this connection through the term "adoption." As a set of preexisting and "inherited" determinants, conditions, and structures, language seems to most native speakers a natural and unproblematic principle of identity, a "mother tongue." Only lawyers and writers, perhaps, regard it as a medium with its own hidden rules, mechanisms, and possibilities; and a native speaker who sets out to master the language always struggles against a prior sense that language requires no conscious effort at all. For Conrad, by contrast, command of the English language, and therefore of a means of self-expression, was attainable only through labor. What was natural for others was alien for him, and the miracle was that he discovered that the foreign language expressed him perfectly, and he rapidly and eagerly became "its own" as a way—his way—of becoming himself.

"Adoption" thus became for Conrad a way of conceptualizing both his struggle to master the English language and his struggle to achieve his own identity. The point on which I want to insist is that these struggles only lasted for a short time, that charmed interval when the still-"resistant" language itself had become, in his powerful grasp, at last "pliable" or "obedient" but had not yet disappeared as a problem. This was, as I have said, the same time when the theme of identification dominated his work and his imagination. We might begin to explain this striking fact by noting that both adoption and identification involve similar principles— the assumption of another's identity, the inner assent to, or assumption of, an external principle of being. The hypothesis, in other words, is that by depicting the identification of one character with another, Conrad was casting into narrative form the very struggle he was experiencing with respect to his medium.

How can mastery be measured, or even observed? Consider a series of passages in which we can track Conrad's astonishingly rapid progress in his use of the language. The first is from *Almayer's Folly*, begun in 1889 and published in 1895:

In the middle of a shadowless square of moonlight ... a little shelter-hut perched on high posts, the pile of brushwood near by, and the glowing embers of a fire with a man stretched before it, seemed very small and as if lost in the pale green iridescence reflected from the ground. On three sides of the clearing, the big trees of the forest, lashed together with manifold bonds by a mass of tangled creepers, looked down at the growing young life at their feet with the somber resignation of giants that had lost faith in their strength. And in the midst of them, the merciless creepers clung to the big trunks in cable-like coils, leaped from tree to tree, hung in thorny festoons from the lower boughs, and, sending slender tendrils on high to seek out the smallest branches, carried death to their victims in an exulting riot of silent destruction. (165)

In reading this, we need to keep reminding ourselves that the subject is, after all, only trees and vines, for these have been given a wild energy, even a sentience—even a malignant intentionality.[2] Conrad, who could see for himself the effect his speech produced on his listeners, seems to reflect their view of his early infelicities or gaucheries when he describes a character in *Lord Jim* whose "flowing English seemed to be derived from a dictionary compiled by a lunatic" (175). The author of *Almayer's Folly* was no longer in the lunatic phase, but could not yet be described as master of anything in the domain of language; indeed, the language in this passage seems to cry out for a principle of control, of responsible management, that the author is unable to provide.

Now consider a passage from *Nostromo*, published in 1904, a few years after the charmed interval when Conrad, I am arguing, had been a master of the English language. Once again, the subject is nature, but note the orderly fluency of the exposition:

[T]he head of the calm gulf is filled on most days of the year by a great body of motionless and opaque clouds. On the rare clear mornings another shadow is cast upon the sweep of the gulf. The dawn breaks high behind the towering and serrated wall of the Cordillera, a clear-cut vision of dark peaks rearing their steep slopes on a lofty pedestal of forest rising from the very edge of the shore .... Bare clusters of enormous rocks sprinkle with tiny black dots the smooth dome of snow. (5–6)

Despite an achieved assurance that contrasts markedly with the first passage's chaos, here, once again, we are not tempted to call the author a master of language. The overexcited lunatic has departed, leaving in his place a fine and accomplished writer, in perfect command: no natural objects are compared to gloomy giants or invested with a wild death-force; no verbal oddities suggest limitations, much less incompetence. Instead, we have an animated but "clear-cut vision" of clouds, peaks, rocks, snow. At this point, Conrad can make sense, but, despite a high level of verbal energy, can no longer make magic. The referential grip on the world is much firmer, but the language has been tamed to the point where we scarcely experience it as a separate force at all. The first passage could only have been written by an inexperienced genius, but this passage might have been written by anybody with a high order of competence. If, at the beginning of his career, the language had clearly not yet made Conrad "its own," then by the time of *Nostromo*, Conrad has succeeded in making English altogether *his* own.

Now let's take a passage from the dead center of the period on which I'm focusing, a description of Marlow's approach to the mouth of the Congo River:

> We called at some more places with farcical names, where the merry dance of death and trade goes on in a still and earthy atmosphere as of an overheated catacomb; all along the formless coast bordered by dangerous surf, as if Nature herself had tried to ward off intruders; in and out of rivers, streams of death in life, whose banks were rotting into mud, whose waters, thickened into slime, invaded the contorted mangroves, that seemed to writhe at us in the extremity of an impotent despair . . . . the general sense of vague and oppressive wonder grew upon me. It was like a weary pilgrimage amongst hints for nightmares. (*YOS* 62)

It's difficult to describe the feelings imparted by such a strange and memorable passage, with its extravagant metaphors, the meandering elasticity of its syntax, its oscillation between past and present tenses, its almost garish vitality. But it is precisely such passages that give us the sense of a focused command in which the conventions of the language are being twisted or worked to radically unconventional effect. Early readers of Conrad reported that his prose seemed like an excellent translation from some unknown foreign tongue; others felt that the English language had been invaded by some alien energy; still others felt that Conrad had tapped some facet or dimension that no native speaker or writer had yet discovered. In passages of "purer" description, Fredric Jameson says, "Conrad's sensorium virtually remakes its objects," suggesting "forms of libidinal gratification as unimaginable to us as the possession of additional senses, or the presence of nonearthly colors in the spectrum" (*Political* 231).

During his brief period of linguistic mastery, nobody suggested that Conrad was incompetent, nor did they suggest that he was an effortless professional like Ford. They felt, rather, that he was a master of the English language, and they felt this way because they could actually sense the balance of colossal forces—Conrad's overmastering will to express the truth about things and about his thoughts and sensations, and the conventions of the English language, in which such truths had never yet been expressed. They felt that the language, without being violated, had been forced to yield something unsuspected, in the process being exposed as something less like a passive medium, a lexicon with grammar, and more like a dynamic, almost creative agency with a startling capacity to bring new objects into being—the "earthy atmosphere," the "impotent despair" of the "contorted mangroves," and the notion, novel to many readers even today, of a "weary pilgrimage amongst hints for nightmares." Once again, Conrad precisely describes his own style when he has Marlow characterize Kurtz's speech as consisting of "common everyday words" that nevertheless "had behind them ... the terrific suggestiveness of words heard in dreams, of phrases spoken in nightmares" (*YOS* 144).

I've been arguing that Conrad was fascinated by adoption because it represented a way of acquiring an identity that was not "natural" or given, but externally bestowed. Conrad may, I have suggested, been excited by this possibility because nature had given him so little; and adoption, with its opportunity for self-invention, seemed to offer so much. In the passage from *Almayer's Folly* quoted earlier, we can actually see traces of a half-conscious meditation on the concept of nature itself. In this passage, "a man" appears as an inconspicuous and virtually nonsentient speck in a scene of wild natural vitality; indeed, it's surprisingly easy to read this passage without noticing that human form at all. And, in general, in the first movement of Conrad's career, nature, especially in the form of jungles, rivers, and seas, often seems to dominate the human figures, often appearing as an immense matrix, a heaving rhythm of mindless generation and death, in which human beings are embedded and from which they distinguish themselves only fitfully and with great difficulty. What we seem to be witnessing in the works published before 1897 is a struggle in the roots of Conrad's imagination to pry humanity free from nature, to liberate it from the mass of tangled creepers, in, perhaps, the same manner as Michelangelo's giant unfinished sculptures, known as "Slaves," which seem to be twisting free of the unchiseled rock mass itself in which they are immured, to which they are "enslaved." We can—if we abandon all professional scruples against unfounded speculation—imagine that, during this time, Conrad was trying to imagine himself free from the clutches of nature, trying to see how he might advance, through a series of fortuitous adoptions, from the desolate condition of being an orphan in a defeated country, an unrelated person with no worldly prospects, to being a man of culture, an "author," even a "British" author, a man who fabricates lives, including his own.[3]

Eventually, beginning with *The Nigger*, nature becomes in his work a reduced, merely physical phenomenon—an agency that tries, for example, to ward off intruders, a force against whose periodic furies human beings test and measure themselves, but no longer a metaphysical threat. Exemplified by sea storms, nature becomes a trial one must pass to discover "how good a man I was," as the ubiquitous Marlow, having just endured sea difficulties, says in "Youth" (36). In other words, nature becomes secondary to human concerns, a background and a trial but not a matrix of inhumanity, a challenge to one's very being. And then, passing through this period—passing the test—Conrad seems to lose interest in nature: in *Nostromo*, nature is a setting, if an imposing one; and by 1907 and *The Secret Agent*, Conrad's imagination is predominantly urban, and would remain so. The sword has been pulled from the stone, and human beings emerge fully distinct from their natural context.[4]

But if we probe once again the central text, *Heart of Darkness*, we can see the momentary but disturbing appearance of something far more mysterious than we see either before or after. Take the scene where Marlow describes the natives along the shore as possessing "a wild vitality, an intense energy of movement, that was as natural and true as the surf along their coast" (61). This is, of course, a commonplace, that the natives are closer to nature than the Europeans. But this cliché produces striking effects in context by raising the question of whether Kurtz's gesture of disengaging from the imperial project and paddling back upriver to his jungle hut represents a rejection of a culture become criminal in favor of nature and natural law. Many readers have seen the text in this light, but to do so means understanding as "natural" the practices of the natives, including cannibalism, skulls on stakes, and a willingness to worship a crazed European. Reading *Heart of Darkness*, we are forced to wonder—does nature represent a moral standard or the negation of moral standards? Ought we to be more, or less natural? Do Europeans have a different nature from Africans; do men have a different nature from women? Is human nature "natural" or "un-natural?" None of these questions has an immediate answer, which suggests that, at the moment he composed *Heart of Darkness*, Conrad was temporarily between paradigms, with no clear idea of nature at all.

In *Heart of Darkness* we can truly see what it might mean to be "adopted by the language." Marlow is talking, in the passage below, about the final phase of his penetration into the interior, the last leg of the fateful voyage upriver toward the Inner Station and Kurtz. This account qualifies as one of the very greatest descriptive passages in the English language, and an eloquent testament to the author's mastery. The ostensible subject, once again, is foliage.

> Going up that river was like traveling back to the earliest beginnings of the world, when vegetation rioted on the earth and the big trees were kings. An empty stream, a great silence, an impenetrable forest. The air was warm, thick, heavy, sluggish .... The long stretches of the waterway ran on, deserted, into the gloom of overshadowed distances. On silvery sandbanks hippos and alligators sunned themselves side by side .... You lost your way on that river as you would in a desert and butted all day long against shoals trying to find the channel till you thought yourself bewitched and cut off for ever from everything you had known once—somewhere—far away—in another existence perhaps. (92–93)

Unlike the passage from *Almayer's Folly*, things are actually described in a way that does not suggest that language has invested them with an inappropriate force or character. Despite the extravagant simile ("Going up that river was like traveling back ... you lost your way on that river as you would in a desert ...."), the language is firmly referential, and we get a clear image of the scene rather than a kind of hallucination.

But unlike the passage from *Nostromo*, the language is not transparent or obedient to the author's will; in fact, language itself almost seems to make suggestions to the author, of the kind that we saw earlier in the Preface to *The Nigger*, when the pain of solitude yielded to its own balm in "solidarity." The whole passage seems built on a silent metaphor, "the river of time"; but even more intriguing is the quiet but decisive force of the word *deserted* that Marlow uses to describe the absence of people on the river. This word seems to generate all by itself the next thought, that "you lost your way on that river as you would in a desert." The description of being alone, unable to orient yourself, in a featureless space hostile to humanity, is often applied to deserts, but rarely to rivers. A native speaker, thinking primarily of concepts, might never have made the connection, but Conrad, with his anxious sensitivity to English words—to him, still strange, newly discovered, almost material things—was attentive to the form of words as well as their meanings, and this sensitivity enabled him to make the connection between a *deserted* river and a *desert*. And so, by way of a hidden pun, the passage proceeds from an account of a lonely boat trip to a meditation on the experience of finding yourself bereft of your past, your identity, your humanity itself, adrift in a strange world indifferent to your existence. Bewitched by the river and by his own language, Marlow achieves and articulates a degree of detachment, or "desertion," that might never have been voiced in these terms by a native speaker.

In this instance, we can observe, or almost observe, the genius of the language adopting the author, suggesting new thoughts. But adoption, as I have argued, also implies the possibility of resistance, where limits in the power or adequacy of language are recognized, and the language is wrestled into submission. The task of recognizing these limits is delegated to Marlow, who registers repeated shocks at certain habitual or mechanistic verbal conventions. He is irritated, for example, by his aunt's talk about "weaning those ignorant millions from their horrid ways" (59); discomfited by reports that he and Kurtz are considered two of a kind, partners in "the new gang—the gang of virtue" (79); appalled by the manager's description of Kurtz's "unsound method" (137); and amazed by various labels attached to the chained, enslaved, or dying Africans he sees. "Rebels!" he exclaims to himself on hearing the description of the dried heads impaled on stakes outside Kurtz's hut. "What would be the next definition I was to hear. There had been enemies, criminals, workers—and these were—rebels" (132). Marlow senses that the linguistic categories provided by the Belgians (translated into English) are somehow inadequate, even demonstrably wrong, but his unease takes largely passive forms until this outburst, when it suddenly seems about to become ethically productive.

That potential had been signaled a few pages earlier, in the continuation of the passage on which we're focusing. As he steams upriver, Marlow passes groups of natives on the shoreline who seem to him to be scarcely human:

> ...a burst of yells, a whirl of black limbs, a mass of hands clapping, of feet stamping, of bodies swaying, of eyes rolling under the droop of heavy and motionless foliage. The steamer toiled along slowly on the edge of the black and incomprehensible frenzy. The prehistoric man was cursing us, praying to us, welcoming us—who could tell? .... we were traveling in the night of first ages, of those ages that are gone, leaving hardly a sign—and no memories. (96)

Nothing in Marlow's experience has prepared him for this astonishing scene, except perhaps the conventional presumption that Africans were "prehistoric." Marlow borrows this cliché, as he had borrowed the notion that Africans were "natural," but we can sense his discontent with the language at his disposal in his very next comment: "The earth seemed unearthly" (96). What could this mean? Marlow seems to have discovered a limitation in the language, a gap in coverage, an insufficiency, a failure to provide the right term. And so, in the interests of recording the truth, he produces a statement that seems nonsensical. Surely, if anything should be "earthly," it is the earth, but in this instance, it is not so: here, if only here, the earth is unearthly—even, we recall, as the "atmosphere" is "earthy."

Having imposed himself on the language in describing the earth, Marlow proceeds to an even more daring innovation. The passage reads, "The earth seemed unearthly, and the men were—No, they were not inhuman. Well, you know, that was the worst of it—this suspicion of their not being inhuman. They howled and leaped and spun and made horrid faces, but what thrilled you was just the thought of their humanity—like yours—the thought of your remote kinship with this wild and passionate uproar" (96). Clearly, Marlow had been about to follow an "automatic" tendency of language to parallelism and say that the earth was unearthly and the men were inhuman, but then, in a moment of spontaneous self-revision marked by a dash, he decided that the men were *not* inhuman, that the statement offered him by language was not, after all, precise.

This moment represents the most radical and disturbing insight of Conrad's literary career, when Marlow concedes that the "savages," on whose inhumanity or subhumanity was predicated an entire imperial enterprise, were not, in fact, inhuman—that no metaphysical difference intruded between the European and the howling figures on the shore—and that the lavish rhetoric of religious and humanitarian altruism by which the entire squalid affair had been justified lacked a factual premise. It was disturbing to many of Conrad's contemporaries that Marlow could assert a common humanity binding themselves and the savage cannibals of the African interior, and it is disturbing to some others, and to the majority of his readers today, that he has to work this assertion out laboriously, as if it were a new, strange, and unsettling thought.[5] But what's recorded is momentous: in refusing the routine statement offered him by the linguistic mechanism, Marlow also refuses the thought behind that mechanism, and asserts, or admits, a kinship that official ideology denied.[6]

Mastery of the language, then, is not merely a matter of technical facility, the discovery of clever new ways of putting things. It entails both a responsiveness to language—a willingness to hear the suggestions of language (desert ...- deserted)—and a willingness to question and even refuse a linguistic mechanism whose sufficiency goes largely unquestioned by native speakers, and, more important, to refuse the ideology that goes silently along with it, embedded in its customary phrases and locutions. When Conrad masters the language in the technical sense, he is able to conceive of and even to urge a relinquishing of mastery in the ideological-imperial sense.

Something traumatic happened to Conrad on his own trip up the Congo in 1890. His journals give little clue as to what that might have been, but he later said that his experience converted him from a "perfect animal" with "not a thought in his head" into a "writer" (qtd. in Garnett, *Letters* xii). Perhaps this conversion occurred when Conrad, son of a patriot who had been arrested, shackled, and removed from his homeland, saw Africans described by their European conquerors as workers, enemies, criminals, and rebels. Perhaps Conrad discovered, during this most formative of his travels, that language does not simply record or reflect identity, but, in a brutally pragmatic sense, confers it, and that mastery of language is mastery itself; perhaps he sensed that his own rapidly increasing powers would one day be sufficient to enable him to manipulate language to unravel prejudicial assumptions and to create new truths. By insisting—a decade after the experience itself—that no, they were not workers, enemies, or rebels, and no, they were not inhuman, Conrad took a long step on this arduous path.

III. Universality

I have spoken of Conrad's mastery of the language as though this were a natural and neutral concept, but it is not: it is the product of a specific intellectual environment. If, in their times, Dante, Shakespeare, Flaubert, and Keats were not praised as masters of the language—if they were praised as vessels of the world-spirit, as inspired geniuses, as national heroes, as voices of the people— the reason is not that they had failed to achieve Conrad's facility, but that the concept of "the language" then in place did not support the notion of mastery. People who regard language as a gift bestowed by God will not praise mere individuals as masters of language; nor will those who understand language as a matching of things and names. And if, like the rationalist thinkers of the French Enlightenment, we hold language to be a species endowment that distinguishes human beings from brutes, it will not occur to us that a particular individual might be a singular master. Finally, if, like the nineteenth century's linguistic nationalists, we maintain that language represents the accreted and concretized spirit of a people, then we will not regard individuals as masters, especially not an individual like Conrad, a latecomer and outsider to the language.

For anyone to be praised as a master of a given language, language must be conceptualized in a certain way, and in one of those marvelous coincidences that gives people faith in the notion of a *Zeitgeist*, that very conception was being developed by an obscure Swiss linguist at just the time Conrad was gaining a reputation. In lectures given at the University of Geneva beginning in 1906, Ferdinand de Saussure invented modern linguistics by identifying what he called the integral and concrete object of linguistics—language as such, the

MANNER OF FETTERING SLAVES.

(a)

(b)

Fig. 1.1 Signifying chains. (a) From: Verney Lovett Cameron. *Across Africa*. 2 vols. London: Daldy, Isbister & Co., 1877. 1.166; (b) From Ferdinand de Saussure. *Cours de linguiste générale*. Eds. Charles Bally, Albert Sechehaye, with Albert Redlinger. Paris: Payot, 1916.

system of signs that enables members of a linguistic community to communicate. In signs, sounds are bonded with concepts to produce meaningful utterances, or words; these, when heard by another person, can be decoded so that the original thought is transferred to the mind of another. Since, in his account, thoughts are conveyed mechanically from head to head without reference to context, Saussure's theory represents the most influential version of "the language machine," a metaphor that, according to Roy Harris, dominates all of twentieth-century linguistics (see Harris *passim*).

Because the language machine is constructed by society, its signs are, as Saussure argued, "arbitrary" and non-natural: Each linguistic community has its own categories and concepts. This part of Saussure's theory would have been intuitively apparent to the multilingual Conrad, and also Marlow, who seems to creep on toward Saussure as relentlessly as he approaches Kurtz. (Indeed, the famous talking heads of Saussure's speaking circuit are a kind of theoretical third to both the skulls surrounding Kurtz's hut and the men Marlow sees at the Outer Station, "advancing in a file … connected together with a chain whose bights swung between them" [*YOS* 19]—a "signifying chain" indeed. (See Figure 1.1.)) Marlow's experience of losing his way on the river, feeling cut off from everything he had known, also has unexpected Saussurean resonance. To Saussure's early readers, his most unconventional feature was undoubtedly the way in which he located language entirely in the heads of speakers and hearers, where concepts were joined to sounds.[7] Where previous linguists stressed the matching of word to object, Saussure set the world off to one side, relegating it, as Marlow might say, "to another existence perhaps." Conrad also grasped the devastating consequence of this account of the sign, an acute sense of unreality deriving from the fact that things can be called whatever the dominant power in the community chooses. "All is illusion," he wrote to a friend during a particularly bleak period, "—the words written, the mind at which they are aimed, the truth they are intended to express, the hands that will hold the paper, the eyes that will glance at the lines" (*Letters* 2: 198). "The 'things as they are,'" he wrote to a friend in despair, "exist only in words" (*Letters* 2: 200).[8] And in another *Zeitgeist* coincidence, Conrad wrote in *Under Western Eyes*, a book largely set in Geneva and published at the very time Saussure was lecturing there, that "Words, as is well known, are the great foes of reality" (3).

There is, however, another consequence of language conceived this way, and this one proved to be beneficial to Conrad, or at least his reputation. Language that floats free of the world assumes the character of a game or instrument, a system that one can learn and a skill that one deploys, like playing the flute or chess, which any competent person may do, but some may do better than others. In the ethos of Saussure, it becomes possible for the first time to speak of linguistic "mastery." Conrad's use of the alien English language provided the best possible example of mastery, since his facility was learned, laboriously, as an adult. In this respect, Conrad was an exemplary Saussurean writer.

But in other respects, Conrad exceeded or eluded the Saussurean model, and the ways he did so actually provide the grounds for a compelling critique of Saussure and the whole idea of a language machine. Strangely, for a Swiss citizen, Saussure based his theory of language on the self-contained system of signs in a given linguistic community. But Conrad's thronging, multilingual mind operated on a completely different principle. For him, homonyms, cognate forms, common roots, and interlinguistic puns crowded around each word, which came accompanied, as it were, by adjacencies and distractions, including immediate translations into several other languages.[9] It would have been impossible for Conrad to think of natural languages as tidy little self-contained packages, as Saussure does. But the fluidity and interpenetration Conrad experienced actually corresponded to the real world, beginning with Switzerland, where no lines on maps or gates at the borders seal off one language from another.

Another weakness in Saussure's theory that Conrad exposes concerns Saussure's implicit conservatism. Society determines the meaning of signs, Saussure says, and solidarity with the past checks individual initiative. We cannot simply make up new signs, or decide one day that a given sound will represent a new thought. But people are "generally content with the language they have inherited," and so language is stabilized and held in place by a general acceptance of the status quo (Saussure 73). Not having inherited English, Conrad never achieved this unquestioning ease; but his practice of relentless and probing innovation as he strove to express his thoughts and represent the world suggests the real mutability and pliability of language in a way Saussure does not. After all, if Saussure were right and language was a fixed code inherited from the past—an essentially conservative system displaying "collective inertia toward innovation" and even "the impossibility of revolution," the social institution that is "least amenable to initiative," a system in which "at every moment solidarity with the past checks freedom of choice"—then nobody could do what Conrad is said to have done, to disclose within the language resources unsuspected by native speakers (Saussure 73, 74).

But Saussure's most glaring limitation lies in positing a mental world of clear and conscious thoughts, proceeding in crisp succession from mind to mind in obedience to intentions with an efficiency that can only be called Swiss. For Conrad, this was simply never the case. His daily experience of being misunderstood or not understood as a speaker instilled or perhaps reinforced a constant doubt that he could communicate with his readers, or even put his own thought into words at all. After noting, with one of those provocatively ambiguous phrases that define Conrad's peculiar stylistic richness, that Kurtz was "just a word for me," Marlow asks his listeners, "Do you see him? Do you see the story? Do you see anything? It seems to me I am trying to tell you a dream. . . . it is impossible to convey the life-sensation of any given epoch of one's existence—that which makes its truth, its meaning—its subtle and penetrating essence. . . . We live as we dream—alone" (*YOS* 82). Such an insight, so characteristic of Conrad—so indicative of his particular kind of literary achievement, in which words seem to have meaning in excess of intention, and the transfer of thoughts is only a vain illusion—simply never occurred to Saussure. Indeed, we can measure the immense distance between the two by considering the portrait of "the Intended" in *Heart of Darkness*—a pathetic and deluded creature living entirely in her illusions, shown to be complicit with "the horror"—as a Conradian commentary (unintended, of course) on intentions in general. Perhaps, in a Swiss mood, we might prefer to live in a Saussurean world; but Conrad's corrosive doubt surely reflects, admittedly in extreme form, the actual experience of language users more accurately than Saussure's theoretical idealization.

Language seemed to Saussure and others to be primarily a vehicle of communication, but Conrad's experience of language was, in general, one of intense groping solitude and isolation. He did, however, manage to communicate this experience so effectively that, for many readers, especially in the twentieth century, his most compelling narratives represent profound explorations of the inner world of the mind. This approach replaced an earlier "nineteenth-century" understanding of Conrad in which the subject of his tales seemed to be what happens to men when they venture into remote parts of the world where they have to exist in conditions of extreme heat and humidity without a supportive social structure.[10] In the nineteenth-century reading, Conrad's work was valuable insofar as it extended the range of European literature, in a spirit of what one reviewer called "annexation," all the way to the ends of the earth (qtd. in Watt, *Almayer* xliii). In the twentieth century, however, Conrad was assimilated, perhaps too rapidly, to Freud and the general notion of the unconscious; the relationship between Kurtz and Marlow eclipsed that between Kurtz and the natives, and the paradigmatic Conradian issue became not annexation but "penetration," a word that grasps, in a Freudian spirit, the cognitive and the sexual together. As Morton Zabel put it, "The facts of human action and conscience which most of [his contemporaries] were content to record passively, detachedly, critically, theoretically, he brought all his forces to the task of *penetrating*" (13). Marlow's desperate statement that it seemed to him he was trying to tell us a dream indicated, to many twentieth-century readers, that the narrative itself was a form of therapy. So powerfully did Conrad exemplify certain Freudian themes that he may in fact have exerted a reciprocal influence on Freud's reception. At least for literary critics, it almost goes without saying that Freud is Conradian; as Frederick Karl says, "Freud, too, returned from the world of dreams—an equally dark Congo—with an interpretation and a method" ("*Danse Macabre*" 125). But neither Freud nor Conrad had any interest—any conscious interest—in the other, and we should not feel obliged to staple them together, especially if this prevents us from fashioning a Conrad for the twenty-first century.

In fact, as the twentieth century drew to a close, many readers were dissatis-fied with explanations of Conrad that confined themselves to the mind. The issues that arose over the past generation concerning the position of Africans, women, and colonized peoples in his work suggested a new concern with broader social, moral, and political issues. These issues, while interesting and productive in themselves, also prepared the way for a new reading that looks outward, beyond the individual mind.

Such a reading might begin with the famous description at the beginning of *Heart of Darkness* of Marlow's narrative methods. The mysterious narrator—the man who listens to Marlow and reports his speech, the man who never ap-pears, whose name and identity we never know—comments that "the yarns of seamen have a direct simplicity, the whole meaning of which lies within the shell of a cracked nut" (48). Coming at the very moment Freud published *The Interpretation of Dreams*, this seems a casual but decisive dismissal of "inner" meaning as vulgar and naïve, something any ordinary sailor could pull off. But Marlow, the narrator suggests, is different. In Marlow's tales, "the meaning of an episode was not inside like a kernel but outside, enveloping the tale which brought it out only as a glow brings out a haze." When Marlow, lounging on the deck of the *Nellie*, gestures back upriver toward England's interior and says, "this also has been one of the dark places of the earth," he does seem to be telling a different kind of story, one that refers not to the inside of the individ-ual mind but to some hazy interpersonal space beyond time and conscious-ness, a space in which people can be different from what they are, and comparable to those from whom they are (at the moment) different (48). In this space, one's position on the timeline of modernity determines cultural and even personal identity. In other circumstances, Marlow suggests, we could be not merely different, but radically and repellently different from what we are, without being *completely* different.

The language has no preexisting name for this space, but perhaps it is pli-able enough to accommodate a new term, the "surconscious," which might be described as a domain of meaningfulness that exists ambiguously among peo-ple, beyond and between their individual minds, at the margins of linguistic categories and concepts. Where the unconscious, with its dark inadmissible secrets, isolates, the surconscious envelops and unites. There are no secrets in the surconscious, no privacies, only collectively felt intimations of thoughts or feelings. But the surconscious shares with the unconscious a resistance to translation into clear propositions, clear sentences, or clear stories, an insis-tence on something beyond the thoughts we can formulate in rational terms. This account must itself remain blurred and unsatisfying, if provocative.

Yet the surconscious might turn out to be Conrad's contribution to the eth-ical and political thought of the twenty-first century. This new era's challenges, insofar as they can be glimpsed in these very early days, do not involve a heroic confrontation with the depths of our being, but rather an acknowledgment, which has its own form of heroism, that those whom political or cultural ideology casts as subhuman or inhuman—barbarians, criminals, cannibals, terrorists, those ignorant millions with their horrid ways—are co-participants in a single human commonality; an acknowledgment that, no, they are not inhuman. Reaching back to a common prehistory, gesturing out toward the enveloping ocean, and venturing deep upriver to the absolute savage, Marlow, an ordinary man in most respects, heralds a new effort to reach beyond rather than within for the source of our deepest being.

In an era of enlightened cosmopolitanism, when we seem to be able to transcend our cultural limitations by accessing vast stores of information and doing away, once and for all, with myths and ancient prejudices about the peoples of the world, we would do well to remind ourselves of Marlow's struggle to admit the humanity of savages, of the real difficulty of establishing positive, transcultural, pan-ideological relationships on a purely "human" or universal level. We cannot simply proclaim an untroubled oneness with that humanity so far away any more than we can speak, or make ourselves want to speak, a world language. Identification, in Conrad, is never easy, for it is an involuntary and traumatic experience that forces us to recognize that the things we cherish about ourselves—the very terms of our cultural, historical, and individual identity, not to mention the moral and legal codes by which we live—are not universal, necessary, or even benign, but are, like Saussurean signs, arbitrary and contingent, with a disturbing capacity for violence.

But if contemporary proponents of the cosmopolitan point of view typically come to rest in a state of heightened self-satisfaction—enrichment for ourselves, great benefit to the other, at no cost—that actually mimics rather than contradicts the colonial-imperial attitude, Marlow comes to rest in a profound despair, obsessively telling his tale to such audiences as he can command. His insight into a universal humanity seems only to have deepened his isolation, and his compulsive narration of his experiences produces as little good effect on him as it did on Coleridge's ancient mariner.

A little story from the end of the twentieth century, different from Marlow's but similar in some respects, might point the way out.

Several years ago, the State Department, in its wisdom, sent me to lecture at a couple of universities in Croatia, including the university at Osijek, a nineteenth-century city that had seen better days. These better days were a long time ago; in recent years, the city had come under attack from the Yugoslav army in a conflict that had left its mark on each building in the city center, and on everyone in it. I had never been in Croatia or a recent war zone; I had only rarely been in places where I simply could not communicate linguistically. Even in the town's one Western institution, a McDonald's installed with great fanfare the year before, I had to point in order to get my sandwich. The English-speaking students and faculty to whom I was delivering my last lecture in a sweltering third-floor room had, just a few years before, been trembling in their cellars as shells and bombs exploded around them; and now they were listening to me as I presented them with *Heart of Darkness*, a text that almost all of them were reading for the first time.

I drew their attention to the passage where Marlow, at the very beginning of his tale, notes that England, too, had been one of the dark places of the earth, in the "savage" position with respect to the conquering Romans. "What do you know about dark places of the earth?" I asked; "what happens in dark places? What must happen for a place to be called 'dark'?" After a difficult period of silence—it is impossible to render the painful sluggishness of the time that followed; I felt as if I were trying to find my way on a deserted river, cut off from everything I had known—one student raised her hand. "Murder," she said quietly, and the word hung in the air. Others eventually had their own answers: "bombs" . . . "killing" . . . "rape." I didn't understand this last word, and had to ask her to repeat it. "Look around you," one said; and the others responded by staring at their desks. I thought of the six-foot hole I had seen in the corner of an apartment house, a space where people might have been sitting, watching at the window, at the time the shell ripped through; of the shrapnel marks on every single building; of the sunburst pattern of grooves gouged in the pavement of the streets by cluster bombs; and of something I had seen just that morning, a staccato trail of machine gun bullets running diagonally up the image of the Virgin Mary in the church in the middle of the town. "And yet," said one, "a few years ago we were all Yugoslavs—almost Europeans."

I took this comment to refer to an understanding, rare in the world at large but common in that room, that people who belong one moment to the civilized world can abruptly find themselves in a "jungle" where "savagery" reigns; that they can suddenly find themselves called enemies and criminals by their former compatriots, and can even find themselves calling those compatriots the same. But these students, as I will call them, were now crowded into a classroom, stretching their imaginations in a different direction, enlarging their minds by considering things from other points of view, imagining a bond with that humanity so far away—Congolese natives, English sailors, Conrad, me. What lingers in my mind is the experience of watching these young people come to terms with the fact that *Heart of Darkness* described them, too, that it contained "words for them." I find myself hoping that this recognition helped alleviate their sense of helpless isolation and exposure, even as it provided a well-nigh mythic account of them.

The world contains so many dark places that "darkness" might be considered a kind of common denominator, the underlying basis of all our identifications. What this means, I think, is that we share with all humans not just a capacity for savagery, but a common vulnerability to being called savage. Since signs are arbitrary, we are all exposed, in theory, to the possibility of being slotted into the dark place reserved for the absolute Other, and treated accordingly. This fact, while not exactly heartening in itself, might still open onto the more promising prospect of two linked insights whose combination is distinctly Conradian: first, that we are inhibited by psychology, ideology, and language from realizing a universal identity: we live as we dream, alone. And second, that since all human beings are isolated in these and other ways, we are in fact identified with each other, all others, even if we cannot fully express or realize this universal identification. Our subjective and linguistic isolation is precisely what we hold in common. The passionate mind-to-mind identifications Conrad depicted between characters who are, as personalities, utterly alone only begin to suggest the real dimensions of Conrad's insight. If we could learn to think isolation and universality together, we might yet gain a certain perspective on our common lot, as well as on our common predicament, and thereby open a pinprick of light within the immense darkness that Marlow confronts but—as a man on the cusp of the nineteenth and twentieth centuries—only half understands.

Notes

1. Listening to his peculiar speech in 1913, Lady Ottoline Morrell found it "difficult to believe that this charming gentleman ... was ... a master of English prose" (qtd. in Gathorne-Hardy 233–34). The compliment is also found in, and indeed presumed by, F.R. Leavis, Edward Said, and Fredric Jameson.

2. For discussions of Conrad's linguistic difficulties in *Almayer's Folly*, see Watt, *Almayer* lxviii–lii; see also Pulc.

3. Note that Conrad describes Yanko Gooral, whom readers often identify as Polish, as immured in nature: "lithe, supple, long-limbed, straight as a pine ... his humanity suggested to me the nature of a woodland creature" ("Amy Foster," *TOT* 111).

4. I do not mean to imply that Conrad never again creates powerful images of nature, only that when he does so (as in *The Shadow-Line*) he often seems to retrieve earlier formulae. We can, incidentally, track a comparable diminishment in the concept of paternal authority. Conrad never depicts strong biological fathers, but at first, he tended to depict powerful male authority figures. Tom Lingard, for example, was described by a contemporary as "a personage of almost mythical renown, a sort of ubiquitous sea-hero, perhaps at times a sort of terror to evil-doers (W.G. St. Clair qtd. in Sherry, *Conrad's Eastern* 315–16). In the world of *Nostromo*, authority is no longer mythical, terrible, or paternal; rather, in this book and others, Conrad depicts complex webs and skeins of relationships in which no single figure dominates, a network in which the concepts of charisma, paternity, and moral authority are relentlessly exposed as mere semblances. In *The Secret Agent*, both paternity and nature have become remote, almost inconceivable concepts.

5. According to Chinua Achebe's notorious argument, Conrad never did work it out, and continued to regard Africans as subhuman (see Achebe, "An Image of Africa"). In African studies, Conrad is also routinely described in these terms. In their influential *The Africa that Never Was: Four Centuries of British Writing about Africa* (1970), Dorothy Hammond and Alta Jablow comment that most European writing about Africa depicts Africans as "stock figures ... never completely human," so that the image of Africa "became and remains the Africa of H. Rider Haggard and Joseph Conrad" (14).

6. One fact readers have difficulty keeping in mind is that the language in which these events occurred, as it were, must have been French. In listening to suggestions arising within English, Conrad-Marlow is actually pitting the resources of English against the Belgian colonial enterprise.

7. I've already noted Conrad's sensitivity to acoustic images as a way of linking words whose meanings were unrelated. This phonic overaccentuation was also a feature of his speech itself. As Lady Ottoline Morrell noted after meeting Conrad, "he talked English with a strong accent, as if he tasted his words in his mouth before pronouncing them" (Gathorne-Hardy 233).

2

The Moment and Afterlife of *Heart of Darkness*

BENITA PARRY

There is no material content, no formal category of artistic creation, however mysteriously transmitted and itself unaware of the process, which did not originate in the empirical reality from which it breaks free.

Fredric Jameson, *Aesthetics and Politics*

I.

Heart of Darkness must be among the most interpreted books in English fiction. It reaches us already glossed—and this is a short list—as a night journey into the unconscious, a mythic descent into the underworld, a meditation on transgression, an allegory of narrative representation, and a key text in both modernism and colonial fiction. In the current climate it is hard to recall that there was a time when the critical literature was awash with commentaries wholly indifferent to the novel's historical, political and ideological materials; or to remember that, among those who were aware of a looming geophysical presence, some offered opinion with an indiscrimination now alien to the intellectual discussion. "It is one of the great points of Conrad's story," wrote Lionel Trilling, "that Marlow speaks of the primitive life of the jungle not as being noble or charming or even free but as being base and sordid—and for *that* reason compelling" (qtd. Cox 64); while K.K. Ruthven described Kurtz as a "pioneer in the psychic wilderness of Africa" (qtd. Cox 80); and Walter Allen mused, "The heart of darkness of the title is at once the heart of Africa, the heart of evil—everything that is nihilistic, corrupt and malign—and perhaps the heart of man" (Allen 291). Perhaps Chinua Achebe's indignation at the racism of Conrad and *Heart of Darkness* should rather have been directed at such portentous and ill-informed ruminations construing a minatory African primitivism, especially since Achebe did recognize that Conrad had set up "layers of insulation between himself and the moral universe of his story" (Achebe 256).

That recent commentaries are now more properly attuned to the novel's historical resonances must in part be attributed to the work done under the banner of postcolonial studies, and because such discussion has infiltrated mainstream literary studies, we now find that *Heart of Darkness* is being read as an ironic re-presentation of the authorized colonialist narrative and an ethical critique of European imperialism. Still, because the book does rehearse the very discourses it also distances, its racist idiom cannot be overlooked or wished away. Although critics have observed that "Africa" is never named, few readers could doubt that the continent is a referent in a novel that draws on and elaborates images long familiar to a Western readership from prior ideologically saturated texts—an unearthly landscape of immense, matted jungle, an impenetrable forest, a human environment inhabited by naked black bodies bearing spears and bows "who howled and leaped and spun and made horrid faces" (*YOS* 96), whose speech is heard as a savage discord and whose souls are perceived as rudimentary.

A few years after the fiction had appeared, Conrad, in his contribution to protests against Belgian rule in the Congo, wrote of the European's obligation to the African who "shares with us the consciousness of the universe in which we live" (qtd in Harrison 56). This acknowledgement of a common human intelligence is in large part absent from *Heart of Darkness*, which reinscribes the normative European ignorance of African societies prevalent at the time of its writing. Indeed, so constrained is the book's view of the peoples' faculties that had Conrad known about the many mutinies and rebellions against the European invasion—ranging from opposition led by traditional and religious leaders to the struggles of workers and peasants[1]—no narrative room would have remained to accommodate such sentient opposition. Yet awareness of resistance to the European physical presence and its metaphysical gaze *is* recognized—even as it is displaced onto an unnamed and autonomous "Africa" that withholds its meanings from a narrator whose story of a voyage into the unknown, by virtue of its generic form, promises revelation.

This manifest frustration of intellectual and imaginative mastery renders Achebe's charge as inadequate to comprehending the novel's plural and contradictory discourses, as does V.S. Naipaul's claim that Conrad's fiction constitutes "totally accurate reportage" about "the world's half-made societies" lacking in any goal and that "seemed doomed to remain half-made" (Naipaul, *Return* 204, 214, 216). By reading the book as either a misinformed or an informed representation of a specific location, both Achebe and Naipaul close off the possibility of considering how *Heart of Darkness* reflects on its own misrecognitions, the rhetorical extravagances of Marlow's narrative performance opening up a chasm between words intended to communicate an extraordinary experience to identified auditors already acquainted with, and implicated in Europe's overseas adventures, and words connoting that which Marlow cannot properly articulate. Consider: "It was the stillness of an implacable force brooding over an inscrutable intention" (93).

Whereas significant sections of the fiction have the eloquent specificity of a realist text, this stylistic register coexists with an opacity that is already apparent in both the first narrator's introduction and the beginning of Marlow's tale, and intensifies as the novel moves spatially and psychologically away from familiar terrains. On the one hand this allusive and indirect language denotes a failure of representation inseparable from the epistemological constraints of the imperialist moment during which the book was conceived; and on the other hand it signifies an apprehension of "overwhelming realities" (93) that lie beyond the fiction's cognitive horizons. If an oblique idiom can imply the unsayable in the philosophical sense of the ineffable and transcendental, in *Heart of Darkness* a deliberated linguistic obscurity gestures toward meanings that the novel cannot understand, but that are perceived as *there* and awaiting a time when they will be spoken.

Perhaps then, the book's singular afterlife can be attributed to its simultaneous habitation of both the temporal and the proleptic, and indeed my sense of the novel's futurity exceeds its well-charted posthumous influences. This is not to suggest that we should neglect the significance of the many rewritings the book has generated. Over the years the fiction's imagined "Africa" has been coarsely appropriated by H.G. Wells in *Tono-Bungay;* echoed in Andre Gide's journal, Graham Greene's *Journey Without Maps* and his novel *A Burnt-Out Case;* and commandeered in V.S. Naipaul's *A Bend in the River* by an author intent on denigrating an entire continent. Critics have also maintained that the unintelligible "Africa" of *Heart of Darkness* inspired writers as various as Chinua Achebe, Ngugi wa Thiong'o, Tayeb Salih, Nadine Gordimer, Ama Ata Aidoo and Zakes Mda[2] to invoke the vibrant cognitive traditions and volatile cultural forms of a vast and heterogeneous continent in ways that implicitly contest what they read as the novel's configurations of a world immutable and epistemologically empty—a construction of Conrad's "Africa" that I will contest.

If journalists and commentators reporting on the present-day crises of Africa are liable to cite *Heart of Darkness* as proof of the continent's entrenched and incorrigible traditions,[3] the book has also prompted more judicious reflections. Looking back to *Heart of Darkness* and preserving some of its geophysical imagery are two recent fictions set in the Congo at the time of independence, Ronan Bennett's *The Catastrophist* (1997) and Barbara Kingsolver's *The Poisonwood Bible* (1998). Written respectively by an Irish and a North American writer, these have conscience-stricken white protagonists confronting colonialism's legacies, and the voice of a people flagrantly disarticulated by Conrad's book can be heard offstage castigating colonialism. We should also note two English-language films claiming descent from *Heart of Darkness,* Francis Ford Coppola's *Apocalypse Now!* (1979) and Nicholas Roeg's more recent *Heart of Darkness* (1993), both communicating a present-tense dismay at past and continuing imperial violations.

An exhibition entitled *Heart of Darkness* held at the Institute of Culture in Barcelona in 2002 is further evidence of the fiction's relevance to contemporary concerns. This installation included audio-film of the sights and sounds of the book's terrain, sepia photographs of mutilated Africans punished by the Belgian administration of the Congo, maps coloured to represent Europe's late-nineteenth-century territorial appropriations in Africa, clips from colonialist documentaries featuring near-naked childlike natives and benignly patriarchal colonial officers in full uniform, and two specially filmed sequences from the novel—the version of a diseased Kurtz in a dilapidated hut surrounded by the accoutrements of European civilization and ministered to by his devoted denizens, as arresting as the professional performances of Marlon Brando and John Malkovich. This openly political exhibition—accompanied by conferences on Conrad, Conrad in Cinema, and the present-day migration of Africans—displayed images and texts testifying to both Europe's historic incursions into sub-Saharan Africa and the contemporary afflictions of globalization in that zone.

Such rewritings, retrospects, and homages revisit Conrad's story of imperialism in Africa. Laura Chrisman, however, has urged attention to the novel's "imperial metropolitan perspective" (22), arguing that this would enable us to read *Heart of Darkness* as "a critique of the ways in which that metropolitan culture and economy is so totally yet casually involved in the process of imperialism" (24), the book's concrete references to the social locations and functions of protagonists converging as a criticism "of the material structures of imperial capitalism" (26). This reading reminds us that if we do not want to talk about capitalism, then we should remain silent about colonialism; and it draws attention to the paradox of a politically conservative writer who does not address the cruelties of dispossession and exploitation within the imperial homeland—and whose hatred of revolution produced the grotesque figures of *The Secret Agent, Under Western Eyes*, and *Nostromo*—but who in *Heart of Darkness* shows capitalism naked in the colonies.

We could, then, describe Conrad, in words borrowed from Walter Benjamin when writing about Baudelaire, as "a secret agent, an agent of the secret discontent of his class with its own rule" (Marcuse 20). For in *Heart of Darkness* the violence of an expansionist colonial capitalism emerges not only in the graphic description of insatiable greed and gratuitous callousness, but also from the sardonic scrutiny of an ideology that enabled and justified aggression. Excoriating imperialism's claim to a noble and disinterested mission, Marlow in characteristically florid language remembers an abject colonialism, "a sordid farce acted in front of a sinister back-cloth" (61), recalling how he foresaw "that in the blinding sunshine I would become acquainted with a flabby, pretending, weak-eyed devil of a rapacious and pitiless folly" (65). Moreover, at a time when lies about a benevolent empire circulated widely within the imperial homeland, *Heart of Darkness* casts a cold eye on imperialism as a world system managed from the metropolitan centers in the interest of these centers.[4]

If in abandoning the provisional title, "*The* Heart of Darkness," Conrad freed the fiction of temporal and spatial constraints, history and geography remain inscribed in rhetoric, tropological design, and structure. Here the austerity of the language enhances the realism of an appalling scene that was also represented in nonfictional accounts:

> Black shapes crouched, lay, sat between the trees leaning against the trunks, clinging to the earth, half coming out, half effaced within the dim light, in all the attitudes of pain, abandonment and despair ... lost in uncongenial surroundings, fed on unfamiliar food, they sickened, became inefficient, and were allowed to crawl away and rest. (66)

In another register, the diction of *Heart of Darkness* parodies the new accents brought to colonial discourse by imperialism, its engorging territorial and political ambition envisaged in Marlow's recall of Kurtz opening his mouth "voracious[ly] ... as though he had wanted to swallow all the air, all the earth, all the men before him" (134). This same historically concrete imagination is brought to Kurtz's Report for the International Society for the Suppression of Savage Customs, a document that rehearses and estranges imperialism's grandiloquent propaganda—the heavenly mission to civilize, the noble, exalted cause, high and just proceedings—for which the speeches of King Leopold of the Belgians provided a readily available source.

So too the book's chiaroscuro of light and dark, which simultaneously reiterates and compromises the customary evaluation attaching to white and black in colonial discourse, is imbued by historical usage. On the one hand the received European associations of white with truth, probity, and purity are reinstalled: one of many such examples is Kurtz's Intended, her fair hair and white brow offered by Marlow as visible signs of a "soul as translucently pure as a cliff of crystal" (152). On the other hand, white light comes to denote lies, greed, confusion, and corruption: the immaculate city of Brussels, the heart of Belgium's heartless imperialism is described as a whited sepulchre; white fog is more blinding than the night, and sunlight can be made to lie; the eyes of the avaricious traders are mica discs; the visible object of colonialist desire is ivory, and the psychotic footnote to Kurtz's Report ("Exterminate all the brutes !") "blazed at you, luminous and terrifying, like a flash of lightning in a serene sky" (118).[5]

Moreover, whereas the use of black and dark repeats the established connotations of the terms with death, the obscure, the sinister, the inauspicious, the evil, and the savage, it also effects a significant realignment of the positive meanings attached to the empire of light. Now it is Europe that is plunged into gloom by its own imperialist project, a gloom that invades the house of Kurtz's Intended, casting the biggest and greatest town on earth in mournful shades, and overshadowing the tranquil and luminous waters of the Thames, the place from which an expedition carrying its freight of moral darkness departs for the benighted continent of the imperial imagination.

If the novel's iconography of white and black reprises and disturbs established tropes of cultural and moral hierarchy, then metaphors and metonyms signifying the link between metropole and colony juxtapose and override difference in configuring the interdependence of a divided and inequitable world-system:[6] grass sprouting through stones in a European city reemerges as vegetation growing among a dead man's ribs in a jungle; the bones of the domino set laid out on the deck of a ship anchored off an English coast reappear in the bodies of emaciated black laborers; a piece of white worsted manufactured in England is seen around the neck of a ragged black man; the brooding gloom of English waters recurs as the tenebrous darkness of a faraway river; the marmoreal betrothed and the barbaric black woman make identical gestures of despair at losing Kurtz; for Marlow the sound of the Intended's voice heard in Brussels "seemed to have the accompaniment of all the other sounds . . . the ripple of the river, the soughing of the trees . . . the murmurs of the crowds, the faint ring of incomprehensible words cried from afar" (159). This dispersed but integral ornamentation is embedded in a narrative architecture supported by an arc between the Thames and a distant, unnamed river, between the capital cities of London and Brussels, and a remote, nameless forest. Thus do structure and trope map a differential imperial totality.[7]

II.

In his short study *The Aesthetic Dimension: Toward a Critique of Marxist Aesthetic*, Herbert Marcuse proposes that:

> The radical qualities of art, that is to say, its indictment of established realities and its invocation of the beautiful image (*schöner Schein*) are grounded precisely in the dimensions where art transcends its social determination and emancipates itself from the given universe of discourse and behaviour while preserving its overwhelming presence . . . . The aesthetic transformation becomes a vehicle of recognition and indictment . . . . [O]nly as estrangement does art fulfill a cognitive function: it communicates truths not communicable in any other language; it contradicts. (6, 10) [8]

Marcuse's remarks are singularly appropriate to a novel that preserves and breaks free from its origins in empirical reality, that is immersed in and alienated from the consciousness and unconscious of the imperialist moment when it was written; that, by telling a story of catastrophe and nescience, alludes to and disparages the triumphalist rhetoric of imperialist ideology, and that invokes images of auspicious expectation.

Rosa Luxemburg in 1913 had described imperialism as "the political expression of the accumulation of capital in its competitive struggle for what remains still open of the non-capitalist environment" (446). This is a striking description of Europe's "scramble for Africa." During the last decades of the nineteenth century, the European powers had divided Africa among themselves, the lion's share going to England; while France, Germany, Portugal, and

Belgium either initiated or enlarged their overseas empires. Following the Berlin Conference of 1884–5, the vast area of the Congo had come under Belgian rule, to be administered as the personal property of King Leopold II, whose appetite for an African empire had been stimulated by *In the Heart of Africa* (1873), written by a German, Georg Schweinfurth (see Harrison 11), and was further whetted by Henry Morton Stanley's sensational account of his African journeys, published in 1878 as *Through the Dark Continent.*[9] Stanley's reports of Africa's immeasurable and untapped wealth were supported by other sources, and already in 1876 an article had appeared in *The Times* referring to the "unspeakable riches" potentially available in the Congo Basin regions, a prescient observation. Although the Congo's great mineral wealth was yet to be discovered, by the late nineteenth century Europe was exploiting its vast reserves of ivory and rubber for use in the consumer and transport industries of the imperial homelands.[10]

Leopold's punitive regime in the Congo came to attract attention in Europe for a scale of rapacity exceeding normal colonialist practice in Africa. When news of Belgian atrocities reached England and North America, public figures— Roger Casement, E.D. Morel, R. Cunninghame Graham, Charles Dilke, Conan Doyle and later Mark Twain—reviled these outrages in print and public meetings, and although the attacks were in large directed at the intemperance of Belgian exploitation, a few of the protesters were vigorous in denouncing the entire imperialist enterprise in Africa.[11] What until recently has been overlooked is the role of African Americans in the exposure of Leopold's enterprise. In 1890 a journalist, George Washington Williams, who had journeyed to the Congo in the hope of finding a place for the settlement of black Americans only to encounter exploitation and cruelty, produced an "Open Letter to Leopold" indicting his rule. In the same year, the missionary William Sheppard persuaded the Southern Presbyterian Church to send him to the Congo, where through personal observation he came to realize how the Belgian administration was using violence to coerce the African peoples into producing rubber and collecting ivory; and although his major exposure did not appear until 1907, he had by the 1890s published numerous accounts of Belgium's reign of terror in the Congo.[12]

On December 17, 1898, the *Saturday Review*, a newspaper that Conrad is known to have admired, carried a speech by the chairman of the Royal Statistical Society, which read: "Of what certain Belgians can do in the way of barbarity [while claiming to promote civilization in the Congo], Englishmen are painfully aware. Mr. Courtney mentions an instance of a Captain Rom, who ornamented his flower-beds with the heads of twenty-one natives killed in a punitive expedition."[13] When Conrad embarked on *Heart of Darkness*, he may possibly have seen this report and he would in all likelihood have been exposed to the wide coverage given to Stanley's expedition in the Sudan in 1889, published as *In Darkest Africa* in 1890, as well as to the publicity surrounding the

Ashanti War of 1896 and Kitchener's vengeful victory against the Mahdi regime at Omdurman in 1898. All these ventures had involved the promiscuous killing of Africans and had been condemned in journals such as *Cosmopolis*, where Conrad's "An Outpost of Progress" had first appeared in 1897.[14] I am not suggesting that Conrad set out to write a book directed at exposing colonialism in Africa—indeed he was at pains to dissociate himself from such an undertaking.[15] I am suggesting that what he wrote was a powerful critique of imperialism as historical undertaking and ethos.

Nicholas Harrison has cautioned that if *Heart of Darkness* "is viewed as being, at least in part, an intervention in a political debate, it seems inevitable that we should want to quantify its effectiveness" (52–3); and he goes on to show that whereas many who were Conrad's close associates worked tirelessly to expose and protest conditions in the Congo, Conrad's contribution in his capacity as a public figure was limited to a letter that E.D. Morel solicited for incorporation in his report *King Leopold's Rule in the Congo* (1904). Here Conrad wrote: "It is an extraordinary thing that the conscience of Europe, which seventy years ago put down the slave trade on humanitarian grounds, tolerates the Congo state to-day. It is as if the moral clock had been put back many hours" (qtd. in Harrison 55). Observing that it would constitute a punishable offense to deal with animals in the way that the Africans of the Congo were treated, Conrad declared that the happiness and misery of the black man were "deserving of greater regard. He shares with us the consciousness of the universe in which we live" (Harrison 56). Yet long after the labors of the Congo Reform Association have been forgotten by all but some scholars of the period, it is Conrad's novel, as he had hoped when writing a preface to the 1917 edition, that continues to vibrate, "to hang in the air and dwell on the ear" (*YOS* xi).[16] That it does so is in some part because the new social experience of imperialism saturates and is estranged by the book.

This is not to scant the extent to which the novella is implicated in received opinion about Africa as a place of moral darkness and mindless obscurantism. By the time Conrad was writing his book, sub-Saharan Africa had long since impinged on Europe's awareness as an undisturbed treasure trove of untold and unused resources. But Africa also occupied another place in the European imagination. Travelers, missionaries, explorers, and adventurers were scouts for imperialism, mapping the terrain, signposting potential sources of wealth, warning of natural hazards and unfriendly natives. They were also prolific authors of negative representations that were neither amenable nor ever subjected to scrutiny of their truth (see Youngs). Hence, ritual killing and cannibalism were assumed to be commonplace. Included in the memoir of one such informant, Sir Harry Johnston, British consul, explorer, geographer, ethnographer, enthusiastic imperialist, and traveler in the Congo, is a drawing he called "Approach to a Chief's Hut Decorated with Human Heads" (153). Here atrocity is joined with normalcy in both title and configuration, the tidiness of the squat dwellings in the background, the tame and pretty vultures in the foreground and the tranquil expressions on the faces of the severed heads nicely registering a view of how Africa had domesticated the monstrous.[17] As a measure of Conrad's familiarity with reputable rumor, he has Marlow refer casually to the cannibalism of his riverboat crew, and more consequently he shows Marlow viewing Kurtz's garden of dismembered heads with some composure, remarking that this was "only a savage sight" with "a right to exist—obviously—in the sunshine" (132).

Christopher Miller has observed that the unnamed and phantasmagoric Africa of a fiction that was to become the consummate text of "Africanist discourse" drew on and embellished the images already familiar to a Western readership. Certainly the plethora of negatives deployed in narrating a mythopoeic journey into a primordial physical space and a minatory metaphysical landscape,[18] can be read as signifying a world without history or culture, a depraved Eden emanating "the unseen presence of victorious corruption" (138). (That this is not all it signifies is the burden of my argument, to which I will return.) The narration, moreover, appears to ascribe a symbiotic relationship to the baseness of imperialism's agents and the moral dangers emanating from the land.[19] Its most significant recruit is Kurtz, the sophisticated product of Europe whose lack of virtue predisposes him to the lure of the environment's malignant spell: "… the wilderness had found him out early, and had taken on him a terrible vengeance for the fantastic invasion. I think it had whispered to him things about himself which he did not know…. It echoed loudly within him because he was hollow at the core" (131). If Kurtz's innate susceptibility to depravity appears to be induced by the appeal of the dumb and immobile earth, then it is completed by his interactions with its people,[20] a lakeside tribe among whom "he forgot himself" (129), whom he had subdued and subjugated with his guns, and from whom he could not break away.

The fiction is most complicit with the imperial imaginary, I suggest, in the figure of Kurtz as heroic transgressor, to the extent that a fear of the concupiscent satisfactions believed to be on offer to the European in a primitive environment threatens to displace an insight into the material and psychic gratifications known to be available to the European colonialist. Thus, whereas Marlow can retain his equanimity when looking upon the display of severed heads, this being "only a savage sight," intelligence of Kurtz presiding "at certain midnight dances ending with unspeakable rites" (118) transports him—Marlow— "into some lightless region of subtle horrors" (132), delivering a "moral shock … as if something altogether monstrous, intolerable to thought and odious to the soul, had been thrust upon me unexpectedly" (141).

The fiction then, it seems, does narrate the regression of the libertine who violates the taboos of his own culture and is captivated by the primitive, participating in ritual killing, bowing to fetishism, and initiating ceremonies celebrating his own divinity—indeed whose conduct parodies the ethnographic accounts of an "Africa" hospitable to every sin and vice outlawed by civilization. Is Kurtz then to be read as corrupted by the metaphysical evil intrinsic to a physical location? Is he to be understood as debauched by the polymorphous perversity of an extant prehistoric society? When Marlow overhears a company agent saying "Anything—anything can be done in this country" (91), does this refer to "Africa" as a licentious social environment in which everything is permitted or to a colonial location that licenses the excesses of its agents? Does the permissiveness Kurtz accords to himself inhere in his position as a colonialist in the lawless Congo Free State or is he the prototype of the colonizer whom Marlow describes at the start of his tale as the man who had to face the darkness of "utter savagery" closing around him:

> ... all that mysterious life of the wilderness that stirs in the forest, in the jungles, in the hearts of wild men. ... He has to live in the midst of the incomprehensible, which is also detestable. And it has a fascination, too, that goes to work upon him. The fascination of the abomination—you know, imagine the growing regrets, the longing to escape, the powerless disgust, the surrender, the hate. (50)

This generalized compassion for the vulnerability of the intrepid tamer of wild places is later bestowed on Kurtz, and when witnessing the self-consciousness attained in his last moment, Marlow celebrates this as a "supreme moment of complete knowledge," as "a moral victory, paid for by innumerable defeats, by abominable terrors, by abominable satisfactions" (149, 151). Thus does the iconoclast of Europe's social and moral conventions repent his transgressions. Thus is the violator of imperialism's elastic laws in the tropics given the status of the redeemed demonic hero.

Yet the historical specificity of Kurtz's social formation and agency is not dissipated, for he is also the ruthlessly ambitious colonialist to whose making "All Europe" had contributed. In Sven Lindqvist's maverick and informative book *Exterminate the Brutes* are two illustrations relating to the second Ashanti War of 1896, one from *The Illustrated London News* of February 26, 1896, entitled "The Submission of King Prempeh," the other "The Submission of King Prempeh, The Final Humiliation," printed in *The Graphic* of February 29, 1896. Both depict the king (in one case with his mother) crawling to British officers who are seated on a makeshift throne of biscuit tins, and who appear to be healthy in body, sound of mind, and untroubled by unlawful desires (55, 56). The obeisance demanded by colonial officials is well documented and returns us to the possibility of perceiving Kurtz as a dedicated servant of imperialism, who "had collected, bartered, swindled or stolen more ivory than all the other agents together" (113), who is eloquent in declaiming notions of an entrusted cause and high purpose, has a voracious appetite for possession— "'My Intended, my ivory, my station, my river, my'—everything belonged to him" (116) and whose sensual intemperance and commercial aggression derived from his unimpeded power as a colonialist in the Congo Free State.

III.

I have attempted to consider the novel's perceptions of a degraded imperialism in the spirit of Marcuse's remarks on locating the radical qualities of art; and it is in the same spirit that I now want to look beyond the book's manifest recoil from a mythic "Africa" and toward its inchoate apprehensions of what lies beyond its own cognitive compass. In invoking the "overwhelming realities" of an Africa that is represented as both a physical space and a metaphysical realm, *Heart of Darkness* alludes to another semantic universe that its own discourse cannot decipher. To his audience, Marlow confesses that he had been unable to tell what the roll of drums might signify (95), if the piece of cloth round a black man's neck is "a badge, an ornament, a propitiatory charm," and if indeed it was connected to "any idea at all" (67); or whether the "prehistoric man was cursing us, praying to us, welcoming us" (96). Such nescience informs his attempts to represent the "mysterious life" of the immense expanse he looks on but cannot fathom:

> And outside, the silent wilderness surrounding the cleared speck on the earth struck me as something great and invincible, like evil or truth, waiting patiently for the passing away of this fantastic invasion ... the silence of the land went home to one's very heart—the amazing reality of its concealed life .... What was in there? .... The woods were unmoved, like a mask ... they looked with their air of hidden knowledge, of patient expectation, of unapproachable silence .... The long reaches that were like one and the same reach ... slipped past the steamer with their multitude of secular trees looking patiently after this grimy fragment of another world, the forerunner of change, of conquest, of trade, of massacres, of blessings. (76, 80, 81, 93, 129, 148, 48, 81, 98)[21]

Marlow repeatedly laments an incapacity to convey the oneiric quality of his encounter with Kurtz:

> It was the farthest point of navigation and the culminating point of my experience. It seemed somehow to throw a kind of light on everything about me—and into my thoughts. It was sombre enough, too—and pitiful—not extraordinary in any way—not very clear either. No, not very clear, And yet it seemed to throw a kind of light .... Do you see him ? Do you see the story? Do you see anything? It seems to me I am trying to tell you a dream. (51, 82)

This admission extends to his venture into a space whose signs he *sees* but cannot *read*. Just as physical obstacles impede the steamboat's progress upriver into the interior, so does "Africa" resist Marlow's narrative invasion, the very obscurity of his ornate and enigmatic language a confession of imperfect understanding and hermeneutic failure—but also and as significantly an acknowledgment of another continent of meaning. For as I read *Heart of Darkness*, and as I have already indicated, what the narrative encounters is not the ineffable and transcendental beyond enunciation, but a "hidden knowledge" that its available conceptual language *cannot* articulate—not mystery, but secret.

I have tried to suggest that *Heart of Darkness,* in Marcuse's phrase, condenses an "indictment of established realities." But more, in its intimations of what may yet come out of an "Africa" that in the fiction cannot speak its name, the book alludes to a reality that lies beyond its own epistemologically constrained field of vision. This Africa, to whose age-old voice Europe had for long remained deaf, was to acquire new accents that Conrad, ignorant of Africa's histories, cosmologies, social forms, and cultures, could not have imagined when intuiting those indiscernible possibilities that the silently expectant continent was holding in abeyance. Indeed, whereas the people are effectively silenced, the landscape is rendered eloquent.

It has been suggested that what is told in the novel is the impossibility of narrating a silence and a void, since narrative is the passage of time, and the fiction's "Africa" condenses the absence of time.[22] This reading, it seems to me, overlooks the book's pervasive consciousness of both historical time and time anticipated. There is then a paradoxical connection between what can appear disjunctive, between a turn-of-the-nineteenth-century novel written in an era saturated in confident notions about cultural hierarchy and imperial destiny, but that concedes its inability to speak of a world into which it has journeyed, and the Congo that some 50 years later spoke for itself by rejecting Belgian colonialism. At the Independence ceremony in 1960 and in response to King Baudouin's arrogant and patently false declamation that "The independence of the Congo is the result of the undertaking conceived by the genius of King Leopold II,"[23] Patrice Lumumba, the elected prime minister, addressed himself not to the former masters but to "Congolese men and women, fighters for independence," recalling that the people had seen their lands despoiled and had witnessed terrible punishments meted out to those who would not submit "to a rule where justice meant oppression and exploitation," reminding them that "it is by struggle we have won . . . a passionate and idealistic struggle" (qtd. in De Witte 1, 2). Lumumba was to be assassinated and the short-lived post-independence regime over which he presided, destroyed at the behest of the imperialist powers of Europe and North America, who continue to covet the Congo's diamonds, copper, zinc, cobalt, cadmium, uranium, europium, niobium, tantalum, germanium, and coltan (a metal used in mobile phones and lap-top computers) with the same appetite as their predecessors had once lusted after its rubber and ivory.

In the brief moment of an achievement won through the social agency of Africans, Conrad's apprehensions of what would emerge from the continent's "concealed life" and its "patient expectation" came into being, although in a form he could not have predicted. With the defeat of Lumumba's regime, the novel was to have another sort of after-life. Writing of the Congo under Mobutu's egregiously corrupt regime, which the imperial powers, and especially the United States, opportunistically underwrote, Michaela Wrong remarks:

Rebel uprisings, bodies rotting in the sun, a sickening megalomaniac. In newsrooms across the globe, shaking their heads over yet another unfathomable African crisis, producers and sub-editors dusted off memories of school literature courses and reached for the clichés. Zaire was Joseph Conrad's original "Heart of Darkness," they reminded the public. How prophetic the famous cry of despair voiced by the dying Mr. Kurtz at Africa's seemingly boundless capacity for bedlam and brutality had proved yet again. "The horror, the horror." Was nothing more promising ever to emerge from that benighted continent? (7–8)

With somewhat less critical distance, a commentator when writing about the downfall of Laurent Kabila observed:

> The Congo, perhaps unfairly, has always been a symbol of the anarchic. The horror of Joseph Conrad's Kurtz was the unspeakable fear of humankind which knows no humanity. It was also the fear that anyone caught in it could regress to the savage. The belief that the Congo has remained stuck in the morass of ignorance and violence is pervasive .... For a Westerner, the idea that there is a country where normal rules do not apply is strangely disturbing .... There is also the fear that somehow a place like this can drag you down.[24]

When a literary text enters the public domain, the danger exists that ideologically purposeful appropriations will do violence to its heterogeneity and occlude its contradictions. This has been the unjust fate of a fiction in which Conrad saw and critically reconfigured imperialism's pursuit of power, its territorial aggression, and economic exploitation. He was unable to foresee the forces that were to confront its dominion, as he was to do, even if with misgiving, in *Nostromo*. Yet, it is because the novel produces a negative knowledge of a real historical era, looks upon another world in awe and incomprehension, and anticipates a time after "the passing away" of imperialism's "fantastic invasion," that it continues to vibrate, "to hang in the air and dwell on the ear after the last note had been struck."

Notes

1. See Nzongola-Ntalja 41-54. See also Hochschild 124, 164; and Ndaywel è Nziem's researches cited in Harrison 53–4.
2. The Francophone Congolese writer Sony Labou Tansi should be included here.
3. See, for example, Wrong.
4. Laura Chrisman has shown that "The metropole was flooded during the period of modernism with representations of imperialism itself as a system and a totality, with representations of its contestation by colonised peoples and with examples of colonised culture and knowledge-systems" (58). And indeed in *Howards End*, the imperial system does impinge on the bounded domestic scene both in the ghostly form of the unspecified investments enabling the Schlegels's condition of permanent leisure, and most materially as the source of the Wilcox wealth in the Anglo-Imperial Rubber Company of Nigeria.
5. In the context of the fiction, the phrase signifies Kurtz's madness; however Sven Lindqvist argues that extermination of the lower races pervaded nineteenth-century racial thinking and had indeed been carried out in Tasmania. See *Exterminate All the Brutes*.
6. Compare Fredric Jameson, who maintains that the impossibility of representing an absent imperial order meant that the effects of imperialism came to be inscribed in "the very syntax of poetic language itself," thus prompting a generic shift to modernism in literary form. ("Cognitive Mapping" 349) This is a compelling suggestion and can be brought to the reading of those domestic fictions whose consciousness of imperialism has

been overlooked, as Jameson does in his gloss on *Howards End*. (See *Modernism and Empire* 12ff). (Concerning this connection see also my "*Tono-Bungay:* The Failed Electrification of the Empire of Light".) However, in claiming that "a systematic block on any adequate consciousness of the structure of the imperial system" made it impossible for literature to map the new imperial world order, Jameson preempts attention to just such a realization in *Heart of Darkness* (*Modernism and Empire* 10–11).

7. Nico Israel has made a convincing case for these connections: "As emphasized by the text's semiotic glut of rivets, connecting rods, ship's chains and tackle, sealing wax and bits of string and yarn, *Heart of Darkness* portrays the colonial enterprise as a vast circuit of material and imaginary connections— between metropole(s) and periphery, colonizer and colonized, sites of production and consumption, a global circuit subject at any moment to fraying, coming apart, or breaking down" (40).

8. See also Bloch et al.

9. Hochschild relates how avidly Leopold followed reports of Stanley's expeditions and set about courting him.

10. Ivory was "shaped into knife handles, billiard balls, combs, fans, napkin rings, piano and organ keys, chess pieces, crucifixes, snuff boxes and statuettes, as well as false teeth." The demand for rubber in manufacture of tires for carriages and bicycles as well as waterproof clothing generated a worldwide rubber boom in the 1890s. See Hochschild 64, 159.

11. Although here it must be noted that J.A. Hobson, the man subsequently remembered as an arch anti-imperialist who expressed his disgust at King Leopold's claim that the only program of government of the Congo was "the moral and material regeneration of the country," had conceded that Europe owed an imperial responsibility to the lower races of Africa. See *Imperialism* 198.

12. See Hochschild. There are two recent biographies on Sheppard: Pagan Kennedy, *Black Livingstone: A True Tale of Adventure in Nineteenth-Century Congo* and William E. Phipps, *William Sheppard: Congo's African American Livingstone.*

13. Qtd. in Lindqvist (28-29). According to Lindqvist, the report drew on an article by E. J. Glave in *The Century Magazine* of 1897.

14. See Lindqvist, who also draws attention to the French Central African Expedition of 1898 that involved massacres.

15. However, Conrad's scruples should not be taken as proof that works of art committed to a cause or a social struggle are doomed to be crude and stultified, since there are spectacularly innovative paintings, fictions, plays, films, and music inspired by political passion and placed in the public domain as political acts—and without artistic integrity being fatally compromised or the autonomy of formal aesthetic practices being infringed.

16. "'Heart of Darkness'" is experience... pushed a little (and only very little) beyond the actual facts of the case for the perfectly legitimate, I believe, purpose of bringing it home to the minds and bosoms of the readers. There it was no longer a matter of sincere colouring. It was like another art altogether. That sombre theme had to be given a sinister resonance, a tonality of its own, a continued vibration that, I hoped, would hang in the air and dwell on the ear, after the last note had been struck" (*YOS* xi).

17. Johnston traveled in the Congo during the 1880s. Among his official appointments was that as Consul-General for Portuguese South-East Africa in 1889.

18. "Going up that river was like traveling back to the earliest beginnings of the world . . . . We were wanderers on prehistoric earth, on an earth that wore the aspect of an unknown planet. . . . We were cut off from comprehension of our surroundings. . . . We could not understand because we were too far and could not remember. . . . we were traveling in the night of first ages. . . . never before did this land, this river, this jungle, the very arch of this blazing sky, appear to me so hopeless and so dark, so impenetrable to human thought, so pitiless to human weakness" (92, 95, 96, 127).

19. "I saw him [the leader of the Eldorado Exploring Expedition] extend his short flipper of an arm for a gesture that took in the forest, the creek, the mud, the river—seemed to beckon with a dishonouring flourish before the sunlit face of the land a treacherous appeal to the lurking death, to the hidden evil, to the profound darkness of its heart" (92).

20. One reviewer, a then prominent man of letters, Hugh Clifford, writing in the *Spectator*, commended the marvelous force with which Conrad conveyed "the power of the wilderness, of contact with barbarism and elemental men and facts, to effect the demoralization of the white man" (qtd. in Harrison 49).

21. Edward Said has written that "much of Conrad's narrative is preoccupied with what eludes articulate expression—the jungle, the desperate natives, the great river, Africa's magnificent, ineffable dark life" (*Culture* 199). In an earlier commentary Said found in *Heart of Darkness* an act of discursive power, its narrative form a paradigm of a colonial discourse that is totalizing and all-enveloping in its attitudes and gestures, shutting out as much as it includes, compresses, and asserts. For despite Conrad's skepticism about the imperialist enterprise, Said argued, the text restores Africa to European hegemony by historicizing and narrating its strangeness. See "intellectuals," *Passim.*
22. See Christopher Miller.
23. Brittain 133. See also Brittain 133–144.
24. See Cartwright 14. Kabila's short-lived revolution had displaced Mobutu's government.

3
Some Millennial Footnotes on *Heart of Darkness*

DAPHNA ERDINAST-VULCAN

I.

A reading of *Heart of Darkness* shortly after the close of the twentieth century and the turn of the millennium cannot evade a certain apocalyptic or eschato-logical tone. It is not only the temporal-cultural context of the reading, but the text itself that sets up an apocalyptic frame of reading, staking out its own range of reference— "all of Europe," all of the "dark continent," all of Western civilization—as no less than total. The spectrum of critical responses to this claim through the century can be read symptomatically as a record of a cultural itinerary, shifting from the initial acquiescence of allegorical reading to selfconscious deconstruction and finally to passionate ideological engagement with what the apocalyptic framework seems to exclude or, at the very least, to occlude. But this in itself is not sufficient to account for the prophetic power of the text and for its apparently increasing relevance on the threshold of the twenty-first century.

To open this apparently outmoded question of canonicity, I will go back to Hans Robert Jauss's essay on the historical dynamics of aesthetic reception, which predicates the aesthetic value of a literary text on the "horizontal change" it commands, the degree to which it negates familiar norms, expectations, conventions, and assumptions of contemporary readers. This may sound like a clear echo of the formalist concept of "defamiliarization," and Jauss does indeed give Shklovsky due credit (32), but his conceptualization of horizontal change involves not only a formal but also, primarily perhaps, an ideological dimension, and his "aesthetics of negativity" evolves out of a profound faith in the socially formative power of literature. The obvious problem with this position is that the "original negativity" of a text wears out in time, when social and cultural changes catch up with it. When a literary work's value rests entirely on its revolutionary potency at a particular time and place, it remains interesting only in a narrowly historical sense. Anticipating this challenge, Jauss proposes that the canonical status of the text, i.e., the consensus regarding its enduring value, is actually "the successive development of the potential meaning ... which is gradually realized" in the historical reception of the text (21).

If we read *Heart of Darkness* in its historical context—against contemporary imperial and colonial practices—it is possible to evoke its "original negativity" and illuminate the horizonal change that must have presented formidable aesthetic and ideological challenges to readers of *Blackwood's Magazine* at the turn of the century. But that original negativity has so eroded that subsequent readers, from Chinua Achebe to Edward Said, have charged Conrad with unwitting complicity with the very ideology ostensibly challenged by the novella. Here the concept of the "potential meaning" of the text, hazy as it is, becomes relevant: *Heart of Darkness* is a paradigmatic text for the twentieth century primarily because it embodies a cultural diagnosis that can only be fully recognized and perhaps transcended at the beginning of the new millennium. Roots of the diagnosis appear in Freud's writings on the Oedipal foundations of human civilization; and the "millennial footnote" promised in the title of this essay offers a view of the Oedipal paradigm itself as a historical cultural construct.

II.

The following discussion is a sequel to an earlier essay entitled "*Heart of Darkness* and the Ends of Man," which revolved—as the title implies—on the teleological and eschatological aspects of the novella and their implications for a psychotextual reading. A brief overview of some of the main points in that essay will serve as introduction to the present study, which approaches the text through beginnings rather than ends.

Heart of Darkness is notoriously difficult to read, primarily because Marlow's narrative seems to be generated by a "double vision" and is refracted into a series of unresolved paradoxes, both rhetorical and ethical. Even when Marlow realizes that Kurtz had "collected, bartered, swindled, or stolen more ivory than all the other agents together," he blandly acknowledges that "that was not the point":

> The point was in his being a gifted creature, and that of all his gifts the one that stood out pre-eminently, that carried with it a sense of real presence, was his ability to talk, his words—the gift of expression, *the bewildering, the illuminating, the most exalted and the most contemptuous, the pulsating stream of light, or the deceitful flow from the heart of an impenetrable darkness.* (113, emphasis added)

This narrative refraction is, I have argued, closely related to Marlow's wavering between his own metaphysical desire for the Word—Kurtz's voice—which promises some revelation of Truth, and his eyewitness knowledge of brute historical actuality, which underlies the Great Cause of Progress. Driven by his desire for the "pulsating stream of light," he will try to suppress the knowledge of "the deceitful flow from the heart of an impenetrable darkness" (113).

Heart of Darkness is a narrative of failure, the belated testimony of a witness haunted by his own failure to testify. The truth toward which Marlow's narrative inches its way is the truth of his own lie, and his silent complicity in the atrocities he has witnessed. The return of the repressed becomes evident through a failure of language in Marlow's account. Toward the end of his journey, Marlow envisages an "open talk" with Kurtz, whom he is about to meet, intending to tell him what he has seen and learned on his way to the station. But the very idea of passing on his knowledge seems impossible: "My speech or my silence, indeed any action of mine, would be a mere futility. What did it matter what anyone knew or ignored? ... The essentials of this affair lay deep under the surface, beyond my reach, and beyond my power of meddling" (100).

The structure of the utterance, beginning with the antithesis of speech/silence, calls for a parallel construction of binary oppositional verbs: i.e., "what did it matter what anyone knew or didn't know?" But Marlow uses the verb "ignore," which indicates the very opposite. This slippage can be read as just another one of Conrad's notorious Gallicisms, an interference of the French *ignorer,* which means "not to know." But we cannot overlook the deeper significance of this. The meaning of the English verb is the opposite of the French denotation, as it points to a knowledge that has been suppressed. What is at stake for Marlow, then, is not his lack of knowledge, but his suppression of knowledge, his failure to respond and to testify to what he has known all along. It is only a short step from erasure of the distinction between speech and silence to abdication of moral agency and action: "My speech or my silence, indeed any action of mine, would be a mere futility."

Following Shoshana Felman's conception of psychoanalytic truth, I have suggested that Marlow's narrative should be read as performative speech act because it does not represent a given truth but generates its truth in the act of telling. The psychoanalytic recognition, says Felman, "is itself essentially a speech act, whose symbolic action modifies the subject's history rather than cerebrally observing or recording it at last correctly" (*Adventure of Insight* 131). In accord with the frame narrator's enigmatic instructions, the "truth" of the text should, then, be approached through the narrative act—not like a kernel within the shell of a cracked nut, i.e., that which is inside, already there, waiting to be uncovered, but "outside, enveloping the tale which brought it out only as a glow brings out a haze, in the likeness of one of these misty halos that sometimes are made visible by the spectral illumination of moonshine" (*YOS* 48). Not at the center, not at the heart of darkness will meaning be found, but outside the tale, in the act of telling. Having failed to testify at the time, Marlow himself seems to be blindly groping for the meaning of what he has seen and heard, what he has silenced and repressed. Only in and through the narrative can Marlow recognize and attempt to name the horror of his metaphysical desire. He makes his ultimate choice at the point of narration: "I have a voice, too, and for good or evil mine is the speech that cannot be silenced" (97). In the act of narration and the recognition of his own silence and complicity, Marlow undertakes—to use the Lacanian phrase—the "assumption of his own history" (*Ecrits* 48). The narrative act itself is a return from metaphysics to history.

III.

Having set our point of departure at the point of *aporia*, this failure of language that has opened up the unconscious of the text, we must return to the problematic concept of the "textual unconscious," which produces this double vision. I approach this concept through what I have elsewhere called a "heterobiographical"—as opposed to traditional "autobiographical"—approach (see *Strange Short* 11–29). Rather than scan the fictional text for autobiographical traces—fictional renderings of historical events, or representations of "real" psychological states of mind, relationships, and dilemmas—I outline an isomorphic relationship between the historical subject who has authored the text and the fictional character "within" the text. The same desire or anxiety resonates within and without the text. *Heart of Darkness* is "heterobiographical" because, underlying Marlow's familiar role as Conrad's public persona is a relationship of surrogacy that is rather more complex and interesting.

Heart of Darkness is based on Conrad's journey up the Congo in 1890–1891 on behalf of the *Société Anonyme Belge pour le Commerce du Haut-Congo,* and Conrad's Author's Note of 1917 claims that the novella "is experience pushed a little (and only very little) beyond the actual facts of the case" (xi). Conrad reinforces this autobiographical claim in his later evocation of himself as a young boy with a passion for maps who had pointed to the map's blank space, saying, "when I grow up, I shall *go there*" (*PR* 13, emphasis in original). However, when one looks to these "actual facts," as documented in Korzeniowski's Congo Diary and contemporary letters, the connection seems extremely tenuous. For part of the voyage, from November 1890 to January 1891, no account of any kind exists. After a period of silence—a blank space, as it were— Conrad "turned up in Brussels towards the end of January 1891, his health permanently wrecked and a changed man in other respects, his letters and memoirs forever silent on this critical period" (Najder, *Chronicle* 139). Nor does the earlier extant biographical evidence offer much, beyond a few names and a general itinerary, that anticipates the fictional account. As Conrad's biographers note, the diary entries are stark factual notations, discussing mainly difficulties of navigation, terrain, and weather, or referring to the traveler's discomfort and ill health (Karl, *Three Lives* 290–291; Najder, *Chronicle* 128).

However inconvenient for the literary biographer, this discrepancy of attitude, focus, and tone, and even the silence during the journey's final months, are what is so significant for the present discussion. Ten years later, in mid-December 1898, Conrad began writing *Heart of Darkness.* He finished it within an amazingly short while in February 1899. Not surprisingly, the letters written during these two months reverberate with verbal echoes of the novel, but some meta-textual points are worth noting. The text, which was to have been a short story of fewer than 20,000 words, grew—as Conrad writes to his literary friends—"like a genie from the bottle in the Arabian Tale" (*Letters* 2: 146). This is more than a literary conceit: the image suggests a volcanic eruption of something that has been bottled up that the author himself is powerless to master and contain.

On December 31, 1898, Conrad wrote to William Blackwood: "The title I am thinking of is 'The Heart of Darkness' but the narrative is not gloomy. The criminality of inefficiency and pure selfishness when tackling the civilizing work in Africa is a justifiable idea" (*Letters* 2: 139–140). This is indeed an odd, not to say misleading, representation of the novella. There are no ironic quotation marks around "the civilizing work," and the "criminality of inefficiency" looks highly suspicious when we remember that Kurtz was, after all, the most efficient agent of the company. What should we make of this misrepresentation? Conrad, not to put too fine a point on it, was trying to sell the idea of the story to Blackwood. Did he consciously lie to the arch-conservative publisher who might have been deterred by the truth? Or perhaps, as is just barely conceivable at this point, Conrad himself had no clear idea yet of what the novella was turning out to be, both in terms of its length and in its very substance.

Even granting this latter more charitable explanation, we cannot rule out the suspicion of some doubt lurking in Conrad's mind as to his own integrity. Apparently, the story did grow like a genie out of a bottle. Two weeks later, on January 13, 1899, Conrad wrote to Crane: "I am coming to see you directly I finish a rotten thing I am writing for B'woods. It is rotten—and I can't help it. All I write is rotten now" (*Letters* 2: 151). Is this an echo of the association of lying with "something rotten?" Was the novella conceived in the same spirit as Marlow's lie to the Intended? Is Conrad himself struggling with the horror?

Some ghost of an explanation suggests itself when we consider Conrad's relation to Roger Casement. Conrad met Casement in the Congo in spring 1890, recording the meeting in his June 13 diary entry: "Made the acquaintance of Mr. Roger Casement, which I should consider as a great pleasure under any circumstances and now it becomes a positive piece of luck. Thinks, speaks well, most intelligent and very sympathetic." Casement, at that time employed as supervisor of the projected railway line from Matadi to Kinshasa, was "well acquainted with the area, having already spent several years in the Congo . . . as a manager of an American camp for exploratory expeditions" (Najder, *Chronicle* 127). In 1903–1904, Casement published a report exposing the slave trade and atrocious practices of Belgian colonizers in the Congo, and launched an international campaign that led to the appointment of a Belgian commission, and subsequently to a change in the Congo government. Understandably cautious, Najder writes, "one may assume that Casement, who was later to become famous for his crusade for humanitarian treatment of the natives in the colonies, told Korzeniowski about the practices of European administrators and traders. But we do not know what Casement's attitude was then and in what categories he saw the problem" (*Chronicle* 128). What we do know, however, is that Casement did not remain silent.

Thirteen years later, in the midst of Casement's campaign, Conrad writes to Cunninghame Graham of the "monstrous achievement" of the European *Conquistadores*, suggesting that Graham meet Roger Casement and help him in his "noble cause": "I would help him but it is not in me. I am only a wretched novelist inventing wretched stories and not even up to that miserable game .... [But] he could tell you things! *Things I've tried to forget; things I never did know*" (*Letters* 3: 140, emphasis added). With its sense of helplessness, its emphatic claim of ignorance, and its admission of a deliberate forgetfulness, this last sentence is a poignant echo of Marlow's "what did it matter what one knew or ignored?"[1]

"The unconscious," says Lacan, "is that chapter of my history which is marked by a blank ... it is the censored chapter" (*Ecrits* 50). In Marlow's case, that chapter is blanked over by metaphysical desire, by the pilgrimage to those once-blank spaces in the map of the dark continent. For Conrad, too, the writing of the novella was a Marlovian act of return to the blank chapter in his own history, the chapter that had then been silenced.

IV.

We can understand the eruption of the textual unconscious through an extended Freudian detour. *Heart of Darkness* can be read both as prototype of Freud's conception of the Uncanny, and as fictional precursor of Freud's metapsychological speculations on culture. The ingredients of the Uncanny are all there: the figure of the double; the blurring of boundaries between animate and inanimate objects; and "the factors of silence, solitude and darkness" ("Uncanny" 234, 226, 246–247). But the significance of this "uncanniness" for our present concerns lies not in the presumed response of a reader to these literary motifs or devices, but in the explicit analogy between the evolution of civilized society and the psychosexual development of the individual subject.

Freud introduces his essay with a proto-deconstructive analysis of the German word "*heimlich*," which denotes both that which is "familiar, homely" and that which is "hidden, concealed from sight," that is, *unheimlich*, uncanny. "*Heimlich* is a word the meaning of which develops in the direction of ambivalence, until it finally coincides with its opposite, *unheimlich*" (226). He then proceeds with a discussion of Hoffman's "The Sandman," suggesting that the story's uncanny effect is related to "the castration complex of childhood" (233) and a regression to a primitive anxiety that has presumably been "surmounted" (237):

> An uncanny experience occurs either when infantile complexes which have been repressed are once more revived by some impression, or when primitive beliefs which have been surmounted seem once more to be confirmed .... [T]hese two classes of uncanny experience are not always sharply distinguishable. When we consider that primitive beliefs are most intimately connected with infantile complexes, and are, in fact, based on them, we shall not be greatly astonished to find that the distinction is often a hazy one. (249)

This analogy between "surmounted" atavistic fears and the repressed anxieties of the individual child, originating in the fear of "the dreaded father" (241), is presented in Freud's metapsychological speculation on culture in the earlier *Totem and Taboo* (1913), which predicates the genesis of civilization on the paradigm of the Oedipal crisis. Drawing on contemporary observations of totemistic cultures and noting the ambivalence of the totem, perceived as the primal father or ancestor, Freud argues that taboo customs structuring these societies are invariably related to the dread of incest and patricide, the "oldest and strongest desires of mankind" (41), and thus accord with the psychic life of the neurotic individual and parallel the symptoms of neurotic compulsion (28, 36). The totemic system, he argues, "resulted from the conditions underlying the Oedipus complex" (133).

For Freud, this is not merely a conceptual analogy, but a potentially valid historical reconstruction of the evolution of social organization from primal hordes dominated by a violent father to brother clans and to the subsequent development of religion and morality. "The totem may have been the first form of father substitute and the god a later one in which the father regained his human form. Such a new creation forms the root of all religious evolution, namely, the longing for the father" (147).

Thirty-six years later, in *Moses and Monotheism* (1939), Freud returned to his early theory, taking it one step further to speculate, rather wildly, on the origins of monotheism. Once again, Freud returns to the analogy between the development of the Oedipal neurosis in the individual and the evolution of social organization:

> Mankind as a whole also passed though conflicts of a sexual-aggressive nature, which left permanent traces, but which were for the most part warded off and forgotten; later, after a long period of latency, they came to life again and created phenomena similar in structure and tendency to neurotic symptoms. I have, I believe, divined these processes and wish to show that their consequences, which bear a strong resemblance to neurotic symptoms, are the phenomena of religion. (101)

The regressive aspects of *Heart of Darkness*, obvious and insistent as they are, have escaped few readers in the course of the century, but the "heavy, mute spell of the wilderness," the "gleam of fires, the throb of drums," and "the drone of incantations" have mostly been related to the "monstrous passions" of Kurtz, which have taken him beyond the bounds of permitted aspirations" (144). In 1965, Lionel Trilling wrote—with a shudder, as it were—of "the strange and terrible message of ambivalence toward the life of civilization" in *Heart of Darkness*, and of Kurtz's degeneration, which recalls "the darker pages of *The Golden Bough*" (19–20). Trilling's evident discomfort is rather more than the recoil of a refined spirit in the face of the unspeakable. The "fascination of the abomination" is not merely a piece of exotica, a residue of savagery that remains in the heart of the civilized man. According to Freud, it is the very foundation of civilization itself.

Marlow's journey into the heart of darkness is described in terms of a return to the "earliest beginnings of the world" (92), and to the atavistic beginnings of the human race. He talks of the smell of "primeval mud," the "primeval forest" (81); of being a wanderer "on a prehistoric earth" (95); and of feeling like "the first of men taking possession of an accursed inheritance, to be subdued at the cost of profound anguish and of excessive toil" (95). The uncanny quality of the experience is evoked by a paradoxical sense of total strangeness—"The prehistoric man was cursing us, welcoming us—who could tell? . . . we could not understand because we were too far and could not remember, because we were travelling in the night of first ages, of those ages that are gone, leaving hardly a sign—and no memories" (96)—and a concurrent sense of kinship with the howling natives:

> It was unearthly, and the men were—no, they were not inhuman. Well, you know, that was the worst of it—this suspicion of their not being inhuman. It would come slowly to one. They howled and leaped, and spun, and made horrid faces; but what thrilled you was just the thought of their humanity—like yours—the thought of your remote kinship with this wild and passionate uproar . . . . You wonder I didn't go ashore for a howl and a dance? Well, no—I didn't . . . . I had no time. (96)

The totemic object of worship and fear for the natives is the voracious Kurtz, who "had taken a high seat among the devils of the land—I mean literally" (116); who came to the natives "with thunder and lightening" (144); presided over "unspeakable rites which were offered up to him" (118); and "had the power to charm or frighten rudimentary souls into an aggravated witch-dance in his honor" (119).

Not only rudimentary souls, as it happens. In the course of his journey through the nightmarish scenes of the dark continent, Kurtz becomes a totemic being for Marlow as well, an embodiment of some originary presence to which Marlow addresses his faith. As with a God-figure, there is no image attached to his name (*YOS* 82). Like the Freudian *Das Ding*, he is a "Word" and a "voice," and Marlow envisages their encounter as a promise of a homecoming, a recovery of some lost truth, and a return to some authentic point of origin. When it looks as though he might be too late to hear Kurtz's voice, Marlow becomes one of the worshiping natives: "I will never hear that chap speak after all—and my sorrow had a startling extravagance of emotion, even such as I had noticed in the howling sorrow of these savages in the bush. I couldn't have felt more of lonely desolation somehow, had I been robbed of a belief or had missed my destiny in life . . . ." (113). What was perceived as savage, abominable, and strange is now recognized as inherent in the civilized subject. Or, to borrow the Freudian formulation, the *unheimlich* has become all-too-*heimlich*.

V.

Had Freud read Conrad's work? The evocations of *Heart of Darkness* in his work are indeed uncanny in the broadest possible sense, but we do not need evidence of direct influence to account for these inter-textual echoes which, I would argue, should be historicized and read in the context of a profound cultural affinity.

However, before we probe the significance of this affinity, we should note that the Oedipal paradigm that emerges from Freud's own texts is more complex than the conventional dichotomy of "Desire vs. the Law." Freud stops short of fully articulating this complexity, but Lacan later recognizes the symbiotic and paradoxical relationship, insisting on the "tight bond between desire and the Law" that contributes to what "might be called patriarchal civility" (*Ethics* 177). Lacan actually reverses the conventional order when he claims that it is the law that constitutes desire. "The dialectical relationship between desire and the Law causes our desire to flare up only in relation to the Law" (*Ethics* 83–84). We can go a step further: If desire is both prohibited and generated by the Law, as Lacan seems to imply, it is actually desire for the absent father who has been replaced by the Name-of-the-Father.

Writing at the turn of the twentieth century or shortly afterward, both Conrad and Freud are citizens of a post-Nietzschean world, marked by the final explicit diagnosis of the Death of God. Both are acutely aware of the paradox implied in Freud's text and fully articulated by Lacan: the reinforcement of the desire for the Word precisely because it seems to have withdrawn. *Deus absconditus* is more powerful that any divine presence, more powerful in the various guises it has taken on when the process of European secularization is ostensibly concluded.

When Marlow finally meets Kurtz in person, he seems to have shrunk, to have become "a hollow sham" (147), an "atrocious phantom," a grotesque "apparition," a "pitiful Jupiter" (134). But his voice—"grave, profound, vibrating" (135)— remains remarkably powerful: "it sounded to me far off and yet loud, like a hail through a speaking trumpet" (143). The man is nearly gone, but the voice remains, and so does Marlow's sense of the "fascination of the abomination" (50).

Here, too, it would seem as if Freud had actually modeled his theory on the fictional text, as he writes of "the great man," the leader of the masses, and the secret of his power: "We know that the great majority of people have a strong need for authority which they can admire, to which they can submit, and which dominates and sometimes even ill-treats them .... It is the longing for the father that lives in each of us from his childhood days .... the features with which we furnish the great man are traits of the father .... He must be admired, he may be trusted, but one cannot help also being afraid of him" (*Moses* 139–140).

However, it is not the fictional character of Kurtz that serves Freud as a model for the Great Man, but a far closer and more terrifyingly real embodiment of this authority. Four decades after *Heart of Darkness*, as a victim of and witness to the rise of Fascism, totalitarian communism, and Nazism, Freud must have been painfully aware of that force that Conrad's novella had already anticipated. Freud's re-articulation of the speculative thesis of *Totem and Taboo* 26 years later, in *Moses and Monotheism*, suggests that the question of civilization became pressingly relevant for him in the face of the alliance between "progress" and "barbarism" (*Moses* 67). Fleeing the Nazi regime, Freud felt that he could not publish the third part of the essay in Vienna, where he lived on borrowed time under the protection of the Catholic Church, whose displeasure he could not afford to incur. It was only after June 1938, when Freud fled to London after the German invasion of Austria, that he could write: "I have never doubted that religious phenomena are to be understood only on the model of the neurotic symptoms of the individual .... that they owe their obsessive character to that very origin" (*Moses* 71).

Heart of Darkness, written at the turn of the twentieth century, is uncannily prophetic in its view of a civilization that has ostensibly gone through a process of secularization and the death of the absolute, but that—true to the Freudian paradox that Lacan notes—has amplified the desire for the Absolute and turned it into a monstrous force. In terms of the Oedipal paradigm, it is the desire *for* the Law, *for* the Word, *for* the Father, or for his pathetic surrogates, which, it seems, is much more invasive and deadly than any ostensibly transgressive desire. This is visible in the drama played out in the historical-cultural arena, no less today than in Conrad's time. Translated into ideological terms, it is the desire for totalizing ideological systems, religious or political, or for the Leader figure, that has discharged the most destructive energies in the history of humanity.

VI.

"At the level of the unconscious the subject lies," writes Lacan, "and this lying is his way of telling the truth of the matter" (*Ethics* 73). Less cryptic than Lacan's usual aphorisms, this can be taken as a reference to the various mechanisms of displacement, projection, or denial through which the truth transforms into a verbal or behavioral symptom. But when we think of Marlow's lies—or of Conrad's evasion of the truth in his letter to Blackwood—it becomes clear that for both the fictional character and his author the lie is a symptom of the desire to remain within the patriarchal system of the law.

Let us return again to the writing of *Heart of Darkness* which, biographers agree, marked Conrad's transformation from sailor to writer. Najder perceptively notes that Conrad's African experience is his

> ... last attempt to become a *homo socialis*, a cog in the mechanism of society. By accepting the job in the Trading Company, he joined, for once in his life, an organized, large-scale group activity on land .... It is not accidental that the Congo expedition remained an isolated event in Conrad's life. Until his death he remained a recluse in the social sense and never became involved with any institution or clearly defined group of people (*Chronicle* 141–142).

This observation becomes even more telling when we recall Bernard Meyer's suggestion that the Congo venture was motivated by Conrad's need to still the gnawing doubt of his own identity and shore up a distinct self-image by aligning himself with idealized and manly explorers of the wilderness like Henry Morton Stanley (97–99). Conrad's metamorphosis from colonial agent and writer of the Congo Diary ("one of them") to the reclusive, disillusioned author of *Heart of Darkness* must have been directly related to his letting the genie out of the bottle; and, since it severed an alignment essential to his sense of selfhood, the act must have been almost unbearably painful.

On February 8, when Conrad was about to finish the novella, he wrote a rather obscure and rambling letter to Cunninghame Graham. That this letter is interspersed with echoes of the fictional text—"general extermination," "a forest where no one knows the way," "the ghosts of dead eloquence"—is hardly surprising. But one long and almost incoherent paragraph seems to illuminate, or rather to darken, Conrad's metamorphosis: "Man is a vicious animal. His viciousness must be organized. Crime is a necessary condition of organized existence. Society is fundamentally criminal—or it would not exist" (*Letters* 2: 157–161). When read in the Freudian context, these desperate ramblings become much more coherent. If "the beginnings of religion, ethics, society, and art meet in the Oedipus complex" (*Totem* 155), does not Freud, too, speculate on the criminal origins of human civilization?

It is not, however, only a question of origins. Both Freud and Lacan view the resolution of the Oedipal crisis, the submission to and identification with the father, as necessary for the survival of the subject within the social matrix. Whether it is the father as a gender-model or the Name-of-the-Father as the key to the Symbolic Order makes no difference to their fundamental affinity on this crucial point. Freud's painful insights on the eve of the Holocaust, on the brink of his own death, have not been assimilated into the collective consciousness of the twenty-first century. This, I believe, is where *Heart of Darkness* poses the most awesome conceptual challenge: the "metaphysical blindness" of Marlow (a more-or-less decent person, like the rest of us), which turns him into a passive accomplice is, after all, symptomatic of the need for a redeeming idea, "something you can set up, and bow down before, and offer a sacrifice to . . . ." (57–58). It is precisely the submission to and identification with the Symbolic Order that licenses the atrocities he has witnessed. The Oedipal paradigm may have had its day. It certainly does not feel intuitively right any more. Perhaps at the end of the blood-gorged century and the beginning of a new millennium we can finally begin to ask ourselves, as Conrad may have done when he "assumed his own history," just what it *is* to which we bow down in the Name-of-the-Father.

Notes

1. I am indebted to Carola Kaplan for drawing my attention to the echo of the Harlequin's words about Kurtz, who had made him "see things—things" (127). This phrase, which recalls the famous formula of the Preface to *The Nigger of the Narcissus*, is particularly significant when we note the shift from Kurtz as the idolized artist-figure who could make his worshippers "see things" to Casement, who could merely "tell things." Casement was all too human, as we know, but his was "the speech that could not be silenced."

4

Conrad's Darkness Revisited: Mediated Warfare and Modern(ist) Propaganda in *Heart of Darkness* and "The Unlighted Coast"

MARK WOLLAEGER

I.

One night in the winter of 1991 I was starting to review my notes for an under-graduate lecture on *Heart of Darkness* when my wife called me downstairs to witness the opening salvoes of the Gulf War, the bombing of Baghdad narrated on CNN by a terrified Bernard Shaw. We watched the tracer fire's greenish streaks crisscross the dark screen for a while until my wife became physically ill, and I felt compelled to turn from the television to the computer screen to think about what I would say the next morning to an audience of a hundred students expecting a lecture on Conrad. If I have properly deciphered my scribblings in the margins, I took some time that day to discuss what I called the political abuse of language, and *Heart of Darkness* proved even more effec-tive on this issue than George Orwell's famous essay, "Politics and the English Language" (1946). I reminded them of Marlow's skeptical response to the French gunboat, "incomprehensible, firing into a continent" at a camp of unseen natives referred to as "enemies" (*YOS* 62), and later his disgust on seeing a string of chained Africans: "They were called criminals," Marlow says, "and the outraged law, like the bursting shells, had come to them, an insoluble mystery from the sea" (64). This yoking of idealizing abstractions to an alien particu-larity, I suggested, should make them suspicious of the duplicity of state-sponsored rhetoric, such as the technological wonder of "Patriot" missiles, a military invasion called "Operation Just Cause," or foreign leaders stigmatized as mad men. I could have gone on more polemically to suggest analogies between ivory and oil and the language deployed to secure them, but instead I moved into my planned discussion of the difficulties of distinguishing truth from untruth in modernity and Conrad's investment in the idea of necessary fictions, a topic that seemed to take on greater pointedness than it had when I first delivered the lecture a year earlier, and one that subsequent wars have made sharper yet. What I was almost discovering in Conrad then is my topic now, the complex entwining of modernism and propaganda in the early twentieth century.

The first Gulf War has become a touchstone for postmodern media studies, and despite the grotesque inanity of such efforts as Jean Baudrillard's *The Gulf War Did Not Take Place* (1995)—a classic case of heat with no light—other studies have done much to illuminate how propaganda operates in late modernity.[1] John MacArthur, for instance, details how a former Kuwaiti education minister, Hassan al-Ebraheem, hired Hill and Knowlton, a large politically connected public relations firm, to spread a fabricated atrocity story about Iraqi soldiers dumping hundreds of babies out of incubators; the story gained currency largely through a false eyewitness account presented to a congressional committee by a 15-year-old girl who was later discovered to be the daughter of Kuwait's ambassador to the United States (37–77). Later, with popular support secured and the war having begun, over and over again TV news footage situated the viewer astride a "smart" bomb like some latter-day Slim Pickens in *Dr. Strangelove* as it seemed to navigate into a building through a window. Visual proof of the intelligence with which war could now be prosecuted distracted attention from the debatable justice of the conflict, and tight control over journalistic access to actual battle made the licensed flow of electronic images support rather than undermine the war effort, as it had in Vietnam. A decade later, post 9/11, as I watched for small flashes of light within the otherwise blank screen of Kabul, I was again struck by the aptness of Conrad's French gunboat. Uncomfortably more comfortable with what was being billed as "America's New War," I couldn't help feeling that firing cruise missiles into the mountains of Afghanistan ultimately might have all the effect of Conrad's impotent man-of-war: "a small flame would dart and vanish, a little white smoke would disappear, a tiny projectile would give a feeble screech—and nothing happened" (*YOS* 62).

Modern media, propaganda, and war: The first signs of this conjunction can be located in late nineteenth- and early twentieth-century England. By rethinking Conrad's modernism in this context, I aim to articulate the particular value *Heart of Darkness* holds in today's culture of perpetual war. One way to do this is to pose the question, what does *Heart of Darkness* look like when read through the retrospective lens of Conrad's ill-fated attempt in 1916 to write World War I propaganda for the Admiralty, "The Unlighted Coast"? Answering that question requires some attention to the invention of modern propaganda and its relation to the concurrent emergence of modernism.

II.

J.A. Hobson commented in 1901 on the "spectatorial passion" elicited by war, a fact that newly emergent mass newspapers had discovered in the closing decades of the century (12). As John MacKenzie has observed, war sold papers at a time when "the locus of hero-worship" was moving "from Europe to the Empire; colonial exploits were enthusiastically followed by the public; [and] war became a remote adventure in which heroism was enhanced by both distance and exotic locales" (6). Modern propaganda is sometimes thought to have developed only with the advent of mass media, such as the wireless, film, and television, but if new media extended propaganda's reach, propaganda by saturation began in the late nineteenth century as soon as "printed and visual materials became available at prices so low as to place them in almost every home" (MacKenzie 16). Before World War I, the British government largely refrained from official propaganda, yet with the expansion of various media industries (printing, photographic, and advertising among others) and the consequent diffusion of pro-imperial messages in picture postcards, advertisements, cigarette cards, newspapers, and posters, along with growing respect for the military and new reverence for royalty promoted by the new imperialism, it became increasingly difficult to draw a line between a "self-generating ethos" that reinforces itself through repetition—think national identity—and "conscious manipulation" of public opinion by those who controlled "powerful religious, commercial, military, and official agencies" (MacKenzie 3).

One might expect that the First World War would sharpen the distinction between manipulation orchestrated by the state and forms of belonging more or less intrinsic to citizenship. After all, during the war, the British government virtually invented propaganda as we now know it, doing such an effective job that in 1925 Hitler wrote admiringly of it in *Mein Kampf* (227–242), and Joseph Goebbels reportedly modeled the Nazi propaganda machine on England's Ministry of Information. Yet the British propaganda campaign was in fact instrumental in blurring the distinction between information and propaganda, a distinction that often seems wholly lost today.

The history of British propaganda efforts during the war records the emergence of modern propaganda's professionalization under the aegis of the state. When war broke out on August 4, 1914, England felt itself well behind the curve. In the British view, Germany had been using official state channels to ply the world with its version of political tensions in Europe for decades, and it is true that as early as the wars of German unification in 1866 and 1870 Germany had imposed strict censorship on the press to shape the news. By contrast, although the press in England throughout the nineteenth century was more powerful and thus more independent, military control was not seriously considered until 1898, when war with France seemed imminent and the newspapers competed to describe British defenses and preparations ("Military Press Control" 3). The Defense of the Realm Act in August 1916 finally granted the government extensive censorship powers over the press, even though government records indicate that the newspapers were already, in effect, censoring themselves in response to guidelines issued by the Press Bureau, a civilian committee established when the war began ("Military Press Control" 7).

Government documents tracing the development of England's effort to catch up on the propaganda front typically begin by acknowledging that German propaganda had put the nation on the defensive in the opening months of the war. By October 1915, however, German newspapers were attacking their own government for not following British methods and complaining about "the uselessness of their own" (Masterman, *Second Report* 10). By the end of the war, it was generally agreed that British propaganda completely dominated the field, and most historians today believe that the British campaign played some role in persuading the United States to enter the war, contributed materially to shortening it by undermining German morale, and was a significant influence on the punitive nature of the Treaty of Versailles.[2]

The most benign view of Britain's propaganda machine is that it attempted to disseminate factual accounts to counter the rumors, gossip, incomplete accounts, fabrications, and lies that were already in circulation. To the extent that German propagandists, confident of a quick victory, sometimes resorted early in the war to lies or misrepresentations concerning enemy losses, landmarks destroyed, or territory captured, counter-propaganda could indeed respond effectively simply by means of factual enumeration. As Lord Robert Cecil observed in a confidential memo, ". . . in war-time it is the facts that count, not words. All we can do to help by propaganda is to let foreigners know what is actually happening."

But if the British were right to see that lies would fail over the long haul, their propaganda techniques indicate that they also knew that information flows best when channels are properly greased, that factual accounts must be tailored to suit different audiences around the world, and that the power of facts to make an impression varies according to the media through which they are disseminated. Germany had grounds, in other words, for its clever glossing of the Allies' information services as "All-lies." Indeed, the British manipulation of facts throws into relief the epistemological peculiarity of what Mary Poovey has termed "the modern fact." Poovey offers a historical account of how "facts" came to be conceived as both prior to systematic knowledge—as raw untheorized data—and inextricable from the theories they support. Tracing the emergence of this duality back to the seventeenth century, Poovey argues that the ambiguity of facts as both preinterpretive and wholly derived from theory is fundamental to modern epistemology (*Modern Fact* 1–28). In this context twentieth-century propaganda looks like a late chapter in the history of the modern fact, for propaganda exploits the internal bifurcation of modern facts by amplifying their rhetorical appeal even while insisting on their value-free neutrality. In propaganda, the supposed independence of facts, their imperviousness to the assimilative power of systematic knowledge or suasion, is aggressively mobilized as part of the fact's rhetorical appeal. Conrad was sensitive to the potential duplicity of facts and debunks them in *Lord Jim* through Jim's response to the *Patna* inquiry, in which the publicity surrounding the affair invests Jim's efforts to tell the truth with meanings he cannot control: "Facts! They demanded facts from him, as if facts could explain anything!" (29).

During World War I, new strategies for massaging facts made it easier for British officials to declare their fidelity to the factual while also committing themselves to the manipulation of public opinion. With advertising techniques already available, the war effort produced, in turn, public relations as a profession and media studies as an emergent discipline. Advances in psychology, such as new research into stimulus and response, were tapped in the interwar years, all of which eventually made possible what is now called the fine art of spin. The trick to spinning effectively is to conceal the bias of the information one disseminates, and as the war moved past its expected end in the fall of 1914, many European neutrals grew tired of the seemingly endless stream of German propaganda emanating from official information bureaus. For this reason, C.F.G. Masterman, the Liberal M.P. charged with initiating the British campaign in September 1914, ruled out direct appeals to neutral countries: "Every recipient of material distributed gratuitously should receive it from an unofficial source" (*Report* 2). Officially named the Propaganda Bureau, Masterman's project soon came to be known by the building in which it was housed, Wellington House.

Wellington House would eventually become only one branch—the literature division—of a dynamic, increasingly complex organization that in February 1917, after Lloyd George came to power, became the Department of Information, run by Buchan, and then in March 1918 the Ministry of Information, run by Lord Beaverbrook and, briefly, by Arnold Bennett. It was Masterman who started the operation by inviting 25 of England's most influential men of letters to his office at Wellington House in September 1914. The invitees included Arnold Bennett, G.K. Chesterton, Arthur Conan Doyle, John Galsworthy, Thomas Hardy, H.G. Wells, J.M. Barrie, William Archer, Anthony Hope Hawkins, Robert Bridges, G.M. Trevelyan, and Israel Zangwill; Rudyard Kipling and Arthur Quiller-Couch couldn't make it but sent messages offering their services.[3] With the exception of Hardy, all who attended agreed to help.[4] Many others joined in the campaign later, including Arnold Toynbee, who wrote several books for Wellington House, and Ford Madox Ford (then Hueffer), who in 1915 published two propaganda books, *When Blood is Their Argument* and *Between St. Dennis and St. George*. Conrad was not contacted until the fall of 1916, when Admiral Brownrigg decided that the doings of the Mercantile Navy needed publicity.[5] Authors published under their own names through well known commercial and university presses that were secretly subsidized by the government. Masterman held a second meeting on September 7 for influential editors and journalists, including representatives from all the leading newspapers. The British campaign was so effectively secretive that most members of Parliament remained unaware of it for two years, and the public did not learn of the participation of so many well known writers until the early 1930s.[6]

Where does modernism come into this? Jacques Ellul, the foremost theorist of propaganda and its effects, explains what might seem the unlikely conjunction of modernism and propaganda. Ellul's importance in propaganda studies derives from his focus on propaganda as a sociological phenomenon made necessary by the nature of modern society rather than as a particular regime or organization's political weapon. When Ellul declares that modern propaganda is "the effect of a technological society that embraces the entire man," he is thinking of sociological propaganda, which he defines as "the penetration of an ideology by means of its sociological context" (*Propaganda* 63). Slower and more diffuse than political propaganda, sociological or "integration" propaganda, operating through political, economic, and cultural structures, produces "a progressive adaptation to a certain order of things, a certain concept of human relations, which unconsciously molds individuals and makes them conform to society" (*Propaganda* 64). Integration propaganda includes not just the usual state-sponsored suspects—political broadcasting, censorship, atrocity stories, and the manipulation of news—but also more diffusely constellated organizations and institutions, such as advertising, public relations, and popular films, whose interactions effectively reinforce official political propaganda without necessarily setting out to do so. From Ellul's perspective, then, what Mackenzie calls a "self-generating ethos" is simply one aspect of the integration propaganda that pervades society. Modern citizens need this sort of propaganda because it offers people increasingly deprived of traditional support groups, such as church, family, or village, precisely what they need: personal involvement in public events and a justification for otherwise useless feelings of discontent. In a very real sense, then, British propaganda techniques from the beginning were suited to the alienated protagonists of modernist narrative.

British propaganda techniques also contributed to the alienation they were designed to alleviate. As the emerging information age began to engulf people in more information than they could assimilate, people who formerly felt well informed became frustrated by their growing confusion and uncertainty. Ford Madox Ford spoke for many when he complained in 1911 that "the Englishman is overwhelmed every morning with a white spray of facts" from the popular press and that excessive factual enumeration was undermining the foundations of citizenship (*Critical* 115, 125). Ford blamed the new mass newspapers in particular, but with the rise of radio the problem of information overload became even more acute and invasive. Mass media thus became both cause and cure: the propagation of too much information by the media created the need for the pervasive integration propaganda made possible by media.

One imagines that Marlow, having returned to the city from the Congo, probably wouldn't have felt such resentment and disdain at "the sight of people hurrying through the streets to filch a little money from each other, to devour their infamous cookery, to gulp their unwholesome beer, to dream their insignificant and silly dreams" (*YOS* 152) if he had been able to swallow more imperial propaganda, not to mention the ads for beer and Bovril that plastered the urban scene. If Marlow's emotional state derives from a feverish sense of superior wisdom gained at the brink of death, his free-floating hostility was not an unusual response to the onslaught of stimuli in the modern metropolis. It is to this milieu that Conrad's Jackson responds on his return to London in "Karain" (1898): "It is there; it pants, it runs, it rolls; it is strong and alive; it would smash you if you didn't look out" (*TU* 55).

Marlow's alienation and Jackson's defensive personification would seem to argue for an antithetical relation between modernism and propaganda. Both men would benefit from the consoling explanations of propaganda, whether it be the notion that urban bustle is a sign of the productivity made possible by empire or that extended stays in outposts of progress are necessary to the revitalization of manhood that sustains empire. Instead, Marlow despises the sleepwalking Londoners who remain oblivious to the fact that they too live in the heart of darkness, and Jackson, while conceding London's palpable *thereness*, refuses to grant that it is "as real" as the memory of his exotic adventures in Malaysia (see Wollaeger, *Joseph Conrad* 42–51). Thus, where propaganda aims to give alienated individuals precisely what they need by channeling discontent into safely xenophobic forms, modernism tends to *elicit* resentment by equating civilization with its discontents. Propaganda suggests techniques of political deception and persuasion designed to influence a mass audience. Modernism, in contrast, has been described as a withdrawal from mass culture and society through the cultivation of aesthetic autonomy, arcane mythopoesis, and private symbolism.

And yet the validity of such claims must be balanced against the equally valid claim that modernism also engages with propaganda, and in several ways. For while some modernist works seem to seal themselves off from the persuasive aims of propaganda, others seek to undo its work, and still others self-consciously shoulder propaganda's burden. Thus where T.S. Eliot constructed an aesthetic order of myth to give "a shape and a significance to the immense panorama of futility and chaos which is contemporary history" (177), Ford redeployed the modernist techniques he perfected in *The Good Soldier* (1915) in his propaganda books for Wellington House. However various the relations between modernism and propaganda, and however diverse the artistic practices grouped under the rubric of modernism, it is important to recognize their common roots in the new media ecology of the early twentieth century. The intuition that new communications technologies were transforming everyday life even more radically than were new forms of transportation, and the conviction that the era required new principles of order—aesthetic, social, and political—were shared by modernists and propagandists alike. Each drew on the new disciplines of depth psychology and sociology, each devoted growing attention to unconscious motivation, each sought new forms of order.

Neither antithetical nor identical, modernism and propaganda were sometimes agonistic, sometimes allies, and sometimes their complex engagement, as in Ford, made them indistinguishable. Even the issue of ambiguity, which (paradoxically enough) might seem to provide a bright line of separation, becomes more complex with the realization that the erasure of the distinction between information and propaganda caused by modern media's information overload, first remarked by Ellul in 1957, was already under way during World War I, owing to the efforts of propagandists on all sides. Whether by design or not, then, both England's Ministry of Information and modernism cultivated ambiguity.

Heart of Darkness is in many ways prophetic of this tangled history. Well in advance of the world wars that would help make public relations a dominant force in society, Conrad already sensed in *Heart of Darkness* that the elusiveness of truth bore directly on his ability to distinguish his own writing from propaganda. The novella gets at both sides of the equation: the eroding distinction between truth and lies in Marlow's ambivalent loyalty to Kurtz, for whom Marlow lies to preserve a different order of truth, and the emergence of the professional propagandist in Kurtz, a man whose seductive eloquence, as one character remarks, would make him a terrific candidate to lead *any* political party. All readings of *Heart of Darkness* must make sense of the pivotal relation between Marlow and Kurtz, and the information-propaganda matrix helps illuminate the underpinnings of Marlow's ambivalent discipleship. In part Marlow sees Kurtz as a symbol of the capacity for belief for which he longs. The death of his helmsman, killed by a spear, is pivotal. The helmsman had carried out one of the most valuable services possible in Conrad's world: like the aptly named Singleton in *The Nigger of the "Narcissus,"* he had steered. With his Palinurus gone, Marlow's mind turns instantly to Kurtz, a figure who might provide the guidance formerly supplied by the helmsman. But what Kurtz supplies is the consoling coherence that is the special province of propaganda. The helmsman's death makes Marlow realize that he had "never imagined [Kurtz] as doing, you know, but as discoursing" (*YOS* 113), and his famous description of Kurtz's "gift of expression"—"the pulsating stream of light or the deceitful flow from the heart of an impenetrable darkness" (113–14)—speaks directly to the truism that one person's information is another's propaganda. It makes sense, then, that in a compressed moment of calculation and instinctive reaction, Marlow later turns away from the Russian adventurer's account of the Africans' ceremonial deference to Kurtz to find comfort in the heads on stakes with which Kurtz has ringed his compound: "pure, uncomplicated savagery was a positive relief" (132). A staple of propaganda, atrocity stories have always counted on the appeal of uncomplicated savagery. If a loss of moral compass is implied by the helmsman's death, in Kurtz Marlow seeks clarity at the expense of moral value.

Propaganda mediates other relations as well. Kurtz's Intended, like Marlow's aunt, remains serenely impervious to the painful contradictions Marlow experiences in the Congo because the "rot let loose in print and talk just about that time" (59) inoculates her against thinking too hard about the actual fate of emissaries of light sent into the darkness. Like British journalists who preemptively censored themselves during World War I, Marlow helps keep the Intended safely cocooned in propaganda by suppressing information. He lies about Kurtz's last words to give her the romantic ending life withheld, and he tears off the savage postscript to Kurtz's report on the suppression of savage customs—"Exterminate the brutes!"—to prevent the degradation of Kurtz's original intentions from seeing the light of day. In many ways, Marlow is Conrad's agent for debunking the myths that Kurtz's Intended and Marlow's aunt drink in. Thus, if Marlow indulges in primitivist stereotypes by seeing Africans who paddle up in canoes as emblems of the real—"they had bone, muscle, a wild vitality, an intense energy of movement, that was as natural and true as the surf along their coast" (61)—he also undercuts such stereotypes when he acknowledges that the cannibals on board his steamers show more "restraint" than the armed white men alongside them (105). But such subversions notwithstanding, Marlow is far from immune to popular myths. His celebrated denunciation of "the conquest of the earth" as "the taking it away from those who have a different complexion or slightly flatter noses than ourselves" is undermined not only by the equivocal language of idolatry in which it culminates—that is, Marlow's praise for a belief "you can set up and bow down before, and offer a sacrifice to"—but also by the peroration on the virtue of British "efficiency" that introduces it (50–51). Indeed, Marlow's "devotion to efficiency" betrays no ethical coordinates. A highly political term at this time and a touchstone for British politics for decades to come (see Hawkins), efficiency for its own sake is also for Ellul a defining feature of the technological society, which fetishizes efficient means at the expense of considered ends (Ellul, *Technological Society* 3–7). It's good for trains to run on time, but one wonders how much of Marlow's horror at the Company Station derives from humanitarian outrage over the treatment of enslaved African workers and how much from disgust at "a wanton smash-up" in which workers became "inefficient, and were then allowed to crawl away and rest" (66). Holding in suspension the values implicit in Marlow's diction and a critique of those values, Conrad's complex ironies register the degree to which the propagandistic "rot let loose in print" at this time was not easily shrugged off, even by a skeptical humanist like Marlow.

Conrad's aims as a writer made it difficult for him to shrug off propaganda as well. For a writer who desired, in the famous words of the preface to *The Nigger of the "Narcissus,"* to harness "the power of the written word" *to make* his readers see, *to make* them hear and feel as he wanted them to (xiv), propaganda must have seemed plugged into the popular imagination to a degree

Conrad could only envy. His complicated relation to the persuasive power of propaganda in *Heart of Darkness*, sharply focused in Marlow's loyalty to Kurtz, first comes into view as a writerly matter in Marlow's ambivalent response to the company's chief accountant, who is at once a hollow man and a kind of "miracle." "Bent over his high desk," the accountant is a writer devoted to facts, and Marlow occasionally seeks shelter in his office from "the chaos" of the station (*YOS* 67, 68). Soothed by the "apple-pie order" of the accountant's books, Marlow ends up situated smack in the middle of Poovey's modern fact.[7] The accountant's precise numerical entries, along with his immaculate collars, cuffs, and hair, constitute part of what Marlow considers his achievement of character: "... in the great demoralization of the land he kept up his appearance. That's backbone" (68). But the accountant's bookkeeping cannot be divorced from the violence of the colonial system he facilitates: "When one has got to make correct entries,' he tells Marlow," "one comes to hate those savages—hate them to the death" (70). Marlow's fascination registers the incongruity between the accountant's writing and "the grove of death" in which inefficient workers fade away, but the intense appeal of his devotion to order blinds him to the incongruity of his own assertion that the exoskeleton of the accountant's starched clothes amounts to "backbone." Marlow's blindness does not entirely negate the latent critique of the accountant implied by Conrad's irony. It would be nice, Conrad seems to be musing, if facts could remain independent of the systems of meaning that generate them, if they could be free from ideological taint or spin, but as he remarks in another context, "a book is a deed, [and] the writing of it is an enterprise, as much as the conquest of a colony" (*LE* 132).

In a world headed toward the propaganda flood that would begin to wash over the globe in 1914, the desire "to make you *see*" is always in danger of being coopted by forces beyond one's control, just as in the Congo Marlow, despite his qualms, anxieties, and resentment, is always working, moment by moment, for the same trading company that pays the Africans in worthless coils of copper wire. If Kurtz's death constitutes Conrad's disavowal of propaganda's powers of persuasion, his lingering appeal, mirroring the appeal of the accountant, testifies to Conrad's ambivalent engagement with the eroding distinction between information and propaganda that characterizes the early twentieth century.

In "The Unlighted Coast" Conrad returns to the problem of truth and lies posed by *Heart of Darkness* in a way that suggests that the first person to rethink *Heart of Darkness* in light of the subsequent history of modern propaganda was Conrad himself. Asked in 1916 to write a propaganda piece on the merchant marines for the Admiralty, on November 6 Conrad sailed out for 10 days on the *Ready*, a brigantine disguised as a merchant vessel. A month later, he wrote an essay in which he recounts being off the coast of England during the blackout. Reminiscent of the *Nellie* anchored in the dying light on the Thames, the situation evidently returned Conrad to the book in which he represented England as "one of the dark places of the earth" (*YOS* 48). Shared generic conventions reinforce numerous links between the essay and *Heart of Darkness*. Both are instances of late imperial romance in which the historical conditions that motivate Conrad's romance are equally responsible for his modernism.[8] In "The Unlighted Coast" Conrad's modernism emerges from a modernization of romance forged under the pressure of trying to figure out what it might mean to write propaganda from within the blank darkness he encounters at sea. Deprived of obvious coordinates for propaganda—the heroism of one's own side, say, versus the ignominy of the enemy—Conrad was left with the truth of his impressions. For Ford, reconciling the truth of the impression with propaganda was not a problem; indeed, in *When Blood Is Their Argument* and *Between St. Dennis and St. George* the two are indistinguishable. But for Conrad, focusing on impressions in "The Unlighted Coast" ultimately meant turning toward the medium of his message—toward the place of the written word in wartime—and toward competing media that were transforming the status of his own.

It is worth noting at the outset that the ineptitude of "The Unlighted Coast" as propaganda is all the more stark when compared with the success of *Heart of Darkness* as fiction. In many ways it is not surprising that propaganda did not come easily to Conrad. Although always eager to declare his fidelity to his adopted country, Conrad was more invested in Englishness as part of his authorial identity than he was in British citizenship. Conrad's eagerness, that is, to wrap himself in the mantle of Englishness has more to do with projecting himself as an English author (as opposed to a Pole writing in English) than with a fundamentally political identification. Conrad certainly wanted England to win the war, but his deepest concern always lay with the Polish question: Would the war result in the reestablishment of an independent Polish state? Indeed, Conrad's participation in the British war effort was very likely a direct consequence of his having written and presented to the British Foreign Office in August 1916 "a memorandum concerning the restoration of the Polish state as a hereditary monarchy under the joint protectorate of England and France" (Najder, *Chronicle* 416). A month after writing the memo, later published as "Note on the Polish Problem" in *Notes on Life and Letters*, Conrad observed naval firing practice at Lowestoft, took a two-day trip on a minesweeper, and enjoyed a short flight on a patrolling biplane. But, deeply skeptical by nature, Conrad was not inclined to credit overblown language touting British heroism; he was also largely immune to the anti-German propaganda sweeping the nation and "treated the shrill, simplistic exhortations of the press with contempt" (Najder, *Chronicle* 424). Still, he planned to write more than one essay for the Admiralty, perhaps because his son Borys, who later fought at the Somme, was stationed near the front, perhaps because he thought his participation might bolster his influence on Polish matters. "The

Unlighted Coast" ended those plans. But more important than Conrad's failure is how he fails. For Conrad's failure as a propagandist is his success as a modernist.

To be sure, Conrad's task for the Admiralty was made all the more difficult by the uneventfulness of the trip. From on board, Conrad telegraphed to his agent J.B. Pinker that he had high hopes of "bagging Fritz," but according to an independent account, the *Ready* (traveling under a *nom de guerre*, the *Freya*, supplied by Conrad) encountered only three submarines, the first two turning out to be British, and the third disappearing with destroyers in pursuit before the *Ready* could get involved (Jean-Aubry 2: 179; Sutherland 119, 137, 139). Lacking an obvious story of uncommon British valor or the even more popular alternative of a German atrocity, Conrad chose to dwell on two things: his impressions of the darkness while cruising the coastline at night, and his interview with a young seaman who had had a relatively inconclusive close encounter with a zeppelin. The German airship had emerged in classic Conradian fashion from a dense fog, was shot at twice, and departed to points unknown, perhaps to Norway, where newspapers reported sometime afterward a damaged zeppelin had alighted. Conrad seems most struck by the encounter as a rare interruption of what he takes to be the crushing monotony of night patrol at sea: for the most part, he is sure, nothing happens. While the essay expresses admiration for the clear-sighted planning and efficiency of the patrol, it was unlikely to produce recruits or trigger a surge of patriotism and consequently was not published until after Conrad's death. The Admiralty even seems to have lost its copy.

But just as Marlow is ultimately more interesting than Kurtz, so too the essay's frame is more interesting than the "Zeppelin-strafer" (*LE* 52). Conrad revisits two favorite tropes, darkness and silence, in a self-consciously revisionary way. The first sentence reveals what most engaged his imagination—"I came ashore bringing with me strongest of all, and most persistent, the impression of a great darkness" (48)—and he immediately distinguishes this darkness from the "brooding gloom" over London in *Heart of Darkness* by assuring the reader that he does not mean darkness in "a symbolic or spiritual sense" (48). This darkness is rather the literal fact of England under blackout. And yet Conrad does not remain in the realm of fact for long: The multiple temporalities of *Heart of Darkness*, in which Marlow spins the historical fantasy of a Roman commander of a trireme and "a decent young citizen in a toga" facing the darkness that was England (*YOS* 50), return in the very sentence that insists on darkness as a "fact." What also returns is a foundational trope of imperial romance. For it is a darkness "such as wrapped up early mariners' landfalls on their voyages of exploration" (*LE* 48); "surely neither Caesar's galleys nor the ships of the Danish rovers had ever found on their approach this land so absolutely and scrupulously lightless as this" (49). With this gesture the pre-modern is uneasily superimposed over the modern: the

Zeppelin will emerge from the fog as a phantasm of modernity within an older darkness understood as the epitome of romance. This darkness, blacking out the familiar landmarks and geography of the English coast, recreates the "blank spaces" on the map that make adventure possible (*YOS* 52).

What makes Conrad's imperial romance *late* imperial romance is his acute awareness that with colonialism and modern travel completely mapping the world, "the glamour's off" (*YOS* 52). Reinvented for nineteenth-century fiction by Sir Walter Scott, modern romance represents modernity's uncanny vision of the worlds it has superseded (Duncan 1–19), but by the late nineteenth century it seemed virtually impossible for romance writers to appropriate unexplored locales for the staging of imperial adventure at the lawless boundaries of civilization. In his late essay "Travel," Conrad laments that the profusion of new travel books is "more devastating to the world's freshness of impression than a swarm of locusts in a field of young corn" (*LE* 86). He goes on to praise the books of the "real travellers" of former times, regretting that

> the time for such books of travel is past on this earth girt about with cables, with an atmosphere made restless by the waves of ether, lighted by that sun of the twentieth century under which there is nothing new left now, and but very little of what may still be called obscure. (88)

To recover traces of what might have existed prior to the global reach of new media and colonialism, late imperial romance had to effect an imaginary unmapping of the world to escape from the grid of the rational and the known (McClure 111–130). Hence Conan Doyle's dinosaurs on an undiscovered plateau in South America in *The Lost World* (1911), one of many early century novels that allude directly to Conrad's blank spot on the map, and Conrad's darkness, in which a submarine might slide silently beneath a Roman galley, or Marlow might witness a spiritual drama of loss and redemption in the dark continent, or Nostromo and Martin Decoud might drift away from the "material interests" of Sulaco into the existential void of the utterly black Golfo Placido.

Yet if such blackness evokes pre-modernity, it also paradoxically discloses the inescapably modern. While the "placid sea gleaming faintly" in "The Unlighted Coast" recalls the atavistic space of *Nostromo*'s Placid Gulf, the silence within that darkness—the second of Conrad's recycled tropes—is also modernized. No longer conveying "the usual meaning . . . to a human mind, that of being cut off from communication with its kind" (*LE* 49), this silence is not empty but full. For two messages arrive on board, one a report about a submarine sighting, the other about floating mines, both picked up by wireless. The unlighted coast, "emitting no sound waves, no waves of light, was talking to its watchers at sea; filling the silence with words" (49).[9] Conrad, who helps decode the messages, is fascinated by "the talk that flows on unheard" (50).[10] In contrast to the usual empty banter of the "war talk we hear on the lips of men," "the grouped-letters war talk" is "full of sense, of meaning, and single-minded purpose; inquiries, information, orders, reports." It is, in short, a perfectly transparent language: "words in direct relation to things and facts" (50).

The darkness and silence of "The Unlighted Coast," operating at once as a form of negation and plenitude, throw into relief the link between Conrad's modernism and his foregrounding of competing media. In *The Political Unconscious*, Fredric Jameson locates Conrad's modernism in his "will to style," which at once expresses and compensates for the rationalization and fragmentation of life under modernity (225–232). Arguing that the senses begin to split apart and become autonomous under late capitalism, and that the hallucinatory quality of Conrad's impressionistic style conjures a Utopian realm of sensuality beyond rationalization even as it embodies rationalization, Jameson observes that "the realm of nonperception" Nostromo and Decoud experience in the blackness of the Golfo Placido is "a heightened form of perception in its own right, a realm of heightened yet blank intensity" (241). What's missing in Jameson's otherwise incisive account is media's role in producing the historical conditions that his analysis presupposes. Explicitly linked to the wireless, war talk that is not propagated by the lips of men also recalls the primary narrator's description of Marlow's story, told in pitch darkness, as a "narrative that seemed to shape itself without human lips" (83). Ivan Kreilkamp, resituating early modernism in relation to new media, has linked these words to the phonograph, arguing that Conrad's treatment of voice places *Heart of Darkness* within the same problematic of disembodiment and fragmentation raised by the phonograph's recording and reproduction of the human voice. These two technologies—the phonograph dating from 1877, the wireless invented 20 years later but not licensed to the public in Britain for another 20—mark two moments within media ecology's broader evolution that had begun to change the status of the word during the later nineteenth century. Conrad's understanding of the coded wireless messages as "grouped-letters war talk," evoking not only the transparent language of fact but also the alphabetic opacities of Mallarmé, thus resonates with literary accounts that locate modernism at the confluence of naturalism and symbolism even as it acknowledges the formative role of new media that such accounts overlook.[11]

Jameson's failure to acknowledge that most of his examples of perception as an end in itself come from Conrad's representations of the space of exoticism only underscores the degree to which Conrad understood new media as a defining feature of modernity. When Conrad focuses on sense data in the metropolitan world of *The Secret Agent*, sound is clinically registered as "waves of air of the proper length, propagated in accordance with correct mathematical formulas" (260). In the remote Malaysia of "Karain" and the never-never land of *Lord Jim*'s Patusan, in contrast, the senses are typically reintegrated through the agency of synaesthesia and the sensory phantasmagoria Jameson describes. Locating rationalization in the city and its negation in places such as

Patusan, which Marlow describes as lying "three hundred miles beyond the end of telegraph cables and mail-boat lines" (*LU* 282), Conrad remains true to the conventions of imperial romance by erasing the network of cables and "waves of ether" that were rapidly shrinking the world.

What makes the romance of "The Unlighted Coast" so distinctive is that Conrad's darkness not only performs the usual function of erasure; it also operates as a kind of ether for the new medium of the radio. The unheard messages propagating through darkness simultaneously create in literature the romance they were erasing in historical experience by producing a new space of mystery. That mystery, moreover, has a suggestively literary quality, for when Conrad exalts the clarity of the wireless messages—"words in direct relation to things"—he simultaneously recodes his own language by indulging in the essay's only literary allusions. The usual war blather from "the lips of men" obscures "the one and only question: To be or not to be—the great alternative of an appeal to arms. The other, grouped-letters war talk, almost without sound and altogether without fury, is full of sense, of meaning and single-minded purpose" (50). Becoming a matter for self-conscious reflection in "The Unlighted Coast," the cultural agon between modernism and propaganda that emerges in *Heart of Darkness* would find multiple provisional resolutions in the coming decades. Conrad returned forcefully to the conjunction in *The Secret Agent*, in which Ossipon's ineffective propaganda pamphlets operate as a negative image of the rhetorical power to which the novel aspires, and the Professor's chilling commitment to what contemporary anarchists called "propaganda by the deed" (Joll 99–129) embodies Conrad's ambivalent fantasy of the power he would like to wield in the marketplace. Other modernists also responded to the increasing power of propaganda and the manipulation of public opinion. Ford, less concerned than Conrad by the eroding distinction between information and propaganda, nearly conflates modernism and propaganda in his Wellington House books. In *Ulysses* James Joyce debunks British propaganda disseminated by World War I recruiting posters in Ireland (see Wollaeger, "Posters, Modernism, Cosmopolitanism" 87–131). Less elaborately systematic in his response than Joyce, Conrad's lessons from the early days of modernism remain instructive. In a way that illuminates our own predicament in front of the dark television screen, awaiting new streaks of tracer fire over the next target in the war on terrorism, Conrad's darkness, simultaneously suppressing and producing information, evokes the space of contestation in which the frontiers of modernism and propaganda, and propaganda and information, are always being negotiated.

Notes

1. "Late modernity" is preferable to "postmodernity" in this context because the propaganda techniques employed in the Gulf War were logical extensions of methods pioneered by the British in World War I and did not constitute the kind of break implied by the prefix "post." For a comparison of the terms, see Fornäs 35–38.

2. The intrinsic difficulties of assessing the effectiveness of propaganda are magnified in the case of World War I because no official history of the British campaign was ever commissioned or written. For persuasive attempts, see Bruntz (188–221), and Sanders and Taylor (251–265). Also of interest, though hampered by lack of historical perspective, is Lasswell's foundational *Propaganda Technique in the World War* (216–222). For a critical overview of historical studies, see Sanders and Taylor's preface (vii–x).

3. For the literary activities of Wellington House, see Buitenhuis and Messinger; Messinger devotes separate chapters to individual figures, including Buchan, Bennett, and Wells.

4. H.G. Wells later ended up running the propaganda campaign in Germany for Lord Northcliffe, who organized propaganda against enemy countries out of Crewe House; Anthony Hope Hawkins served as literary advisor to Wellington House; Gilbert Parker ran the crucial propaganda campaign in the United States.

5. Sutherland (126) mistakes the year as 1917.

6. Buitenhuis (15) claims that the news broke only with Squires' book in 1935, but Squires (27, 30–31) cites at least two publications from 1931, including Nicholson's important article on his Wellington House work.

7. Poovey begins her historical account with double-entry bookkeeping (29–91).

8. For an account of modernism and the late nineteenth-century romance revival as entwined responses to modernity, see Nicholas Daly 1–29.

9. Wireless in Britain at this time was largely controlled by the military. Though invented almost 20 years earlier, wireless had been made available to the public only two years earlier, in July 1914, and then, only two months later with the outbreak of war, all public licenses were withdrawn.

10. Sutherland corroborates that Conrad learned how to work the wireless and decode messages, though one wonders how much to trust an account by someone whose first impressions are that Conrad is a man interested in "seeing only the bright side of things" (12) and who judges their trip "the most memorable and exciting experience of [Conrad's] seafaring career" (1).

11. For the inaugural version of this account of modernism, see Edmund Wilson 1–25.

2
Global Conrad

5

Between Men: Conrad in the Fiction of Two Contemporary Indian Writers

PADMINI MONGIA

I. Introduction

Conrad Lives!

"Conrad Lives." With these resounding words, Peter Nazareth ends his essay, "Conrad's Descendants" (1990). Another decade has passed, a new century has begun, and interest in Conrad continues unabated. Indeed, Conrad enters the twenty-first century at a steady high: Conferences all over the world are devoted to his work, and from 1993 onward, the MLA bibliography averages over 100 listings a year with Conrad as their subject. No doubt there are numerous ways of understanding this popularity, but one concerns changes within literary criticism and its provenance in recent decades. Whereas an earlier critical tradition separated the literature of empire and colony from the high tradition of English literature, much attention has recently been paid to the ways in which colonial encounter shaped metropolitan culture, including its literature. The boundaries between metropole and colony, high literature and colonial fictions, seem now so tenuous to have almost disintegrated.

Contemporary Indian literature in English[1]—itself a troubling category in a world ever more porous—also appears to be enjoying great success in both India and metropolitan centers the world over. While Indians have been writing in English since the early nineteenth century and producing novels in English since shortly after, Salman Rushdie's *Midnight's Children* (1980) signaled the advent of a new kind of novel in English. Earlier Indian writers were self-consciously aware of using the colonizer's language, a language considered inherently limited for the rendering of an Indian reality. Such were considered the divisive tensions between the opposing claims of Indian-English, that Meenakshi Mukherjee called this literature "twice-born" (5). Rushdie, on the other hand, and many other writers during the last two decades, use English as one of the Indian languages. Their success, in both India and elsewhere, stems in part from this ease with the English language and also from affinities between their works and sophisticated prose fiction. The new cosmopolitan novel is visible everywhere; just a quick glance at recent awardees of the prestigious Booker prize is instructive. In two of the most successful novels of the recent "boom" in Indian fiction—Amitav Ghosh's *The Shadow Lines* (1988) and Arundhati Roy's *The God of Small Things* (1997)—Conrad's works provide a familiar vocabulary within a tradition of the novel that might more fruitfully be considered the novel in English rather than British or Indian. Like other contemporary writers who choose to write in English, Roy and Ghosh do so for a global audience and accept the legacy of English literature of which they are also a part. Both writers are at once inheritors of an Indian and a wider cosmopolitan prose tradition, and their works have found niches with audiences worldwide, not just Indian and British. Ghosh and Roy echo Conrad—sometimes explicitly, sometimes less so—as they use Conradian elements in their own fictions. Below, I address how these two writers work with what appears at first an almost insignificant feature of Conrad's tales—male homosocial desire. Before doing so, I locate Conrad's colonial novel within the broader history of the novel and place Roy and Ghosh in the context of what has been understood as "writing back" to Conrad.

II. Conrad's Colonial Novel

Amitav Ghosh's essay, "The March of the Novel through History: the Testimony of my Grandfather's Bookcase," demonstrates how "thoroughly international" is the history of the novel. While reading habits in Britain's former colonies demonstrate this internationality, Ghosh suggests that "this truth has nowhere been more stoutly denied than in those places where the novel has its deepest roots" (294). Location, Ghosh goes on to suggest, is an integral part of the novel and conceptions of it "came into being at exactly the times when the world was beginning to experience the greatest dislocation it has ever known" (294). Indeed, the specificity of location in the British domestic novel is necessary, as has been argued, because of the dislocation being experienced within the social and economic spheres. By now, the less than obvious awareness of a colonial world within the tradition of the British domestic novel has been well explored. Martin Green's *Dreams of Adventure, Deeds of Empire* offers a compelling history of the development of the novel in Britain from its beginnings in the separate trajectories initiated by *Robinson Crusoe* and *Moll Flanders*. Green notes that the tradition of the novel regarded as serious literature paid little direct attention to the world of trade, empire, and colony—features inseparable from the lives of people in Britain from the seventeenth century onward. By contrast, the adventure tradition spawned by *Robinson Crusoe* was regarded as dismissable although or *because* it dealt explicitly with Britain's ever-expanding empire.[2] The world of shrinking opportunity that the domestic novel explores is totally at odds with the one of expanding opportunity in which the colonial novel revels. As

Edward Said has so powerfully argued in the context of Kipling's *Kim*, knowledge in Kipling's India may be translated directly into power for Kim, whereas the Judes and Dorotheas of the domestic novel must come to terms with the impossibility of finding sufficient outlets for their hard-earned wisdom.[3]

The colonial novel in English as it has evolved and developed over the last two centuries—a novel built on the encounter between different peoples in so-called exotic settings, with essentially male characters discovering their capacities and limits as individuals—has been shaped by Kipling, Stevenson and Conrad. Of these three writers, Conrad introduced into the nascent genre features that helped break down distinctions between high and low literature. Conrad's fictions, many well anchored in the adventure tradition, significantly revise both the trajectories Green identifies. Conrad's adventures question the genre even as his concerns—psychological, sociological, formal—share more in common with the traditions of serious literature. His explicit psychological and existential concerns add a density that the colonial novel doesn't always have. In his essay "Conrad's Darkness," V.S. Naipaul poignantly spells out the burden placed on a writer like himself—by Conrad (not Kipling or Stevenson)—when he first started writing: "I found that Conrad—sixty years before, in the time of a great peace—had been everywhere before me" (385). Conrad, a writer depicting the colonial world (the "world's half-made societies" as Naipaul derogatorily puts it), producing fictions exploring tenuous and difficult encounters between peoples of different races and cultures, must inevitably be before the writer who traverses similar terrain. Given Conrad's canonical status as one of the writers of the "great tradition," he is encountered—whether one wants to or not—in school syllabi and college courses all over the world.[4] Conrad has been everywhere before all of us who were schooled in English literature, whether we come from the areas he wrote about or not.

What happens to the colonial novel after decolonization? What happens to it in the hands of indigenous writers? Within the Indian context, one could argue that writers such as G.V. Desani and Salman Rushdie continue working and reworking the genre, rather than relying on social realism, also a significant strain in the Indian novel in English throughout this last century. Not surprisingly, Kipling's *Kim* is the story that has haunted these writers. Desani's *All About H. Hatterr* (1950) and Rushdie's *Midnight's Children* are just two examples of works responding to the Indian disease, the "urge to encapsulate the whole of reality" (Rushdie 75). Just as Kim traverses all of India in his dual roles as the lama's guide and a spy in the "great game," Desani's and Rushdie's heroes also journey across India encountering its myriad marvels, holy men, and variegated excesses. Kipling's importance for the contemporary Indian novel in English is no surprise. Conrad's legacy is a more complicated, less obvious, but nevertheless significant one. The quality of Conrad's presence in

Roy's and Ghosh's novels, for instance, is diffuse yet palpable as both writers examine fragmented subjects shaped by colonial encounter.

III. Conrad's "Descendants," Conrad's Interlocutors

"Conrad lives." Once Nazareth started writing his essay, he found Conrad's "descendants" so numerous that several small courses could be developed around them. Considering mostly writers of West Indian or African origin, Nazareth's essay examines Conrad's impact on these writers as a form of signification. Possibly part imitation, part parody, and part homage, signification isn't fully explained by any one or even necessarily a combination of the features mentioned above. Asako Nakai, in *The English Book and its Marginalia*, calls *Heart of Darkness* "a model for the English Book of the twentieth century" (18). Using an approach very different from Nazareth's, Nakai builds on Homi Bhabha's trope of the discovery of the English book within a colonial context. Nakai examines the trope in works by writers such as Naipaul, Isak Dinesen, and Ngugi wa Thiong'o. In her approach, the notes in cipher in the margins of the seamanship book in *Heart of Darkness* may be read as the "locus of the internalized other" (27). Paralleling this document with Kurtz's pamphlet containing another marginal comment, Nakai suggests that the "deciphered marginalia points to nothing but an outburst of colonialist paranoia" (27). Chinua Achebe's *Things Fall Apart* starkly demonstrates the stakes inherent in the dissemination of authoritative texts within the colonial context. Many writers and critics concerned with Conrad's colonial depictions "write back" to Conrad, using aspects of his fictions to tell alternate stories of the peoples and places with which Conrad familiarized a British reading public. The phrase "writing back" was popularized in the late '80s by the influential *The Empire Writes Back: Theory and Practice in Post-Colonial Literatures*. In the Conradian context, no essay or book I can name explicitly uses the phrase to describe new imaginative works. However, works examining the uses to which Conrad has been put in writings from the once-colonized world often include—in varying degrees—this premise.[5] The model's popularity—in anthologies, college courses, conferences—deserves greater critical scrutiny than it has been granted.

The impulse of writers from the once-colonized world, writing in the decades immediately after decolonization, often led to a rewriting of the dominant narrative. Within the Indian context, the dominant colonial narratives generating responses were ones produced by Kipling and Forster, whereas Conrad was the towering presence in works by West Indian and African writers.[6] These writers often focused on the Conrad whose works were so in tandem with the construction of Western disciplinary knowledge, the Conrad of the English book. Differences between Conrad's constructions of Africa and the Orient might also help to explain why Indian writers have not been as compelled to respond to Conrad as African and West Indian ones. Conrad's

Africa in *Heart of Darkness*, many critics have argued, closely replicates the Africa popular in late-Victorian anthropological, sociological, and newspaper discourses.[7] The novella, we remember, was first published in *Blackwood's* magazine, a magazine popular with readers not unlike Marlow's closed circle on the *Nellie*. James Clifford's reading of Kurtz's postscript, "Exterminate all the brutes," draws attention to the tremendous impact of the English book on constructing literary and other authority (155–162). The corrective gesture inherent in "writing back" could hardly be a burden not shared by the many writers who chose to write in English in the early decades leading up to and beyond decolonization.[8] Offering stories of Africa alternative to Conrad's, these writers focused on the impact of Conrad and writers like him as articulative engines of a particular Africa, an Africa of darkness, present throughout the many discourses flourishing at the end of the century. It is this Conrad Naipaul evokes in *The Bend in the River*.

However, in the model of "writing back," the central narrative remains the narrative of the West, with the new narrative supplementing a previous lack. Such a model echoes the patriarchal model of "descendants" and of "anxieties of influence" explored by many Conradian critics, where the father's authority is replaced by his progeny's. It is important to underscore that the model of "writing back" is primarily one crafted by the critical tradition rather than an approach that has compelled the imaginative works of creative writers. While it would be misleading to suggest that Ghosh and Roy aren't also engaged in a revisionary enterprise questioning the worlds that colonial fictions and history have popularized, the inversion implied by "writing back" is not the model either writer finds most compelling. Both writers are drawn to the Conrad interested in the less than clear distinctions between a protagonist and a shadow self, a face in the mirror that is and is not one's own. Interestingly, in the two novels I consider here, Roy and Ghosh use what appears at first glance to be an insignificant feature in many Conradian tales—desire between men. In *The God of Small Things*, a Kurtz figure—an embodiment of sexual deviance—haunts the story, while Ghosh's exploration of the homosocial ties that bind the nameless narrator of *The Shadow Lines* to Nick has a distinctly Conradian flavor. Not a "writing back" nor even necessarily an "influence," Conrad is nevertheless very much present in the two novels.

IV. Shadows, Lines, and Small Things

Heart of Darkness, Lord Jim, The Shadow-Line, to name just a few of Conrad's fictions, all obliquely, at least, pay some attention to love between men and the circulation of desire within the colonial arena.[9] Desire between men—Ransome and the young captain, Giles and the captain, Marlow and Kurtz, Kurtz and the Harlequin—are just a few of the relations that come easily to mind when one thinks of same-sex desire in *The Shadow-Line* and *Heart of Darkness*. In Conrad criticism, it is now quite commonplace to encounter work exploring these "other" sexual relations and placing them within the context of late-Victorian morals and mores. Jeremy Hawthorn's recent introduction to the Oxford *The Shadow-Line* and Donald Wilson's "The Beast in the Congo: How Victorian Homophobia Inflects Marlow's *Heart of Darkness*" are two recent works addressing aspects of same-sex desire in Conrad's fictions. Wilson's essay, in particular, contextualizes *Heart of Darkness* by arguing that Marlow's discourse is acutely responsive to the homophobic milieu of late-Victorian England.

Offering the site where sins may be buried and transgressions hidden, the colonial location reveals the sexual (and other) opportunities made available by empire.[10] As Roger Hyam has shown in his "Empire and Sexual Opportunity," empire afforded sexual opportunities not just for heterosexual relations but for relations between men. Indeed, Hyam argues, the colonial context especially facilitated the exploration of same-sex relations between men and between men and boys. Probably no single figure in twentieth-century English literature better embodies these opportunities than Conrad's Kurtz. Transgression is his domain, and miscegenation is, perhaps, the least of his excesses. Given, as Wilson argues, the homophobic environment of contemporary England, it's unlikely that Conrad's novella isn't speaking of and to that environment. That Marlow never spells out Kurtz's excesses shows the novel responding to the repressive atmosphere surrounding same-sex desire. In Wilson's reading, "Marlow's highly abstruse discourse" (99) leaves open the possibility that the horror of the jungle lies in its homoerotic and homosexual dimensions (99–101). Closeted in his own jungle fiefdom, Kurtz lives out the potential and possibility afforded white men in the colonial arena, a potential only restricted by Marlow and the reader's imagination. Of the many boundaries Kurtz crosses, same-sex desire is as likely one of them as any other "transgression" we can imagine.

In his colonial fictions, Conrad's interest in the white men who go soft in the heat and dust of colonial outposts is always attentive to the possibilities the colonial context makes available to these men. Indeed, it is this context of easy luxury (based on race and the accidents of history) that tests their mettle. Location is crucial to Conrad's colonial tales. The African woman in *Heart of Darkness* is inseparable from the surrounding wilderness that sees in her its own "passionate soul" (*YOS* 101). Similarly, in *Lord Jim*, Jewel, like the place with which she's associated, Patusan, is eroticized in the vocabulary of desire often employed in late-Victorian Orientalist constructions. Highlighted by explicit sexual markers like her long, dark hair and flowing white clothes, Jewel is both sensual and domesticated, at least by comparison with the "primitive," more explicitly sexual woman in *Heart of Darkness*. Deploying, as many critics have argued, late-Victorian stereotypes of the Orient and Africa, Conrad links the sensualized Orient with a responsiveness to domesticity unlike a "primitive" Africa, which resists domestication and therefore retains more threatening aspects. Both regions are, of course, eroticized and represent forbidden desires to which the white male protagonists respond.[11]

Relying on a similar erotics of space, Roy creates Ayemenem as the site of sexual transgressions and devastating physical betrayals. Unlike Conrad's sensual but domesticated Orient, Roy's Ayemenem is sensual yet oppressive. More like Conrad's Africa, Ayemenem is a place of tropical excess, where forbidden desire may be explored.[12] An abandoned house where the novel's critical events unfold is the chief site of past and future transgressions. Located in the middle of an abandoned rubber estate, this house had once belonged to Kari Saipu, the "Englishman who had 'gone native.' … Ayemenem's own Kurtz, Ayemenem his private Heart of Darkness" (*Roy* 51). Deliberately making explicit the homoeroticism and sexual exploitation that inflects *Heart of Darkness*, Roy makes Kari Saipu a pedophile for whom the colonial arena also affords opportunities for expressing same-sex desire. Kari Saipu commits suicide after the parents of his young lover take the boy away, ten years before the novel's main events.

However, Roy is not chiefly interested in excavating Kari Saipu's story. Instead, Roy's novel emphasizes the forbidden love shared by Ammu and the "untouchable" carpenter, Velutha, a love transgressing both class and caste boundaries. Yet this expression of transgressive desire is presented to the reader as a latter-day manifestation of an older impulse. "The white man's demon had entered them" (242), Vellya Paapen says of his son Velutha's transgression. Vellya Paapen believes he put "an end to the bloodthirsty wanderings of a pedophile ghost" (190), by pinning Kari Saipu's ghost to a tree with his sickle. But Ayemenem's own Kurtz exerts control over his fiefdom long after his death and indeed long after the termination of his ghostly wanderings. Having bequeathed his capacity for expressing unsanctioned desire to the likes of Ammu and Velutha, Kari Saipu seems maliciously to oversee the unfolding of traumatic events in Roy's novel, even granting them a peculiar legitimacy. Going native goes native and takes on another shape entirely in the desire shared by Ammu and Velutha.

Kari Saipu's abandoned house on his abandoned rubber estate offers the physical site for Velutha and Ammu to express their desire. For the young twins Estha and Rahel, from whose perspective the novel unfolds, this abandoned house becomes associated with history, thanks to their Uncle Chacko: "He explained to them that history was like an old house at night. With all the lamps lit. And ancestors whispering inside" (51). The children immediately conclude that the house to which Chacko refers is the house on the other side of the river, where they've never been. If history is a house, it is a house haunted by the empire and by the white sahibs it allowed to "go native." Chacko's focus on history suggests the outsider status of the once-colonized, of people like him and his family: "They were a *family* of Anglophiles. Pointed in the wrong direction, trapped outside their own history and unable to retrace their steps because their footprints had been swept away" (51). Condemned to be always outside history, they are desperate to go into the house and overhear the whispers, "But we can't go in ... because we've been locked out" (52). In Chacko's understanding, the world's events that matter will never happen to him or his family in their specific location: History happens elsewhere, in Europe, and to other people. His views are very specific and aren't shared by his sister, Ammu, who finds his explanations tedious.

The twins, however, sense their difference from those to whom History happens, from those who seem to matter, like their half-English cousin Sophie Mol, who arrives in Ayemenem with her mother (Chacko's ex-wife), Margaret Kochamma. The fuss made around Sophie is inseparable from her whiteness and the young children are quite aware of it. Brilliantly presented as a one-act play, "Welcome Home, Our Sophie Mol" offers only bit parts to Estha, Rahel, and Ammu. Yet these bit parts fuel the crucial events occurring offstage. A brief moment when "History was wrong-footed, caught off guard" (167) allows Ammu and Velutha to see each other with desire and to recognize each other's awareness of that desire. Propelled by her alienation from her family, Ammu "hoped that ... he [Velutha] housed a living, breathing anger against the smug, ordered world she so raged against" (167). That night, Ammu acts on her desire and sets in motion the events that culminate in Velutha's death and her own and Estha's departure from Ayemenem.

Chacko never pays attention to these layers of history, able only to see himself as an outsider in a narrative where he has no part. Always the "colonial" outside History, Chacko's focus is unable to acknowledge the weight of tradition in what happens and also his own part as the privileged son and patriarch of the Ayemenem household. Desire between peoples of different castes and classes is only unsanctioned for Ammu, not for Chacko. When Chacko first returns home from his position as a teacher in Madras, his mother, Ammachi, has a separate entrance built to his room, since Chacko cannot help having a "Man's Needs" (160). Through this door, the women who satisfy Chacko's libido enter and leave freely, without Ammachi having to encounter them. Unable to see the contradictions between his stated political positions and his private propensities, between, as Roy puts it, his "Marxist mind and feudal libido" (160), Chacko behaves like a feudal patriarch when Ammu wrests agency for herself through her sexual liaison with Velutha.

As if demanding Velutha's death for his sexual transgression, History "claims its dues" (190). Using the same language Chacko used earlier to describe the war within the once-colonized, a "war that captures dreams and re-dreams them" (52), Kari Saipu, the white man who "captured dreams and re-dreams them" (190) is history's agent, a Kurtz figure offering stale dreams to the once-colonized. What initially appears to be an insignificant detail—Kari Saipu's pedophilia—is grimly mirrored in Estha's sexual exploitation by the Orangedrink Lemondrink man at the movie theatre. Estha's terror after this event mirrors other terrors—that of Sophie's death by drowning, Velutha's death at the hands of the police, and Estha's own part in betraying Velutha. Like the house he's associated with, Kari Saipu exerts control over Roy's protagonists and circumscribes their dreams of freedom or safety: Ammu, her twins, and Velutha are unable to shape their own destinies.

Overseen by the Kurtz figure, men in Roy's novel must accept a greater responsibility for the brutal events that occur, whether they act inadvertently or not. "Man's subliminal urge to destroy what he could neither subdue nor deify. Men's Needs" (292), Roy says of the brutal beating Velutha receives from the police. Even Estha corroborates the lies surrounding Velutha's death, thereby contributing to an "official" story that reinscribes a colonial tale—a white child's death at the hands of an "untouchable" black man. More distressing, Ammu and Estha's expulsion from the Ayemenem estate is Chacko's decision, as he ruthlessly exerts his rights over his inherited property to express his anger against his divorced sister and her children. The circulation of power between men is aided by caste and class privilege, by inheritance laws and political power, but Roy is careful to suggest that the exploitation predates the colonial encounter, perhaps going as far back as when the love-laws were made. Early in the novel, Roy says that although possibly "it all began when Sophie Mol came to Ayemenem ... it could be argued that it actually began thousands of years ago. Long before the Marxists came. Before the British took Malabar, before the Dutch Ascendancy, before Vasco da Gama arrived ... That it really began in the days when the Love Laws were made" (32–33). Indeed, it could be argued that Sophie and Margaret's journey to the heart of darkness is the chief cause of the deaths of Sophie and Velutha. And Roy does. Yet Sophie Mol is just one small feature in a vast canvas, a canvas in which responsibility can be ascribed to the Marxists, the feudal landlords, the Syrian Christians, the caste system in India, and to gender inequities. Assessing the part played by each of these institutions, Roy excavates events carefully as she examines how responsibility can be ascribed to the many participants who share it.

Chacko's and Ammu's views present two different ways of understanding history. Chacko seems to approach history as academic, history produced at the institutional site of the university, a history with Europe at the center. Ammu's understanding of history is quite different. Akin to an archaeological peeling away of layers, as suggested in the narrator's claims quoted above, taking us back to the earliest beginnings of social relations when the "love laws" regulating desire between human beings were developed, Ammu's understanding of history is subaltern in impulse. Through this tension between conflicting understandings of history, Roy's novel explicitly challenges the truths presented by Western modes of knowledge production—both historical and imaginative—while offering an alternate version of events.

Conrad's *Heart of Darkness* offered twentieth-century readers unforgettable portraits of a region and white men negotiating a masculine world of opportunity. Roy utilizes many of the novella's features while giving them a disturbing twist: Sexual liaisons between unsanctioned heterosexual partners become unsavory liaisons between men and boys. White male pedophiles oversee the replaying of transgressive desire at several different levels. Power is exerted and maintained by men—through physical force, class privilege, political ambition, and inheritance laws. Yet, Roy's novel does more than suggest a colonial legacy to the issues she examines. *The God of Small Things* provides a compelling view of the sordid heart of the heart of darkness, even as Roy suggests the limits of Conradian echoes for a writer such as herself.

Although Kari Saipu's house initially falls into disrepair, by the novel's end it is transformed into a "heritage" hotel, where "History and Literature [are] enlisted by commerce" (120), so that "Kurtz and Karl Marx" may be found "joining palms to greet rich guests" (120). The History House in Roy's novel is overburdened with symbolic weight: it is the heart of the Heart of Darkness, it is the site for burials of transgressions, the site for the expression of forbidden desire, and for the execution of power over the powerless in a brutal, excessive manner. As the ruined house within Roy's heart of darkness functions as the site of desire and transgression, so does a house burdened by history in Ghosh's *The Shadow Lines*. On a family picnic to Ila's grandfather's house outside Calcutta, the young (nameless) narrator finds himself led by his cousin Ila to an underground room. Ila whips off the dust cover (which itself disintegrates into dust) to reveal an impossibly large table her grandfather had shipped in pieces from England, after he had seen it in an exhibition at the Crystal Palace. Beneath this table, Ila makes the narrator play Houses, playing the wife to his husband in a house she draws in the dust. This make-believe house is modeled on the house of family friends in West Hampstead, where she currently lives with her mother. Houses, Ila says, is the game she plays with Nick Price, Mrs. Price's son in West Hampstead. When the narrator asks who Nick is, Ila's response creates him as her close friend, with whom she goes to school and plays houses in the evening in the cellar. Suddenly alert, the narrator is suspicious of this Nick: "After that day, Nick Price, whom I had never seen ... became a spectral presence beside me in my looking glass; growing with me, but always bigger and better, and in some ways more desirable .... And yet if I tried to look into the face of that ghostly presence ... there was never anything there" (49). After this introduction to Nick Price, he is always in the narrator's mirror, an image reminding the narrator of his more tenuous masculinity, as he imagines it. In Ila's game of Houses, their child, Magda, is rescued from racist school children by a gallant Nick. Only three years later does the narrator learn that Ila's narration of this episode is false; Nick didn't rescue Ila but abandoned her. Meanwhile, Nick has shared space in the narrator's mirror, always bigger, stronger, and more handsome. Of course, the narrator's hopeless and unreciprocated love for Ila feeds this feeling, placing him in a permanently unequal relationship with Nick. Although Nick and the narrator only meet years later, the narrator's identification with and competitive feeling toward Nick shape his journey into adulthood.

By introducing Nick into the family romance being enacted under the table, Ila initiates a triangulation that continues well into their adulthood. Dependent economically on Ila, Nick enacts small rebellions through numerous affairs he conducts even after their marriage. The narrator finds some sympathy for this Nick: "Looking at him, I tried to think of the future as it must have appeared to him: of helpless dependence coupled with despairing little acts of rebellion. I wanted to get up then and hold him, chest to chest, his shoulders to mine" (186). As Suvir Kaul points out, "in keeping with his [the narrator's] long identification with Nick ... he feels sorry for Nick's economic dependence on her, and on the punishment she would mete out to him for his extramarital sexual activities" (144). Although so close to Ila that they have been regarded as inseparable as children, the narrator now finds, in a moment of surprising homosocial bonding, great sympathy for Nick's unenviable position in his marriage.

Another moment of seamless affinity with Nick Price occurs when the narrator discovers—as he thinks—their shared passion for travel. As a boy of fourteen he hears, through his own father, that, when he grows up, Nick would like to be like his grandfather Tresawsen. Tridib, his archaeologist uncle, tells the narrator of Tresawsen's life: Like a latter-day Robinson Crusoe, he left his family farm in Cornwall and spent much of his young adulthood as an inventor and entrepreneur traveling in different parts of the world. As the narrator imagines Tresawsen's life, he grants it impossibly romantic features and feels he knows instinctively why Nick would want to be like his grandfather. For our young narrator, sedentary in Calcutta, a shared passion for travel, which he attributes to Nick, makes him "the kindred spirit whom I had never been able to discover among my friends" (52). This passion for travel has been nurtured and developed in the narrator through Tridib; they spend hours poring over Tridib's tattered copy of *Bartholomew's Atlas*, as Tridib tells him stories of places with magical names. "[T]hose names, which were to me a set of magical talismans because Tridib had pointed them out to me" (20) help train the young narrator to use his "imagination with precision" (24), laying the groundwork for the narrative imagination that leads him to construct the moving and cathartic tale he tells.

Those hours spent gazing at the atlas recall the childhood passion for maps Conrad describes in "Geography and Some Explorers": "[M]ap gazing ... brings the problems of the great spaces of the earth into stimulating and directing contact with sane curiosity and gives an honest precision to one's imaginative faculty" (13). Just as young Marlow once dreamed of visiting the white heart of Africa as a boy, so did the young Conrad. As a white European male coming of age in the second half of the nineteenth century, Conrad took advantage of the opportunities available to someone with his background and skills. That magic associated with travel and discovery that so compels Marlow's urge to the Congo in *Heart of Darkness* certainly has a particular flavor, given the time Conrad evokes in the novella. The excitement and childish wonder associated with unknown spaces and a world newly discovered that both Marlow and Conrad recall from their boyhoods is shared by the nameless narrator of Ghosh's *The Shadow Lines*. Tridib gives his nephew, through their map gazing, "worlds to travel in and . . . eyes to see them with" (20). Not only capable of using his imagination precisely, the narrator becomes a storyteller who uses his passion for travel and adventure to muse upon many shadow lines. His awareness of Nick as a spectral presence through their boyhood gives way to more complex discoveries of lines that are meant to separate. The adult narrator realizes how a riot in Calcutta resonates across the border in Dacca even as its impetus is an event in faraway Kashmir. The image of war-torn London is mirrored in a subcontinent ripped by violence. Among the most difficult truths the narrator learns is that borders don't separate; instead the border is a "looking-glass" (228), reflecting not difference but sameness.

In the context of the partition of India, Ghosh's meditation on borders has particular poignancy and throws up for scrutiny the artificiality behind the division of the subcontinent. Toward the end of the novel, when the narrator realizes how events in one part of the world resonate in unexpected ways in a supposedly unrelated part of the world, he takes a compass and arbitrarily draws circles from random points he selects on his copy of Tridib's atlas. Like Conrad's meditation on map gazing, "which brings the problems of the great spaces of the earth into stimulating and directing contact with sane curiosity" (13), the narrator's meditation on space reveals nothing but the mystery of distance. Despite the honest intentions of map-makers who believed in the "enchantment of lines" (228), the narrator discovers the tenuousness of borders that do not keep apart but reflect sameness, so that Calcutta and Dacca become the "inverted image of the other, locked into an irreversible symmetry by the line that was to set us free—our looking-glass border" (228). Inevitably, Ghosh's meditation on borders and distance has a different inflection from Conrad's boyhood passion for maps. The rapid cartographical changes between "known" and "unknown" that fascinated Conrad have given way to new realities in Ghosh's novel. While the mystery and attraction of the unknown compel both, Ghosh's novel struggles with a late-twentieth-century concern: the imagined community of the nation.

Nick is a spectral presence for the narrator as a child; the story he tells as an adult holds up for scrutiny many other moments that question shadow lines. Ironically, the adult Nick has none of the features our young narrator has granted him. His method of travel turns out to be rather different from his grandfather's: he travels through his affairs with women from different parts of the world. As Nick Price's world of opportunity has shrunk with the smaller opportunities afforded to him, those of our narrator have grown in inverse proportion. In his passage to London, Ghosh's narrator reveals an almost disturbingly profound capacity for travel—both real and imagined. Contemplating the difference between "coming home" and "going home," the narrator touches one of the most poignant shadow lines of the late twentieth century: "a journey that was a search for precisely that fixed point which permits the proper use of verbs of movement" (150). Not a journey marking the transition between youth and adulthood as in Conrad's novella, Ghosh's shadow lines comment on the tenuous, nebulous, yet persistent boundaries between home and abroad.

While the difficult journey from youth to adulthood may be the most significant shadow-line in Conrad's novel, its very title demands that the reader connect what appear, at first glance, to be two unrelated events: World War I and Conrad's first command. In his Author's Note to the novel, Conrad elaborates on the connection between two seemingly disconnected events: "There could be no question here of any parallelism .... But there was a feeling of identity" (40), an identity expressed through the mood coloring Conrad's rendition of his autobiographical experience and the world war he connected it with. Appropriately pluralized, shadow lines in Ghosh's novel have multiplied frighteningly as peoples traverse space and nations change boundaries in his novel. Yet Ghosh offers a "feeling of identity" with the earlier work he echoes, not only though his reliance on travel and the imagination but also by addressing the shadow lines of his own generation and produced by his specific location: the tenuous difference between home and abroad.

Discussing *The Shadow Lines*, John Thieme suggests in his article "Passages to England," that the contemporary Indo-British encounter as rendered in current fiction by Indians might be termed a gothic one, haunted as it is by layers of uncomfortable history. It's a provocative suggestion and offers a vocabulary for the myriad tensions that mark relations between the Indians and the British in novels like Ghosh's and Roy's. However, I would suggest that the gothic aspects of the contemporary Indo-British encounter reveal not only a haunted history but also the force of transgressive desire. In traditional gothic novels, terror and horror are created in large part from their flirtation with forbidden desire, particularly—but not only—incestuous desire. This exploration of desire functions in the gothic novel to help demarcate boundaries of identity, particularly female identity. In Ghosh's and Roy's novels, incestuous sexual relations are consummated rather than feared, although desire hardly seems the appropriate term for describing them. Of the sexual union between brother and sister, Roy says, "what they shared that night was not happiness, but hideous grief" (311). In Ghosh's novel, the union of the narrator with May (his uncle Tridib's girlfriend) allows the narrator a glimpse into a "final redemptive mystery" (246). Breaking the "love laws," as Roy would put it, operates in both novels as cathartic, a gesture crucial to the acceptance of the traumatic events that have unfolded earlier. The encounter with the British—with either a Sophie Mol or a Nick Price—reveals a conflicted response, at least partially propelled by desire. Just as Nick is always in the mirror when the narrator glances at himself, so too are the boundaries nebulous between the nations/individuals in these novels.

V. Conclusion

In "Postcoloniality and the Artifice of History: Who Speaks for 'Indian' Pasts?," Dipesh Chakrabarty has argued that "insofar as the academic discourse of history—that is, 'history' as a discourse produced at the institutional site of the university—is concerned, 'Europe' remains the sovereign, theoretical subject of all histories, including the ones we call 'Indian,' 'Chinese,' 'Kenyan' and so on" (263). All other histories become "variations on a master narrative that could be called 'the history of Europe'" (263). In a similar fashion, approaches to Conrad emphasizing "influence" or "writing back" keep Conrad at the center of a Western master narrative of the history of the novel. In the subtler ways that Conrad's presence is felt in *The God of Small Things* and *The Shadow Lines*, Roy and Ghosh offer a different alternative: one that might be seen as "provincializing Europe." For neither writer takes Conrad as their point of departure, despite the fact that he's a significant presence in their works, elaborated through a fluid and multivalent vocabulary of homosocial desire.

To speak of provincializing Conrad is to offer an alternate map of the novel, one in which Conrad is significant but not central. Regarded as one of the provinces rather than the metropolis, Conrad's position helps open the space for an examination of the novel that takes into account the new cultural processes that shape our contemporary world. To approach Conrad as part of the globalizing forces that have made national histories of the novel limited if not spurious is to allow him a place in the twenty-first century that accounts for the changes that have taken place over the last hundred years. In the mainstream critical tradition, two Conrads have lived this last half-century: the first a Conrad of high literature and of an attendant literary-critical tradition, and the second the Conrad who not only wrote of empire and colony but is associated with the "third world." Ironically, the separation between these two Conrads is at odds with the fictional worlds Conrad himself created, where both metropole and colony are brought under scrutiny.

Indeed, the separation of these two Conrads creates divisions that replicate a disturbing hierarchy of interests. Consider, for example, the monumental and wonderfully useful four-volume work *Joseph Conrad: Critical Assessments*, reproducing critical assessments of Conrad from the earliest commentaries through 1992.[13] The scale and scope of these volumes ensure they will be among the first tomes students and researchers will turn to in the twenty-first century, much as scholars and students turned to *The Critical Tradition* series in the latter half of the twentieth century. But only once in the more than 2,800 pages of text covering the critical response to Conrad does the "third world" merit attention. Unsurprisingly, this attention is granted because of Achebe's essay on *Heart of Darkness*, which Carabine tells us "has also engaged the finest writers of the post-colonial era who manifest in different ways 'Anxieties of Influence'" (1: 6). While Russia, Poland, France, and America each merit separate sections of attention, the colonial world that Conrad rendered with such long-lasting impact is never allocated a separate section nor any sustained analysis, although it receives more space than "Conrad's influence with regard to England, France, America, Russia, and Poland" (1: 6). Instead, the "third world" is approached as both hardly consequential and separable—geographically, critically, and theoretically—from the "first," so that the "third world" is kept at arm's length. In such a critical tradition, the reach of the colonial world doesn't stretch to the metropolis by becoming a part of it. Such approaches replicate a disturbing dichotomy between "first" and "third" worlds; even the uncritical use of the term "third world" does its part to suggest a hierarchy of interests. In the twenty-first century, I hope this hierarchy of difference will be shaken so that Conrad and his interlocutors can be approached as part of the tradition of literature in English rather than as members of a patriarchal familial structure.

Notes

1. The cumbersome phrase "Indian writing in English" emphasizes that English is just one of contemporary India's many thriving literary languages.
2. Green argues that the adventure tale was the "energizing myth of English imperialism" (3) although these tales were regarded as light reading. Fredric Jameson describes as "degraded" the "sub-genres into which mass culture will be articulated (adventure story, gothic, science fiction, bestseller, detective story, and the like)" (*Political* 207).
3. See Said's Introduction 36–40.
4. *Lord Jim*, for instance, has been on the English honors undergraduate reading list at Delhi University for over 25 years; Kipling is not. Although I have not conducted formal research on the subject, I think it likely that Conrad is taught—in undergraduate syllabi worldwide—more often than Kipling, Stevenson, or Forster.
5. Consider Hamner, Hamner, *Joseph Conrad: Third World Perspectives*; Nazareth, "Out of Darkness; Huggan; Nakai; and Carabine, *Critical Assessments*.
6. G.S. Amur writes: "Conrad who has been such a formative influence on the African writers has never had much of an appeal to the Indian writer" (qtd. in Nazareth, "Out of Darkness" 174). If one accepts Nazareth's explanation for this—"Conrad does not make sense to persons belonging to monolithic societies" (174) such as the Indian—then Conrad's presence in contemporary Indian fiction must speak to changes in the "monolithic" nature of Indian society and culture.
7. See, for instance, Shetty; Hammond and Jablow.
8. See, for instance, Achebe's *Things Fall Apart*, Ngugi wa Thiongo's *A Grain of Wheat*, and Wilson Harris's *The Palace of the Peacock*.
9. Eve Kosofsky Sedgwick's *Between Men: English Literature and Male Homosocial Desire* loosely shapes my reading of Roy and Ghosh. The "potential unbrokenness of a continuum between homosocial and homosexual" (1) desire allows for a discussion of relations between men, including power and sexual relationships.
10. Marlow in *Lord Jim* says, "I can only guess that once before Patusan had been used as a grave for some sin, transgression, or misfortune" (157).
11. For more on differences between Conrad's eroticization of Africa and the Orient, see Mongia, "Empire, Narrative."
12. Africa, in Roy's novel, also functions as a place of desire. Impossibly distant, it is the region the twins evoke whenever they need to imagine some safe place, away from the world of adults.
13. I refer to these volumes in particular since their scale makes them the best example of the sort of anthology I have in mind. Lest I be misunderstood, let me clarify that I speak of the volumes, not Keith Carabine, a personal friend. It does seem important, though, to note that he is the product of a particular moment of literary scholarship, just as I am of another.

6

Opera and the Passage of Literature: Joseph Conrad, Pramoedya Ananta Toer, and the Cultural Dialectic of Abysmal Taste

CHRISTOPHER GOGWILT

Readers have often been struck by the operatic qualities of Conrad's early Malay tales, and Conrad's own comments in letters suggest that he thought of the Malay (or "Lingard") trilogy of his first projected novel sequence in terms of a specifically operatic aesthetic.[1] While the operatic effects in these Malay novels would seem to confirm the exoticist distortion critics have found in their Southeast Asian settings, I argue here that this operatic aesthetic helps identify the historical and cultural specificity of Conrad's Malay Archipelago. This argument follows, in part, a recent trend in reading Conrad historically, and with renewed attention to the way his fiction registers the historical facts of colonial and anti-colonial contest. The significance of opera in Conrad's East Indies fiction, however, is by no means only a matter of historical representation. As with all the approaches variously classified as "postcolonial" or "new historicist," the question of aesthetic form remains a fundamental theoretical problem. To situate Conrad's interest in opera historically also entails examining the theoretical challenge Conrad's work presents for literary criticism at the beginning of the twenty-first century: in particular, the imperative to find a viable model for studying literature within a global and comparative historical-cultural perspective.[2]

One such model is the "contrapuntal reading" of texts proposed by Edward Said in *Culture and Imperialism*: "As we look back at the cultural archive, we begin to reread it not univocally but *contrapuntally*, with a simultaneous awareness both of the metropolitan history that is narrated and of those other histories against which (and together with which) the dominating discourse acts" (51). Conrad's Malay novels might usefully be read in "contrapuntal" relation to Pramoedya Ananta Toer's "Buru" quartet of novels, composed in prison exile on Buru Island during the 1970s and published—but immediately banned in Indonesia itself—in the 1980s. The historical settings for both novel sequences overlap with the period of high Dutch colonialism between the 1870s and the 1920s: Conrad's trilogy moving backward historically from the late 1880s to the 1860s; Pramoedya's tetralogy moving forward historically from the 1890s to the 1920s.

This period (which also coincides with Conrad's writing career) is often "re-called nostalgically" (as John Pemberton puts it) "through the haunting compound linguistic expression *tempo* (Dutch) *doeloe* (Malay), 'the old days,' 'former times'" (20). Three photographs from Rob Nieuwenhuys' photo anthology, *Tempo Doeloe*, associate this nostalgic sense with a specific kind of operatic performance. The first photo, of an "amateur krontjong band from Semarang, 1910," illustrates the cultural mix of instruments used to play the popular "krontjong" music that often accompanied a form of opera variously called "Komedi Bangsawan," "Komedi Stamboul," or "East Indies opera" (Figure 5.1). This hybrid opera form is evoked in the second photo of "a Stamboul women's orchestra," which illustrates the multiracial (and often mixed-gender) cast of traveling opera groups performing plots drawn from Arab, European, and Chinese stories (Figure 5.2).[3] The third photo (from 1912) shows a group of young Indo (Eurasian) men and women *pretending* to be an orchestra group—a spatula, tennis-racket, and rattan-stick masquerade here as musical instruments (Figure 5.3). It is difficult to read with what sort of humor of ironic cultural, racial, class, or gender identification the photographic record is framed. One thing that makes for the puzzle is the object around which the photo-image is composed—the hand-organ—which not only mimics whatever form of musical performance the group is imitating, but also mirrors the mechanical means of photographic reproduction that records the composition.

In what follows, I examine two particular passages from Conrad's and Pramoedya's novel sequences, both of which foreground problems of opera appreciation. I call this "abysmal taste" because both concern questionable aesthetic judgments and because both involve a narrative mirroring effect of *mise-en-abyme*.[4] In both cases, Verdi opera—rather than East Indies opera—presents a problem of aesthetic taste that reiterates, in miniature, the overall question of global and comparative cultural perspective raised by the novel sequences as a whole. Despite the significance of opera for each, the form of East Indies opera depicted in the photographs is mostly absent from the historical vision of each writer's novel sequence. Measuring each against the historical specificity of *tempo doeloe*, I follow a "contrapuntal reading" of the way Conrad and Pramoedya each grasps, respectively, the period designated by that phrase. This reading explores how Said's critical model, too, is implicated in the cultural dialectic of abysmal taste at work in each of the literary passages.

Our first passage, a memorable moment from almost exactly mid-way through Conrad's first novel, *Almayer's Folly* (1895), depicts the playing of a Verdi opera in the novel's East Indies setting:

Fig. 6.1 Amateur krontjong band from Semarang (1910).

Fig. 6.2 A Stamboul women's orchestra.

Lakamba listened with closed eyes and a delighted smile; Babalatchi turned, at times dozing off and swaying over, then catching himself up in a great fright with a few quick turns of the handle. Nature slept ... while under the unsteady hand of the statesman of Sambir the Trovatore fitfully wept, wailed, and bade good-bye to his Leonore again and again in a mournful round of tearful and endless iteration. (*AF* 89)

The hand-organ rendition of Manrico's farewell aria from Verdi's *Il Trovatore* locks into place a set of incongruous contrasts on which the irony of the passage depends—recapitulating, in turn, the ironic narrative perspective of the whole novel's grasp of the deluded European dreams of the Indies-born title character (whose death by poisoning has just been planned by Lakamba and Babalatchi). In some ways, this is merely a humorous digression from the main unfolding of plot—light relief from the climax to come in the next chapter, when the reader, along with Almayer, will momentarily be confronted with the death of Dain Maroola, a Balinese prince to whom Almayer is trading gunpowder, and (as Almayer has yet to learn and will refuse to acknowledge) the lover of his daughter, Nina. But the humor of the passage is not easy to decode. Deploying the stereotypes of lazy chief and wily schemer—Lakamba and Babalatchi, respectively—the passage replicates what Frantz Fanon called the "perverted logic" of colonialism: "not satisfied merely with ... emptying the native's brain of all form and content, ... it turns to the past of the oppressed people, and distorts, disfigures, and destroys it" (210). Conrad, however, ironically inverts the set of implied oppositions between native barbarism and European civilization with which the whole passage plays. In order to decode the racist "native" stereotypes, a reader must measure the incongruity of Lakamba's and Babalatchi's appreciation of opera against his or her own. And so the troubling racism is troubled in turn by the work of irony, in a sort of vicious circle of racist stereotyping and its critique. This problem of abysmal taste frames a set of assumptions of race, civilization, and modernity, whose very unsettling ensures a foundational instability in the inauguration of an implied Conradian readership, generating not only the ironies of his first novel, but organizing, too, the entire corpus of his work and the way it continues to be received critically today.

A contrasting question of opera emerges in *Footsteps* (*Jejak Langkah* [1985]), the third volume of Pramoedya's quartet of novels about the period of Indonesian anti-colonial nationalism over the turn of the century. In the midst of this increasingly historical narrative account of mass political organizing throughout the Dutch-controlled East Indies, Minke, the narrator of the first three books of the quartet (a figure based on the historical journalist and political activist Tirto Adi Suryo), pauses to account for "something that I will always remember," hearing a recording of Verdi's *Rigoletto*:

> Sandiman was just putting on a recording of Verdi's opera *Rigoletto*. I'd started the practice of setting aside three hours a week to listen to European music, copying what had been the practice of Mama and her children.
>
> Perhaps because this had been our practice in Surabaya, Verdi always took me back to old memories, to Mama and her business, to Annelies and to all the happiness that had ended with tragedy.
>
> It was true that I didn't yet appreciate European music as fully as I did gamelan. European music stimulated in me many different thoughts. Gamelan music instead enveloped me in beauty, in a harmony of feeling that was without form, in an atmosphere that rocked my emotions to an eternal sleep. (*Footsteps* 200–201)

As with Conrad's *Almayer's Folly*, Verdi presents a problem of opera appreciation, although here it is internalized in the narrator's judgment of his own non-European appreciation of European opera. Complicating this problem, and making it all the more abysmal in the formal narrative sense in which the Conrad passage implicates its readership, is the further comparison between European and Javanese gamelan music.

Both passages serve as miniature narrative cues for the larger unfolding of the plots within which they appear. Minke's split musical sensibility recalls the conflict of racial and cultural identification between his native Javanese and educated European identity, recapitulating one of the main thematic

Fig. 6.3 A group of young Indo (Eurasian) men and women "pretending" to be an orchestra group (1912).

elements of his sentimental education in the first two novels, *This Earth of Mankind* and *Child of All Nations*. Verdi serves as a metonym for those lost attachments of youth, recalling the tragic loss of his first wife, the "creole beauty" Annelies and—as if invoked by the very playing of European opera—bringing back into the narrative that mixed racial cast of characters from the first novel that constitutes what might be called Minke's "creole" family romance.[5] Verdi opera thus signals a riddle of European cultural capital embedded in the narrative form of the tetralogy. Where one expects a critique of colonial nostalgia, as the narrative approaches the historic founding of the proto-nationalist organization Boedi Oetomo in 1908,[6] the narrative seems to evoke the colonial nostalgia of *tempo doeloe* as the reader's own nostalgic attachment to Minke's narrative voice. This attachment is strengthened all the more with the abrupt dislocation of narrative voice that occurs in the transition from the third to the fourth volume, *House of Glass*, when Minke's narrative voice is replaced by that of the native Menadonese police commissioner charged with containing and ultimately eliminating him as a political threat to the colonial regime. Minke's abysmal taste in opera, a *mise-en-abyme* of narrative form, marks the disjuncture between narrative and history on which the entire tetralogy is premised. Ostensibly tracing the "awakening" of Indonesian nationalism over the turn of the century, the narrative inquest into the erasure of Tirto Adi Suryo from the historical record provides a genealogy of official amnesia about twentieth-century Indonesia, retracing the lineaments of the post-colonial state around the policing apparatus of colonial governance and its systematic subversion of early anti-colonial nationalist organizations.

Verdi opera provides a corresponding *mise-en-abyme* of narrative form for Conrad's Malay or Lingard trilogy. Set in the remote Borneo region of Conrad's fictional Sambir—that "model state" (*AF* 34) whose independence from European interests Lakamba and Babalatchi seek to maintain through nominal dependence on Dutch colonial rule—*Almayer's Folly* plots the premise for the trilogy on a retrospective grasp of the contemporary politics of archipelago-wide anti-colonial nationalism.[7] The full significance of this for the historical scope of the trilogy remains contingent on the ironic force of racial stereotyping. Already split between the appreciative repose of Lakamba and the less-than-appreciative position of Babalatchi, the "native" stereotype is itself complicated by what Cedric Watts identifies as the "covert plot" of *Almayer's Folly*—the betrayal of Dain Maroola to the Dutch authorities by Lingard's rival, the Arab trader Abdulla. Although Watts argues that the novel's "ironic complex of racial, national and sexual revenge" (*Deceptive Text* 51) transcends racial stereotypes, Babalatchi's role as arch-schemer suggests, on the contrary, that racial stereotype is the very motor force of Conrad's "covert plotting." As the most distorted of racialized figures, Babalatchi's voyeuristic manipulation of the Nina-Dain love affair taints romance with the insinuation of perversity in interracial desire. *An Outcast of the Islands* adds to his one-eyed disfigurement the completely blind Omar el-Badavi who, with his daughter Aissa and Babalatchi, constitute a sinister counter-family to the other mixed racial families of the first two novels: Willems's respectably creolized family in Macassar (undermined by the Aissa-Willems affair, again manipulated by Babalatchi); and the somewhat less respectably mixed racial Almayer family at Sambir. By contrast to Minke's nostalgic association of Verdi with a creole family romance, any such association here must be viewed—as Verdi is heard—through the distorted perspective of Babalatchi. To the extent that the romance plot of *Il Trovatore* mirrors the romance plot of the Nina-Dain affair, it only serves to reinforce the distortion of racial stereotype at the heart of each story of "racial, national and sexual revenge." Far from providing some final interpretive key, the allusion produces a permanent ellipsis of relation between narration and plot, forever deferring comparison of the story of *Il Trovatore* to the plot of *Almayer's Folly* and to the novel sequence it inaugurates.

Both passages confirm the argument Said develops in his own reading of another Verdi opera, *Aida*. As "an imperial spectacle designed to alienate and impress an almost exclusively European audience" (Culture 130), *Aida* exemplifies the riddle of European cultural capital Conrad and Pramoedya each take as the point of reference for their non-European characters' appreciation of European opera. In all three cases, dependence on European cultural capital stands in varying degrees of ironic contrast to aspirations of independence from European political power. In contrast to Said's extended reading of *Aida*, however, neither Conrad nor Pramoedya offers a "full contrapuntal appreciation" of the operas—*Il Trovatore* and *Rigoletto*, respectively—to which they allude. In each case, the problem of operatic appreciation is refracted through the medium of mechanical reproduction—the hand-organ rendition in *Almayer's Folly*, and the phonograph recording in *Footsteps*.

As if to confirm Walter Benjamin's famous thesis— "that which withers in the age of mechanical reproduction is the aura of the work of art" (*Illuminations* 221)—each citation invokes an operatic aesthetic in the very moment of its distortion through the agency of mechanical mass reproduction. Far from realizing their "revolutionary potential," however, in each case the instrument of mechanical reproduction becomes a fetishized luxury item, emphasizing the negative moment in Benjamin's cultural dialectic and anticipating Adorno's more pessimistic application of Benjamin's argument to the regressive "fetish-character" of music appreciation. It is indeed a fetishized pleasure Lakamba takes in having Babalatchi bring out the "box of music the white captain gave me" (*AF* 88). This comic fetish of European modernity emblematizes the ironic situation of Lingard's betrayal by Lakamba—the "covert plot" more fully explored in *An Outcast of the Islands*. The fact that it was once Lingard's hand organ makes it an emblem, too, of what in *The Rescue* will be revealed as Lingard's own sentimental attachment to opera. The phonograph plays an analogous function in Pramoedya's tetralogy. An early instance of Minke's fascination for all things modern, the phonograph is singled out, on his first visit to the Mellema house in *This Earth of Mankind*, as a luxury item of furniture whose beauty is associated with the stunning "creole beauty" of Annelies. This combination of erotic, racial, and commodity fetishism will again be attached to the image of the phonograph when, in the final volume, Pangemenann describes the scene of his early seduction into the political work of subversive police activities against Minke: by means of the prostitute Rientje de Roo and to the accompaniment of Verdi's *La Traviata* played on an expensive new phonograph.

Both opera citations illustrate the fetishism Adorno decried in the practice of making musical arrangements that "snatch the reified bits and pieces out of their context and set them up as a potpourri ... destroy[ing] the multilevel unity of the whole work and bring[ing] forward only isolated popular passages" (298–299). Conrad's choice of "what used to be the best-known of all *Trovatore* melodies in the days of the barrel organ and the street piano" (Budden 100) compounds racial stereotyping with the insinuation of a class distinction between the bad taste pedaled by street musicians and the fuller appreciation of opera goers who knows their place within the context of the work as a whole. Although it is Verdi's *Rigoletto* that is cited in Pramoedya's novel, what Minke recalls hearing a few lines later is, through some phonographic distortion of memory, "The Last Rose of Summer," a popular aria from Flotow's *Martha*. Opera's very diminishment enacted by the work of mechanical reproduction calls attention to the literary text's paradoxical and exemplary estrangement at the very heart of the operatic aesthetic. The barrel-organ theme from *Il Trovatore* may once have evoked the text of the song, but now the *trovatore's* "mournful round of tearful and endless iteration" repeats itself wordlessly. And although Minke remembers the title of an aria, the song itself, based on an Irish folk melody adapted by Thomas Moore, confirms the estrangement opera typically effects in literary form.

Hegel's *Aesthetics* grasps this estrangement of the literary in the formal question of priority in the relation between music and text. By contrast to either "operetta" or "vaudeville," in "real opera" the music transcends the words (951). This operatic moment of musical transcendence and subordination of words leaves its mark both on the Hegelian dialectic and the grand narrative assumptions of nineteenth-century Europe.[8] Grasping opera as the epitome of just such European grand narrative claims, Conrad and Pramoedya use their operatic examples to foreground a crisis of literary consciousness, one that ruptures the very form of developmental narrative with which their projected novel sequences engage.

The crisis of European literary consciousness foregrounded in Conrad's Verdi passage is premised, like much in Conrad, on the example of Flaubert.[9] It recalls two scenes from *Madame Bovary*—Emma Bovary's enraptured identification with the soprano (in contrast to her husband's incomprehension) at a performance of Donizetti's *Lucia di Lammermoor*; and an earlier description of Emma's enchantment with the tunes of an organ grinder in the street.[10] Conrad alludes to both scenes in the playing of Verdi on a barrel organ in Borneo, pushing the "bovarysme" of his own novel to an extreme and widening the gap Flaubert explores between romantic illusion and the banalities of middle-class consumer culture. Conrad's corresponding dissection of European literary sensibilities, however, stakes its claim to recognition by an *English*-reading public on a projected long-term narrative investment in *Malay* culture. The linguistic register may be more fundamental than the cultural, historical, or ethnological resonance of these two designations for assessing Conrad's place in the formation of English literary modernism. As Michael North has discussed, one thing that makes Conrad so paradigmatic for modernist experimentations with linguistic and racial difference is the fact that his English was rooted in the *lingua franca* of shipboard English (49–50). The affinities between Malay and English each as a *lingua franca* are foregrounded in significant moments, such as the very opening of the novel—"Kaspar! Makan!"— and in Conrad's proposed pseudonym, "Kamudi" (the Malay word for rudder). As the spoken language of the characters, and as the linguistic disguise of pseudonymous authorship, Malay provides something of a foil for what Conrad was attempting to achieve using English as his literary medium: to reorient European literary traditions' coordinates through the translingual, transnational, literary *lingua franca* of English. If *Almayer's Folly* implies a cosmopolitan readership (familiar both with Verdi opera and barrel-organ renditions), it also places that cosmopolitan perspective within a wider global context. The center of literary consciousness is located neither in an English nor in a Malay literary tradition, but rather in the gap between the two marked by the problem of an abysmal taste in opera.

This point is foregrounded in the last novel of the sequence, *The Rescue*. Edith Travers, one of the shipwrecked Europeans Lingard will rescue at the cost of the plans—and lives—of his Malay friends, compares her involvement in the political intrigues of Lingard's Wajo romance to the "unreal" and "artificial" feeling of "walking on a splendid stage in a scene from an opera, in a gorgeous show fit to make an audience hold its breath" (*Re* 300). Not only does Lingard share a knowledge of opera. It is the illiterate sailor who has a passion for opera, finding it "more real than anything in life," while the refined Edith Travers "never knew anything" of that kind of "feeling." "Would real people go singing through their life anywhere except in a fairy tale?" (*Re* 300-01). Whereas *Almayer's Folly* measures the ironic limits of cross-cultural perspective against the musical taste of two Malay characters, in *The Rescue* this perspectival limit is measured against the operatic taste of two English characters. At both ends of the trilogy, an abysmal taste in opera marks the limitation of an English investment in Malay culture.

In the middle novel, *An Outcast of the Islands*, the vanishing point of comparative English-Malay cultural-historical perspectives is grasped through the distorted viewpoint of Babalatchi's "frivolous desire to sing"—prompted, significantly, by the voyeuristic sight of the lovers Aissa and Willems:

> It could hardly be called a song; it was more in the nature of a recitative without any rhythm, delivered rapidly but distinctly in a croaking and unsteady voice; and if Babalatchi considered it a song, then it was a song with a purpose and, perhaps for that reason, artistically defective. It had all the imperfections of unskillful improvisation and its subject was gruesome. (*OI* 138)

Like the contrast between European music and gamelan in Pramoedya's novel, Babalatchi's song appears to introduce an alternative cultural category of artistic performance to that of European opera—perhaps some form of Malay *pantun*. The narrative, however, immediately denigrates that form, suggesting even more strongly what Fanon calls the colonial work of "devaluing precolonial history." Despite the "inartistic" privileging of words over music, the words themselves—along with any sense of a Malay literary context—remain closed to the text. Its "subject" is, however, briefly described: "It told a tale of shipwreck and of thirst, and of one brother killing another for the sake of a gourd of water. A repulsive story which might have had a purpose but possessed no moral whatever" (*OI* 138). An ornamental coda to the rumors of how Babalatchi arrived in Sambir, Babalatchi's song proves to be a grotesque miniature inversion of the plot of *The Rescue*—another story of shipwreck and brotherly betrayal, whose motif repeatedly punctuates the narrative of the second novel.

Babalatchi's song suggests a further twist to what Cedric Watts describes as the "covert plotting" that resiliently defies successive interpretations. Anticipating the link between Babalatchi and Lingard's failed rescue plot, made explicit halfway through *An Outcast of the Islands*, the cryptic doubling of shipwreck plots signals an untold story: indeed, Conrad never will tell of their prior meeting, although Babalatchi's reminder precipitates Lingard's disturbed memories of "the past sweetness and strife of Carimata days" (*OI* 223). This untold story emphasizes all the more the shared masculine romance of a piratical past that defines both Babalatchi's and Lingard's sense of the "good old days" (*OI* 196).[11] This overlapping and contested Malay-English grasp of piracy is historically grounded in Conrad's use of Brooke's journals that record his celebrated campaign against piracy along the coast of northwest Borneo. As Robert Hampson has pointed out, the trilogy enacts a reversal of that archival perspective, retelling Brooke's destruction of pirate villages from the Malay point of view. Babalatchi's exploits with Omar el-Badavi following the Brooke campaign register both heroic and distinctly unheroic possibilities.[12] According to Hampson, for example, the Virgilian allusion to "that piratical and son-less Aeneas" (*OI* 54) "vacillates between ironic discrepancy and genuine equivalence" (Hampson, *Cross-Cultural* 109).[13] What enables this fundamental ambiguity of perspective, moreover, is a drastic foreshortening of epic scale. This is precisely the effect produced by the *mise-en-abyme* of Conrad's operatic aesthetic. As with the disfigured form of Babalatchi's song, or the operatic allusion to *Il Trovatore*, the scope of romance or epic is truncated, reducing grand narrative to fragments, turning the literary passage into what Lyotard calls the "differend."

This can be seen in the distorting effects of racial stereotype, most particularly in Babalatchi. In *Almayer's Folly* his background is specified as Sulu in origin, and in *An Outcast of the Islands* he is associated with the Islamic militancy of Omar. Even as Conrad manipulates these distinctly negative racial stereotypes, however, the narrative insists on a historical specificity that refuses fixation on any one racist stereotype. The description of his role in *Almayer's Folly* as "prime minister, harbour master, financial advisor, and general factotum" (*AF* 38)—confirmed in *An Outcast* through Almayer's disparaging comments on his status as "shahbandar" (*OI* 364)—situates Babalatchi's role as a quite specific functionary. This simultaneous indexing and disfigurement of historical fact is encoded in his name. Although suggestively orientalist, evoking Ali Baba of *The Arabian Nights*, the name is based in historical fact—a bill of lading found in Conrad's possession shows goods shipped by "Babalatchie" on the west coast of Sulawesi.[14] It conveys, moreover, a distinctly Chinese resonance—"Baba" (the specific form of address for an elderly Chinese man) and "La-Tchi" suggest an ethnic Chinese, rather than (or perhaps in addition to) his purported Sulu origin.[15] Whether Conrad was aware of the possibility or not, the name marks a highly volatile repertoire of unresolvable racial identifications and antagonisms (Malay and Sulu, possibly also Bugis; Moslem and Chinese). This chain of racial stereotypes ensures a fundamental ambiguity of historical perspective whichever way one attempts to read the trilogy's plot—whether chronologically, toward the Indies-wide rebellion imagined in *Almayer's Folly*, or sequentially as a retrospective account of Lingard's role in the failed restoration of a Wajo Bugis kingdom in southern Celebes. In this sense the perversity of Babalatchi's racial stereotype—as "the statesman of Sambir" condemned to crank out the music of Verdi, and maligned for his "artistically defective" singing—epitomizes the fragmentary narrative logic at work in the trilogy's operatic aesthetic.

Pramoedya's own reading of Conrad emphasizes the significance of this distorting aesthetic.[16] "In Conrad's works," he once said, "there are historical facts which have not been recorded elsewhere" (GoGwilt, "Pramoedya's Fiction" 156). Far from suggesting that the text is simply the repository of historical facts, this positions the literary work in counterpoint to the archival record. With his use of the Brooke journals, Conrad's fiction engages in a critical reading of the cultural archive, in Said's terms, "not univocally but *contrapuntally*." With the name Babalatchi, Conrad's fiction also registers what is "not recorded" elsewhere. The operatic qualities of Conrad's Malay fiction are not merely exoticist distortions of history. In the very deformation of their effects, they constitute questions of political and cultural identity and identification that haunt the historical record.

The corresponding function of operatic taste in Pramoedya's tetralogy reveals the shared problem of global and comparative perspective in each of these novel sequences, as well as in the musical metaphor of Said's model of "contrapuntal" comparative analysis. In all three, music foregrounds a crisis of literary form. The phonographic replaying and distortion of European operatic tradition in Pramoedya's tetralogy presents a crisis not only of European, but also of Javanese literary consciousness. As a Dutch-educated Javanese noble ("priyayi"), whose narrative is based on notes written in Dutch according to his European training, rearranged and rewritten according to later experience, Minke constitutes a self-evidently hybrid, split literary consciousness.[17] This "double consciousness" is reflected in a doubly abysmal problem of taste. As a man of European taste, his appreciation of opera reenacts the pathologies of opera appreciation and the distortions of literary tradition that constitute the European operatic aesthetic.[18] More significantly, as a man of Javanese taste, loss of appreciation for Javanese opera threatens the very essence of the Javanese "priyayi" world view. Gamelan music and the wayang shadow puppet performances it traditionally accompanies are defining features of cultural refinement for the Javanese "priyayi," inseparable from the Javanese notion of taste, or "rasa" in its full, traditional, and ineffable spiritual sense.[19] By the end of *Footsteps*, however, Minke has come to reject that world in his critique of the forms of superstitious thinking he calls "Javanism" (373). Although European and Javanese operatic forms seem to present opposing registers of aesthetic taste, Minke's problem of opera appreciation in fact signals a fundamental collusion of both forms.

"Javanism" is the term used to articulate this abysmal doubling and splitting of Minke's aesthetic sensibility in *Footsteps*, and it reflects Pramoedya's own use of modern Indonesian against the complex hierarchies of Javanese.[20] Recalling Edward Said's celebrated critique of "Orientalism," "Javanism" names the European colonial sponsorship of ossified Javanese traditions and "superstitious thinking"—"those beliefs that had become so embedded in people's consciousness over centuries of colonization" (*Footsteps* 374). Minke's reflections on his own abysmal sense of musical taste coincides, indeed, with a crisis of political consciousness signaled by the word "priyayi" in the name of the first native political organization, *Sarekat Priyayi*. In the preceding chapter, Sandiman—the man operating Minke's phonograph in our opera passage—has questioned the use of that exclusive designation "priyayi" for an organization that purports to be Indies-wide, embracing those of all classes and reaching beyond Java, too. Since the critique of "Javanism" and Minke's "priyayi" taste is implied in the very language Pramoedya uses, however, this passage foregrounds a problem of abysmal taste that has informed the tetralogy from the very start—attending each comment on gamelan and wayang, reduplicating a simultaneously European and Javanese sensibility in the same passage, whether transmitted through the voice of a European, a native Javanese, an Indo, or some other voice.

The specifically musical effects of gamelan, moreover, call attention to a philological problem of literary form at the heart of both European and Javanese operatic forms. In the prison memoirs, in a passage that echoes Minke's reflections in *Footsteps*, Pramoedya reflects on the mesmeric effect of the gamelan accompaniment to wayang performance:

> All is accompanied by gamelan music and women's voices, those wayang recitations that connect all at once wisdom, prayer, and worship, drugging and putting the mind to sleep, and absorbing the people in an illusory world of stasis. Alone. Empty. *Non-existing.*
>
> And that gamelan—what polyphony! [kepolifonikannya!] reaching such heights as have also been reached by Western music. (*Nyanyi Sunyi Seorang Bisu*, I, 35; italics added to show English in original)

Pramoedya here refers to the special songs called *suluk* in the interconnected accompaniment of *gamelan* to *wayang*. As Geertz explains, "As the *suluk* are derived from ancient Javanese versions of Hindu poems, and so are in great part incomprehensible both to the *wajang* audience and to the *dalang* himself, the emphasis tends not to be on their intrinsic meaning but, as in the music generally, on the mood they suggest" (280). This "mood" or "feeling" is what Minke describes, in comparison to the mood evoked by Verdi, as "a harmony of feeling that was without form" ("ketenangan perasaan yang menyangkal wujud").[21] Revealing his own abysmal taste for gamelan and wayang, Pramoedya associates gamelan with the most sublime, most refined annihilation of Javanese literariness.

This exegetical abyss—the rendering meaningless, or "nonexisting," the sacred text of song—defines, both for European and for Javanese opera, the aesthetic power of polyphonic counterpoint. In Javanese opera it is not only the *suluk* songs that are accompanied by the polyphonic "stratification" of gamelan; the "recitations" to which Pramoedya refers constitute only one of the many kinds of voices or themes developed to the accompaniment of gamelan, since, as A.L. Becker points out, "A wayang includes within it, in each performance, the entire history of the literary language."[22] One of the best examples of a comparable effect in European opera is the familiar barrel-organ tune from *Il Trovatore*. The troubadour's song, set in counterpoint to the lamentations of Leonora's voice, has, as its contrapuntal backdrop, the "Miserere" of the chorus, a homophonic imitation of the polyphonic performance of the sacred text of Psalm 51. Opera here too recapitulates an entire history of literary language. Stereotypically, as a repetitively sung fragment of text that acquires familiarity in translation across languages and artistic media, the operatic aria performs a paradoxical and exemplary estrangement of literature: the simultaneous *passing away* of literary form, and its reconstitution in the isolated *passage* of text held up for exegetical analysis. The philological problem staged in both Conrad's hand-organ and Pramoedya's gramophone renditions of Verdi concerns not only the negation of an original literary text or prior literary tradition (European or Javanese), but also the loss of origin for literary tradition.

In applying a "contrapuntal analysis" to the novel sequences of Conrad and Pramoedya, the contrast that emerges between European and Javanese polyphonic musical systems productively complicates Said's musical metaphor. Applied to the historical period of colonialism—roughly 1600 to 1900—during which European counterpoint and the polyphony of Javanese gamelan music formed discrete and discrepant tonal systems, Said's use of the specifically "Western classical" musical term "counterpoint" at first suggests a markedly Eurocentric philological model.[23] When Said associates the art of musical counterpoint with the exegetical and interpretive practice of philology—as he repeatedly does—he usually invokes the heroic figure of Eric Auerbach. As Emily Apter has argued, however, Leo Spitzer may be a more revealing precursor for contemporary literary theory. Spitzer's projected *opus magnum, Classical and Christian Ideas of World Harmony*, traces the German philological tradition in which Auerbach and Spitzer were both trained back to those "ideas of world harmony" that bring medieval counterpoint, literature, and Biblical hermeneutics together into a single historical evolution. Spitzer notes that the Latin terms "contropare, adtropare" from the Greek term ("tropologein") used "to explain or compare biblical passages by harmonizing them" "led to *contropare*, 'to compare, corroborate legal documents'" (173). Said's "contrapuntal analysis" may indeed echo the sense of this Spitzerian insight. But for Said—as arguably for Spitzer, too—this philological sense of "contropare" provides a model for a post-philological discordant analysis of textual passages. Toward the end of *Culture and Imperialism*, a sort of covert plot emerges in Said's argument when he writes: "But this global, contrapuntal analysis should be modeled not (as earlier notions of comparative literature were) on a symphony but rather on an atonal ensemble" (318). The shift from a model of "tonal" to "atonal" music recalls Adorno's argument, developed in his *Philosophy of Modern Music* and used for the plot of Thomas Mann's *Doctor Faustus*, about the collapse of tonal music at the turn of the twentieth century. Within this argument, the autonomous work of art's aura is threatened, and with it the continuity of a presumed whole organic historical tradition. The contrast between European and Javanese systems of musical counterpoint foregrounds this philological problem of textual exegesis informing the model of Said's "contrapuntal analysis." For Conrad and Pramoedya, opera stages the lost origins of European and Javanese literary traditions. For all three, Said included, the philological problem of abysmal operatic taste precipitates new models of global comparative and historical analysis.

This question of philology brings us back to the significance of the kind of East Indies opera depicted in the photo images from Nieuwenhuys's *Tempo Doeloe*. These images provide something of an answer to the philological question of global comparative analysis at the heart of both examples from Conrad and Pramoedya. As Pramoedya himself discusses, in his own anthology *Tempo Doeloe* (an anthology of stories, not photographs), East Indies opera provides a crucial linguistic and literary record of what he calls "pre-Indonesian literature." Like the tales Pramoedya anthologizes, East Indies opera records not some nostalgic evocation of a lost colonial world, but the "structure of feeling of the time" (1). Written and performed by European, Indo, or Chinese writers, the stories and theatrical performances record the shared linguistic medium of that matrix of Indies-wide social, political, and cultural exchanges that shaped the climate of anti-colonial nationalism. One of the tales Pramoedya anthologizes, *Nyai Dasima* (a key text for the Buru tetralogy), was also part of the stock repertoire for *Komedi Bangsawan*. More significant, however, is the fact that most of the repertoire of East Indies opera vanished with the eclipse of this form of popular opera in the 1920s. Whatever the reasons for this disappearance, the phenomenon of East Indies opera remains the record of a *lost* moment of cultural cross-fertilization between different literary traditions. Even more graphically than Conrad's and Pramoedya's examples, then, these photos show how an abysmal taste in opera constitutes the literary as a fundamental vanishing point of cultural perspective.

This cultural logic emerges politically and historically in the puzzle of each of the figures operating the mechanical object of operatic reproduction (whether hand-organ or phonograph). Babalatchi's racial stereotype embeds a central historical and perspectival deformation in Conrad's Malay or Lingard trilogy. Sandiman, who operates the phonograph for Minke, remains a shadowy figure in Pramoedya's Buru tetralogy: A fictional character among increasingly historical names, his presence in *House of Glass* is invoked by Pangemenann as a "dalang" figure: "I think it is Sandiman who is Marko's *dalang*. He lives in the shadows" (*House of Glass* 175). Such figures necessarily complicate the historical record of what Nieuwenhuys's photographs evoke as *tempo doeloe*. The hand-organ and its technological cousin the phonograph bind together each of these examples into a single dialectical image of the relation between opera and the passage of literature. In all three of our examples, regardless of the different forms and traditions of opera on display (East Indies opera, European grand opera, or Javanese *wayang*), the hand-organ and phonograph provide points of ironic and distorting perspective from which to grasp opera in general as a fundamental cultural—and political—problem of taste. Simultaneously signaling the formation and the deformation of culture, opera performs a *mise-en-abyme* of modern cultural capital.

In the third photograph from Nieuwenhuys' *Tempo Doeloe*, East Indies opera is illustrated without actually being depicted (Figure 5.3)– there are just so many people and objects mimicking the form of an orchestral opera troupe. So, too, in a sense, with Pramoedya's and Conrad's novel sequences. If they do not *represent* East Indies opera, their novels themselves have a great deal in common with this hybrid cultural and artistic form. Both draw on its characteristic multi-ethnic masquerade and melodramatic grasp of exotic stories. Both draw on the same *linguistic* medium: For Pramoedya, the *lingua franca* Melayu is the precursor for modern *bahasa Indonesia*; for Conrad's Malay fiction, it is the common language of the characters, and the mirror-image, as it were, of what he himself does with the translingual, transcultural medium of English. Both also grasp opera as the performance of literary tradition's fundamental estrangement: the loss of origin, and the loss of temporality, for literature. This abysmal operatic taste in the work of Conrad and Pramoedya thus confirms the way literature, radically unmoored from tradition, continues to mediate for us the very idea of cultural tradition.

Acknowledgments

This essay began to take its current shape as a talk delivered at the "Conrad and Territoriality Conference" in Vancouver, BC, in August 2002, but it has its origins further back: in a discussion of the Verdi passage with participants of the international Conrad conference in Gdansk in October 1997; and in discussions in Jakarta in January 1995 with G.J. Resink. For their comments on various drafts, I'd like to thank Madeleine Brainerd, Fraser Easton, Peter Mallios, and Andrea White.

Notes

1. Reporting to his aunt Marguerite Poradowska in May 1894 about his completion of the last chapter of *Almayer's Folly*, Conrad writes: "Il commence avec un *trio* Nina. Dain. Almayer. Et il finit dans un long *solo* pour Almayer qui est presque aussi long que le Tristan-solo de Wagner" (*Letters* 1: 155–156). Reporting to Edward Garnett in September 1895 about his completion of *An Outcast of the Islands*, Conrad writes: "It is my painful duty to inform you of the sad death of Mr Peter Willems late of Rotterdam and Macassar who has been murdered on the 16th inst at 4 p.m. while the sun shone joyously and the barrel organ sang on the pavement the abominable Intermezzo of the ghastly Cavalleria" (*Letters* 1: 245).
2. For a most useful discussion of such models, see Apter, "Global *Translatio*."
3. In this photo we see the star singer, Marietje Oord (the figure standing in the middle background); and, although this is a "woman's orchestra," Nieuwenhuys notes that the figure seated in the middle foreground is a transvestite star called Theo Mac Lennan. On East Indies opera, see Manusama, Tan Sooi Beng, and Pramoedya's *Tempo Doeloe*. See also Mrazek 147.
4. Dupriez traces the naming of this literary device back to André Gide's use of the heraldic term "abyme" to explain the narrative effect of "disappearing repetition" (285). Jacques Derrida makes extensive use of the term (and the device), posing the question of Mallarmé, for example, "isn't it precisely such writing *en abyme* that thematic criticism—and no doubt criticism as such—can never, to the letter, account for?" (265).
5. The phonograph music almost literally calls forth the characters from the first book. (See *Footsteps* 201.)
6. On "what is now celebrated annually in Indonesia as the Day of National Awakening" (Anderson *Language and Power* 243).
7. Just before the opera passage, the contemporary moment of *Almayer's Folly* is described as occurring "at the time when the hostilities between Dutch and Malays threatened to spread from Sumatra over the whole archipelago" (*AF* 81). In 1995, Pramoedya described the plot of *Almayer's Folly* as "the story about a Balinese prince who is smuggling guns to organize resistance against Dutch colonial rule" (GoGwilt "Pramoedya's Fiction" 156).
8. In the *Phenomenology of Spirit*, that touchstone for the grand narrative tradition, the figure of the "Minstrel" appears in the penultimate chapter before "Absolute Knowing" as "the organ that vanishes in its content" to sing the "universal song" or Epic of the dialectic of individual, national, and universal unfolding of self-consciousness into absolute knowledge (Hegel, *Phenomenology* 441).

9. After Conrad himself, Ford Madox Ford was the first to emphasize Conrad's debt to Flaubert. For more recent assessments, see Watt, *Conrad in the Nineteenth*, and Hervouet.

10. In the opening to *A Personal Record*, Conrad associates the first of these scenes with the scene of his own writing of *Almayer's Folly* "in the neighbourhood of the [Rouen] Opera House" in view of "the very" *café* "where the worthy Bovary and his wife … had some refreshment after the memorable performance of an opera which was the tragic story of Lucia di Lammermoor in a setting of light music" (*PR* 5). The famous scene of abysmal operatic taste in *Madame Bovary* is itself informed by the earlier description of a vulgar street organ grinder playing "tunes that were heard elsewhere—tunes played in the theatre, sung in drawing-rooms, danced to at night beneath lighted chandeliers—echoes reaching Emma from the great world outside" (Flaubert 78). Splicing together these two moments to grasp the double displacement of a European romance tradition—operatic adaptation of literary works; barrel-organ arrangements of operatic aria—Conrad displaces, in turn, that literary consciousness (Emma Bovary's) Flaubert dissects as the novel's pathological point of literary identification.

11. Compare Hampson 100.

12. The heroism of their exploits is both deflated and inflated in a single sentence: "On the cool mats in breezy verandahs of Rajahs' houses it is alluded to disdainfully by impassive statesmen, but amongst armed men that throng the courtyards it is a tale which stills the murmur of voices and the tinkle of anklets; arrests the passage of the siri vessel, and fixes the eyes in absorbed gaze" (*OI* 54–55).

13. Hampson and Stape disagree over whether this allusion refers to Babalatchi or Omar (see Hampson *Cross-Cultural Encounters* 215). The truncated form of the allusion surely contributes to this interesting dispute—as does, more significantly, the perverse negation of epic narrative genealogy encoded in the implication of a "son-less Aeneas."

14. See van Marle's note on Babalatchi (Stape and van Marle 375).

15. This suggestion was first made to me by the poet, legal historian, and Conrad critic G.J. Resink in Jakarta in 1995, in a discussion in which he spoke of a last essay he knew he would never write on the topic of Conrad and music.

16. One Conrad passage to which Pramoedya twice returns is from "Karain: A Memory," when Karain, on arriving in Java, finds "every man … a slave." Introducing the nonfictional work of Tirto Adi Suryo (on whom Minke is based), the citation serves to illustrate the historical moment of extreme Dutch colonial subjection. Although Pramoedya does not here explain that this is the perspective of a Bugis Malay character—a non-Javanese judgment on the state of Javanese society at the height of Dutch colonial rule—it is precisely this non-Javanese outsider perspective that defines the second allusion, from the Buru prison notes. Recording his response to a journalist's question about the Indonesian "psyche," Pramoedya writes: "We should not be offended by what that Polish-born sailor-turned-writer wrote about the Javanese people: that everyone, from beggars to kings, is a slave" (*Nyanyi* 1: 183).

17. His very name marks a problem of fictional Europeanized consciousness: as revealed in the first novel, the name comes from the half-articulated Dutch pronunciation of the English word "monkey," a racist epithet directed at him by his Dutch high school teacher, immediately adopted by his grandfather on the assumption that it signaled a sign of respect, although Minke's own suspicions are confirmed in English classes. Thereafter, the name signals a paradigmatic "double consciousness," to borrow W.E.B. Du Bois' celebrated formulation for the internalized experience of racial stereotype.

18. According to Giorgio Agamben's examination of aesthetic taste, Minke fits the profile of that figure—the man of taste—who appears in Hegel's *Phenomenology of Spirit* as the very measure of "pure culture": the "absolute and universal perversion and alienation of the actual world and of thought … *pure culture*" (qtd. in Agamben 25).

19. Clifford Geertz has explained the significance of gamelan as an essential component of the "prijaji"—aristocratic Javanese—world view. Shaped by all three of the "major foci" of "prijaji" belief—"etiquette, art, and mystical practice"—gamelan music is inseparable from that "common element in them all which ties them together and makes them but different modes of the same reality": "what the Javanese, borrowing a concept from India, call *rasa*" (238). Although, as Nancy Florida has pointed out, "there is no translating the polysemic *rasa*" (176), Geertz explains that it "has two primary meanings: 'feeling' and 'meaning,'" covering—with the first—all of the traditional five senses and their figurative application

beyond sense-perception; and—with the second—"As 'meaning,' *rasa* is applied to the words in a letter, in a poem, or even in speech, to indicate the ... type of allusive suggestion that is so important in Javanese communication" (238).

20. As Benedict Anderson points out, *bahasa Indonesia* "is a cultural fortress from which to cross swords with his heritage" (*Language and Power* 219).

21. The English translation imposes a European musical sensibility—"harmony"—not suggested by the Indonesian words (literally: "a calm feeling that defies form"—and we might note in "perasaan," the presence of that all-important Javanese word "rasa"). "Harmony," indeed, seems in some respects precisely the wrong term to capture the particularly complex structure of *gamelan* music. According to Mantle Hood—"Unlike the primary tradition of the Western orchestra, founded on a large harmonic complex which moves in vertical structures, the gamelan moves in as many as twenty-five different horizontal strata" (452).

22. That history stretches "from Old Javanese, pre-Hindu incantation and mythology to the era of the Sanskrit gods and their language, blending with Javanese in the works of ancient poets (the suluks), adding Arabic and Colonial elements, changing with the power of Java to new locations and dialects, up to the present Bahasa Indonesia and even a bit of American English (in which one clown often instructs another)" (Becker 232).

23. "Counterpoint," for Said, is specifically "Western": "In the counterpoint of Western classical music, various themes play off one another, with only a provisional privilege being given to any particular one; yet in the resulting polyphony there is concert and order, an organized interplay that derives from the themes, not from a rigorous melodic or formal principle outside the work" (*Culture and Imperialism* 51).

7

Conrad's Heterotopic Fiction: Composite Maps, Superimposed Sites, and Impossible Spaces

ROBERT HAMPSON

At the end of "A Passion for Maps," I called attention to a series of maps included in one of the "dull, wise books" Conrad drew on for his Malay fiction, Henry Keppel's *The Expedition to Borneo of HMS Dido for the Suppression of Piracy* (1846) (*Letters* 2: 129–130). These maps included a plan of the River Sarebus, marked with soundings of the channel and notes about the nature of the banks: "Mangrove;" "Thick Jungle;" "Cleared Land." The map's legend shows the usefulness (and use) of this knowledge: "taken on Board the Boats of the H.M.S. Dido when employed destroying the nests of the pirates at Rembos, Pakoo & Paddi. June 1843." The next map is a plan of the Batang Lupar River. It gives channel soundings, and again the legend is revealing: "laid off from Compass bearings etc. taken on board the Boats of H.M.S. Dido when in pursuit of the Piratical Chief Seriff Sahib, August 1844." After this comes a plan of the "Forts & Villages of Patusan," with indications of the channel and the nature of the banks, and, again, a revealing legend: "stormed and taken by the boats of H.M.S. Dido ... Aug.1844." In other words, Patusan was mapped at the moment of its destruction.

As I demonstrated in "A Passion for Maps," this succession of maps presents a system of surveying, naming, and recording that combines particular professional practices with supporting institutions for the construction of a scientific and imperial archive. More concretely, what we see is not only how these professional practices (and the maps they produced) had obvious strategic purposes, but also how the maps themselves, far from being objective and disinterested, are ideologically slanted texts. The above examples are the very tip of an iceberg of European cartography effectively produced for military purposes. The tradition of cartographic reconnaissance was part of a military intelligence-gathering process. As Jeremy Black observes, such a mapping of territory also effectively "sanitises the process of battle" (156). This is obvious in the mapping of Patusan, and we have become very familiar with this use of maps again at the start of the twenty-first century (see Black 156).

Below, I will be exploring Conrad's heterotopic fiction. These are works in which different places have been superimposed in what is, effectively, a process of composite map-making. These composite maps produce impossible sites: not a unified, homogeneous fictional space, but a collage of heterogeneous spaces. In Conrad's hands, these are extraordinarily productive fictional strategies. Through these composite mappings, Conrad conducts a highly complex engagement with imperialist practices; through collage, Conrad's heterotopic fictions engage and question the world of his time through dismantling and reassembling. More importantly, this heterotopic paradigm, as it continually questions the relations between local specificities across a range of world cultures, also provides a counter-model to the monolithic mapping of all in the false and reified image of the capitalist West— what Pierre Bourdieu calls "the false universalism of the West" (19)— that dominates the start of this century. This "false universalism" means, in practice, that "American society and its way of life are understood as standing in for 'universal' qualities or characteristics—humanity, reason, freedom, human rights, democracy, and the 'good of mankind'" (Schirato and Webb 6). Furthermore, the identification of the U.S. with civilization, democracy, and modernity has the effect of defining all three in terms of each other and in relation to a particular neo-liberal economic model. The coercive embrace of this discourse makes it difficult to imagine modernity or civilization outside that particular narrow grid. Thus, for Britain's Prime Minister Tony Blair, "modernization" always means privatization, American models, and neo-liberal economic solutions. This identification further reduces the difference of "the other" to "the status of an adjunct of, or stage in a path to, 'the same'" (Schirato and Webb 191). In this respect, "modernization" merely reproduces the "progress" model of nineteenth-century imperialism. We have seen, in the aftermath of the Afghanistan and Iraq invasions, some of the dangers of this way of thinking. Conrad's heterotopic fiction, with its depth of historical awareness and emphases on local specificities, heterogeneity, and difference, provides a continuingly effective antidote. Indeed, Conrad's fictions not only open onto a number of world cultures in relation to which they, in turn, can be productively mapped, but have the very idea and project of mapping at their heart. Conrad is the maker and unmaker of maps, and this engagement with his cartographic project also provides a conceptual model for rethinking the project of mapping a global literary history.

I. Occupied Territories

In *Mapping and Empire*, Matthew Edney traces the intersection of imperialism and map-making in the construction of "India": "The maps came to define the empire itself, to give it territorial integrity and its basic existence. The empire exists because it can be mapped; the meaning of empire is inscribed into each map." (2)

From James Rennell's survey of Bengal (1765–1771) and the 1769 surveys of the northern districts of the Carnatic to the Great Trigonometrical Survey of 1831-43, surveying and map-making were an integral part of the East India Company's territorial administration of India. Maps were "fundamental tools of rule" (Edney 295). However, the Great Trigonometrical Survey went beyond "the pragmatic need for information" to ideological affirmation: "the trigonometrical surveys held the promise of a perfect geographical panopticon"; they promised to "reduce India to a rigidly coherent, geometrically accurate, and uniformly precise imperial space ... within which a systematic archive of knowledge about the Indian landscapes and people might be constructed" (Edney 299, 318). In short, the uniform map of India was a precursor to "the establishment of a single, India-wide administration" (Edney 322). At the same time, this "cartographic ideal," the ideal "cartographic perfection" necessitating the "critique of maps as paradigmatic tools of modernity's totalizing and all-engulfing culture," has to be set against the actualities of map-making, which are exercises in "negotiation, mediation, and contestation" (Edney 24, 25). The knowledge from which the geographic archive is constructed is "circumscribed by the numerous contingencies of knowledge acquisition" (Edney 26). First, the Company's early map-makers compiled their maps "from a widely disparate archive": "Surveys and maps were made by a host of military and civil officials, some explicitly trained in map-making, others working from general knowledge" (Edney 162). And surveys could be suddenly halted due to "funding, political, personnel or health problems" so that the archive was full of "the products of incidental or organised surveys in various stages of completion" (Edney 162). Second, surveys and map-making transpired within a range of institutional constraints: company finance and patronage structures; the lack of skilled personnel; a fragmented administrative structure; and the rivalries between the Company's three Indian governments (Calcutta, Bombay, and Madras) and the Court and Board in London (Edney 300). Third, practical problems existed on the ground: Not only were there linguistic and conceptual barriers between British surveyors and their Indian informants, but frequently the surveyors faced active resistance. Edney notes an 1836 riot in Chittagong prompted by a revenue survey and the 1837 destruction of survey towers by armed villagers in Gwalior (326, 330). The surveyors' use of flags as signals was a potential source of misunderstandings, while their removing trees to clear sight-lines also, at times, provoked resistance.

Victory begins by invoking, if not the East India Company's mapping of India, then the naval mapping of the archipelago—some of which, at least, was the product of the Company's trading activities in the region since 1603. Thus, Samburan is introduced cartographically at the outset as "the 'Round Island' of the charts" (*Vi* 5). It makes a second cartographic appearance as the central point of the Tropical Belt Coal Company's promotional map:

> On it Samburan was represented as the central spot of the Eastern Hemisphere with its name engraved in enormous capitals. Heavy lines radiated from it in all directions through the tropics, figuring a mysterious and effective star—lines of influence or lines of distance, or something of that sort. (23)

This map is clearly not concerned with objective description, but with conveying a very particular commercial message. The use of font size, capitals, and heavy lines all work to this end. Samburan is the company's "central station" (*Vi* 23), and it is clearly commercially important to assert the centrality of this out-of-the-way little island. As the narrator observes, "Company promoters have an imagination of their own" (24). In this case, the imaginative mastery of territory is directed not to the administration of land but to the support of sea routes. Control of the archipelago's sea routes had been the basis of European contestation for centuries—between the Portuguese and Spanish, and, later, between the French, Dutch, and British. The coaling station is represented in this map as the center of a network of communications that is also a network of control and influence. The map thus asserts commercial penetration as a form of power.

However, while the map asserts this imaginative possession of the territory, no "corresponding power," as Christopher GoGwilt notes, exists in reality (*Invention* 67). In the first place, the Tropical Belt Coal Company fails to take off. As the narrator observes: "Engineers came out, coolies were imported, bungalows were put upon Samburan, a gallery driven into the hillside, and actually some coal got out" (*Vi* 24). However, subsequently: "The T.B.C. Co. went into liquidation .... The Tesmans washed their hands of it. The government cancelled those famous contracts. The talk died out, and presently it was remarked here and there that Heyst had faded completely away" (25).

Also, the map's implicit claim to mastery of the island itself is challenged on the ground: while the heavy radiating lines imply a freedom of movement and communication, the narrative makes clear that the part of the island occupied by the Alfuros is a no-go area for Europeans. Thus, in Part IV Chapter 8, having found Wang's hut empty, Heyst and Lena follow the path he has taken "towards the upper limit of the forest" (343). However, the path is blocked by "a barricade of felled trees," which Heyst, with conscious irony, describes as "a barrier against the march of civilisation" (344). The Alfuros are visible only as spear blades poking through the barricade. This incident echoes the first reference to the Alfuros in the novel: in Part III Chapter 1, we are told that Wang had married one of the women from the Alfuro village "on the west shore of the island, beyond the central ridge," although the Alfuros, taking fright at the arrival of so many Chinese coolies for the coal mine, "had blocked the path over the ridge by felling a few trees" (179). Their territory is, in effect, an exclusion zone beyond the barrier they have erected. As Douglas Kerr suggests, their part of the island is a blind spot in the European panoptical map (359). At the same time, it is not empty space. The Alfuros are neither seen nor heard in the novel, yet there is clearly a fully functioning small society with seasons for fishing and trading beyond this barricade. This is a lived space and a space resistant to European domination. A contemporary analogue to the charts and commercial maps invoked by *Victory* would be the nineteenth-century United States maps, which, as Jack Forbes observes, substituted the "cartographic pretensions of the U.S. government" for the "realities of native power" (19). In both cases, the maps lay claim to territory that is already occupied.

Finally, the implied cartographical accuracy of "the charts" in which Samburan figures as "Round Island" and the cartographical explicitness of the promotional map for the Tropical Belt Coal Company are set against (and undermined by) the actual impossibility of locating Samburan. The U.S. first edition of *Victory* had an end map that confidently locates Samburan in the Java Sea, just as it finds locations for all of Conrad's prior fictions. It is an assertion of imaginative colonization, a mastery that *Victory* itself subverts.[1] It is not just that Heyst's island cannot be positively identified nor even precisely located. Samburan is not just a nonexistent place, but an impossible space. Its location within shallow seas, its coal deposits, and its proximity to a volcano "just above the northern horizon" (*Vi* 4) constitute an impossible set of conditions (see Hampson, "Passion" 46). As Peter Hulme has shown, in *The Tempest*, Shakespeare produces a dual location for Prospero's island as West Indian and Mediterranean voyages overlap (88-134). The play engages with both the "New World" encounter and, as Jerry Brotton observes, the neglected "eastern frontier" of maritime expansion: it is situated precisely at the "geopolitical bifurcation between the Old World and the New" (31). As we will see in relation to Patusan, Conrad too uses composite maps and impossible spaces to articulate a complex engagement with contemporary imperialist practices.

II. Settlers

In *Lord Jim*, by choosing the name "Patusan," Conrad commemorates the west Borneo riverine village that British naval action destroyed in the "war against the pirates" of 1843–44. In *An Outcast of the Islands*, Babalatchi recalls this campaign from the receiving end: "Over the hill and over the forest … they dropped whistling fireballs into the creek where our praus took refuge"(*OI* 46). Babalatchi graphically recollects "the flames of the burning stronghold" (52), the praus "wedged together in the narrow creek … burning fiercely," and "the crews of the man-of-war's boats dashing to the attack of the rover's village" (53). Babalatchi's memories supply the human presence that the H.M.S. Dido's maps studiously remove.

In *Lord Jim*, Conrad carefully situates his Patusan historically by reference to the European competition to control the lucrative spice trade. More specifically, Patusan is approached through sixteenth- and seventeenth-century European explorations and the early European mappings of the archipelago. Chapter 22 begins with a fictional account of how the place name figures in "collections of old voyages": "The seventeenth-century traders went there for pepper, because the passion for pepper seemed to burn like a flame of love in the breast of Dutch and English adventurers about the time of James the First" (226). This clearly alludes to the beginnings of the English and Dutch East India Companies. In 1603, for example, James Lancaster commanded the English East India Company's first voyage, which set up a factory at Bantam and brought 500 tons of peppercorns back to London (Keay 24–25). However, geographically, Patusan is much less stable. As we have seen, the name derives from a west Borneo village the British destroyed in 1843. This name is then attached to a settlement whose social formation (with its local rajah and contesting Arabs and Bugis) derives from Conrad's 1887 experience of east Borneo. However, the route Gentleman Brown follows places it firmly in Sumatra: "down the Straits of Macassar .... across the Java Sea .... in less than a week after clearing the Sunda Straits, he anchored off the Batu Kring mouth" (*LJ* 356–357). As the novel developed, Conrad seems to have changed the location of Patusan from Borneo to Sumatra. (However, it should be noted that James Lancaster's first port of call was Aceh in northern Sumatra, where he was welcomed—and, like Conrad's traders, "impressed"—by the Sultan, Ala-Uddin Shah [Keay 16–18].) Rather than genetically explaining this cartographic instability, I want to offer a spatialized reading of the novel. In particular, I want to consider the effect of Patusan's construction through this superimposition of different times and spaces.

Chapter 22 opens: "The conquest of love, honour, men's confidence—the pride of it, the power of it, are fit materials for a heroic tale" (*LJ* 226). Then it offers a metaphorical rather than a cartographic location for Patusan:

> Thirty miles of forest shut it off from the sight of an indifferent world, and the noise of the white surf along the coast overpowered the voice of fame. The stream of civilisation, as if divided on a headland a hundred miles north of Patusan, branches east and south-east, leaving its plains and valleys, its old trees and its old mankind, neglected and isolated .... (*LJ* 226)

Physical geographical features—forests, coastlines, plains, and valleys—slide into metaphors, abstractions, speculative comparisons. Chris Bongie has argued that Patusan is, from the start, always already an impossible space in the circumstances of global modernity evoked elsewhere in the novel (176). Consider, for example, the apparently arbitrary sighting of the tourists in the Malabar House when Jim and Marlow dine together there:

> Henceforth they would be labelled as having passed through this and that place, and so would be their luggage. They would cherish this distinction of their persons, and preserve the gummed tickets on their portmanteaus as documentary evidence, as the only permanent trace of their improving enterprise. (77)

Bongie cites Conrad's essay on Curle's *Into the East,* where Conrad is similarly critical of modern travel (and travelers), and an essay on travel writing, which ends in an acute apprehension of global modernity. For Conrad, "the days of heroic travel are gone" (*LE* 128). Once the "basic facts of geography" had been "ascertained by the observations of heavenly bodies," the "glance of the modern traveller" was confronted by "the much-surveyed earth" (*LE* 130). The triumph of exploration has produced what Conrad calls "the vanishing mysteries of the earth" (*LE* 132). The Enlightenment project of panoptical knowledge has ended in the nightmare of official surveillance, as Conrad anticipates a time when "there will be no back-yard left in the heart of Central Africa that has not been peeped into by some person more or less commissioned for the purpose" (*LE* 129). Conrad's specific fearful vision has been realized, in a form he could not have anticipated, through modern surveillance satellites, but also more generally through modern globalization. Bongie summarizes Conrad's position: "Everywhere and in everything, this modernity cancels out whatever might once have differed from it, reducing both the earth and those who inhabit it to a single common denominator" (149).

Bongie goes on to explain Conrad's reluctance to complete *The Rescue* in these terms, for as the novel itself comes to appreciate, Lingard was implicated in the excesses of the new imperialism and thus contributed to that "specific fearful vision" of a globalized world Conrad had adumbrated in *Lord Jim.* However, because we are supplied with the grounding of Jim's ambition in his reading of "light holiday literature" (*LJ* 5), Bongie argues: "Not only the heroism Jim aspires to but an entire alternative world" figures as part of a "wholly bookish fiction" (175). Thus, "the other world of Patusan" has "from the beginning, been excluded from the novel as a real possibility" (175). Where, in *The Rescue,* Conrad struggled to bring into coherent relation his nostalgia for an old imperialism, his critical awareness of the new imperialism, and an apprehension of the will-to-power implicit in the imperialism of "noble ideas," in *Lord Jim* he knowingly situates himself "at the impasse of an atomized modernity" (186).

Bongie's compelling reading of Jim's belatedness obviously foregrounds time. I want to pick up on his idea of Patusan as an alternative space. In a 1967 lecture, "*Des Espaces Autres,*" Michel Foucault introduced his idea of "heterotopias" through a brief history of space from the medieval space of emplacement through the post-Galileo space of extension to the modern world's concentration on site.[2] Foucault begins his account of heterotopias with lived and socially produced space: "We do not live inside a void .... we live inside a set of relations that delineates sites which are irreducible to one another and absolutely not superimposable on one another" ("Other Spaces" 23). He then outlines the idea of heterotopias as sites "that have the curious property of being in relation with all the other sites, but in such a way as to suspect, neutralize, or invert the set of relations that they happen to designate, mirror, or invert" (24). Heterotopias, he then asserts, are "counter-sites," involved in "the simultaneously mythic and real contestation of the space in which we live" (24). He illustrates the first idea through the example of "crisis heterotopias" in "so-called primitive societies"—that is, "privileged or sacred or forbidden places, reserved for individuals who are, in relation to society and to the human environment in which they live, in a state of crisis" (24). He instances spatial rituals for adolescents, menstruating women, pregnant women in "so-called primitive societies"—and the "honeymoon" tradition in our own. We might also think of Jim in Marlow's room in the Malabar House after the Inquiry reaches its verdict. Jim is undeniably in a state of crisis relative to the "human environment" in which he lives. And, as Marlow observes: "On all the round earth" Jim had "no place . . . where he could withdraw" (*LJ* 171). Marlow's room becomes that placeless place. This was "the only place in the world" where "he could have it out with himself without being bothered by the rest of the universe" (*LJ* 171). Foucault suggests that, in the modern world, crisis heterotopias are being replaced by "heterotopias of deviation," places for "individuals whose behavior is deviant in relation to the required mean or norm" ("Other Spaces" 25). Heterotopias of deviation would include rest homes, psychiatric hospitals, and prisons. In *An Outcast of the Islands*, when Lingard had to decide what to do with Willems, he determined to leave him stranded up a Bornean river as a form of imprisonment: "As far as the rest of the world is concerned," Lingard tells him, "your life is finished" (*OI* 277). If Patusan is a heterotopia, what kind of heterotopia is it—and what would be the implications of this designation?

The last trait of heterotopias that Foucault describes is that "they have a function in relation to all the space that remains" ("Other Spaces" 27). The passages quoted above relating to Jim and Willems are marked by just such a consciousness of one place in relation to "all the space that remains." Foucault's account of the two extreme poles of this function is suggestive:

> Either their role is to create a space of illusion that exposes every real space . . . as still more illusory . . . . Or else, on the contrary, their role is to create a space that is other, another real space, as perfect, as meticulous, as well arranged as ours is messy, ill-constructed, and jumbled. The latter type would be the heterotopia, not of illusion, but of compensation, and I wonder if certain colonies have not functioned somewhere in this manner. ("Other Spaces" 27)

Foucault has in mind the Puritan settlements in North America, settlements in which, as he playfully claims, "human perfection was effectively achieved" (27). Patusan clearly functions as a heterotopia of consolation. It provides the conditions in which Jim can live a heroic life and live up to his image of himself. In doing so, it also subtly implies a criticism of the rest of the world that does not provide such opportunities. However, given the fictional basis of Jim's dreams of heroism, that whisper of criticism is disabled in its contestation with other critical voices.

Foucault describes the heterotopia as "capable of juxtaposing in a single real place several spaces, several sites that are in themselves incompatible" (25). Conrad's Patusan is not a real place, but it does, as suggested above, bring together several incompatible sites. More precisely, it brings together different times as well as sites. The name invokes British interests in Borneo and Brooke's mid-century one-man imperialism; it commemorates a village destroyed to advance British interests in the name of a "war against the pirates." If, as Agnes Yeow suggests (132–152), Jim's career is constructed on nostalgia for the *tuan putih*, the white rajah who ruled Sarawak, the name Patusan never allows us to forget the cost of that imperium to the local people. Also, by way of comparison, the east Borneo social formation de-emphasizes and de-centers European imperialist interests. Although nominally under Dutch rule, Berau was historically part of the Sulu Sultanate and was, in Conrad's time, the contested site of overlapping Taosug and Buginese spheres of interest (see Hampson, *Cross-Cultural Encounters* 43). The east coast of Borneo was one of the main foci of the Bugis people's informal political and commercial empire (Tarling 8). Meanwhile, the Sumatra setting points to contemporary Achinese resistance to Dutch imperialism. Aceh, for the region's Muslims, was also "The Gateway to Mecca": "Here pilgrims embark for the *haj* to Arabia and here Arab and Indian traders first brought the teachings of Islam to the Archipelago" (Keay 16). Here, as elsewhere, Conrad picks up on Islam as a focus for resistance to European imperialism. Thus, these three juxtaposed sites imply a history of various European attempts to dominate the region and various local resistance efforts, while also registering a geopolitical history of the region that has no reference to European imperialism. The juxtaposition of these sites brings these different "sets of relations" into dialogue.

III. Nakba[3]

James Corner notes that we now "live in a world where local economies and cultures are tightly bound into global ones": "localities can be more closely connected to sites thousands of miles away than to their immediate surroundings" (226). This awareness is present in Conrad's fiction from the start. Chapter 3 of *Almayer's Folly* begins: "deliberations conducted in London have a far-reaching importance, and so the decision issued from the fog-veiled offices of the Borneo Company darkened for Almayer the brilliant sunshine of the Tropics" (34). In *Nostromo*, Conrad confronts this issue directly: not only is the silver mine run by U.S. finance, but the steamship company, the railway, and the telegraph company all represent the penetration of the economy of Conrad's fictional South American country by European interests. The local is permeated by the global.

Nostromo's general historical context was the emergence of the United States as an imperial power. Partly through his friendship with Cunninghame

Graham, Conrad took a particular interest in the Spanish–American War. In May and July 1898, Conrad wrote to Cunninghame Graham echoing his friend's public opposition to the United States' role in the war and his criticism of U.S. expansionist ambitions. Under the December 1898 treaty that concluded the war, the United States acquired, among other things, Cuba and the Philippines: this clearly marked the decline of Spain and the arrival of the United States as an international player. Another event during the period reinforced this message and is more directly relevant to *Nostromo*. Until November 1903, Panama was part of the Republic of Colombia. In June 1902 the U.S. Congress approved the Panama route for a new canal to link the Atlantic and Pacific oceans. Unfortunately, the Colombian government rejected the terms of the Hay–Herran Treaty to develop the new canal. Representatives of the New Panama Canal Company then promoted a secessionist movement in Panama. U.S. warships prevented Colombian troops from landing to suppress the revolt, and, when Panama seceded from Colombia on November 3 1903, the new country received prompt recognition from the United States. Within a month, Panama had negotiated in its own name the canal treaty that Colombia had rejected. On December 26, 1903, Conrad wrote to Cunninghame Graham, reflecting on "the Yankee Conquistadores in Panama" (*Letters* 3: 102). Cunninghame Graham's strategy of drawing parallels between the *conquistadores* and the new imperialism also plays its part in *Nostromo*, the novel Conrad was writing at the time.

In constructing his fictional country, it is well known that Conrad drew on a range of works such as George Frederick Masterman's *Seven Eventful Years in Paraguay* (1869) and Edward B. Eastwick's *Venezuela: Sketches of Life in a South American Republic* (1868). He deliberately aimed at producing a composite. As he wrote Cunninghame Graham on October 31, 1904, Costaguana was "meant for a S. American state in general: thence the mixture of customs and expressions" (*Letters* 3: 175). Conrad's "mapping of a new American imperialism" (GoGwilt, *Invention* 216) involved not just a "mixture of customs and expressions" but also a cartographical composite. Thus, Costaguana, with its Caribbean and Pacific seaboard, most closely resembles Colombia; its location corresponds roughly to the present border of Ecuador and Colombia, but the description of Sulaco harbor derives from Eastwick's account of Puerto Calbello in the Golfo Triste, Venezuela (Watts, Everyman *Nostromo* 418–419). Gould's mine is compared to the Atacama nitrate fields (which stretch from Copiapo in Chile to Arica in Peru), and its precursor is obviously the Potosi silver mine in the Bolivian province of Peru. At the same time, Costaguana is also referred to as "the bottomless pit of 10 per cent loans," which Watts reads as alluding to the Venezuela government offer of 1863–1864 (Everyman *Nostromo* 425–26).

Jacques Berthoud has delineated the similarly composite nature of the city of Sulaco:

To be sure, every reader can see that it was founded by the conquistadores, that it developed under Spanish colonial rule, and that it contains many survivals from that period: the name "Camino Real" for the road into a hinterland originally colonised by the Jesuits; ... the crumbling town walls and gates built, like those of Lima and Cartagena, against the incursions of pirates; ... Giorgio Viola's inn which, according to Decoud, "may have been contrived by a Conquistador farmer of the pearl fishery three hundred years ago," which recalls the famed pearl deposits of Venezuela and Colombia; the surviving statue of the last Bourbon king, Charles IV, like a similar statue that once stood in the Plaza Mayor of Mexico City; the Alameda or public gardens, like those of Lima or Mexico City .... ("Modernization of Sulaco" 143)

Berthoud describes Conrad's creation of "the prototype of a Spanish American state at the end of the nineteenth century" (143) and of "an exemplary Hispano-American city" (147). He praises Conrad's "powers of assimilation" and "capacity for synthesis," his ability to make the assembled details "cohere" (143). However, his own reading practice (as exemplified in the passage above) operates in terms of disassembling rather than coherence. The effect is like that in Malcolm Bradbury's *Rates of Exchange*, where the informed reader picks up on the collage of Eastern European events, references, and expressions. Where a reading through coherence produces archetypal South American politics and economics, a reading through collage (as in the composite mapping of Patusan) foregrounds specificities and the dialogue between the different sets of relations designated by the different sites. Instead of synthesizing differences, reading through montage operates through maintaining differences dialogically. As James Corner suggests, in the context of "layering" in urban and landscape design by architects such as Bernard Tschumi and Rem Koolhaas, the construction of a composite space produces a "field of multiple orders" (235), a "*milieu* that is heterogeneous and multiple in its effects" (239). The "heterogeneous and multiple" spaces of *Nostromo* offer a reflection of what de Certeau calls the "plurality of the real" (94).

Berthoud's account of *Nostromo* demonstrates two further ways in which the spaces of the novel are "multiple and heterogeneous." First, drawing on Watts' plan of Sulaco, he shows how Conrad not only changes his sources but also varies the topography in the course of the narrative "to achieve a local effect" ("Modernization of Sulaco" 145). Thus, Watts drew attention to Eastwick's description of Caracas as a model for Sulaco: "a large plaza, government buildings on the western side, and a cathedral 'at the south-eastern angle'" (Penguin *Nostromo* 30). Berthoud notes, however, that Watts' plan of Sulaco changes the orientation so that the square has a northwest–southeast axis rather than the north–south axis of the square in Caracas. This orientation takes account of various topographical details in the novel—such as "the fact that the harbour gate must be facing the harbour, which is to the north-west, since Nostromo from his vantage-point in the old fort will have direct sight of it" ("Modernization" 144). On the other hand, other details—such as Charles Gould looking over the square from the audience chamber of the Intendencia and seeing "the snowy curve of Higuerota" next to "the perpendicular lines of the cathedral towers"— require a north–south orientation of the square, since the mountain is due east of Sulaco ("Modernization" 145). Sulaco is thus not only a composite city but an unstable space in which we can never confidently orientate ourselves.

Second, Berthoud notes selective similarities between Sulaco and Cracow that, while they do not amount to an identification, suggest "a less direct inspiration" (154). Berthoud complements his case by drawing attention to Conrad's "Author's Note," where Conrad claims that the model for Antonia Avellanos drew on his memories of schoolboy love for a girl "just out of the classroom herself" (*No* xx). Keith Carabine has also drawn attention to the Tres de Mayo coffee, one of the rituals that contribute to the identity formation of the new republic of Costaguana (*Nostromo* 587). As Carabine notes, the third of May is an important date in Polish history: the Constitution of the Third of May (1791) was Poland's first written constitution. Behind the new republic of Costaguana is the ghostly presence of the suppressed and yet to be reborn Polish nation.

From one perspective, *Nostromo* could be said to be about the drawing of a boundary and the creation of a new nation.[4] One of the novel's many ironies is that the firming up of the new republic's identity is set against the destabilizing of the identities of the major characters. Charles Gould, for example, having originally told his wife "we Goulds are no adventurers" (*No* 64) is eventually forced to admit "that he was an adventurer in Costaguana, the descendant of adventurers" (365). Similarly, Captain Mitchell presents Nostromo, from the start, as an epic hero, but, as GoGwilt points out, "Nostromo's emerging consciousness of his own position in historical events is plotted in terms of the eclipse of his heroic stature as a 'man of the people'" (*Invention* 205). Indeed, as GoGwilt shows, Nostromo's status as a "man of the people" and the collective "the people" are both problematic. Nostromo is an Italian immigrant in Costaguana, and the "people" he most directly leads, the OSN lighter-men, are "natives of the Republic," an "outcast lot of very mixed blood, mainly negroes" (*No* 14). As Nostromo comes to realize, he has used his control over this group to protect the interests of the creole aristocracy and the foreign investors—a "betrayal of a dispossessed people to the propertied interests of the 'European residents'" (GoGwilt, *Invention* 205). GoGwilt also notes "a strangely collective double for the organized group of 'outcasts' under Nostromo's leadership" in the people of the mine who march on the town of Sulaco "at the decisive moment in events" under the leadership of Don Pepe (*Invention* 215, 214). Don Pepe, like Nostromo, is a man of "humble origin" who serves Blanco interests (*No* 87), but what GoGwilt fails to mention is that the miners he leads were "all Indians from the Sierra" (*No* 476). Furthermore, "the decisive moment" ends with these Indians from the mine joining the Indian troops led by Barrios (*No* 167), himself regarded by the creoles as an "ignorant, boastful Indio" (*No* 171), in defeating the "wild llaneros" (*No* 145), nomadic mestizos from the plains, "violent men but little removed from a state of utter savagery" (*No* 385), in order to save the "European residents," the US-backed Ribierists.[5]

Nostromo and Decoud, in their different ways, are taken over by the myth-making involved in establishing the new republic. The ride to Cayta makes "the Capataz de Cargadores famous from one end of America to the other" (*No* 464), and "the famous ride to Cayta" becomes a "historical event" (*No* 473), one of the new republic's founding myths (see Hampson, "Formation of Legends" 167–186). The "Frenchified" Decoud, with his "most un French cosmopolitanism" (*No* 152), who "imagined himself Parisian to the tips of his fingers" (*No* 153), becomes "the Journalist of Sulaco" (*No* 158) and the new nation's founding father. The founding of the new republic preserves the Blancos, the creole aristocracy, and protects the investments of the U.S. and European capitalists, but at the expense of the indigenous peoples. The defeated rhetoric of the Monterist uprising is thus justified by the events of the novel. Whatever the Monteros' real motives, the basic charges underlying the military revolt they lead are justified: "the national honour" has been "sold to foreigners" by the Ribierists (*No* 145); the country has, indeed, been made "a prey to foreign speculators" (*No* 146). The Monteros have their roots in Costaguana's indigenous peoples: they are rumored to be the sons of "a charcoal burner in the woods" and "a baptised Indian woman from the far interior" (*No* 39). At the same time, they represent another form of hybridization. At the lunch on board the *Juno*, General Montero, with his "hooked nose flattened on the tip" and the "coppery tint of his broad face" (*No* 120), is described as having "the atrocious grotesqueness of some military idol of Aztec conception and European bedecking" (*No* 122), while the "bunches of crisp hair" above his ears is read in terms of "the presence of some negro blood" (*No* 386). For his part, his brother, Pedro, has acquired his political ideas from reading "the lighter sort of historical works in the French language, such, for instance as the books of Imbert de Saint Amand upon the Second Empire" (*No* 387). Where the new republic owes its existence to the deracinated "Frenchified" Decoud, the "Monterist Revolution" has, among its "immediate causes" (*No* 387), the "light literature" of the Second Empire—and, indeed, as Pedro confides to Gould, the Second Empire provides him with his model for the direction of the revolution—not toward democracy, but toward "Caesarism." However, unlike Jim, Pedro is not given an "other place" to develop this vision: his "light literature" dream of the Second Empire is overwhelmed by the more powerful economic forces through which it attempts to work.

Meanwhile, the indigenous people, while playing a decisive part in the Sulaco crisis, are politically marginalized and disempowered. Their history is one of exploitation and genocide. The novel begins by evoking the arrival of the conquistadores ("the time of Spanish rule"), and the narrative is scattered with memorials of this history: "The heavy stonework of bridges and churches left by the conquerors proclaimed the disregard of human labour, the tribute-labour of vanished nations" (*No* 89). The early history of the San Tomé mine conveys the same message: "Worked in the early days mostly by the means of lashes on the backs of slaves, its yield had been paid for in its own weight of human bones. Whole tribes of Indians had perished in the exploitation" (52). At the same time, the novel's opening also implies the continuity between the time of "deep-sea galleons" and modern times. The indigenous people appear in the novel primarily as a source of labor. Above all, they are visible as the miners of the San Tomé mine. GoGwilt has commented on the description of the mine and its workings as a "picture of exploitation—exploitation of people, and exploitation of nature" (*Invention* 214): "the mountain would swallow one half of the silent crowd, while the other half would move off in long files down the zigzag paths leading to the bottom of the gorge" (*No* 100). In the green and white uniform of the mine, they are also represented as having undergone a process of homogenization. The indigenous peoples in the remote areas of the country have been the object of Father Corbelan's missionary activities (*No* 194–195), and the mining communities have undergone a similar process of deculturization under Father Roman, producing "the innumerable Marias and Brigidas" of the mine's villages (*No* 399).

IV. Conclusion

Conrad's Malay fiction negotiates between residual nostalgia for an earlier version of imperialism that he would have found in his sources and his post-Congo understanding of the "new imperialism" of his own day. In *Nostromo*, he engages with an even newer form of imperialism: the form that was to dominate the twentieth century. In *Nostromo*, as in his essay "Travel," Conrad presents a fearful anticipation of modern globalization. Thus, the novel notes early on that the "material apparatus of perfected civilisation which obliterates the individuality of old towns under the stereotyped conveniences of modern life had not intruded as yet" upon Sulaco (*No* 96), but, at the novel's end, we see how this process is overtaking Sulaco through the glancing reference to the "American Bar" on the Plaza Major (*No* 479). At the same time, as Schirato and Webb note, contemporary globalization has also been accompanied by a "turn to the local," and Conrad shows how this aspect of globalization, too, was already evident at the start of the last century. Thus, at the end of *Nostromo*, alongside the triumph of "material interests," we glimpse the existence of "the secret societies amongst immigrants and natives" working to resist the new world order (*No* 511). This reintroduces the difference within the Americas that the discursive regime of globalization occludes (and also those for whom the new economic order is a threat to civilization rather than synonymous with civilization). However, Conrad's heterotopic fictions offer not just a critical engagement with imperialism on a thematic level, but, through the collaging of heterogeneous sites, provide also a form of resistance—a vitally necessary way of thinking against the grain.

Notes

1. I am grateful to Peter Mallios for reminding me of this map, which is reproduced in Mallios' recent edition of *Victory*. The "Key to the Map" ends with the note: "It must be borne in mind that the markings on the map are only approximations based many times on invented names" (lviii).

2. Compare Con Coroneos's discussion of Patusan as a heterotopia: he relates the "new space" of Patusan to Winnicot's "third space" of play—which is neither fantasy nor shared reality (146).

3. The Nakba (the catastrophe) was the expulsion in 1948–1949 of 750,000 Palestinians from their homes by massacres and intimidation in a process of "ethnic [cleansing:" 40 Palestinian] villages were obliterated and 78% of Palestine was taken over.

4. In the same way, in 1921 the British Colonial Office drew a "line in the sand" and carved a border across southern Iraq to create the new nation of Kuwait. See Ritter and Pitt (10).

5. Don Pepe is a *llanero* (*No* 112), as are the soldiers led by Pedro Montero (*No* 476). I am grateful to Professor Will Rowe, Birkbeck College, University of London, for information about the *llaneros*.

8

Connoisseurs of Terror and the Political Aesthetics of Anarchism
Nostromo and *A Set of Six*

ANTHONY FOTHERGILL

How is the world governed and how do wars begin? Politicians tell lies to journalists and when they read them in print they believe them.

Karl Kraus, *Die Fackel*

I.

On March 29, 1892, the Paris correspondent to *The Times*, London, reported on the latest spate of anarchist outrages, François Ravachol's bombing of the homes of the judge and prosecutor who had tried and sentenced May Day anarchist protestors the year before:

> No possible political end can be adduced to justify or explain the detestable acts which have startled us all. It is clearly the war of disorder and chaos against order and law. It is crime for crime's sake. It is murder and havoc acting in the service of covetousness, hatred and all evil. Undoubtedly all Anarchists are not assassins but all assassins are ready to increase the army of Anarchists and it really is with an army of murderers that society has now to deal.

The crucial *political* agenda comes a few sentences later:

> In the stress of so wide a danger there should certainly be an international league preventing every murderer of this sort from finding a place to linger even for a night in any country under the sun. Anarchists should not be regarded as members of a political party, and it should not be possible for an Anarchist to hurry away from Paris to find an asylum in Brussels, in Geneva or in London. (qtd. in Quail 118)

Notwithstanding the overheated rhetoric (characteristic, then as now, of the "outrage" genre of journalism), police suspicions, and contemporary fiction, no great Europe-wide anarchist conspiracy to kill off heads of state and destabilize governments actually existed. Rather, lone men like Ravachol (a petty-criminal-turned-anarchist) were most often responsible for targeted attacks avenging the death or imprisonment of comrades; they were not part of a program of indiscriminate violence. Indeed, most anarchists were critical of bombings endangering human life, and for many the very idea of a coherent movement was a contradiction in terms.[1] But the tone of the report reflected and helped to create conditions of social and political anxiety and to publicize the "war of chaos" that it sought to combat. Even the awkward syntax—"undoubtedly all anarchists are not assassins"—proposes what it ostensibly negates, and within a single sentence "anarchists" are elided with "murderers." The mythologizing of anarchist perpetrators (as devils or martyrs, by state authorities or anarchist sympathizers, respectively) fed on this hyperbole, usually absent anything like factual evidence. In short, a symbiotic relationship developed between state power and oppositional terrorism. In this relationship, each "side" sees the other as the embodiment of oppressive violence, which must be met by an even greater punitive and spectacular violence, or violent preemptive counter-violence. This destructive symbiosis constitutes aspects of what Derrida, in a recent reflection on "9/11," has called a structure of "autoimmunity." The body (politic) produces antibodies that act against the defense mechanisms naturally within the body: "a living being, in quasi-*suicidal* fashion, 'itself' works to destroy its own protection, to immunize itself *against* its 'own' immunity" (Borradori 94). I will return to this model for thinking about the bourgeois order, law, and anarchism.

The Times' report evokes a number of tropes current then and over a century later. They are as follows: Anarchism is virtually synonymous with terrorism. It is incomprehensible. Liberally inclined states are safe havens, constituting a threat through their implicit support for terrorism. The threat is both internal and international, requiring a coalition of states to fight against it with legislation and increased state control. Terrorists do not belong to a political party (and so submit to no "normal" structures of organized, controllable, political processes). Above all, anarchy is a transgression not just against the law, like common murder, but against the authority of the law, against the very terms by which law understands itself. These accumulated tropes constituted the state's political reaction to terrorism in the late nineteenth century.

The anarchists, too, offered a political reaction to the bombing, a reaction unexpected and in some ways startling, as it proposes an aesthetic of the politics of performance. It is expressed most notoriously by the anarchist writer, wit, and dandy Laurent Tailhade, after Vaillant's 1893 bombing of the Chamber of Deputies (which caused no injuries): "What do the victims matter if the gesture is beautiful? What does the death of some unidentified persons matter, if, by it, the individual is affirmed?" (Sonn, *Anarchism* 257). Intended to outrage, the remark is itself an outraged gesture against the bourgeois status quo.

It was into this political and cultural territory of violent antagonism that Joseph Conrad, rather anachronistically, ventured when in 1905 and 1906 he wrote three works notionally on anarchists: two short stories, "An Anarchist: A Desperate Tale" and "The Informer: An Ironic Tale," published in *A Set of Six*

(1908); and a novel, *The Secret Agent: A Simple Tale* (1907), loosely based on the Greenwich Observatory explosion of November 15, 1894. Widespread anxiety about plotting foreign conspirators "in our midst," which government and the popular media helped fuel, and which the last two decades' numerous "dynamite novels" exploited, had both real and imaginary causes. The most local imagined danger came from Fenian activists (whom many blamed, falsely, for the Greenwich bombing). But they were said to work out of Paris or Brussels and so fed unspecific but potent fears of a foreign menace. In fact, the active phase of anarchist terrorism in Britain, which they called "propaganda by the deed," when "something (generally an explosion) more or less deplorable does happen" (*SA* 85), was fairly short-lived, from roughly 1881 through the mid-1890s, and much more extensive abroad. (Greenwich was the only bombing on Britain's "mainland.") By 1906, with the rise of anarcho-syndicalism and the formation of workers' associations, revolutionary strikes had become favored forms of anarchist action. But the *fear* of terror was much more widespread and persistent, and the importation of fear into Britain through frightening newspaper reports was as great as the immigration of "anarchists" themselves.

We may speculate about an "epidemic" of fear as a response to terrorism. Evidence of such an epidemic exists today, stemming not from September 11 (though that has intensified it) but from the late 1960s, generated by the wide (mis-)use of the word "anarchistic" for any form of mass political action. Hence, when an electricity blackout occurs in New York or London, or a car backfires in the wrong street in Belfast, the specter of a terrorist attack is immediately evoked. It is deeply ironic that actual victims of actual acts of violence may get subsumed within this epidemic, dying, because of it, two deaths. The appalling horror of September 11, 2001, reduced to the metonymic "9/11," is a case in point.[2] Politicians' fear of an epidemic of unmanaged fear (for a fearful population may act in politically unpredictable ways) spirals as "threatened" states impose increasingly repressive laws in the name of freedom and security, and adopt measures breaching international law and their own liberal constitutions and civil rights. One commentator on Victorian history, after noting the diplomatic pressure put by autocratic European states upon more liberal ones, states that:

> as far as native British chauvinism went, the cry for anti-Anarchist legislation was mixed in with "fair trade" demands, demands for the throwing out of "pauper aliens" and so on. The smokescreen thrown up by professionally excitable fellows [of the media] allowed the authorities a certain latitude in their handling of immigrants. (Quail 118–119)

This is, of course, the reaction that the foreign (possibly Russian) diplomat, Mr. Vladimir, hopes to provoke in *The Secret Agent*.

"Anarchism is the crime of crimes." That is, it is crime for crime's sake. The phrase evokes that other "decadent" form of autonomy and self-centeredness contemporary with the height of the active terrorist phase, "Art for art's sake."

Both accusations hung in the air in the 1890s, and the offended bourgeoisie reacted in more or less the same materialist way to both. Crime for money's sake was understandable, art for profit's sake, acceptable. But crime for crime's sake, art for art's sake? Willfully purposeless, they defy all reasonable terms and offend civilized values. "Autonomy," "*l'Autonomie*"—the political cry of the anarchists as well as the generic name of their political clubs—was echoed in the aesthetic espoused by many among the late nineteenth-century artistic avant-garde, particularly in what Walter Benjamin called "the Capital of the Nineteenth Century," Paris, from which center it spread to other European capitals. Both defiantly renounced the dominant order, with outsiderly independence and individualism the paradoxically unifying vision. From within the bourgeois order, such renunciation did not, does not, make sense. "Why do they hate us?" "Why do they undermine and seek to overturn what is self-evidently true and proper?" Calling someone an "anarchist" or "terrorist" means not having to answer such questions. Thus, *anarchy* provided the English populace with a potent repressive "explanatory" power that did not bear much looking into.

Conrad, however, *does* look into anarchy and the culture within which, for a while, it flourished. He has a much better-informed insiderly knowledge of the cultural and political complexities of the anarchist movement than his evasive prefatory comments on *The Secret Agent* and *A Set of Six* would imply. Indeed, his literary intervention into the movement offers a subtle and complex analysis of the interrelationship between bourgeois society and anarchism. Examining his other writings (the letters to Cunninghame Graham, for instance) to find either a straightforward denunciation of anarchism or, simply, clarification, instead reveals more complexity. Paragraphs and phrases stand out as if Conrad is aware of their quotability, as if he deliberately dramatizes his voice to match or outdo Cunninghame Graham's theatrical flamboyance. This is particularly clear in a letter of October 7, 1907, when he defends himself against the accusation that *The Secret Agent* satirizes revolutionaries. "All these people are not revolutionaries—they are shams. And as regards the Professor I did not intend to make him despicable. He is incorruptible at any rate .... I wanted to give him a note of perfect sincerity. At the worst he is a megalomaniac of an extreme type. And every extremist is respectable" (*Letters* 2: 491).

Besides the political judgments offered here, Conrad's audacious formulations—"Every extremist is respectable"; "The Professor is incorruptible"—appeal to the transgressive. That is, Conrad appears not only to endorse an apparently reprehensible character; but the language he uses to defend the Professor jars against common usage: "respectable," "incorruptible," "perfect sincerity," indeed "Professor." These terms, which would happily confirm the self image of the liberal humanist bourgeoisie, have been explosively co-opted to describe a figure seeking its destruction. Conrad's rhetoric is an aesthetic (and political) mischief-making with linguistic transgression. It counters the normal maintenance of boundaries and order to deconstruct the language and modes of thinking within which both sides of the mirroring and destructive equation are entrapped. Conrad's critique of a capitalist bourgeoisie and of so-called anarchists and "sham revolutionaries" works toward establishing an aesthetic position from which these mutually dependent forces can be understood. The autonomy of a critical aesthetics, Conrad's approach suggests, *might* be able to resist the illusions and inhumanities both forces exercise. Political thinking and its rhetoric tend to legitimate ideologies, policy, and action predicated on (uninterrogated) categories of absolute difference: liberty/oppression, civilized/primitive, progress/decadence, us/them—and, in the clash of terrorisms, internal/external, civilian/non-civilian, native/foreigner, legitimate/illegitimate. Conrad's aesthetic engages the liminal, the trouble at the boundaries between these concepts, by inviting us into fictional worlds that confound assumed order. This aesthetic task's political and moral responsibilities lie not in endorsing a particular position but in comprehending, with compassion, what's at stake in imposing the borders.

II.

What we have witnessed is the greatest work of art there has ever been.
Karlheinz Stockhausen on the attack on WTC, September 11, 2001[3]
PENTAGON SCRAPS PLAN FOR BETTING ON TERROR STRIKES
Daily Telegraph, July 30, 2003

The World Trade Center attacks brought together in manifold ways spectacle and speculation, even as it buried the suffering human body. In almost all accounts of "9/11," much has been made of the phantasmagoric, cinematic quality of the event as "experienced" by those not immediately involved or physically present. Without our necessarily being fully conscious of it, the spectacular collapse had already been rehearsed in our imaginations in Hollywood scenarios. Just as the Greenwich Observatory represents for *The Secret Agent*'s Mr. Vladimir the closest target he can imagine to the (scientifically) pure Absolute "worthy" of attack, so the WTC's physical and symbolic centrality and mightiness, standing at the gateway to the world at "the end of history," apparently called to terrorists for a symbolic counter-blast. We now know they used for that counterblast what an advanced capitalist economy depends upon for its existence: the latest techniques of communication, ubiquity of efficient transportation, advanced technology, and availability of training—all gained in America. That is, the event of September 11, 2001 revealed the destructive symbiotic relationship between forms of advanced capitalist society, the forces of "civilized law and order," and terrorism. Nowhere is this nexus more apparent than in the recent Pentagon project, now abandoned, to establish an online futures market for betting on terrorist attacks, assassinations, coups, and other violent political crises. Its purpose was to flush out intelligence on potential attacks. At first stoutly defended, the idea was soon dropped by the Pentagon, political embarrassment, not ideological or material rethinking, winning the day. The abandoned project is nonetheless instructive for considering the systematic interrelation of the modern state (especially under globalized commodity capitalism) and its terrorist opponents. For it is symptomatic of certain structures of thought and military, political, and economic practice that embody the symbiosis between state power and "stateless" terrorism. The contradictions and paradoxes involved in this nexus are ones I want to examine as they illuminate and are illuminated by preoccupations Conrad pursued in his thinking about modern society and its discontents almost exactly 100 years ago.

Conrad would have received news of the Pentagon's stock market project, I suspect, with fascinated horror and profoundly ironic contempt—but not with complete surprise. This is not just because he once disastrously burned his fingers in futures speculations. Rather, the scheme combines motifs Conrad explored in his own cultural diagnosis of late nineteenth-century bourgeois society: the collision and collusion of business and violence (if not terror), and the dominance of new technologies, influencing all areas of industrial production, economics, information, and communications, with the attendant growth in the commodification of knowledge. Nor does Conrad hesitate to depict the amorality of those at the power centers and their exploitation of "material interests."

For his political critique we can turn briefly to *Nostromo*. Through the figure of arch-capitalist Holroyd, we have a sense of the acuity with which Conrad was already articulating what we now call "globalization," specifically a modernity under the aegis of U.S. domination. Analyzing a politics and history of imperial expansionism and failed revolutions, the novel pinpoints some of the crucial manifestations of this modernity. Conrad describes Holroyd as a "great personage" (79) with "the profile of a Caesar's head on an old Roman coin," an American with a parentage made up of half of Europe, and "the temperament of a Puritan and an insatiable imagination of conquest" (76). Expounding to Charles Gould his "vast conceptions of destiny" (78), Holroyd exudes forthright, if not lyrical, confidence:

> Now, what is Costaguana? It is the bottomless pit of 10 per cent loans and other fool investments. European capital had been flung into it with both hands for years. Not ours, though. We in this country [USA] know just about enough to keep indoors when it rains. We can sit and watch. Of course, some day we shall step in. We are bound to. But there's no hurry. Time itself has got to wait on the greatest country in the whole of God's universe. We shall be giving the word for everything; industry, trade, law, journalism, art, politics, and religion, from Cape Horn clear over to Smith's Sound, and beyond too, if anything worth taking hold of turns up at the North Pole. And then we shall have the leisure to take in hand the out-lying islands and continents of the earth. We shall run the world's business whether the world likes it or not. The world can't help it—and neither can we, I guess. (76–77)

It would be invidious to draw close comparison between Holroyd and any current world leaders, and, in a sense, wrong. For Conrad makes clear that Holroyd, a man of immense wealth, is not a politician but a businessman—a distinction, admittedly, more easily made then than now, when we consider the nearly absolute identification of the two in the current U.S. administration (and others). More important is the total penetration and global reach of the processes, institutions, and territories of which Conrad has Holroyd talk. It's a mistake to identify this penetration and reach with powerful individuals or even powerful states. Neither "the World" nor Holroyd can help it. Holroyd's "we" is generalized, unspecific; its very vagueness articulates the power of the processes, barely locatable and not reducible to individuals, of which he speaks. "Holroyd," one might say, is an immensely wealthy metonym. Conrad seems to say that human agency, intention, and interest *do* determine global politico-economic developments; but they cannot be reduced to James Bond-like world conspiracies, to an "axis of evil" (or "good"), easily comprehensible, tangible, and tractable.

In *Nostromo*, Conrad's narrator satirically comments on the unequivocal, unilateral politics of Holroyd's rhetoric, a rhetoric that steamrollers any alternative:

> By this he meant to express his faith in destiny in words suitable to his intelligence, which was unskilled in the presentation of general ideas. His intelligence was nourished on facts; and Charles Gould, whose imagination had been permanently affected by the one great fact of a silver mine, had no objection to this theory of the world's future. If it seemed distasteful for a moment it was because the sudden statement of such vast eventualities dwarfed almost to nothingness the actual matter in hand. (77)

Gould "had no objection"; he knows where power lies. For Holroyd, however, the mine is a "caprice." "He was not running a great enterprise. He was running a man," and he bluntly states that Gould and the San Tomé mine are completely dispensable. "A man may be thrown off .... You may rest assured that in a given case we shall know how to drop you in time" (81–82). Holroyd's "legitimate" power over Gould makes any kind of threat redundant; he needs only to "infuse an added grimness into his assurances." It is Emilia Gould (who, of course, as a woman does not count in this linguistic economy) who voices resistance to this globalizing power: "And do you believe that, Charley?" Mrs. Gould asked. "This seems to me most awful materialism, and ...." Gould brushes this off, disrupting her doubts in a reasonable tone: "My dear, it's nothing to me .... I make use of what I see. What's it to me whether his talk is the voice of destiny or simply a bit of clap-trap eloquence? There's a good deal of eloquence of one sort or another produced in both Americas" (82–83). Gould's "reasonable" compliance with Holroyd interrupts and suppresses the "interests" of his wife, who comes to realize quite how this "clap-trap" can, in its potent emptiness, empty out, like a wasting disease, the life from those who serve it. The Goulds' childless marriage can be read metaphorically as, among other things, symptomatic: The family line and its inherited interests are at an end. Politico-economic power has long since moved elsewhere. We can see in the world hegemony that Holroyd describes a *real* anarchy—at least as that label is popularly understood, but on a global scale. This force will arbitrarily exert its will, defying any sense of international law and disregarding the interests even of those it employs to achieve its ends. The "true anarchist," the one Conrad said he would like to "go for" if he had the talent, "is the millionaire," Holroyd (*Letters* 3:491).

Holroyd's paean to a particular version of modernity (its epitome, the envisaged capitalist Empire of the U.S.) embodies one of its most powerful and arguably most problematic forces: the drive to futurity and perfectibility. Its destined realization is monologic, homogeneous, and global. This form of modernity (by no means its only imaginable one) permits of no difference and asserts its own perfection. In this, it has structural parallels with Marxism and other post-Enlightenment radical social revolutionary movements, including, indeed, aspects of radical Islam: modernity's future perfect project.[4] Notwithstanding their ideological differences, all believe in and exploit the power of scientific technology and sophisticated communications to transform the human condition in the direction of their chosen utopias beyond the contemporary struggle between (their) good and evil. Their fundamentalist "faith" (to use Conrad's religious word) in the legitimacy, moral value, and destined inevitability of their monolithic future "justifies" the force they all exert, indeed the violence they all perpetrate, to achieve and sustain their ends.[5]

As we see from Holroyd's "dialogue" with Gould and will further explore in "An Anarchist," the forms of this force, or violence, the uninvited exercise of power by the stronger over the weaker, can vary. Hegemony is not always maintained by blatant physical or military force, of course. Indeed, the more embedded hegemony is in everyday political and cultural discourses, the less easily we can identify its structures or feel ourselves subservient to them. Derrida interrogates this embeddedness in his reflections on "9/11," deconstructing, as Conrad does, not abstract philosophical beliefs but the semantics of state power and its terrorist "antibody." "If one is not to trust blindly in the prevailing language, which remains most often subservient to the rhetoric of the media and to the banter of the political powers, we must be very careful using the term 'terrorism' and especially 'international terrorism'" (Borradori 102). How do we distinguish terror from fear or from keen anxiety? How do we distinguish between terror at a bomb going off, and fear that one might? Or, as Derrida asks, "How does a terror that is organized, provoked, and instrumentalized differ from that *fear* that an entire tradition, from Hobbes, to [Carl] Schmitt and even to Benjamin, holds to be the very condition of the authority of law and of the sovereign exercise of power, the very condition of the political and of the state?" (102). Derrida reminds us that the word *terrorism* is largely derived from the revolutionary terrorism of Robespierre and the Reign of Terror, which was carried out in the state's name and in fact presupposed its legal monopoly on violence. This might best be understood in terms offered by Walter Benjamin in his essay "Critique of Violence" ["Kritik der Gewalt"] (1921), to which Derrida also alludes. In this highly exacting essay, Benjamin offers an account of, indeed deconstructs, the conventional binary oppositions by which all states and their supporting institutions legitimate their monopoly on power. Helpful—but not logically crucial—to Benjamin's argument is the fact that *Gewalt* in German may be translated in English variously as "power," "force," "authority," "violence," "might," "control," "domination"— depending on the specific context and idiom. The dialectical relationship of law and violence (*Gewalt*) might in English be recognized in such idioms as "the force of law" or "to enforce the law." Benjamin's use of the word exposes the euphemisms through which authority's power is usually named and conceptualized (see Benjamin, *Reflections* 277–300).

Conrad would not have been surprised at the semantic, political, and conceptual minefield *Gewalt* evokes. His whole moral, linguistic, and political sensibility, not to mention his youthful experiences as an imperial subject, was thoroughly attuned to the politics of rhetoric and the rhetoric of politics, and the need for their linguistic deconstruction. Demagogic "eloquence"—almost an antonym to *le mot juste* and truth-telling in Conrad's dictionary—as well as brutal laws can terrorize or entrance listeners into subjection to any political order.

III.

These men could by no stretch of the imagination be called enemies. They were called criminals, and the outraged law, like the bursting shells, had come to them, an insoluble mystery from the sea.

Conrad, Heart of Darkness

That force (or violence) and fear are dual sources of legitimating power is made explicit in Conrad's short story "An Anarchist: A Desperate Tale," which also articulates the destructive symbiosis between this power and "anarchism" and terror, ostensibly its antagonistic Other. The story presents a triangulation of figures roughly reducible to capital, enslaved labor, and culture, in a relationship of asymmetrical power: Harry Gee, the ranch manager of a world-renowned meat-extract company, B.O.S., the brutally dutiful agent of international capitalism; Paul, a working-class artisan, now a prison escapee and forced-laborer; and the unnamed narrator, a butterfly collector and observing bystander. The story's setting, a remote South American ranch, is both "a sort of penal settlement for condemned cattle" and "the only known habitat of an extremely rare and gorgeous butterfly" (*SS* 137). This ironic juxtaposition of brutality and beauty brings into an uncomfortable liaison (both real and symbolic) exploitative capital, the raw material of its profits (cattle and the condemned engineer Paul), and cultural, quasi-artistic sensibility. Although the narrator considers himself independent—almost an outsider, almost an aesthete, for "I traveled at that time, but strictly for myself" (137)—his butterfly collecting depends on the manager's good offices for (overcharged) accommodation. He prefaces his tale with a lively criticism of capitalism: i.e., a bitingly satirical account of the company, its barely quaffable product, and more precisely its discursive global presence embodied in its worldwide advertising program. He justifies this prelude as demonstrating to the reader his general lack of gullibility and thus the veracity of what he is about to relate, Paul's story. But the witty sarcasm vented against B.O.S. and its advertising reflects, one confidently feels, Conrad's political perceptions more than the narrator's. Moreover, as thought rather than speech, the viewpoint implied cannot be easily, openly stated within that fictional world. This "suppressed" prelude gives way to the narrator's account of meeting Gee, the bullying, brutish manager of the ranch, who in turn introduces him to Paul, whom Gee calls variously "Crocodile" and "the anarchist from Barcelona," the engineer who maintains the estate's steam launch. Paul's pathetic history is one of unremitting exploitation, after unjust and unwarrantedly harsh imprisonment first in France, then in French Guyana, for "anarchist" sloganeering, and then for involvement in a mismanaged robbery with his disloyal "anarchist" *compagnons*. The butterfly collector hears all this sympathetically and ineffectually passes on, leaving us with Paul's less-than-incisive "principal truth … that a little thing may bring about the undoing of a man" (144).

The tale offers several versions of coerced silence. In the triangulation of power, both the narrator (the voice of culture, of sorts) and, more extremely, Paul (dumb and criminalized labor) are marginalized and muted by the real and metaphorical volubility and authority of capital's local agent, Gee. The narrator is unable or unwilling to voice disagreement after the manager's diatribe against anarchists, workers, or indeed anybody who would "[do] away with all law and order in the world" (144). Assumed by the manager to be "one of us," that is, "decent, respectable hard-working people," the narrator can only complicitly answer, or rather mumble, "that doubtless there was much subtle truth in [the manager's] view" (144), a sentiment significantly rendered in indirect speech. Such coerced silence is also a condition suffered by Paul, "the anarchist," by virtue of his having been construed and named as such by others. Inebriated speech, "*Vive l'anarchie! Death to the capitalists*" (147), first landed him in jail in Paris, with some help from the "magnificent" eloquence of his self-serving upwardly mobile socialist defense lawyer. Now he is effectively imprisoned on the B.O.S. estate and working for slave wages because he has been sentenced, literally and metaphorically, by a speech act, a performative utterance, on the manager's part. Gee names Paul "the anarchist from Barcelona," and that name justifies any violence toward him, as the narrator discovers to his (unspoken) shock:

"Is he really an anarchist?" I asked, when out of earshot.
"I don't give a hang what he is," answered the humorous official of the B.O.S. Co.
"I gave him the name because it suited me to label him in that way. It's good for the company."
"For the company!" I exclaimed, stopping short. (139–140)

> Over the jocular addition of "de Barcelona" Mr Harry Gee chuckled with immense satisfaction. "That breed is particularly murderous, isn't it? It makes the sawmills crowd still more afraid of having anything to do with him—see?" he exulted, candidly. "I hold him by that name better than if I had him chained by the leg to the deck of the steam-launch." (143)

Alongside his physical threats to Paul (trampling him underfoot with his horse or letting his cattle do so), Gee monopolizes discursive power, the underside of that equally mendacious and illusory rhetoric of the advertisement. Both exploit uninvestigated general desire or fear in the interests of capital. To misquote Hamlet slightly, "There is nothing either good or bad, but naming makes it so" (2.2.259). Like the floating symptom of fear that it generates, the word *anarchist* is a floating signifier, appropriable by the law (in Paris) or the dominant economic system's agents and media, to apply to whomsoever it will. Those so named are forcibly held in control.

Conrad makes clear in Paul's story that whatever barely articulate resistance to this linguistic and physical domination he makes is a reaction to, not a cause of, the "legitimated" use of force. Says Gee of the "anarchist": "he does not deny it. I am not wronging him in any way. He is a convict of some sort, anyhow" (143). The nearest Paul comes to anything like resistance, embodied in a double negation, is in the non-denial of a denial, his repeated and desperate mantra, "I deny nothing, nothing, nothing!"; "I deny nothing. It is no good denying anything" (139, 142). In negating normal grammatical rules of affirmation or denial, Paul's "statement" is a sort of pathetic refusal to play Gee's language game; but he remains enslaved within the linguistic "order" and economic "reality" Gee represents.

IV.

"An Anarchist," like its partner "anarchist" story, "The Informer," is only very superficially, I think, a discussion about anarchism in a systematically philosophical sense. Both stories, rather like *The Secret Agent*, are studies of the political, social, and psychological reactions of those living in the ambit of so-called anarchism.[6] That we have in Conrad's stories no dramatized acts of violent terrorism or anarchy but, at most, representations of them from others—acts displaced, that is, by the secondary act of narration—implies that the action Conrad is interested in is reaction, reflection, interpretation. *The Secret Agent*'s use of an ironic narrator and the implicit authorial irony of the other tales creates for Conrad (and his "discriminating reader") a grounded distance from the internal perspectives of the characters inhabiting the fictional worlds, an autonomous aesthetic counter-space from which we can try to perceive truths that are not spoken, but shown.

As for Conrad's aims, there is a studied unhelpfulness about his "Author's Note" (1920) to *A Set of Six*. Getting one title wrong he says:

> Of The Informer and The Anarchist I will say next to nothing. The pedigree of these tales is hopelessly complicated and not worth disentangling at this distance of time. I found them and here they are. The discriminating reader will guess that I have found them within my mind; but how they or their elements came in there I have forgotten for the most part; and for the rest I really don't see why I should give myself away more than I have done already. (vii–viii)

Refusing to divulge his sources, Conrad with blustering evasion casts himself in a clandestine role. The same has been said of the "Author's Note" to *The Secret Agent* (Berthoud, *Secret Agent* 100–103). There is textual evidence in "The Informer," and the other two "anarchist" works, that Conrad knew much more about anarchist affairs than he let on; and by disingenuously saying of the *Six* that "they are not studies—they touch no problem" (*Letters* 4: 300), Conrad covers his artistic tracks to expose those of the deeply dissembling and self-deluding characters in his fictions.

"The Informer" abounds in category confusions and transgressions: social positions; assumed ideological allegiances; emotional convictions; play-acting; and, at the level of plot, a play-within-the-story. It's a tale of a double double-crossing; betrayal and deception are crucial motifs, of course, but one must ask who is transgressing whose trust in this Chinese-boxes of a story. Information is provided narratively by three connoisseurs, all of whom know less than they think they do: two minor ones, the framing narrator ("I") who collects porcelain, and his unnamed Parisian friend, a collector of interesting people; and the main narrator of the story within the story, Mr. X, a connoisseur anarchist. In this looking-glass war of allegiances and floating identities, Comrade Sevrin (the traitor and informer in Mr. X's narrative) is a would-be anarchist convicted as a crypto-bourgeois on whom the other anarchists can take "legitimate vengeance" (99). He is fascinated by the bourgeois Lady Amateur of Anarchism, who indulges her bourgeois taste and upper-class fascination for those who would abolish the bourgeoisie. Their aristocratic leader, Mr. X, earns from his bourgeois readership a healthy living with his "venomous pen," writing pamphlets demolishing the bourgeoisie. He shares with the first-person narrator, who is otherwise aghast at "this [polished] monster" (76), a connoisseur's passion for "monstrously precious" Chinese bronzes and porcelain—not the least vulnerable of art objects when anarchist bombs go off. (These objects themselves, we may surmise with Benjamin, have their own violent pedigree as cultural spoils carried off by history's victors [*Illuminations* 256].) The interpenetration of identities and conflicting values moves well beyond a question of disguises and mistaken identity, notwithstanding the almost comedic structure of the ironies Conrad elaborates.

"The Informer" may be seen as an early sortie into the terrain of bourgeois–anarchist–artist relations more seriously developed in *The Secret Agent*. There, Conrad employs (as his Author's Note states) an ironic tone to capture the near-absurdity of the symbiosis between the state and its opponents, a symbiosis that occludes real human suffering. An anti-statist act is (planned but not successfully) carried out, sponsored by a (foreign autocratic) state, to subvert "anarchist" subversion. The home state's legal agents are effective insofar as they work largely outside the law and in secrecy, to protect their personal interests, positions, and anarchist connections, all in the name of the maintenance of legal civil society. Covert anarchic acts and illegality are shown being exploited to pacify a fearful and outraged society, to maintain order. At the still moral center of this churning world lie the remnants of innocence, Stevie.

Derrida's model of an auto-immune process to describe what I have called the destructive symbiosis of capitalist order and its subversive other stresses precisely the internality of the "antibody." That which represents the (force of) law is seen as an object of aggression, threatened by that which comes as if from its inside, trained within its own house to destroy it.[7] This is embodied almost allegorically in "The Informer," in the Hermione Street building in which the anarchists are secretly housed. In what at first appears to be a bizarre parody of capitalism's division of labor is a description of activities in the house, floor by floor. In the cellars are the workers, anarchist printers ("propagandists by the word") and others tunneling through to their next bombing target ("propagandists by the deed"). On the first floor is an Italian restaurant (representing consumption); on the second, a music-hall theater agency run by a certain "Bomm" (mass culture); on the top floor, a small grocery business set up as a cover for an anarchist chemistry lab. We might read this as an allegorical abbreviation of the complex cultural political relations between the "above-ground" legitimate production and consumer practices and its underground, the whole being (unwittingly) funded by a "distinguished government official." With characteristic black humor, Conrad conjoins capitalist over-production and advertising with the tools of their destruction, as the anarchist Professor uses the remaindered stock of highly advertised tinned soup as packaging for his explosive devices.

One aesthetic device has, however, been burning on a slow fuse from the outset, as the reader becomes aware. By multiplying narrators but privileging Mr. X's anarchist perspective and judgments, Conrad effectively positions the reader to accept the transgressive and "criminal" as normative and the bourgeois norm as contemptible. Conversely, the first-person narrator—reduced to the story's margins—offers by turns only exclamations of outrage, fascination, bewilderment, and complacency. He provides nothing like an intellectually more stable alternative perspective. As a result, words like "genuine," "sincere," "legitimate," "fanatic," "real," "high-minded," and "conviction" get disturbingly re-appropriated in the cause of "criminality." We thus have, if not a transvaluation of values, at least a transgressive probing of them.

The explosion of appearances this involves exploits an aesthetics of performance, Mr. X's play-within-the-tale: gestures to betray real and false gestures, performance to expose performance. Besides Sevrin, the betrayer betrayed, the target object of this troubling aesthetic is the Lady Shamateur of Anarchism: "She had acquired all the appropriate gestures of revolutionary convictions—the gestures of pity, of anger, of indignation against the anti-humanitarian vices of the social class to which she belonged herself" (81).

She wears her convictions as she wears her other costumes; she is a representative of "an idle and selfish class [which] loves to see mischief being made, even if it is made at its own expense" (78). From Mr. X's viewpoint, she is one of Conrad's "sham revolutionaries." But gestures and theatricality are not synonymous. Recalling that it is by a *coup de théâtre* that Sevrin is exposed—he does not see through "the game" as Mr. X at one point suspects—we should not too quickly assume that theater or acting *as such* is being condemned. The idea of sincerity in symbolic theatrical performance is quite other than the "play-acting" of the shams who are unconscious of their mimicry. Theirs are the signs of "the amateurs of emotion" perpetrated by the indolent classes. "Its own life being all a matter of pose and gesture, it is unable to realize the power and danger of a real movement and of words that have no sham meaning" (78). What is suggested here is a performative aesthetics that could almost have come from "A Glance at Two Books," an essay in which Conrad criticizes the (generalized) English novelist for his easy emotions and his failure to regard his work—the exercise of his Art—as an "achievement of active life by which he will produce certain definite effects upon the emotions of his readers .... It never occurs to him that a book is a deed, that the writing of it is an enterprise as much as the conquest of a colony" (*LE* 132).

For Conrad, "books are deeds," symbolic actions as potent as political ones. Zdzisław Najder attributes this view to Polish Romantic writers (*Chronicle* 297). But another source for the cultural–political analogy lies just across the Channel, in the links between the modernist avant-garde and anarchist thinking. Seeking to annihilate the prevailing order of significance, but at a literary not a physical level, by word rather than by dynamite, many artists saw an expressive link between bombs and books. Stéphane Mallarmé commented after the Vaillant bombing, "I know of no other bomb but a book," and said of his friend, Felix Fénéon, prolific writer, artist, dandy, and avowed anarchist, tried (and acquitted) for allegedly possessing detonators: "Certainly, there were not any better detonators for Fénéon than his articles. And I do not think that one can use a more effective weapon than literature" (qtd. in Lewis 78).

With his deep familiarity with French culture of the period, Conrad could not have been unaware of the most important literary cultural movement of the day, nor of the notorious trials of leading anarchists and writers in the 1890s. Both Fénéon and Tailhade may have lent their outrageous wit and dandy radicalism to Conrad's imagining of Mr. X, just as he borrowed the bomber Ravachol's devoted assistant, one Simon called Biscuit, for "An Anarchist." These links are interesting, not as models or influences, but as markers of a shared undercurrent of feeling, something like a family resemblance. Appropriating the language of violent gestures to describe their own work, the artistic avant-garde declare a functional similarity between the bomb and the work of art, though they believed that the poem could be more efficacious in jolting consciousness into creative lucidity. Mallarmé saw writing, like all serious art, as performative; the right word is a deed, "the presentation, as an explosive, of a very pure concept to society" (qtd. in Lewis 78). Reminding us of another Stevie seeking social justice, for Mallarmé literary works are constantly compared to fireworks—but more lasting. Art, the product of artifice, fiction, and fashioning, may explode into startling light and make one see.

These tropes occur in a letter to Edward Garnett when Conrad describes the effect of his words:

> Where do you think the illumination—the short and vivid flash of which I have been boasting to you came from? Why! from your words, words, words. They exploded like stored powder barrels—while another man's words would have fizzled out in speaking and left darkness unrelieved by a forgotten spurt of futile sparks. An explosion is the most lasting thing in the universe. It leaves disorder, remembrance, room to move, a clear space. Ask your Nihilist friends. (*Letters* 1: 344)

Writing to his French translator, Davray, Conrad insists that his novelistic aims lie less in the content than in the effect of style. "That is always my object. That's why I am so much an English writer who lends himself so little to translation. [Kipling's] interest is in the *subject*: the interest of my work is in the *effect* it produces. He talks about *his compatriots*. I write *for them*" (*Letters* 4: 29). While Flaubert was Conrad's declared master, Conrad could not have been unaware of Mallarmé's declaration some 40 years earlier of his need to invent a new poetic language, whereby the poet painted "not the thing but the effect it produces." This idea of language as explosive helps to explain the disturbing congruence of some of Conrad's statements with those of *The Secret Agent*'s Professor. The Professor declares, "Give me madness and despair and I will move the world," and Conrad famously says in *A Personal Record*: "You cannot fail to see the power of mere words; such words as Glory, for instance, or Pity .... Give me the right word and the right accent and I will move the world" (xi).

Does this affinity between anarchist explosions and an "effective" aesthetics imply that Conrad sees Mr. X, like the Professor, as a "respectable" extremist? Does the scathing critique of bourgeois sham, which Mr. X provides in a privileged narrative account, imply that Mr. X carries the writer's authority? Or do we, as law-abiding, bourgeois, sensitive readers, share the "I" narrator's horrified fear of a secret sharing, along with a deep repugnance for Mr. X's callously detached vision in this "Ironic Tale"?

> This monster was polished—in a sense even exquisite. He was alive and European. He had the manner of good society, wore a coat and hat like mine, and had pretty near the same taste in cooking. It was too frightful to think of. (76)

Mr. X figures for the narrator as an abominable travesty of class allegiance. He makes real the fear of an "underground life," vital and dynamic beneath the veneer of respectability, an energy that, like the repressed, is never defeated and will always return to threaten the very fabric of rational social bourgeois existence. Conrad uses the narrator, like the teacher of languages in *Under Western Eyes*, to ventilate quintessentially English bourgeois shock at these transgressions of social and artistic category. Conversely, the European Mr. X uses the word "amateur"—that quintessential component of the self-image of the English national identity—as a mildly satiric term, equivalent to "sham." The narrator finds this an abomination. But in so doing, he registers a distinctly English form of political and psychological self-image and anxiety, unable to imagine that the educated élite *could* be revolutionary. But in continental Europe—the Poland of Apollo Korzeniowski seeking national liberation; Russia under the Tsars; or the France of the defeated Paris Commune and its corrupt aftermath, the increasingly oppressive Third Republic—opposition to the prevailing political and social order often brought together (across class and ostensible political lines) groups that, in the eyes of the middle- and upper-class English, made very curious bedfellows. Sympathies and alignments transgressed "proper" categories. The anti-establishment individualism inherent in anarchist thinking found friends and forged alignments in other seemingly disparate quarters of the déclassé, the intelligentsia, and the artistic avant garde. My view is that Conrad's political sensitivity made him alert to these transgressive alliances and that he found it artistically challenging to test them out, to "make the reader see" them.

Perhaps Conrad himself did not wish (unlike some of his commentators) to drive to moral conclusions, position himself, as it were, by defining how close or distant he "was" from Mr. X. Writing to Davray about the forthcoming French collection of *A Set of Six*, Conrad explains that "in order to alert the reader to the book's *artistic* intention," the tales will appear with subtitles. "This offers the *tone* of each tale." He calls "The Informer" ["*Le Traître*"] "A Cynical Tale."[8] Conrad's hovering between "cynical" and "ironic" perfectly conjures the liminality that the work of art can embody and hold in suspension. Conrad insisted on art's autonomy, at least in the sense that its aim should not lie "in the clear logic of a triumphant conclusion" (*NIN* xi). Rather, "Art for me *is* an end in itself. Conclusions are not for it" (*Letters* 5: 237). "The only legitimate basis of creative work lies in the courageous recognition of all the irreconcilable antagonisms that make our life so enigmatic, so burdensome, so fascinating—so full of hope" (*Letters* 2: 349). This "hope" is not the monocular "absolute optimism" that engenders the fundamentalism, the fanaticism of political or religious self-right(eous)ness. These irreconcilable antagonisms, these "many cruel and absurd contradictions," led Conrad "to suspect that the aim of creation cannot be ethical at all. I would fondly believe that its object is purely spectacular: a spectacle for awe, love, adoration or hate, if you like, but ... never for despair! Those visions, delicious or poignant, are a moral end in themselves. The rest is our affair—laughter, the tears, the tenderness, the indignation, the high tranquility of a steeled heart, the detached curiosity of a subtle mind—that's our affair" (*PR* 92).

Is "the steeled heart" and "the high tranquility," with which Conrad then leaves us our affair in deciding how we may look on this "sublime spectacle" of wonder and haunting terror—is this steely tranquility the modality of a cynical or an ironic sensibility? Cynicism implies an aloof indifference to the absence of hope for things to be otherwise; irony, the disinterested, skeptical but compassionate comprehending of things so that they might be. For an antipolitical political ironist like Conrad, the morality of a work of art does not consist in the self-satisfaction of taking sides, of showing commitment to a particular ideological position. Rather, it lies in irony's doubled aesthetic effect, destructive and constructive at once, of offering binocular vision, of holding contradictions in suspension, resolutely defending the no-man's land from both sides.

Notes

1. For general histories of anarchism, see Sonn, *Anarchism*, and Woodcock. As they observe, many anarchists were appalled by indiscriminate, physically violent means of political action, both because of the suffering involved and because this meant adopting, with asymmetrical capability, precisely the repressive means the state used to enforce its own domination.

2. That the experiences of "9/11" have been universally mediated and accepted in this reduced formulation has organized human suffering virtually into its own disappearance. Suffering has disappeared, that is, in direct proportion to "it" being endlessly rehearsed, compulsively replayed with all the ubiquity and image-making power of the communications media, spoken about, analyzed and explained by myriad experts. "Since 9/11" is a coded phrase evoked by policy-makers, stock-marketeers, arms manufacturers, cultural commentators, and many, many others, who decode it to suit their own purposes. Ironically, the manipulation and commodification of "9/11" has reproduced what the twin towers already were: a symbolic spectacle. In that sense, the act's perpetrators, supremely mastering the technology, communications, and world financial systems epitomizing U.S. superiority, have achieved through media-saturation precisely the symbolic ubiquity they sought with their "propaganda by deed." They share with their deadly enemies the common purpose of publicity and the power it bestows.

3. As widely reported in the German press, though the actual words spoken and their context was later disputed (Virillio 45).

4. For persuasive arguments locating radical Islam within the context of (not as "medieval" counter to) modernity, see Gray, *Al Qaeda*, and Kermani.

5. A more philosophically inclined friend of latter-day Holroyd, Francis Fukuyama, offers theologico-economic sustenance to Holroyd's "theory of the world's future." In 1992, following the collapse of the Soviet Marxist project, Fukuyama confidently declared that the future had arrived in its "liberal democratic," "free market," U.S. capitalist form—and with it, "the end of history." Fukuyama's premature claim about this "end" is not, a decade later, without its ironies: "The universal and homogeneous state that appears at the end of history can thus be seen as resting on the twin pillars [sic] of economics and recognition" (204).

9

Reading *The Secret Agent* Now: The Press, the Police, the Premonition of Simulation

PETER LANCELOT MALLIOS

"Ah, the perils of relevance!" writes Judith Shulevitz in the September 27, 2001 issue of *Slate* magazine. "In the aftermath of the attacks of September 11, Joseph Conrad's *The Secret Agent* became one of the three works of literature most frequently cited in the American media." Such has held true well beyond that time and the specific province of U.S. mass media. During the past three years, *The Secret Agent* has been referenced over a hundred times in newspapers, magazines, and online journalistic resources across the world—from Australia, Ireland, and Canada to Indonesia, Chile, and California. Its venues of discussion include *The Times* (London), the *New York Times, Time Out, Newsweek, The National Review* (U.S.), the *Toronto Star*, the *Sydney Morning Herald*, the *Belfast News Letter*, the *Manchester Weekly Guardian*, the *Ottawa Citizen*, the *Vancouver Sun*, the *Washington Post*, the *LA Weekly*, the *San Francisco Chronicle*, and the *Gazette* (Montreal).[1] Its commentators range from George Will, Joan Didion, Terry Eagleton, Paul Theroux, and Harold Bloom, to writer Anne Marlowe, comedian and film star Robin Williams, editorialist and U.S. foreign policy adviser Robert Kaplan, former senior CIA analyst Melvin Goodman, and professors of Health Law and Human Rights at the Australian National University and European Thought at the London School of Economics. It has led some to consider Conrad "a literary Nostrodamus" (Shulevitz), and another to describe Conrad as "the first great novelist of the 21st century" (Gray "NS Essay").

Such are the good fortunes of a novel—serendipitously published on the eve of September 11, 1907, no less—whose plot to bomb the Greenwich Observatory and "terroristic" cast of characters have offered themselves so suggestively to the post-World Trade Center global imaginary. Yet this essay argues that it is less any materiality of terror *per se* just than the very kind of media phenomenon just charted out—in which a "Conrad" becomes produced to explain, contain, and administer threats largely produced by the media as well—that is the true mark of the novel's contemporaneity. Elsewhere, I have argued that the production of Conrad as a prophet in today's news media is significantly a *simulated* phenomenon—both in the conventional sense, that it is frequently unclear whether a genuine interpretive act, as opposed to the empty pretense of reading, is happening in these articles, and in Jean Baudrillard's larger sense of the term, whereby "*The Secret Agent*" that emerges in these articles is largely an artificial phenomenon whose only genetic referent consists of the media procedures and political hysteria of the present moment (see Mallios, "Desert of Conrad"). At the close of that essay, I suggested that *The Secret Agent* forecasts its own fate in this respect; in this essay, I seek to restore the context and the field of textual issues that have their culmination in that claim. My subject is the central but underdiscussed phenomenon of newspapers in the novel,[2] which I discuss first in light of the distinctive political and disciplinary emphases of the British press throughout the nineteenth century, and then in light of commercial developments at the turn of the twentieth century that consolidate a stylistics of "information" and a power of "simulation" that are still with us today. Indeed, the historical hunch that lurks behind this essay, informed by the several press histories cited within it, is that *The Secret Agent*'s special "contemporary" feel for us today derives from its singular responsiveness to material confluences and developments in the British press and mass media in Conrad's time that continue to structure those institutions in our own. But this alone does not determine how the story is told, which historical factors and periods are made to count most, which theorists and critical discourses are conceived as most illuminating, and which Conrad texts are most closely read and how—the quandary of the "contemporary" that lends this essay its contrapuntal relation to other engagements with the politics of the mass-disseminated sign in this volume.

I.

Newspapers fill *The Secret Agent*. In the opening scene, the Verlocs' shop window is presented containing "a few apparently old copies of obscure newspapers, badly printed, with titles like *The Torch*, *The Gong*—rousing titles" (3)—while the window itself, in its discontinuous and distracting aggregation of attention-arousing items, is structured like a newspaper. When Verloc arrives at the Foreign Embassy, he encounters in rapid succession a doorman, who "glanced up from the newspaper he was holding with both hands before his calm and severe face" (15); Privy Councillor Wurmt, who enters "holding a batch of papers before his eyes" and is subsequently identified as "a man of papers" (16, 17); and Mr. Vladimir, who, in the extensive interview that follows, makes much of how "every newspaper has ready-made phrases to explain [threatening] manifestations away" (32), and hatches a plan that will have people "writing to the papers" and also "defy the ingenuity of journalists" (34). At one point, Vladimir asks of Verloc's "ostensible business," to which the secret agent simply replies, "Stationery, newspapers" (36); at another, Verloc reminds the

First Secretary of his "habit of reading the daily papers" (26), a remark later echoed by other characters in the novel (145, 271). Like Vladimir but to different ends, the Professor despises newspapers: he chides (at least in the Dent edition) Ossipon for doing nothing but "talk print" (73), and for him the cruelest insult is the charge that one "thinks [as] independently as any respectable journalist or grocer" (68). Ossipon, on the other hand, nearly incarnates the myriad press forms that perpetually surround him. Not only is he "the principal writer of the F.P. leaflets" (44), the author of other "cheap pamphlets" and "literary propaganda" of a vaguely medical and revolutionist nature (46), and "in touch with a few reporters on the big dailies" (78); he is also the novel's principal vehicle for conveying to the reader and other characters what gets reported in the papers—which he is invariably carrying with him or in earshot of, and which, in the form of the clipping concerning Winnie's suicide at the novel's end, seem to comprehend and determine his existence.

Stevie is also a "man of papers." As Peter Nohrnberg has recently argued, Stevie is introduced by the novel both *as* a reader and as a member of a new historical reading class that emerged from the Reform Bill of 1867 and the Education Bill of 1870: the origins of "our excellent compulsory system of education [in which Stevie] had learned to read" (*SA* 8; Nohrnberg 52). This scene is also one that includes a sketch of Stevie's misadventures as a young errand boy—jostled about by the various disconnected spectacles of the urban roadside—which might be said to inscribe an allegory of mass newspaper reading: an episode, in any event, whose shocked and hysterical reaction on Stevie's part directly prefigures his violent and credulous newspaper-reading habits as an adult. As Winnie complains a bit later in the novel: "He's always taking those newspapers from the window to read. He gets a red face poring over them . . . . I had to take the carving knife from the boy . . . . He was shouting and stamping and sobbing" (60). Yet Stevie, as Nohrnberg splendidly points out, ultimately proves a consummate figure not only of a certain kind of newspaper reader but of the modern newspaper itself. His exploded body—"a heap of mixed things, which seemed to have been collected in shambles and *rag* shops" (*SA* 87, emphasis added)—forms a "palimpsest-image" with the other bits of "newspaper 'rag'" in the novel (Nohrnberg 55). It is, hence, fitting that Chief Inspector Heat, the principal investigator of Stevie's body, is also a man of great insight when it comes to the papers, which he shrewdly manipulates and in which his name is "printed sometimes" (101). Likewise, the assistant commissioner, despite having less patience for newspapers than he does for either Heat or the bureaucratic "litter of papers" heaped on his desk (116), is profoundly sensitive to "the near presence of that strange emotional phenomenon called public opinion [that] weighed upon his spirits" (99), and plays whist with the "gloomily humorous editor of a celebrated magazine" (102). So too Michaelis, the ticket-of-leave apostle who "never reads the newspapers" (302), has his entire fate—from his original jail sentence to the possibility of his release to the possibility, at the hands of Heat, of his re-imprisonment—overwhelmingly determined by newspapers. And even Winnie, despite significant insulation from the papers—"The newsboys never invaded Brett Street" (204)—and a trauma that would seem to blast her free of the very conventionality the novel sardonically associates with "the beauties of . . . journalistic style" (307), has her "torn" "personality" figured as a ripped newspaper (254, 210–212), and finds her final hours haunted by phrases of the gallows that come straight from the press (268).

The ubiquity of these references to the papers suggests they add something more than a mere "motif" in the novel (Berthoud, "*Secret Agent*", 119); something more, indeed, on the order of a vital ground and *terra mirabila* from which the novel extends—a set of generative conditions both inside and outside the novel that occasions its unusual interest in the ideological and genetic power of signs, as if in challenge to both sides of the Professor's easy assertion that "the condemned social order has not been built up by paper and ink, and I don't fancy a combination of paper and ink will ever put an end to it" (70). How, though, does one account for this power of the "peremptory letter" (28) in *The Secret Agent*?

One way is to recall the distinctly political character of the British press throughout the nineteenth century, and to consider *The Secret Agent*'s topography of papers as not only marked by this legacy of politicality, but also crafted in terms commensurate with James Curran's more recent historical account of the modern British press as an evolving "agency of social control" (51).[3] Such an approach would take seriously the claim in Conrad's dedication that the novel is, in an important respect, a "tale of the XIX century" (xxix), bridging its historical developments with the twentieth century and allowing the twenty-first century to look all the way back to nineteenth-century beginnings to locate the novel's contemporaneity. Prior to the repeal of the economic press controls that Richard Cobden denounced as "taxes on knowledge"—i.e., the advertisements duty in 1853; the stamp duty in 1855; and the paper duty in 1861—the structure of the British press in the nineteenth century was directly determined by the government, and in explicitly political terms. Apropos of Lord Castlereagh's concern that "persons exercising the power of the press be men of respectability and power" (xci), the Six Acts of 1819, inaugurating the duties and other press controls, were passed with the express aims of curtailing an incipient "pauper press" and pricing newspapers generally beyond the reach of the growing urban working classes, especially their artisanal elements (Hollis 26–28). The establishment's fear was that through newspapers, especially organs of their own, working people would acquire the education, political and economic self-awareness as a class, and initiative and infrastructure to press for "radical" reforms like franchise extension, labor rights, and the general elimination of arbitrary aristocratic and bourgeois privilege (Hollis vii; Koss 1: 32–34). This, in fact, was very much what happened, for in the void left by the government's heavy-handed attempt to police the disenfranchised by economic exclusion, there quickly emerged, in the 1820s and 1830s, a vibrant, wide-circulating, and pointedly illegal "Unstamped" press that addressed workers in precisely the aggressive class terms conservatives feared the most. This Unstamped press—often vilified under the name of "anarchy,"[4] and featuring titles (rousing titles) like *Black Dwarf, Slap at the Church*, the *Destructive*, and *Poor Man's Guardian*—was a crucial forebear of what Deian Hopkin calls the "climacteric in the history of socialist journalism" witnessed in Conrad's time: i.e., the explosion of nearly 800 labor-identified papers, half of them explicitly socialist, and 25 anarchist papers published between 1890 and 1910 (294).

Yet the Unstamped itself was essentially crushed in 1836 through a strategic reduction of the stamp duty from 4d. to 1d., an event that reveals much about the true political assumptions behind the "free press" cause—and also the meaning of "papers" as they would come to signify in *The Secret Agent*. For, like those middle-class liberals of the 1850s who, with Cobden and John Bright, successfully defeated the "taxes on knowledge" altogether, the bourgeois libertarians of an earlier generation were by no means invested in the autonomy, mobilization, and free expressive rights of the working classes. Rather, in accord with their conservative counterparts, they were principally concerned "to ensure that the press provided institutional support for the social order" (Curran 61); only given that state controls weren't working, and given, indeed, that not only political power but also a large market of potential readers were being ceded to the radical Unstamped for no good reason, reform proponents emphasized that there was no mechanism more powerful than a free and cheap universal press to "instruct" and effectively indoctrinate the working classes in the values of orderliness, economy, and sobriety appropriate to the smooth operation of bourgeois economy (Hollis 11; Curran 57–58). As Edward Bulwer-Lytton, blending the causes of free press and state control, put the matter in 1832: "Is it not time to consider whether the printer and his types may not provide better for the peace and honour of the free state than the gaoler or the hangman? Whether ... cheap knowledge may not be a better political agent than costly punishment?" (qtd. in Stephens 207). Indeed, far from facilitating resistance and dissent, "the cause of a free market press was synonymous with the suppression of trade unionism: *the dream for which [the reformers] fought was an unfettered capitalist press that would police the capitalist system*" (Curran 56, emphasis added). This is not to say that, from Bentham to John Mill to John Stuart Mill to Cobden and John Bright, all the grand ideas in support of a free press—"freedom of expression," "marketplace of ideas," "public opinion," "fourth estate"—were offered disingenuously; but it is to say, in a logic that is essential to both *Nostromo* and the *de facto* police officer who is Nostromo, that such ideas became compelling, convincing, practicable, and dominant precisely insofar as they accommodated the monitoring functions of the capitalized social order.[5]

Let us notice, but bracket for the moment, *The Secret Agent*'s manifest recognition of newspapers both as a "political agent" and one existing in relation to other efforts to "police" and "protect" (Verloc's mantra; *SA* 12) the social order—so as to bring this brief sketch of the politicality of the British press up to date with Conrad's novel. Two factors are of crucial importance here. First, far from liberating or eradicating the essentially political nature of the British press, the repeal of the "taxes on knowledge" had the immediate effect of imbricating the press—and its increasingly colossal powers to mold public opinion—even more firmly within the sectarian operations of government. For though Cobden's victory did engender, as Stephen Koss explains, a "new forum for national debate by according newspapers a vastly enlarged readership and, consequently, an enhanced potential for political influence" (1:1), the fact was that "the natural position of the nineteenth-century political press was being part of the political machine" (Boyce 26); and the next 40 years witnessed the evolution of a profound symbiosis of press and politics, such that institutionally, tactically, personally, and semantically, it was generally very difficult to draw the line between the two (see Koss 2: 3-9, 1: 115-17; *passim*).

At the same time the press was being discovered as such a vital political instrumentation of engaging, administering, and manipulating public opinion on matters foreign and domestic, it was also accruing further dimensions of power as an agency of social control as a function of its fundamentally bourgeois and capitalist coordinates. For the "free" press always meant the capitalization and industrialization of the press: the transfer of its control over time into the hands of a few wealthy entrepreneurs (Curran 69); the aggressive marginalization and dilution of "radical" voices (Curran 71); and the invention, beginning in the 1880s and 1890s, of a new commercial journalistic aesthetic that would revolutionize the institution and, in the opinion of most historiographers, ultimately divorce the British press from its political roots (Koss 1: 1–15; A. Williams 143–183). The political aesthetics of this "new journalism" will be discussed shortly, but what is important to note here is that far from detracting from "the height of . . . prestige and power" that the British newspaper reached between 1880 and 1918 (Boyce 27), the growing commercialization of the press significantly enhanced its social and political force (Koss 2: 3–13). Indeed, very much in the manner of the subtle understanding of "propaganda" that Mark Wollaeger elaborates in his essay in this volume, but less, in my view, as a specifically "modernist" development than as an extension of a bourgeois administrative logic that had been unfolding since the beginning of the nineteenth century, the commercialization of the press, which affected all newspapers to some degree, dramatically expanded not only the base of readers reached by the press but the range and dimension of human issues (sports, amusements, beauty, personal advice, etc.) over which normalizing, authoritarian social control could be exerted. As such, Alfred Harmsworth, the defining figure of the "new journalism," could proudly complain of his *Daily News* in 1904: "The most unfortunate part of the circulation of my paper is the fact that the immense number of people who see everything that appears in it and the comments they make, magnifies its every utterance" (qtd. in Boyce 32). Later, as Lord Northcliffe and owner of the *Times*, the same man would add: "The whole country will think with us when we say the word" (qtd. in Seymour-Ure 276).

Northcliffe's words speak to the nearly totalitarian[6] dimensions of power that *The Secret Agent* imagines at all levels, from the most macrocosmically political to the most intimately psychological, being exercised by and through the press. As a fundamental organizing premise, the novel assumes the press's exceptional facility as an instrumentation of political or state authority: hence, Vladimir's plan to use the press to effectuate a vast civil rights crackdown; Heat's career of manipulating the press to enhance his authority as a police officer and the strength of his "whole system of supervision" (211); Stevie's blind "fanaticism" (229) with respect to whatever newspaper he happens to be reading (see Nohrnberg 54); and the Professor's resistance to newspapers as a matter of general "anarchic" principle. It is for this reason that Vladimir's scheme to trigger the press's attention is explicitly paired with Verloc's stunt of calling "Constable!" out the window to capture a policeman's attention (making him "spin round as if prodded by a sharp instrument" [24]). That is, press and police, instruments of surveillance and coercive authority, are crucially one and the same in this novel that incessantly identifies them. But not entirely. For, just as the assistant commissioner by no means exists in harmony with that "strange emotional phenomenon called public opinion," which "weighs upon his spirits" and which he regards as an "irrational" and often "evil" "power" pulling his office's investigations in unproductive directions (99), so too Inspector Heat, that master of the disciplinary press, finds that the papers control him as much as he uses them to control the public. As becomes clear in his interview with the assistant commissioner, for instance, Heat wants to pin the bombing on the harmless Michaelis *not* to vilify a prominent radical leader in the press, but rather *in the event* the press demands someone should be vilified. "There will be no difficulty in getting up sufficient evidence against *him*," Heat says with smug, self-righteous complacency: ". . . for it seemed to him an excellent thing to have that man [Michaelis] in hand to be thrown down to the public *should it think fit to roar* with any special indignation in this case. It was impossible to say yet whether it would roar or not. That in the last instance depended, of course, on the newspaper press" (114, emphasis added).

Similarly, when Heat later experiences the "sudden illumination" that newspapers are "invariably written by fools for the reading of imbeciles," this is not to be taken as a moment of deep insight on Heat's part, but rather as his frustrated realization that the press—to whom Verloc intends to confess all, to "no end of row in the papers"—has the independent power to lay waste to "fields of knowledge" it has taken him years to cultivate (210, 211). Indeed, "anarchism" suits *The Secret Agent* as its crime *par excellence* significantly because it exposes tensions between press and police, i.e., whereas with "normal" crimes (like burglary), there is a clear referent of behavior and a coincidence of policing interests, with anarchism—"*all* foolishness," Heat muses, but of a kind that "excited the public mind" (97, emphasis added)—the press is encouraged to take notice of a kind of crime that the police know will have force only to the degree it is noticed.

What's at stake here is *The Secret Agent's* recognition of the press's autonomy as a policing agency, and more subtly, its shift in pursuing questions of social control from the levels of political and legal spectacle to the less visible and more internalized domain of monitoring techniques that Foucault associates with the term "discipline" and that D.A. Miller has so compellingly traced to the Victorian novel itself.[7] A key passage in this respect—and one of the most misunderstood passages in Conrad's novel, I believe—comes at the end of Chapter Four, as Ossipon, having just met with the Professor at the Silenus pub, prepares to exit the premises into the street:

> In front of the great doorway a dismal row of newspaper sellers standing clear of the pavement dealt out their wares from the gutter. It was a raw gloomy day of the early spring; and the grimy sky, the mud of the streets, the rags of the dirty men harmonized excellently with the eruption of the damp, rubbishy sheets of paper soiled with printers' ink. The posters, maculated with filth, garnished like tapestry the sweep of the curbstone. The trade in afternoon papers was brisk, yet, in comparison with the swift, constant march of foot traffic, the effect was of indifference, of a disregarded distribution. Ossipon looked hurriedly both ways before stepping out into the cross-currents, but the professor was already out of sight. (79)

At the level of plot, the immediate meaning of this passage—which we are encouraged to identify with the absurdity of extremist endeavors in general—is that Vladimir and Verloc's plan, carried out with the Professor's bomb, did not work. Whereas the Greenwich bombing as reported in the press was supposed to plunge the masses into terror, confusion, and shock, the newspapers' "effect" is one of "indifference," of a "disregarded distribution"—and humanity's dull "swift, constant march" plods assiduously on. But this is less a comment on the power of newspapers, of course, than it is on the fact that Verloc and Stevie botched the bombing, leaving little that is terrifying to report. Indeed, with respect to the conditioning social force of newspapers, the meaning of this passage is precisely the opposite. For not only is the passage's basic premise the *expectation* that the papers could, if given suitable occasion, disrupt the automatized course of humanity; in addition, its clear implication is that the papers *already are* controlling and coordinating the very "traffic" that marches on so implacably, which is why the appearance and movements of the "dirty men" dressed in "rags" "harmonized" so "excellently" with the eruptive flow of the "damp, rubbishy sheets" of newspaper "rag"; why press posters "garnished" the "sweep" of the street like scripting "tapestry"; and why the emphasis ironically falls on the word *effect* in describing what is in reality only the illusion of a "disregarded" press.

In a chapter noteworthy for its images of a player piano and a circumscribing fresco; in a novel existing under the sign of the "circles, circles, circles" through which Stevie depicts the automated recursiveness of human existence (45); in a text that incessantly correlates discourses and institutions of science, bureaucracy, law, and print with the vacant stares, sleepy eyes, fleshy inertness, and general idleness of the utterly "domesticated" (5) subject—newspapers emerge here as a privileged agent of social orchestration, i.e., the domestication that comes before and makes possible the grander political manipulations the novel pursues at the level of "anarchism." It is no coincidence, hence, that this scene pairs up the Professor, who is programmatically averse to all forms of social control, with Ossipon, who is overdetermined in his connections with the press; nor that a few pages later, the Professor begins a series of interiorized rants concerning the one "haunting fear of his sinister loneliness": the "resisting power of numbers, the unattackable stolidity of the great multitude" (95)—which made it so "mankind mighty in its numbers" could swarm "numerous like locusts, industrious like ants, thoughtless like a natural force, pushing on blind and orderly and absorbed, impervious to sentiment, to logic, to terror, too, perhaps" (82). These similes and adjectives all gloss the "swift, constant march" of mechanically industrious humanity described earlier, and what the two scenes point up in conjunction is the power of newspapers—through their "ready-made phrases" (32) and the "optimistic" flush of their "rosy sheets" (70)—to route human beings in flush relation to the social order with wider dissemination and deeper penetration than any other domesticating agency.

Indeed, what's special about *The Secret Agent* is the degree to which it probes and comprehends the depths to which subjectivity is penetrated by the press—a point that is productively illustrated by reconsidering any easy assumptions that Vladimir's plan simply "fails," for as Conrad takes great pains to demonstrate, nearly every major character in the novel is in some way physically or figuratively annihilated by the bombing, and in a fashion that invariably returns to newspapers. Inspector Heat, for instance, is an individual who, though "forced by his calling into an attitude of doubt and suspicion towards his fellow-citizens," relieves the "instinct of credulity implanted in [every] human breast" by placing "unbounded faith" in the "prophets" of the evening sports page (207). But when he is forced to look on the gruesome remains of Stevie's body—a body, one recalls, that is explicitly figured as an exploded newspaper "rag," and an *experience* whose "shattering violence of destruction" and "inconceivable agony" is clearly felt by Heat too (87)—the conditioning grip of the sacrosanct newspaper is by no means blasted away. True, in language that, for very good reason, recalls Walter Benjamin's conceptual ideal of being "blasted" into "homogeneous, empty time" (*Illuminations* 262–263), Heat experiences himself "rising by the force of sympathy, which is a form of fear, above the vulgar conception of time. Instantaneous!" (*SA* 87–88). But in a reversal that I think is useful for questioning the complacency of Benjamin's image too, Conrad makes it absolutely clear that what *feels* to Heat like being blasted completely out of the social order, and what certainly has the effect of making Heat momentarily vulnerable to the impulses of panic and terror that the Professor and Vladimir covet as a threat to the social order, is actually the recovery of the newspaper as a conditioning disciplinary instrument at the most fundamental level. For Heat is by no means "blasted free" of newspapers, but rather now is more radically enslaved by them than ever as the one dictating mechanism of his thoughts, which still remains: "*He remembered all he had ever read in popular publications of long and terrifying dreams* dreamed in the instant of waking; of the whole past life lived with frightful intensity by a drowning man as his head bobs up, streaming, for the last time" (88, emphasis added). This is a horrifying sequence of thoughts, and "the horror" (as it were) in this novel is not simply written *out* of newspapers, but also written *by* newspapers, which are internalized to such a fundamental degree that to be "blasted free" of the usual crutches of the social order (and one's capacity critically to reflect on it) is to have nothing but their conventions to fall back on, to be policed by *their* kind of terrorism, and ultimately to become rehabilitated as the very police officer whose form Heat suddenly resumes. Precisely the same, moreover, is true of Winnie, who, having suffered the twin shocks of losing her brother and killing her husband, is "free" precisely in the sense that she can now, without conventional and temperamental restraints, "look into the very bottom of this thing" that is her life—and see a newspaper (267). What she sees, indeed, is not only a press-derived image of the gallows but the juridical phrase, "as the reports in the newspapers always said, 'in the presence of authorities'" (268); and it is no exaggeration to say that as a consequence of the internalized terror and authority of newspapers, Winnie pronounces sentence on herself and commits suicide.

The most revealing case, though, is Ossipon. Archetypally instantiating the model of "suspense" put forth by William Bonney in this volume, Ossipon ends this novel in a state of paralyzed confliction over a newspaper article whose very subject is suspense: i.e., the "*impenetrable mystery*" of Winnie's suicide that "*seems destined to hang forever over this act of madness and despair*" (307, emphasis in original). Ossipon's problem is the obverse of his earlier claim: "One must use the current words" (71). In the wake of Winnie's suicide, he has lost all the "unbounded trustfulness" that he once was able to and needed to place in the current words of "journalistic style," "sentiment," and "manly tenderness" alike (307). Yet not only does being loosed from a slavishly blind relation to language produce no Promethean glory; in addition, Ossipon is more chained to conventional language's compulsory powers and orchestrating institutions than ever. Ossipon's circumstance at the end of *The Secret Agent* bears an isomorphic relation to Nostromo's at the end of *Nostromo*. Both characters are radically alienated from the very fundamental sociopolitical mechanism—the "knitting machine," by any other name—that not only drives their worlds (as posited by their respective novels) but also defines, with an insistence bordering on the allegorical, the essence of who they are as characters. The mechanism is global capitalism, symbolized and instrumentalized by the silver, in *Nostromo*; in *The Secret Agent* it is the press, symbolized and instrumentalized by papers and signs. This is why, in my view, *The Secret Agent* ends with a pointed return to the characters, setting, and content of Chapter Four, with the final scene of the novel presenting Ossipon on exactly the same street featured in the press scene at the end of Chapter Four—now tormented by the "mystery of a human brain pulsating wrongfully to the rhythm of journalistic phrases" in which he can no longer believe; and "marching in the gutter" whose currents, akin to the "leather yoke of the sandwich board," are controlled by newspapers (311).

The kinship with the "sandwich board," a form of commercial advertisement, is not inconsequential.[8]

II.

The door is open here to Nohrnberg's argument that *The Secret Agent* is a "satire" on the "degraded reading public" of Edwardian England—especially as this public consists of the new historical class of "lowbrow" newspaper readers figured in Stevie, and especially as this lowbrow, lower-*class* group of readers might be induced to violence or social revolution by radical papers like *The Torch*, which sits in the Verlocs' window but was also an actual anarchist journal of the period (Nohrnberg 50–52, 54). But it is unclear whether Conrad's purpose is to satirize rather than train, scapegoat rather than politically register, single out rather than cross-implicate, *any* particular category of reader in the notoriously slippery figure of Stevie. Moreover, the generic category of "satire"—which Nohrnberg compellingly glosses through Swift's metaphor of "a sort of glass, wherein Beholders do generally discover everyone's face but their own" (51)—has trouble fully accommodating a novel whose extreme poles of sympathy and scorn, Stevie and the Professor, both unquestionably bear the specular imprint of the author. With a critical net cast this wide and without safe haven, the novel's investigative emphasis seems to fall on the *medium* of newspapers rather than specific types of presupposed newspaper reader; on what Aaron Fogel and Geoffrey Harpham, in two highly original yet remarkably commensurate discussions of the novel, describe as *externalities* of "coercion" and "necessity" rather than subjectivities formed in antecedent relation to the world (Fogel, *Coercion* 146–179; Harpham, "Abroad"). Given the degree to which *The Secret Agent* registers the penetration of subjectivity by newspapers, the question remains how such power is exerted, and through what terms it takes place.

There are two hypotheses I want to explore in this respect—one deriving from Benjamin, concerning "information" as a political aesthetic of the modern newspaper; the other from Baudrillard, concerning the modern press as an engine of "simulation"—both of which take as a crucial historical coordinate a commercial phenomenon whose discussion I have backgrounded to this point: i.e., the rise of the "new journalism" at the end of the nineteenth century. Pioneered by W.T. Stead at the *Pall Mall Gazette* in the 1880s, and later institutionalized by Northcliffe in the years before the Great War, the "new journalism"—a contemporary phrase coined by Matthew Arnold, but a current one too—comprised a new commercial mode of journalistic production aptly summarized by Boyce as:

> characterised by a bid for mass circulation—a bid aimed at the increasingly prosperous and literate lower classes—with news parcelled up into short and easily digestible portions, produced and sold using improvements in printing and distribution, and with advertising an essential part of newspaper finance. (27)

Physically arresting in its flashy typography and bold headlines and images (Koss 1: 210, 279); affectively sensational and crudely narrative in its presentation of "news" (Smith 152); overwhelmingly dependent on advertising for revenue (Curran 69–70); financially predicated on extreme capital investments, high operating costs, a corporate shareholding structure, and increasing concentration of ownership by syndicates controlled by a few powerful wealthy industrials (Curran 67–69; R. Williams, "Communications" 231–232; Boyce 37); and ideologically responsible for the conversion of the "popular" from an (oppositional) political to an (integrative) capitalized domain (R. Williams, "Popular Culture" 49; Boyce 67)—the "new journalism" presupposed the priority of the newspaper as a money-making commodity and entertainment industry. This was a development and "revolution" that would significantly devastate the British press's unique political vitality by mid-century, but the Edwardian years, as noted above, are best understood in this respect as a period of transition and hybridity, one in which old and new grids of journalistic practice overlapped, and in which newspapers generally did not simply incarnate the (retrospectively theorized) tenets of the "new journalism" so much as they were forced to confront and negotiate its competitive terms (Koss 1: 345; 2: 4–11). And it was in this climate, in which both partisan politics and serious political discussions were compromised by the new priorities of mass circulation and maximal advertising revenue, that a new emphasis on neutral "facts" and a new style Benjamin calls "information" seized hold as a dominant professional norm (Schudson 71–74; Benjamin, *Illuminations* 84–89, 156–160).

Though Nohrnberg casts a brief glance in this direction (50–51), Jonathan Arac has written the most searching consideration of the journalistic form of "information" in relation to *The Secret Agent.* Arac begins by referencing the opening of "Autocracy and War" (1905), where Conrad sharply distinguishes between the "cold, silent, colourless print" of "newspapers"—which leave events like the Russo-Japanese War perceived only "dim[ly]" through the "grey reflection" of a "veil of inadequate words"—and "Direct vision of the fact, or the stimulus of great art," which "can alone" awaken the "slumbering faculty" and "heavy eyes" of human imaginative responsiveness (*NLL* 84, 85). The problem with newspapers, Conrad argues, is that notwithstanding their "precision," statistical "eloquence," and endlessly itemized "stream" of details, the human imagination "remains strangely *impervious to information,* however correctly and even picturesquely conveyed" (84, emphasis added). "Direct vision" and "great art," on the other hand, which are very close to the same thing in Conrad's world (see Preface, *NIN*), seize on the more retentive and deep-seated fields of "common experience" and "the testimony of the senses and the stirring up of emotion" to work their effects (*NLL* 84). As Arac notes, this distinction is so close to the one Benjamin draws between the "information" whose form typifies newspapers—fresh, brief, comprehensible, plausible, promptly verifiable, discontinuous (*Illuminations,* 158–159; 89–90)—and the more lived, longstanding "experience" that characterizes pre-industrial forms like storytelling, that it is clear that Conrad and Benjamin are jointly theorizing "the same complex [problem]" (Arac 79). Indeed, Arac draws on Benjamin's further distinction between two kinds of "experience"—*Erfahrung,* the continuous and deeply assimilated life patterns of the craftsman or tiller of soil, and *Erlebnis,* the sporadic and fragmented nature of existence in the urban metropolis, where jostling crowds and explosive surprises persistently bombard inhabitants with the threat of "shocks"—to conceptualize the place of newspapers in *The Secret Agent* (Arac 79–81).

For Benjamin, the pervasive threat of shocks posed by the urban environment results in a fundamentally shielded mode of existence in which intimate personhood is kept protected and deeply lived experience is kept at bay (*Illuminations* 160–167). So too newspapers, themselves quite capable of engendering shock, are internally possessed of an empty character, their "informational" form locating events in time but sterilizing them of meaningful content (88–89). Arac argues that *The Secret Agent* connects these two as "cultural correlates," and that the novel's principal aesthetic premise, as prescripted by the opening of "Autocracy and War," is to do full imaginative justice to the world's complexities by undoing and undermining—what Said once called "negating as writing"—the tyranny of journalistic modes of expression (Arac 80, 81; Said, *World* 108–110).

These are powerful insights, and ones that could be developed even further to trace *The Secret Agent*'s diagnosis of the newspapers it resists. Mr. Vladimir, for instance, is quite clear that the choice of the Greenwich Observatory as a bombing target has much less to do with "science" than it does with confronting a formal challenge posed by newspapers: "*I defy the ingenuity of journalists* to persuade their public that any given member of the proletariat can have a personal grievance against astronomy. Starvation itself could hardly be dragged in there—eh?" (35, emphasis added). What Vladimir means is that the press's usual battery of conventionalizing narratives—e.g., class warfare ("proletariat"), vengeance ("personal grievance"), material need ("starvation"), all of which derive from the social order and whose taming application to the unknown has the ultimate effect of reproducing status quo values (that one must work, that one is a person, that one has needs that should be honored)—will be radically defied by an act of destruction so gratuitously inexplicable as the bombing of a house of astronomy. Unlike political assassinations, church bombing, murders, and riots, all of which, as Vladimir explains, have so thoroughly entered "the general conception of existence" that "it's almost conventional" (30–32)—there are no "ready-made phrases" (political, religious, personal, sociological) that can recoup an observatory bombing in a manner that ultimately confirms the social order's security, legitimacy, and humanity (32). But the very *difficulty* of coming up with an act of atrocity that *could* "defy the ingenuity of journalists"—which is not only the point here, but an overall point made by the book—confirms an important observation Benjamin makes about newspapers predicated on an aesthetic of "information": "Every morning brings us news of the globe, and yet we are poor in noteworthy stories. This is because *no event comes to us without already being shot through with explanation* (*Illuminations* 89, emphasis added). What seems like the emptied-out nature of "information," in other words, is actually its superabundance of and overdetermination by restrictive explanations and conventions, what the Professor, with customary zeal, would call "a historical fact surrounded by all sorts of restraints and considerations, a complex, organized fact open to attack at every point" (*SA* 68). Information, hence, is neither merely an emptied-out objective correlative for urban "shock," nor simply a defensive means of parrying and filtering unwelcome messages that might be associated with shock. Rather, it is an aggressive, colonizing, preemptive producer of "blunted sensibilities" whose purpose is to explain the world in advance and to render the experience of shocks to the social order impossible (*SA* 36). For how is shock to arise in a world so "shot through" by the press's "optimistic" self-confirming conventions, themselves posing a neutral "fact," that people themselves have become "m[e]n of papers" (70, 17)? How is one to challenge a regime of "information"—broadcast at increasingly full decibel—predicated on the monadic "factual" reduction of essentially dialectical and dialogical questions (Benjamin, *Illuminations* 262–263); on the folly of "knowledge understandable in itself without context" (Schudson 120); on the craven scientism of substantive politics treated in increasingly technical and strategic terms (Hallin 18–19); on "the despotism with which, in journalism, *topicality* sets up its dominion over things" (Benjamin, *Reflections* 240)? These sorts of questions inform the Professor's haunting fear that the public *can't* be shocked, as they further inform his search for a "perfect detonator," whose ideal of "instantaneous" combustion is predicated on the closure of the very gap of fear in which, as we have already seen with Heat, Winnie, and Ossipon, the policing effects of newspapers arise (*SA* 66–67). Indeed, Benjamin's emphasis on the "despotism" of "topicality" in newspapers, which Anthony Smith describes as their "convulsive emphasis on the now" (139), may help account for the time shifts in the middle of *The Secret Agent*; for if Arac is right that this novel is written *against* newspapers, then those time shifts, which have the effect of coordinating all around and pulling everything into the convulsive "now" of Stevie's explosion, may be said to register the *resistance* of the medium Conrad is attempting to un-write.

But a brief return to the opening of "Autocracy and War" suggests that journalistic "information," for all its representational insinuations and ideological implications, may be the lesser of two concerns Conrad ultimately discerns in the press. For the distinction Conrad draws at the outset between journalism and art, "information" and a more engaging aesthetic, is actually much more the essay's *convention*—like some of the more public, standardized language in the "Preface" to *The Nigger of the "Narcissus"*—than its *argument*. Summon the "dim . . . mist of print" though it may (*NLL* 83, 87), the essay itself devotes little if any attention to rescuing from behind the clouds of "information" the material and human realities of its two ostensible subjects—the Russo-Japanese War and Russia—and indeed, demonstrates a fundamental lack of interest in *misrepresentation* altogether, at least insofar as this suggests the distortion or occlusion of a well-defined prior object. Rather, what principally preoccupies Conrad is the ability to *make* realities out of words whose referent in the world is truly nothing at all. It is for this reason that the essay relentlessly assails Russia as a figure of nothing: as a "phantom," a "ghost," a "spectre," an "apparition," a "hallucination," a "nothing that does not exist," an "abyss" "without starting point," "the most baseless thing in the world," an infinite "*Néant*," etc. (86, 87, 90, 91, 100). Conrad does this not simply, or even primarily, to make the moral point that Russia is the "negation of everything worth living for" (100), but rather to make the material point, the ontological point, that Russia is *not* an antecedent something at all, but rather a void in whose name England has fabricated a reality entirely through the generative powers of the sign. In the memorably grim early paragraph in which Conrad describes Russia in words beginning—"This dreaded and strange apparition, bristling with bayonets, armed with chains, hung over with holy images . . . ." (89)—Conrad dramatizes "Russia's" genetic origins in potent effusions of words. But it is clearly the press, in this historical moment whose "real object-lesson" should be Russia's true status as a military, political, and cultural *Néant* (89), which, through its endless "speculations" on Russia's lingering imperial threat, strategic global significance, possible military resurgence, and, no doubt, hidden weapons of mass destruction (89)—it is the press that makes a virtual something out of absolutely nothing:

> All these speculations (with many others) have appeared gravely in print; and if they have been gravely considered by one reader out of each hundred, there must be something subtly noxious to the human brain in the composition of newspaper ink; or else it is that the large page, the column of words, the leaded headings, exalt the mind to a state of feverish credulity. The printed page of the Press makes a sort of still uproar, taking from men both the power to reflect and the faculty of genuine feeling; leaving them only the artificially created need of having something exciting to talk about. (90)

The rhetoric here is ostensibly, superficially, that of representation and ideology. But the power expressed—in the heavy materiality attaching to the newspaper page alone; in the subtle hints of annihilation that run throughout the passage ("gravely"; "noxious"; "still uproar"); in the final circumstance of the "genuine" being "tak[en]" away, leaving only an "artificially created" world of words and an equally synthetic "need" for more of them—the power expressed here is that of language completely overmastering the prescriptives of not only psychology but reality itself. Such that "Russia" can be birthed from the black, inky abyss of the printed page alone; such that words, as *The Secret Agent* would have it of professional spies, demonstrate "every facility to fabricate the very facts themselves" (139). Here we finally arrive in the world of Jean Baudrillard, a vitally untapped resource in Conrad studies, whose idea of "simulation," I have suggested elsewhere, is the ultimate sign of *The Secret Agent*'s contemporaneity. If *The Secret Agent* may be figuratively conceptualized—as I think it productively can be—as Conrad's imaginative attempt to throw a bomb into a newspaper to determine what the terms and dimensions of its authority are,[9] then the answers it reaches at its furthest limits of prescience are those of "simulation"—a reproductive order predicated on the "liquidation of all referentials" and the "generation by models of a real without origin or reality: a hyperreal" (Baudrillard, *Simulacra* 2, 1). What is entertained here is a reproductive relationship to the world—say, in the context of the press, a written relationship to events—that is so powerful that the elements of representation and of a differentiated, autonomous reality drop out entirely, the world instead being *scripted, constituted, supplanted* by the media and models that are brought to bear upon it. It is a matter of "the territory no longer preceding the map, nor [even] surviving it" (1); of a "precession" of the map and model, and a disappearance of the distinction between "map" and "territory," "concept" and "real" (2, 6); of "substituting signs for the real" and developing a relationship to objects that is "no longer specular and discursive" but rather "nuclear and genetic" (2, 3); of the power to make the world over in the image of "a giant simulacrum—not unreal, but a simulacrum, that is to say never exchanged for the real, but exchanged for itself"(6).

As I have suggested elsewhere, these are terms that hold great explanatory power for *The Secret Agent*: not simply with respect to the simulated anarchist plot on which it is premised, or even its larger understanding of the ability of the press to simulate a world in the image of that plot, but in all the attention the text devotes to the extraordinary genetic powers of "paper and ink" (*SA* 17), the disappearance of "origins" and reality known at "first hand" (89, 144), the precession of systems and models ("no details," says Sir Ethelred [136]) in relation to the known world, and the idea of perfectly simulated spectacles like Vladimir's "amazingly genuine English accent" or the assistant commissioner's "foreign appearance" at the shady Italian restaurant (*SA* 35, 148–149). The note I would like to close on here, though, is historically accounting for this premonition of simulation with respect to the institutions of the press that seem to generate "simulation" as a master organizing concept of *The Secret Agent*.

The "new journalism" offers at least two answers. One is its invention, or at least institutional consolidation, of what Daniel Boorstin would later call "pseudo-events," i.e., happenings planned "for the immediate circumstances of being reported or reproduced" (170). Such new developments included the celebrity interview (which Conrad emphasizes in *The Inheritors*, and which prior to Stead was thought to be a "distinctly shocking American practice" [Koss 1: 344]); the circulation-enhancing "stunt" (whose most notorious, and Conradian, example was perhaps the journey of H.M. Stanley of the *New York Herald* to Africa in 1871–1872 to find the lost Dr. Livingstone [A. Smith 157]); the social invention of the supporting roles of "reporter" and "Lobby correspondent" (Schudson 65; Koss 1: 238); and the general priorities of self-advertising and "making news" (Schudson 66)—all of which put the press in the circumstance of *producing* the facts it then reported *as* the facts. The second development was the press's increasingly remarkable power, as a function of empire and technology, of unprecedented distribution and decibel in a world whose information resources it significantly controlled, simply to *make* facts of grave political and social consequence by *declaring* them as such. Most notoriously illustrative here are (i) the Pigott scandal of 1887, in which the *Times* did grave damage to the cause of Irish Home Rule by publishing *as fact* a series of simulated letters in which Parnell appears to confess to having co-planned the Phoenix Park murders of 1882 (see Koss 1: 296–300); and (ii) the entire sequence of sham facts and simulated episodes through which William Randolph Hearst, with the competitive assistance of Joseph Pulitzer, propelled the United States into the Spanish American War (see Swanberg 79–162). "You furnish the pictures. I'll furnish the war," Hearst infamously wrote to one of his photographers stationed in Cuba in 1897 (Schudson 61–64). "You are being called upon to furnish facts," says Vladimir to Verloc (*SA* 31).

Notes

This essay is dedicated to the memory of my grandmother, Mary Mallios Gregory (1912–2004): who gave to my family a fidelity without stint or calculation of recompense, and to my childhood an immeasurable devotion and love.

1. See Mallios, "Desert" for details.

2. Excepting Nohrnberg and Arac, whose valuable discussions I engage below, I have found no other serious treatments of the press in Conrad's novel. I have also learned from Houen's introduction, though his insights concerning the media are not carried over to his discussion of *The Secret Agent*.

3. Curran's essay proved influential in the late 1970s because it challenged, among other orthodoxies, the conventional Cold-War acknowledgement of "the press [as] ... an instrument of social control only in totalitarian societies, whereas in the free world it is the institutional embodiment of the democratic principle of freedom of expression" (51). But if ever an author were early prepared to collapse binaries between democratic and autocratic, British and Russian, free and coerced expression, it is surely the author of *The Secret Agent* and *Under Western Eyes*.

4. As Anthony Smith notes, even as late as the 1850s, "Lord John Russell, Prime Minister, opposed the abolition of the stamp [duty] on the grounds that it would encourage popular newspapers and popular education and therefore tend towards anarchy" (122).

5. For an excellent sketch of the history of ideas as concerns the British press, see Boyce 19–40; for more on Nostromo as police officer, see Mallios, "Undiscovering" 366–368, 379–380.

6. My choice of this adjective is inflected by concerns mentioned in note 3.

7. See D. A. Miller vii–xv, 1–33.

8. Compare the cartoon by R.O. Blechman, reprinted in R. Williams, "Communcations" 232, in which a man wearing a sandwich board confronts another wearing a television with the caption beneath reading: "Who sells the pasta fasta?"

9. Consider in this regard: (i) Stevie's figuring as a newspaper, the novel's predication on the (successful, on Conrad's part) event of his explosion; (ii) Conrad's frequent turn to the seductive silences of newspapers for novelistic inspiration; (iii) Conrad's own newspaper research on Martial Bourdin's historical attempt to bomb the Greenwich Observatory in 1894 (Watt, *Essays* 112–126); and (iv) the grand culminating irony of the novel, that whatever Conrad's success may be in "making us see" what newspapers can't, its final conclusion, offset perhaps slightly by the final hedge of the Professor in the closing paragraph, is that newspapers cannot be resisted.

3
Conrad and Textuality

10
Suspended*

WILLIAM W. BONNEY

This suspense is a thousand times worse than the most horrible event....

Victor Frankenstein

Activité, activité, vitesse.

Napoleon's Motto

A decade ago, scholarly indifference toward Conrad's final novel, *Suspense: A Napoleonic Novel* (1925), was noteworthy. Indeed, "neglect of this novel has been virtually absolute" (Moore, "In Defense" 99), and, in spite of some recent bibliographic work and inquiries into the accuracy of Conrad's real-world references (see Mursia), it largely persists. To be sure, "much of the difficulty of appreciating *Suspense* lies precisely in the nature of the demands it makes on the historical imagination of the reader." Such demands require "a detailed familiarity [with] events leading up to the Hundred Days," including "Italian politics in the time of Napoleon" (van Marle and Moore 147). But it remains to be understood that often these demands quite transcend textbooks of history. For of all Conrad's works, none more effectively demonstrates his lifelong ambivalent fascination with the ideas of rhetoric that erupt into Western European culture at the inception of the Romantic era, precisely the interval wherein *Suspense*'s three-day plot is set. *Suspense*, moreover, provides an invaluable occasion to reconsider the idea and aesthetics of suspense as they have informed Conrad's grapplings with politics and history throughout his fiction.

These are issues of relevance to both the twenty-first century and the several centuries before. Below, I begin by tracing the idea of "suspense" from its Renaissance origins, explaining how, in the nineteenth century, it came to signify and coordinate a wide array of human activities and activism, and how, in the twentieth century, it came consequently to serve Conrad as the perfect target trope through which to disdain such activity. Conrad's earlier fiction, frequently set in distant colonial places, is consistently determined by a thematics of suspense wherein all attempts to act against status quo imperial capitalism are systematically disallowed, suspended, in a paralyzing miasma of existential and psychological confusions. Even more, Conrad's twentieth-century critics, myself included, have become complicit in this affect of suspense wherein questions of "politics" come to turn on *not* delineating possibilities of action but rather contemplating the reinscription or deconstruction of ideas which, regardless, remain suspended in the ineffectual realm of discourse. *Suspense* offers a retrospective anatomy of this process—i.e., reading it closely, which I do below, provides a means of rereading the entire Conrad canon and its critics— at the same time it also affords the twenty-first century the prospective opportunity to come to more aggressive political terms with Conrad in exceptionally relevant ways. *Suspense*, one notes, was not only written "about" the Europe of the Congress of Vienna, a moment of great international upheaval and uncertainty; it was also written *in* a moment—i.e., the years following World War I—in which questions and anxieties of new world order were paramount. As such, *Suspense* offers up a palimpsest of moments quite similar to our own; and if *Suspense* has been suspended as a matter of critical interpretation until now, perhaps the ultimate pay-off lies in the opportunity it offers to consider how the rhetoric and aesthetics of suspense still delimit possibilities of political action and resistance in our own time.

I. Sundry Suspensions

The *OED* shows that "suspense" and variations thereon date from the fifteenth century. Typically, the semantic function of these words is to stress a state of "uncertainty" directly continuous "with expectation of decision or issue" (2094). Although it may be that "of all evils, holding suspense [may] be the most tormenting" (Sterne 219), the pragmatic design of early scientific discourse allows Bacon to claim in *Novum Organum* (1620) that "suspension of the judgment" can lead, not to "what the Greeks call *Acatalepsia*,—a denial of the capacity of the mind to comprehend truth ... but *Eucatalepsia* ... provision for understanding truly," or, what Sprat in his *History of the Royal Society* (1667) calls "suspence ... to a better purpose" (qtd. in Harth 13, 14).

In marked contrast, the French Revolution and post-Kantian philosophy compel a disturbing awareness that, since the late eighteenth century in western Europe, cultural *acatalepsia* may be unavoidable and interminable. Predictably, Hegel in *Lectures on the Philosophy of World History* (ca. 1822) expresses the idea that even super-human efforts to eliminate disorienting mutability may merely inaugurate self destruction. For "Zeus, who sets limits to the depredations of time and [who thus] suspended its constant flux, had no sooner established something inherently enduring than he was himself devoured along with his whole empire" (40). More tangibly, as early as 1783 Montgolfier's hot-air balloon, suspended above Versailles and thereby enabling an ocular democracy, initiated the conceptual displacement of the king that six years later was enacted physically, whereafter it seemed not to matter how many suspensions were contrived—suspensions of Parliament, the *Veto Absolu*, constitutional bishops, the king's role in government, the commissions of military heroes, even the embalmed heart of Marat, "suspended" in an "agate urn" over the heads of "the Cordeliers" (Schama 125, 266, 458, 548, 561, 610, 744)—the citizenry, "one vast suspended-billow of Life" (Carlyle 106), can accomplish little more than cycles of its own personal, political, and cultural retardation.

Ominously, the Latin *suspendere* means "to hang," a linguistic curiosity that connects the French people's political suspension of aristocratic privilege and power with their physical acts of smashing public lighting and hanging victims from lantern-fixtures, in a virtual mockery of the Enlightenment (see Shivelbusch). Small wonder that Wordsworth, in his "Essay, Supplementary" of 1815, while praising the imaginative potential of the word "hung," is careful to cite Virgilian, Shakespearian, and Miltonic uses, for much of his literary output constitutes an effort to qualify anxious intimations of cosmic dangling— the dread that "when I have hung/ ... almost (so it seemed)/Suspended by the blast . . . / . . . I hung alone" (*The Prelude* I. 330–336). But the more skeptical Shelley, doubting both windy metaphysical agents and respondents, mocks Wordsworth in the epigraph to "Alastor" (1818), while featuring the melancholy reflections of a narrator who can use the verb only in a passive-voice form, figuring forth his state of unresolved tension "as a long-forgotten lyre/Suspended in [a] solitary dome/ ... await[ing] ... breath" (ll. 42–45). Less ethereally, even the Bank of England (founded in 1694 by William III to finance French wars) was compelled to respond to this rhetoric when, in response to repeated monetary crises, the Bank Charter Renewal Act of 1844 was suspended by Parliament in 1848, 1858, and 1867 (Poovey, *Financial System* 22–23).

Apart from political, philosophical, and financial crises, the nineteenth century could be called "the age of suspense" in merely a technological sense, for it is the time when the concept of the "catenary curve" (from Latin *catena*, "chain") was found to have many applications. Defined precisely by Johann Bernoulli in 1691 as $y = \cosh x$ (the "hyperbolic cosine of x"), the "chain curve" remained largely a mathematical curiosity until its instrumental use was realized much later. For it describes two opposing forces in balance— i.e., any flexible material in a linear shape that is suspended from two points takes this form. Catenary curves appear, for example, in all overhead wires, in belts connecting two pulleys, in flumes designed from flexible material, in suspension bridges, and in the graph that plots the pressure of a cylinder with respect to its velocity in a Carnot-cycle steam engine. Indeed, so compelling was this shape to the Victorian mind that John Ruskin in *Modern Painters* (1856) defines the catenary as a perfect expression of the "Immortal Curves" that are "absolutely incomprehensible and endless, only to be seen or grasped during a certain moment of their course," and that "universally [are] the class [of curves] to which the human mind is attached for its chief enjoyment" (*Modern* IV. xvii). Finally, as Conrad surely knew, anchor chains take the form of a catenary (and when the curve becomes a straight line, the anchor may pull free).

In fact, scarcely a word other than "suspense" so efficiently evokes Conrad's misgivings about the consequence of human *acts* and the late-nineteenth-century cultural context from which they emerged: though, to be sure, dangling from two cerebral pinions generates not a lovely "Immortal Curve" but rather a terminal imposition comparable to Razumov's surmise, "Between the two he was done for" (*UWE* 31).[1] Interestingly, noting that "an artist is a man of action" (*MS* 33), Conrad is willing to temporize about aesthetic deeds. He thereby implies that the act of writing about action is somehow exempt from the comprehensive scorn of "Action ... the enemy of thought and the friend of flattering illusions" that *Nostromo*'s narrative voice asserts (66; cf. Arnold's aestheticization of "action" in "Preface to *Poems 1853*"). Furthermore, it is obvious that Conrad does not sustain his scorn for action consistently when he ponders the most simplistic kinds of physical assertiveness. As the title of his essay "Well Done" (1918) affirms, it is indeed possible in Conrad's world to perform deeds dissociated from inauthentic, merely personal motives and craven existential evasion.

But when it comes to action as presented in his novels rather than his more pietistic prose; and when it comes to actions not fully commensurate with the norms and needs of the national or imperial capitalistic status quo—the kind of action that may be classified as genuine *resistance*—Conrad answers only with dubiousness and absurdity. One thinks, for instance, of *Nostromo*, wherein several crucial capitalist axioms remain unmentioned and unassailed despite a comprehensive mockery as mere fatuous "belief" of virtually every other strategy whereby aggressive action might be vindicated. As *Nostromo* demonstrates, moreover, one way to assert the invalidity of resistant action, and to project this assertion narratologically, is to vitiate the obvious historical fact that acts of decisive consequence have indeed occurred and continue to occur. There may or may not be "something inherent in the nature of things" that sponsors "oppression, inefficiency, [and] savage brutality," just as it may or may not hold true that the "hostility [of] nature... can always be overcome by the resources of finance" (*No* 109, 39). But clearly, *somehow*—a *somehow* that Conrad's analysis tends to elide—the power to generate "successful action" (*No* 521) in the interest of specific, historically transformative goals is obviously wielded on many scales, regardless of inane "flattering illusions" or exorbitant "imaginative estimate[s]" (*No* 66, 107)—e.g., Spanish conquistadors and their Catholic masters; various accumulators and wielders of capital (including a British "Napoleon of railways" and the credit officers of "the Third Southern Bank" located by "the Holroyd Building"); the miners who "march upon [Sulaco] to save" Gould; Barrios's troops wielding the technically superior breech-loading "Chassepot" rifles (fittingly, first used by the French to destroy Garibaldi's army at Mentana, November 3, 1867); and those accountable for "the international naval demonstration, which put an end to the Costaguana-Sulaco war," and the intimidating arrival of the "United States cruiser *Powhatan*" (*No* 318, 143, 511, 487). More precisely, the inaugural, and clearly successful, colonial acts that Conrad consistently ignores are: the use of superior transportation, communications, and military technology to enable an invasion of distant territory in order generally to terrorize the native population, and particularly to destroy their traditional subsistence economy so that sheer death-anxiety can be wielded against them to compel submission to exploitation and slavery (including wage-labor devoid of alternatives) if the people are to have food and shelter at all.

But if suppressing the actions that make up the status quo is one way of discrediting the actions that could bring resistance and alternatives to it, still another strategy—perhaps the major strategy aesthetically evidenced by Conrad's fiction—is that of suspending action in such an elaborate sea of moral contradictions and psychological and existential confusions that there is no basis upon which to act at all. At the level of character, Conrad invariably employs subjective tension in his aspiring agents as a strategy whereby most any aggressive social intervention can be selectively judged to be illegitimate. Specifically, he relies continually upon venality as a sign of personal unworthiness. In *Nostromo* this judgment involves his own (possibly disingenuous) misuse of the concept "materialism." For instance, when, in response to her husband's prediction that "'the great silver and iron interests ... some day shall get hold of ... the world,'" Emilia Gould protests, "'This seems to me the most awful materialism'" (*No* 82–83), she uses the term in an imprecise, pietistic sense, denoting "desire for wealth." And Conrad leaves this usage uncorrected. As a result, the novel rhetorically can scornfully attribute a political or ethical opacity to capitalist invaders and their clients as they repeatedly use the word "matter" paradoxically and metaphorically, virtually chanting "No matter" (239, 258, 558, 562), even as a complaint arises about "'an awful sense of unreality,'" indeed, "a bizarre sense of unreality, affecting the very ground" (207, 302), although a "legitimate touch of materialism" (75) just might exist here or there.

The fact that characters are never essentially, or at least eventually, disinterested—that there is "something inherent in the necessities of successful action which carries with it the moral degradation of the idea" (*No* 521), as Emilia Gould reflects, and which, as her husband suspects, makes it "impossible to disentangle one's activity from its debasing contacts" (*No* 360)—means that all political action and beliefs are ultimately self-deceiving. The fact that all political views are self-deceiving, moreover, ushers in the open occasion to treat all political beliefs as if they were equal, to probe them as an endlessly equivalent species of arbitrariness and self-contradiction, and to convert them to an overarching narrative whose master terms are self-canceling oppositions and negated courses of action. As a result, a commonplace tactic used by Conrad scholars since the mid-1970s has been to ferret out all manner of rhetorical and conceptual clashes, and then to analyze them as signs of various symmetrical negations that enable Conrad simultaneously to gainsay both sides of the clash. Hence, the frequency of, e.g., grammatical constructions of the "both this + and that" or "even this + as that" variety, where the pronouns stand for substantives that generate some form of oxymoron, and the overall analytic quest is for examples of "contradiction."[2]

Although much of this criticism is indeed sophisticated and innovative with regard to the aesthetic features it discloses, to discover all manner of symmetrically negational, hence "contradictory," rhetoric and content is to identify an artistic feature that is quite easy to contrive. All that is required is the innovation of a sufficiently abstract, inclusive sentence employing both sides of the binary conflict to a single, logically consistent, exemplary purpose—in this case, the two sides function as examples of a single metaphysic that is symptomatized by the dualistic conflict itself. One wonders whether Conrad is naive enough to think that aesthetic constructs are capable of "demonstrating" much of anything about the nature of the phenomenal world, but in any event, the key point to take is that the aesthetic at issue here—that particular exhilaration of being lost in Conrad's usual sea of "irreconcilable antagonisms"—is precisely that of suspense. And what is special about *Suspense* is that it dramatizes how this aesthetic of suspense—which, as we have just seen, is politically immobilizing in its impact—has been at issue in Conrad all the way along.

II. Into *Suspense*

In *Suspense*, the political arena includes not the colonial backwaters of Conrad's earlier novels, but the entirety of Europe, "the wide world" (*Su* 22). Moreover, the political reconstruction of the "world," during its "first breathing time" in decades, unsettles the protagonist, whose first name, "Cosmo" (connoting "world"), suggests that entanglement in the repercussions of restoring "'the whole world'" is likely (*Su* 104, 26).[3] In marked contrast to his other novels, Conrad here need use the word "suspense" only infrequently (three times: 106, 189, 194), for each appearance bears an inclusive import that necessarily and easily invokes all manner of lesser quandaries, since, as the Marquis knows, "'uneasy suspense is the prevailing sentiment all round the basin of the Mediterranean'" (*Su* 106). The novel's very setting emphasizes this unease, as the narrative voice notes: "The inward unrest which pervaded the whole basin of the Western Mediterranean was strongest in Italy" (*Su* 165). Of course, a lengthy essay might be written about Conrad's uses of the signature noun "unrest," especially in relation to the idea of "suspense." Conrad's *Tales of Unrest*, for instance, explores various forms of discontent within the context of militarily enforced colonialism and finance. In *Nostromo*, since the Industrial Revolution "San Tome [is] suspended" globally, "hanging ... more pitiless and autocratic than the worst Government; ready to crush innumerable lives" (*No* 521).[4] This predatory suspension is possible largely because of investors' willingness "'to send half of Sulaco into the air,'" so to speak, "flying sky-high out of a horrified world" (*No* 204, 400), if their wishes are opposed, thus rendering moot at the level of political intervention Marlow's facile assertion that "'We exist only insofar as we hang together'" (*LJ* 223), and ensuring that the "history which bears and determines us has the form of a war rather than that of a language: relations of power, not relations of meaning" (Foucault, *P/K* 114). At least in Conrad's works, then, "'no ... rest'" seems possible (*No* 511), be it "desired unrest" or ferment less welcome (*NIN* 90). Amidst such "awful restlessness" pages of patrician historiography may become "'wads for trabucos loaded with handfuls of type'" (*No* 230, 235), but to no avail, since relatively primitive weapons are wielded solely by the indigent masses, always the inevitable losers, perpetually "armed with muzzle-loaders" (so to speak), unlike their affluent capitalist-client foes.

However, *Suspense* itself is set well before the technological changes that beget the tortured human consequences of steam-powered colonial exploitation and international capital investment. In this novel, then—initially entitled *The Isle of Rest* (Najder, *Chronicle* 453)—the pervasive "inward unrest" (*Su* 165) may be somewhat different from the "unrest" that, for instance, stirs the Professor, and that Privy Counselor Wurmt wishes to "'accentuat[e]'" (*SA* 81, 17). The entirety of pendulous Europe, fragmented and fractious, awaits decisions to be made by the Congress of Vienna that will supposedly stabilize the continent regarding virtually every conceivable structure of power. In no other Conrad novel is dislocation as complete or anticipated restorative action as comprehensive, for "'The fate of nations hangs in the balance'" (*Su* 106). Yet, as Metternich suspected early in 1814, noting "There will be war again within two years" (Paul Johnson 76), this is a balance whose beam is soon to be stirred radically when Napoleon, aboard the *Inconstant*, abandons his "isle of rest," thereby making "inward unrest" (*Su* 165) once more violently manifest. A more precarious historical moment of "benumbed immobility" (*NoN* 78), fraught with greater extremity and, at last, greater abjection, is difficult to cite.

Conrad's biographers observe that the Napoleonic era consistently fascinated him, although only near the end of his life did he attempt directly to incorporate such a momentous context into a work of fiction. This fascination is impossible to explain reductively, of course—though the fact that the fourth division of Poland was consequent upon Napoleon's escape from Elba, while the Triple Alliance at Vienna sought to prevent another union of

French and Polish revolutionaries, is probably implicated. More generally, Conrad exhibits a lifelong preoccupation with all manner of literal and metaphoric "suspended menace" (*LJ* 96), and repeatedly expresses skepticism regarding the motivation and value particularly of individual acts with a political cast.

Consider briefly in this respect *The Rescue*, the novel that occupied intermittently twenty-three years of Conrad's life, and that he completed at the very time he began work on *Suspense*. Conrad obviously is preoccupied with such a concept, for in *The Rescue* "suspended" appears at least five times and "suspense" twice (167, 183, 195, 203, 452; 168, 281). With one exception, these words denote either a character in a state of indecisiveness about personal conduct that bears upon largely private issues, or an object that literally seems to hang in space. The nature of the exception is revealing, for in it the word "suspense" is applied to a leader's indifference to private appeals as he decides whether to perform public, politically crucial deeds upon which the fate of many lives depends: "No words, no blandishments ... or whisperings of a favorite could affect either the resolves or irresolutions of [Belarab] whose action ever seemed to hang in mystic suspense between the contradictory speculations and judgments disputing the possession of his will" (*Re* 281). Apart from the overt meaning of this sentence, the syntax and structure embody Conrad's fascination with an experience of torpor consequent upon an encounter with some sort of binary clash. Any capacity for "action" is (only seemingly) annulled forever, as it is not merely suspended, but redundantly and occultly "hangs in mystic suspense" due to "contradictory speculations and judgments," a phrase whose structure negates the prior order of nouns denoting definiteness and indefiniteness, "resolves or irresolutions," even as "and" abolishes the promise of decisive discrimination previously offered by "or." Finally, the entirety of the sentence asserts the utterly dubious notion that it is preferable to have one's will be subject to contradictory promptings of such mystical potency that they are virtually independent psychic agents, rather than to be vulnerable to the seductive whims of a favorite woman. And the sentence itself is a segment of indirect discourse, summarizing the ruminations of the terminally lingering Lingard, of course. Such a semantic vortex is typically elicited in Conrad's prose whenever the possibility of taking decisive public action looms, for there is little that seems to cause him more anxiety than the prospect of aggressive political intervention, no matter how scrupulous the agents' designs are. In the above passage, after all, even Belarab's potential to act—he's a politically powerful but minor character in *The Rescue*—must be rhetorically and (therefore) philosophically dissolved.

Little in Conrad's work is more predictable than the trivialization of political action by means of such characterological dissolution. In *Suspense*, set in a politically contentious city during the deliberations of the Congress of Vienna, it is highly debatable whether the specific facts of the labyrinthine historical moment have any aesthetic purpose beyond providing a vague occasion for the protagonist's own confusion and resultant indecisiveness. For instance, as Part I closes, Cosmo Latham's servant, Spire, is asked to take action that he perceives as culturally discontinuous. Aware that the present historical moment's "tension" and "restlessness" are "'very extraordinary,'" Spire simply cannot understand "'what's come to them all. Everybody seems excited.'" Worse, his young master then instructs him incongruously to "'follow'" an "'angry gentleman'" [Dr. Martel] "'and try to see where he goes'" (*Su* 52–54). Spire, part of a generation "born to a settled order of things," has literally no words to describe the consequences of "the most agitated ten years of European history," and, in "astonishment" at being ordered to become an ungentlemanly snoop, can only exclaim "'Well, I never!'" (*Su* 99, 91, 54). Both Spire and Cosmo are trying to "lay to rest" anxiety over the nature of the cultural moment, the former by reactive withdrawal from that which he "'never'" conceived, the latter by becoming entangled in others' conspiratorial action that may or may not create "the illusion of a mastered destiny" (*NLL* 109)—or, indeed, of any "'Destiny'" at all, since "'One must live a very long time to even see the hem of her robe'" (*Su* 144). It may be that "'Austerlitz has done it,'" as Sir Charles asseverates, but the referent of "it" remains unclear, though its impact causes "anguish ... acute" (*Su* 36).

Their problem, of course, involves an attempt to comprehend the cultural context of the Revolutionary era, begun formally perhaps by Kant in *The Conflict of the Faculties* (1798), and continued by Ernst Moritz Arndt in *Geist der Zeit* (2 vols., 1805, 1809; the major topic is Napoleon, "*Der Empogekommene*," the Parvenu), and by Hazlitt in *The Spirit of the Age* (1825). However, in *Suspense* there is only the absence of any substantive about which to speculate, only "the wide world filled with the strife of ideas and the struggle of nations" that makes even the recent past seem "'quite another age'" (22, 90). Amidst such "strife," few traditionally determined grounds of assertive social participation remain, for, as Cosmo remarks, " 'The smoke hangs about yet and I cannot see,'" to which Adele responds, "'One doesn't know where to look'" (*Su* 143). Hence, espionage becomes an epistemologically definitive act, since there is little to do as the "world ... enjoy[s] its first breathing time" but "'make use of agents more or less shady'"—"Austrian spies," the "'Piedmontese *sbirri*,'" the "'priests ... poking their noses everywhere'" or the "'spy'" Bernard—to collect information that might help renew explanatory constructs (*Su* 103–104, 11, 151). Moreover, this is the international task of "'settling the frontiers'" conceptually (*Su* 100) during a time when, with regard to social control, techniques of surveillance are displacing techniques of sovereignty, and a new "threshold of efficiency" requires that the formation of a body of knowledge about individuals should take the place of "a power that is manifested through the brilliance of those who exercise it" (Foucault, *Discipline* 220, 224).

So pervasive is Cosmo's sense of dislocation that, unlike even the lovelorn nihilist Decoud, he simply cannot compose letters, although he is determined to "'write, whole reams,'" which, at the urging of others, he tries repeatedly to do (*Su* 42; see 70, 91–92, 100, 176, 188). Increasingly immobilized, as "facts appraised by reason preserved a ... dual character," Cosmo begins "thinking contradictorily," and, in response to Dr. Martel's query concerning the "'end of history,'" can give "no answer" (*Su* 38, 91, 62). In this era "Letters were not spontaneous effusions but ... 'symbols of compromise' between the public and the private, the individual and the social" (Perrot and Martin-Fugier 132). Hence, only those who are simply dull (Lady Latham: *Su* 20), or who remain committed ideologically, preserving rudimentary grounds for action, can correspond in writing, either as reactionaries (the Marquis d'Armand, Talleyrand, the French consul, Bernard the spy: *Su* 106–107, 151) or subversives (Attilio, Cantelucci, the count: *Su* 12, 199, 202). This is why Cosmo, who initially declares "Reason is my only guide" (*Su* 9), begins a transition from faltering private infatuation to halting political involvement when "a bundle of papers, dangerous documents," correspondence from Napoleonic conspirators in Italy, "fell on the top of his head," indeed, with metaphoric impact (*Su* 237, 234).

As might be expected in a novel haunted by a time when "'lots of heads rolled'" (*Su* 64), the narrative voice ominously uses the synecdoche "heads" for persons (see *Su* 22, 43, 62, 68–69, 78, 83–85, 112, 120, 122, 198, 210). To Cosmo, who misses the "peace of his Yorkshire home," and fears getting "knocked on the head," the blow from the packet is physically modest but characterologically profound, for it begins a modest process of psychological transformation that he personally appreciates as the making of a "state of inward peace" (*Su* 40, 43, 240). The word "peace" defines an important motif with regard to international affairs, of course (see *Su* 9, 24, 62, 199). But as the novel moves relentlessly and (for Conrad) predictably toward debilitating subjective tensions, the idea of peace gets personalized. Missing from Genoa in 1814, however, are trenchant cultural expectations that might make possible that "'unswerving fidelity to what is expected of you [that] only ... secures the reward, peace'" (*TU* 156). Consequently, it is precisely Cosmo's search for inward tranquility that brings him into contact with "the whisperers in the tower" (*Su* 261) at the end of Conrad's manuscript.

The privileged son of a "naturally kind and hospitable" baronet, Cosmo lost his mother early in life, a woman with "a drop of Medici blood" who incongruously demonstrated "a marvellously commonplace mind" and a "fear of all initiative" (*Su* 19–20). Her husband, Sir Charles, no doubt poses no threat to his wife's "idle equanimity," since he embraces a politics of virtual stasis; with steadfast "fidelity to national prejudices of every sort," he has "no great liking for ... aristocrats, despised the fashionable world, and would have nothing whatever to do with any kind of 'upstart,'" while his "scorn for men's haphazard

activities and shortsighted views was combined with a calm belief in the future" (Su 20, 23). Small wonder, then, that during *Suspense* Cosmo's befuddle-
ment only increases, since his "faculty of orientation in strange surroundings"
(*Su* 17) has never been seriously tested.

In Italy, Cosmo must struggle with discordant social and political surroundings that remain ever elusive. Hence, his comment in yet another unfinished letter to his sister, "At this rate I will never arrive in Genoa" (*Su* 188), is
unintentionally metaphoric, for the place, "'seething with conspiracies,'"
makes him feel "lost in an enchanted city" (*Su* 108, 44). Then, too, he discovers
a childhood friend, "marvellous" Countess Adele de Montevesso, whose "brilliance," "beauty," and "charm" cause him yet again to be "exasperated," since
the "more he saw of the grown woman, the less connection she seemed to have
with the early Adele. The contrast was too strong," and consequently the "lady
on the sofa . . . may or may not have been Adele d'Armand at one time" (*Su*
95–96, 86, 155). Although her appearance is indeed enthralling, Cosmo is particularly drawn to her when he learns from Aglae, her maid, that "'Miss Adele
had not a moment's peace since she drive away from your big home,'" that she,
too, yearns for "'peace'" (*Su* 82, 135). Disappointingly, Adele is now wed to a
"military adventurer of the commonest type" (*Su* 123), whose identity and
wealth are an accident of the very international upheaval that makes the process of "arriv[ing] in Genoa" so disorienting, and that no one seems able to explain, or even name, since doing that would also mean grasping the essence of
Napoleon—"'what has done it?'"—and the consequences of his collapsed empire—"'what has it done?'" (*Su* 143–144)—that are embodied in Genoa and in
Adele's "nasty upstart" husband, the count (*Su* 42; see 33, 37, 41, 157), with
only a maddening imprecision.

Cosmo has been charged by his sister "to write everything he could find
out, hear, or even guess about Napoleon" (*Su* 72). Small wonder, then, he cannot finish a letter, for there remains little more than a "deconstruction of the
social as a global ground of explanation" and a resultant "political struggle
over the hierarchization of . . . discourses" (Baker 193). A symptom of all this
is the rhetorical and conceptual struggle diagnostically to frame Napoleon as a
historical phenomenon responsible for having discomposed private life into a
mere "'feeling of suspense [which] that man's presence gives rise to'" (*Su* 194).
Can it be that "the Destructor of the Austrians," and "the only man of his
time," is merely "'the power of lies,'" in fact of "'no account,'" indeed, just
"nothing" (*Su* 52, 26, 38, 143)? Although Cosmo had affirmed to his reactionary father that "'Nobody can admire that man more than I do,'" finally he
can adopt "neither of the contrasted views of Napoleon" that are "entertained
by his contemporaries" (*Su* 38). So maybe the only resource is the rhetoric of a
Wordsworthian seance: "'Napoleon is . . . an unseen presence'" (*Su* 93; compare "Tintern Abbey" l. 94), possibly even messianic, since conspirators and

aristocrats alike agree "'whenever two men meet he is a third'" and "'Whenever three people come together he is the presence that is with them'" (*Su* 261, 93; compare Matthew 18:20, and *No* 100 for a parody). Again, "'what has done it?'"—perhaps, indeed, "'Austerlitz has done it'" (*Su* 144, 36, 42), but the enigmatic pronoun persists, surely connoting far more than merely the Treaty of Pressburg (December 26, 1805) and the collapse of the Third Coalition. In *Suspense*, then, "Napoleon" is primarily that ominous, pronominal proper noun—at most "'the idea'" or "'the Other'" (*Su* 182, 165)—that connotes "forces ... that pushed people to rash or unseemly actions," as "'the great man'" (*Su* 36,107) himself had claimed to the Council of Ancients (19 Brumaire 1799): "I will be your agent in action" (qtd. in Durant and Durant 122).

Surrounded primarily by "shadowy figures on the shifting background of a very poignant, very real, and intense drama of contemporary history" in a "'Europe [that] is mysterious ... just now,'" featuring "'Different men, different wisdoms'" (*Su* 38–39, 5), Cosmo is vulnerable to any further enhancement of uncertainty. He finds just such an enhanced enigma in Adele de Montevesso, whose impact he can only understand in terms of "immensely mysterious" Napoleonic "greatness" (*Su* 38). Thoughts of her "interfered with the process of consecutive thinking," and he concludes clumsily, "A woman like that was a great power" (*Su* 95–96; permutations of "great" mark perceptual struggle throughout). Particularly appealing is Adele's figurative language. Embroiled in a marital disaster that embodies and results from the international political and financial upheaval incited by Napoleon, Adele, "like a lost child in a forest" (*Su* 212), resorts to a trope of playacting when she tries to articulate her sense of confusion and inauthenticity, and Cosmo adopts it. Soon after they meet, Adele expresses her sense of the emptiness of the historical moment, saying "'The play is over, the stage seems empty'" (*Su* 90). Later, when toiling to write to his sister simply about the landscape, Cosmo's mental state resembles Adele's, for he feels he is "laboring the description of the scenery of a stage after a great play had come to an end. A vain thing," and he only acknowledges inclusive, debilitating perplexity in a hasty postscript: "You can form no idea of the state of suspense in which *all classes* live here" (*Su* 188–189; my emphasis). Indeed, "no idea" will suffice, for European culture has been suspended by Napoleon, "'the idea'" itself (*Su* 182). Furthermore, the metaphoric vehicle of playacting proves inadequate because it blends ideas of "actor" and "plaything," while leaving director and puppet master unidentified. As Cosmo waits for Adele in the ambivalent Palazzo Rosso—a "red" edifice, "white walls and red benches," inhabited by "white" partisans (*Su* 80, 155)—his thoughts are summarized by the narrative voice: "All these people were mere playthings .... But who or what was playing with them? He thought ... in the manner of people watching the changes on a stage" (*Su* 120). Or, yet again, "'what has done it?'" (*Su* 144).

Fatefully, for Cosmo the tormented woman Adele, "the presence" (*Su* 195), becomes a personified symptom of contemporary historical convulsions fomented by Napoleon, the "'presence'" (*Su* 194). A captivating aristocratic beauty held financially and politically captive by a "'nasty upstart'"—a "common stupid soldier of fortune," the *parvenu* husband who "'has always been inevitable'" (*Su* 42, 185, 130)—Adele persistently rues the loss of a sustaining, salutary culture. Having "had all her illusions about rectitude destroyed ... early," she copes with personal wretchedness in her "'Inevitable'" marriage by "'learn[ing] to suppress every expression of feeling,'" and, "'caring for nothing, as though I had done with the world,'" she thereby achieves "'peace'" (*Su* 35, 148, 135). Significantly, Adele's description of her private state of mind parallels Cosmo's diagnosis of the French collective persona that he experienced while in Paris—a "'sense of security'" achieved as a result of "'the absence ... almost of all feeling'" so extreme that "'one would have thought ... Bonaparte had never existed'" (*Su* 105). Fittingly, then, Adele is reluctant even to name the upstart Napoleon, and calls him merely "'the presence,'" the "'man in Elba,'" a "'mock king,'" while describing the "'baseness of selfish passions'" under which she lived during the Empire, when she found "'All hopes were crushed. It was like a dreadful overdressed masquerade with the everlasting sound of the guns in the distance'" (*Su* 93, 145–50). As if "looking down at the ashes of a burnt-up world" (*Su* 143), she concludes that, because of Napoleon, "'there is nowhere any honesty on earth—nowhere!'" (*Su* 148–49). Indeed, "'Everything is ended already,'" and she finds it therefore "'intolerable'" that emigrés now trifle at getting "'the world ... put back where it was before you and I were born,'" for they have "'come back without a single patriotic feeling ... like merciless spectres out of a grave, hating the world to which they had returned. They had forgotten nothing and learned nothing'" (*Su* 149–150).[5] Like Adele, Cosmo detests "'the work'" of Bourbon restoration going on in Vienna (*Su* 40), and he even shares her metaphor, thinking scornfully of "the royalist-legitimist enthusiasms ... now paraded like a rouged and powdered corpse putting on a swagger of life and revenge" (*Su* 114). But her relentlessly negational history lesson is disquieting, especially since much of it is directed against both herself and Napoleon, about whom Cosmo had affirmed: "'Nobody can admire that man more than I'" (*Su* 38).

Adele's vitiating words leave Cosmo with little more than her remarkable appearance whereby he might preserve a sense of substance and commonweal. And, seeking stability, he consequently becomes enthralled by the surfaces of a woman who is, in fact, in a state of suspension personally and politically. Cosmo long has remembered her as a "'marvel of fairness,'" and, inured to the marvelous, he even acquiesces when Spire at first gets Dr. Martel's name wrong, pronouncing it "'Marvel'" (*Su* 41, 53). Like the doctor, who also finds her "a marvellous being" (*Su* 211), Cosmo immediately sees Adele as "marvellous" when he first meets her in Genoa (*Su* 96). In fact, her presence straightway makes him forget "Lady Jane," the woman who "had, so to speak, attended him all the way from Paris [to] Cantelucci's inn" (*Su* 71). Unaware of the prohibition against marveling in Conrad's world—where "marvellousness is a hidden thing," hence it is best not to "say marvellously or miraculously . . . because these are . . . overstatements of undisciplined minds" (*NLL* 179)—Cosmo finds in Adele's image, "such a marvel," an unprecedented psychological buttress that makes him feel "unconsciously grateful," since her "seductive voice" and the "living profundity" of the "deep dark blue of her eyes" save him from "that acute social awkwardness from which he used to suffer" (*Su* 195, 87; see 76, 86). And, "their eyes [having] remained fastened . . . for a time," the susceptible Cosmo even concludes "Light entered into her composition," and, with "white shoulders" and a "gold mist of hair," she "'actually glows'" (*Su* 88, 129–130; cf. Mrs. Travers: *Re* 139, 214, 236, 264, 315).

This mitigative image is profoundly compelling. Earlier in the day, only briefly and temporarily parted from Adele, Cosmo had already experienced a "solitude" in which he "could not think connectedly," and "even came to the verge of that state in which one sees visions" (*Su* 95). He is an unusually vulnerable young man. Regarding his personal history with women, Cosmo recently bragged "'I can safely say I've never been conquered'" (*Su* 91), which means he most unsafely has "never" had much experience coping with extreme emotional deprivation, either. Later, when his evening with Adele ends, Cosmo can scarcely endure the loss. Beset by "loneliness" for "the first time in his life," realizing he had "nothing to do," had "never made any real friends," and feeling "mortally weary," Cosmo approaches cosmic disorientation, unable "to know what to think of anything in the world" (*Su* 175–176).

The next morning Cosmo feels only "dismay," for he cannot decide "what to do" (*Su* 176). This vocabulary indicates that he is in a transitional state, since discontent, expressed in just these words, historically denotes incipient political agitation and execution, not merely private indecision. Thus, Charles Gould's avowal, "'There were things to be done. We have done them; we have gone on doing them'" (*No* 230), and Haldin's deposition to Razumov, "'When the necessity of this heavy work came to me . . . I understood that it had to be done'" (*UWE* 23), burlesqued by Decoud's insular "'It is done'" (*No* 501). Indeed, Carlyle practically begins *The French Revolution* (1837) with the query "what is to be done?" (15). Charles Kingsley entitles an entire chapter of *Yeast* (1848) "What's to be Done?" Soon thereafter appear Tolstoy's *What Then Must We Do?* and Chernyshevsky's *What Is To Be Done?* And the twentieth century opens with V.I. Lenin's *What Is To Be Done?* (1902), a phrase that is echoed by Jack London's Bishop Morehouse in *The Iron Heel* (1908), "'What is to be done?'" (61). That is, by causing Cosmo to formulate this question in just this way in Genoa in the year 1814, Conrad (writing just after the Bolshevik

Revolution, after all) incorporates a rhetorical pattern that has long been identified with working-class revolt. And in *Suspense*, this phrase heralds a striking psychological change in Cosmo. Finding the very "notion of captivity" to be "odious," he languishes, impotent and isolated, among "triumphant reactionaries" at a time when, at most, "'everybody seems to be doing Elba'" (*Su* 78, 106). He is left with the repulsive thought of "doing the churches" and the cloying realization that "there was no need for him to do anything." Thus, not even the insightful Doctor Martel, who answers the question "'what could you do?'" with "'Nothing,'" can keep Cosmo from "the black waters of melancholia" (*Su* 176–177, 181).

Provocation leading to this imminent change can be explicated more precisely. Cosmo is clearly infatuated with Adele. However, in view of this infatuation, the simile used by the narrative voice to describe Cosmo's state of mind, as he reluctantly abandoned the "solitude" of his chamber the previous evening to go to visit Adele, requires analytic comment: "when he forced himself out of that empty room, it was with a profound disgust of all he was going to see and hear ... like a man tearing himself away from the side of a beloved mistress" (*Su* 96). Since he is in fact "going to" Adele, whose "appearance" that afternoon had created "an impression of living profundity" (*Su* 87), Cosmo's "profound disgust," coupled with the notion of leaving "a beloved mistress" (the vehicle for the tenor, "solitude"), evince a discordant consciousness. Clearly, Cosmo is smitten by two opposed categories of experience, both gendered female. Small wonder that next morning he "felt as if lost in a strange world" (*Su* 194).

Cosmo knows only three places in Genoa: the "wonderful peace" of the harbor tower, qualified by the company of Attilio, the conspirator; Cantelucci's inn, its dining room charged with soldiers' triumphant bluster and losers' political intrigue, but offering "solitude" in a private bedchamber; and the Palazzo Rosso, where lovely, impecunious, aristocratic Adele lives with her wealthy "'Piedmontese upstart'" husband, son of a "dealer in rabbit skins" (*Su* 9, 37, 140). Repeatedly, he takes refuge in his chamber at the inn from the ambiguous political and emotional claims of the other locations. However, on the fateful evening of his last day in Genoa, Cosmo finds his room less than restful, for he feels "lost in a strange world," and doubts that he ever should have "called that day at the Palace, if only to say good-bye" to Adele (*Su* 194). Musing on the excessive impact her appearance had upon him recently, "like the awed recollection of a prophetic vision," Cosmo concludes that the feeling "he had seen her glory before" cannot merely be attributed to vestigial memories he retains from childhood, for "no man ever found the premonition of such a marvel in the obscure promptings of ... flesh" (*Su* 195). He suddenly realizes that the mortal woman's "harmony of aspect" seems actually to be an extension of an aesthetic experience he repeatedly had while growing up, that Adele "must have been foretold to him ... in Latham Hall, where one came on pictures (mostly of the Italian school) in unexpected places ... in spare bedrooms" (*Su* 195).

Immediately hereafter, he is able to re-create, in his (spare) bedroom at the inn, the details of the painting that has long haunted him unawares:

> A luminous oval face on the dark background—the noble full-length woman, stepping out of the narrow frame with long draperies held by jewelled clasps and girdle, with pearls on head and bosom, carrying a book and a pen (or was it a palm?) and—yes! he saw it plainly with terror—with her left breast pierced by a dagger ... as if the blow had been struck before his eyes [the] released hilt seemed to vibrate yet, while the eyes looked straight at him, profound, unconscious in miraculous tranquillity. (*Su* 195)

The novel never makes clear whether such a painting exists at Sir Charles's country house. The only basis for an analytic response to Cosmo's vision is the appearance earlier of the actual Adele, which parallels the figure in the picture in many ways. The "Italian" context of the palazzo goes without saying. Like the "luminous," "noble" figure in the painting, with "long draperies," framed "narrow[ly]," with "book and pen" and "profound" gaze, Adele—the "tall" countess whose very name means "noble" (German *Adel:* "nobleness") and who "'actually glows'" in a long "blue robe"—is at first seen using a "pen," and, with "profundity of ... eyes," subsequently greets Cosmo within the "carved frame" of a sofa with "living profundity" (*Su* 84, 129, 87). Missing from the actual encounter are the "pearls" (which displace Adele's "gold circlet"), the heart-piercing dagger, and the possible modulation of "a pen" into "a palm."

That is, with its corrective supplements connoting innocent perfection and martyred sensibility, Cosmo's aesthetic fantasy creates an icon of a palmary, immolated "pearl of great price" (Matthew 13:46), "dying hart,/ ... transfixed with a cruell dart" (*Faerie Queene* III. xii. 31), devoid of compromising personal and cultural history. The image is therefore far more unified conceptually than the "enchanting" but exhausted Countess, "marvellous" but "not her own mistress," indefinitely suspended in heartbreak, poverty, and political disenchantment, saying, "'I feel very old'" from a couch the color of "pure ashes," and, later, while reminiscing, staring ruefully at "white ashes" on the hearth "as if looking down at the ashes of a burnt-up world" (*Su* 91, 85, 96, 142–143).

Early in the novel Attilio told Cosmo that he had "'marvellous adventures before'" him, and, indeed, he has met "a marvel" of a "marvellous being" named Adele, though in her inclusive enervation she is scarcely an occasion for brisk adventure (*Su* 16, 195, 211). So, as Cosmo, "alone within ... four bare walls" (*Su* 196), sits fecklessly, it remains to be decided which of Attilio's prognostic words will achieve dominance psychologically—petrific admiration or dynamic, transformative "adventures." Yet the issue has already been decided rhetorically, for twice, as Cosmo went to pronounce Adele's name, he could only stammer proleptically the first syllable, "'Ad—'" (*Su* 88, 121). The word "*ad*" in Latin means "to" or "toward," of course, and is the initial syllable of "adventure," or, the ability to be receptive to whatever might be "coming toward" (*ad* + *venio*). Small wonder then that Cosmo, instead of marveling, spellbound, at his aesthetic vision, judges it to be "awful," and "jumped up" in "horror" and "fled" (*Su* 196). For this is the moment of decision, "'a time ... when anything may happen,'" when Cosmo must come to terms with the fact that, literally and metaphorically, "In the whole town he knew only the way to the Palazzo and the way to the port." And, as if responding only to the first syllable of Adele's name, "He took the latter direction," naked toward "fantastic adventure," with "sudden relief ... in the mere resolution to go off secretly with only ... clothes, absolutely without money or anything of value ... not even a watch" (*Su* 192, 196, 255, 270). For Cosmo is simply "impatient to be doing" (*Su* 270).

Just exactly what he's "doing" remains undefined in the novel. Presumably the conspirators, who send clandestine communications to Elba, are part of the network of international informers keeping Napoleon aware of the increasingly negative "mood of his former subjects," the result of Louis XVIII asserting the Charter of 1814 as his "gift" to the nation, thereby suggesting the revolution and Napoleon's reign had never occurred, and permitting his younger brother, the Count of Artois, and his Ultraroyalist faction to obtain unwarranted social control (Breunig 110–111). In any case, Conrad is little interested in the details and dynamics of the political complexities he sporadically invokes. Instead, *Suspense* enacts his usual project of analytically fragmenting his protagonist's psyche into various conflicting private compulsions, thereby undercutting this character's potential to be an informed, authentic participant in any political activity that might challenge established money and power. In so doing, Conrad clarifies the considerable difference between his rather shallow use of specific political details and imperatives, and, for instance, Napoleon's own contention, made on the eve of Austerlitz, that "Policy should take the place in our theater of ancient fatality ... [since] in the exigencies of politics ... it [is] only necessary to place your personages in opposition to other passions ... under the absolute influence of this powerful necessity" (qtd. in Hay 80). For the novel ends with Cosmo still poised confusedly within permutations of the verb "to do," which practically annuls the century-long connotations this word has accumulated as a signature of working-class revolt. While detained by the *sbirri*, who are rowing him across the harbor to deliver him to the gendarmes, Cosmo wonders "what he had better do," although even after Attilio and his accomplices have delivered him from the authorities and taken him aboard their own boat, Cosmo still can only ask of Attilio, "'What can you do?'" (*Su* 243, 266). At this point he may indeed have "completed the cycle of his adventures," having passed from his early encounter on the tower with Attilio, through infatuation at the Palazzo Rosso, and back to Attilio. But Cosmo cannot transcend the notion of an erotic relationship that informed much of this "cycle," for such rhetoric forms the metaphoric vehicle whereby he conceives of his involvement with the conspirators. Even after his rescue, Cosmo can only contemplate the "splendid charm" of his "adventure" as "resembling the power of a great and unfathomable love" (*Su* 255), apparently having little comprehension of prior or pending international conflict.

Yet there is one important difference between his growing attachment to Adele and his sudden entanglement with Attilio's band. His love only provoked a vision and consequently an unbearable degree of agitation that forced him to flee even his bedchamber at Cantelucci's inn, whereas aboard the conspirators' boat Cosmo luxuriates in a paradoxical "feeling of peace that had come to him directly his trouble had begun," and that "like a sacred spell lays to rest all the vividities and ... violences of passionate desire" (*Su* 244, 255). It remains unclear whether this feeling contrasts with the "'peace'" Adele finds after her ruinous engagement to the count, and with the alarming "unconscious ... miraculous tranquillity" exuded by the dying woman in his fantasy (*Su* 135, 195). Conrad's manuscript also leaves undecided whether Cosmo comes to understand the virtually Marlovian remark that Attilio makes while boarding the felucca for Elba, "'You will have to be one of ourselves for a time'" (*Su* 273).

Be this as it may, both Cosmo's response, "'what am I doing here?'" and the ultimate historical fate of "'that man in Elba'" (*Su* 273, 149), suggest the author—who, when asked late in life why he never participated even in Polish affairs, replied "'It is not my watch on deck'" (qtd. in Hay 60)—sank into his own peace as content with visions of abject suspension as he ever was in his earlier political fiction. But an important question remains. If, as Foucault claims, "political action belongs to a category of participation completely different from ... written or bookish acts," and if "to engage in politics ... is to try to know with the greatest possible honesty whether or not the revolution is desirable," then—since Conrad's "political novels" primarily use evasive, reactionary allusions to statecraft, economics, and social station as a context wherein to dramatize little more than recurring personal demise amid social inertia—it seems imperative to consider whether they have anything to do with politics at all. For "politics is a field which was opened by the existence of the revolution, and if the question of revolution can no longer be asked in these terms, then politics risks disappearing" (*Live* 191, 152).[6]

Notes

*   *Note from editors:* This chapter is part of a longer essay on Conrad, the aesthetics of suspense, and politics. Its remaining segments will be appearing in their entirety in the number of *Conradiana* adjunct to this volume.

1.   For "suspense" in some other works, see Bonney, "Conrad's Romanticism" 196–198.

2.   In a fine 20-page essay, Armstrong uses "contradiction(s)" and "contradictory" thirty-one times. Much history may consist, figuratively speaking, of a rebellious Montero, a "shameless Indio," fighting a capitalist-client Barrios, an "'ignorant, boastful Indio,'" whose troops consist of "Indios, only caught the other day" fighting "'Indios [who] know nothing either of reason or politics'" (*No* 190, 171, 167, 181). But such contradiction is not necessarily symmetrically negational and hence the antecedent of an all-consuming suspension, for the "successful" consequences of "political action" (*No* 521, 176)—superior finance and weapons—decide outcomes and bespeak a future. Even during the

nineteenth century, quite a different understanding is already current. Hegel, a founder of modern historiography, "envisages the categories of the Logic becoming richer in a cumulative fashion as they develop out of each other," since a transitional process will generally produce "*more* than one known new category that stands in [the] relation" of the "negative of the negative" to a "given pair of ... contrary categories," whereupon finally "*every* higher category in the Logic stands in this relation to *every* lower pair of contraries" (Forster 146–147, italics original). Given this context, then, as Conrad, in the process of dramatizing the historical process, artistically causes the existence of "contradictions" to generate merely iterations of annulment, he is narrowly limiting his aesthetics to an ideological purpose.

3. Cosmo, the bland young man, is by novel's end primarily an aftereffect of others' words, "a site of the heterogeneous subject positions constituted by ... competing discourses" (Baker 193), analogous to the agitated cultural situation itself. The novel continually presents him listening, with varied degrees of receptivity, to Sir Charles, Attilio, Dr. Martel, Adele, and others, whose remarks then mingle in his memory with enervating results. Interestingly, this name appears in Ludwig Tieck's influential and complex epistolary novel, *Die Geschichte des Herrn William Lovells* (1795), where the character Cosimo turns out to be an Englishman named Waterloo. The name also appears in Scott's *Waverley*.

4. The San Tomé excavation in *Nostromo* aggressively negates the trope of the mine as a *locus* of transcendental insights and encounters that is widespread in the Romantic era. See Ziolkowski, 18–63. Of greater interest is the fact that Gould's *idée fixe*—using both the mine and the capitalist military that protects foreign investments as a means to stabilize Sulaco politically, thus improving its citizens' daily lot—is conceived *entirely* as a personal, even "insane" (*No* 379) reaction to his father's fate. Once again, a maelstrom of private psychology permits Conrad to dodge facts of recent revolutionary history. For a "Napoleonic edict of 1810 made the concession of national mineral rights to private enterprise conditional on the obligation of the entrepreneur to ensure 'good order and security'... among the 'mass of men, women, and children' needed for their exploitation" (C. Gordon 27).

5. The trope of "the return" is prominent throughout nineteenth-century literature and philosophy. See Abrams 141–324; Reed 216–249. Of course, in the uncongenial realm of real-world history, various abortive returns and restorations primarily suggest that "all the great events and characters of world history occur, so to speak, twice. . .the first time as tragedy, the second as farce," whereupon "Men and events appear as Schlemihls in reverse, as shadows which have become detached from their bodies" (Marx 146, 171). In *Suspense*, where a Napoleonic "return" is anticipated that will fail wretchedly (as will efforts to "restore" the Bourbon hegemony), the trope of drama and farce is definitive: see 90, 120, 145, 185, 188, 204. Of course, rejection of the very notion of genuine repetition is a sign of post-Romantic historicism. Foucault is adamant: "One should totally and absolutely suspect anything that claims to be a return. ... there is in fact no such thing as a return" (*Live* 269).

6. In any case, it's doubtful that the aesthetically adroit hopelessness of Conrad's intransigent political posturings can be taken seriously in a world where increasingly ruthless military assaults are necessary merely to safeguard the intellectually vapid, secular transcendentalism (see L. White, H. Daly) of a failing capitalist economy that has demonstrably been an ecological and human disaster for nearly two centuries (see Rifkin). The terms whereby superannuated reactionary visions of political suspension must be rejected are now simply provided by hard science: "If today is a typical day on planet Earth, we will lose 116 square miles of rainforest or about an acre a second. We will lose another 72 square miles to encroaching deserts, the results of ... overpopulation. We will lose 40–100 species, and no one knows whether the number is 40 or 100. Today the human population will increase by 250,000. And today we will add 2,700 tons of chlorofluorocarbons to the atmosphere and 15 million tons of carbon. Tonight the Earth will be a little hotter, its waters more acidic, and the fabric of life more threadbare" (Orr 1). For the sake of brevity, let the very existence of Monsanto's lucrative "Terminator" technology provide a bleak synecdoche: Nature's ability to renew itself annually is now being destroyed selectively to make crops sterile and force farmers to buy new seed each spring from corporate sources (see Margaronis, Shiva). *Ça ira.*

11

Conrad on the Borderlands of Modernism: Maurice Greiffenhagen, Dorothy Richardson and the Case of *Typhoon*

SUSAN JONES

Recently, borders and borderlands have become the common theoretical currency of anthropology, cultural, and postcolonial studies. But in this chapter I re-deploy these terms to offer an alternative perspective on familiar readings of Conrad's contribution to literary modernism in the context of narrative experimentation and literary aesthetics at the turn of the twentieth century. As a focus, I will use Conrad's initial publication of *Typhoon*, first considering the writer's encounter with the artist Maurice Greiffenhagen, who provided illustrations for *Typhoon's* serialization in *Pall Mall Magazine* (1902) and later for *The Rescue* in *Land and Water* (1919).[1] Second, I consider *Typhoon's* impact on a later exponent of high modernism, the writer Dorothy Richardson, whose epic novel series, *Pilgrimage*, is associated with the representation of female consciousness.[2] The relationships of both painter and writer to Conrad, occurring as they did on the "borderlands" of their mainstream artistic engagements, remain largely overlooked in critical discussions of Conrad. Yet a study of these artists' protomodernist and modernist aesthetic practices reveals surprising conjunctions, emending our view of Conrad's development of protomodernist writing while revising our assumptions about his impact on subsequent innovators of high modernist fiction.

By exploring a familiar theme of modernist aesthetics—the representation of spatial and psychological "absences"—we find that Conrad's aesthetic practice took place within a wider field of influence and experimentation than is usually accorded to him. His engagement with Greiffenhagen's illustrations suggests we conceptualize modernism with great attention to the use of visual images in popular contexts. Shifting the viewpoint to Conrad's less obvious "borderland" relations with visual and literary artists also places him in a different relationship to his readers. Here his representation of absence and of the modern subject's "dislocations" of consciousness had an impact on twentieth-century women's writing in startlingly underappreciated ways.

I.

First, we need to look afresh at some of the more traditional views of literary aesthetics and literary production in relation to Conrad's that tend to limit our sense of his aesthetic development. Significantly, this requires a move away from conventional assessment of literary modernism as an event or "rupture" in aesthetics and formal methodology.[3] As twentieth-century critics have constructed the boundaries of a modernist canon, the protomodernist Conrad appears on a linear trajectory leading us toward the high modernism of Woolf, Eliot, Joyce, and Pound. While this paradigm conveniently orders our sense of what constitutes literary modernism, Conrad's engagement with a wider field of artistic endeavor fails to fit precisely the terms of this particular frame. But if we consider modernism in spatial rather than temporal terms, we might imagine Conrad's narratorial experimentation developing in borderlands and "contact zones," to adopt Mary Louise Pratt's phrase describing "social spaces where disparate cultures meet, clash, and grapple with each other" (*Imperial Eyes* 4), and where a variety of agencies collide, allowing for a broader intertextual and interdisciplinary field and the conjunction of a greater range of individuals and forces. Today, this perspective facilitates reading Conrad more broadly than as literary "protomodernist," a prominent member of a relatively limited field of *literati* engaged in rigorous philosophical discussions about textuality, a practitioner of radical experiments in narratology who focused on predominantly masculinist subjective conflicts. The alternative picture emphasizes his important engagements with journal publication, reveals him as an astute reader of popular forms, and, most intriguingly, as a modernist practitioner who specifically appealed to women readers and writers of twentieth-century fiction, shifting not just our sense of the modernist canon, but also the perception of a canon of influence on modernist writing.

Conrad's engagement with particular modernist "contact zones" needs some preliminary explanation. Both Maurice Greiffenhagen and Dorothy Richardson remain somewhat peripheral figures today, yet they enjoyed considerable renown during their respective careers. Greiffenhagen is most noted for his illustrations, in the 1880s, of H.R. Haggard's novels and for his contributions to *The Daily Chronicle*, *The Lady's Pictorial*, and, occasionally, *Punch*. Conrad's relationship to Greiffenhagen occurred not through the acknowledged mainstream of his most distinguished literary encounters, but on the borderlands of artistic exchange where the circulation of modernist aesthetics developed through more obscure conjunctions—in this case, between the literary and visual art forms of serial publication. Dorothy Richardson also belongs to the "contact zones" of modernism, where Conrad's influence on later writers often goes unrecognized. Here, I will explore his unacknowledged impact, not on the usual suspects, Woolf or Eliot, but on Richardson—a now somewhat neglected writer (although during her lifetime she was praised by Ford Madox Ford, H.G. Wells, and Woolf, among many others). Paradoxically it was Richardson, not Woolf, who May Sinclair claimed, in 1918, had invented the "stream of consciousness" novel (Scott 444).[4] Although Richardson's work has never been associated directly with Conrad, both writers owed their advancement in British literary circles to Edward Garnett, whose recognition of up-and-coming practitioners of radical experimentation in the novel is well known. We will see that Richardson's relation to Conrad, allusively cultivated in modernist aesthetics' "borderlands," may have been closer than we currently assume.

However, a further issue arises from the conjunction of Conrad, Greiffenhagen, and Richardson. The term "borderland," suggesting as it does a "peripheral" place, an unexpected area of contact, also urges us to reconsider how, in the twenty-first century, a variety of theoretical developments have facilitated the recovery of Conrad's relationship to previously unacknowledged associates. Thus, aspects of twentieth-century visual theory (arising from the influence of deconstruction, phenomenology, and psychoanalysis), as well as the impact of cultural studies, come into play in assessing Conrad's response to Greiffenhagen. Feminist and gender theories, questioning, as they frequently do, patriarchal notions of authority, canonization, and readership have shifted the balance of masculinist critical perspectives on Conrad, giving us access to the frequently unacknowledged aesthetic and philosophical problems he shared with women writers and readers.[5] Furthermore, such theories advance our perception of his influence, not just on the now "canonized" figures of women's writing, such as Virginia Woolf, but on less prominent figures, of whom Dorothy Richardson is only one unrecognized example.

I have observed elsewhere that French feminist theory prepares the ground for reconsidering Conrad's texts in this respect (Jones 20n). Hélène Cixous's well-known notion of *écriture feminine* suggests an appropriate starting point from which to dismantle conventional suppositions about Conrad's writing as unreservedly "masculine." As we will see, *Heart of Darkness, Lord Jim,* and *Under Western Eyes* provide paradigms of modernist innovation, the interrupted narrative, the gaps and hiatuses that Cixous associates, for example in Joyce's writing, with the libidinal forces of *écriture feminine.* Many feminists have argued that Cixous propagates biological essentialism by reversing the gender status of the Lacanian subject and describing the fragmentation of texts as its "feminine" counterpart. Subsequent developments in gender theory, such as Judith Butler's theories of "performativity," suggest an alternative to the essentialist turn of Cixous's argument, and the opening up of a forum for theoretical discussions of gender has further liberated us from narrow assumptions about Conrad's "masculinist" voice.[6] The emphasis on gender as performance, or indeed on the *text* as performance, has facilitated many alternative readings, promoting us to think beyond the socially dominant assumptions of heterosexuality and to include an exploration of the troubled masculinity or the homoerotic performances of Conrad's writing.[7]

More relevant for the purposes of this argument, feminist theories of the body have frequently emphasized the "tension between women's lived bodily experiences and the cultural meanings inscribed on the female body that always mediate those experiences" (Conboy 1). As we will see from the following account of Dorothy Richardson's "borrowing" from Conrad, a writer like Conrad, while predominantly concerned with a male subject in the fiction, nevertheless seems to have represented the complexities of his protagonists' physical and psychological experiences in a manner not wholly incompatible with later women writers' accounts of the conflict of consciousness and identity.

Moreover, Diana Fuss's work on reader-response theory provides insight into the way in which readerships are shaped by phenomena residing outside the text, an argument that has deep implications for canon formation. She refutes the claims of theorists such as Michael Riffaterre, Wolfgang Iser, and Hans Robert Jauss, who fail to identify the gender of the reader and maintain that the text remains the dominant location of the readers' expectations and responses. Fuss outlines the flaw in their argument, observing that determining the gender of the reader invites a questioning of gender roles in a much larger frame, since, she claims, "readers, like texts, are constructed; they inhabit reading practices rather than create them *ex nihilo*" (Fuss 35). Thus, if we consider that Richardson, as a writer, was encouraged by both Garnett and Ford, and at the same time as a reader she would have been a party to the circulation of texts within that literary circle, it comes as less of a surprise to find that Richardson's "reading practice" included Conrad's work. In this context, it is worthwhile remembering that when *The Nigger of the "Narcissus"* was initially published in 1897, Conrad had made particular reference not to Garnett's reaction, but to Garnett's wife's response to the novel. Conrad valued highly Constance's "most prized words of praise" and found them "specially interesting as disclosing the woman's point of view" (*Letters* 2: 6).

What is more intriguing for today's reader is to find that a writer like Richardson, so exclusively concerned with the representation of *female* interiority might well have been inspired by Conrad's methodology. Here Fuss's thesis of the "construction" of reading practices again lets us broaden our perspective—to think about writers as readers and about the importance of the reader's gender, and to prompt us to pose the question: How might a woman writer of experimental fiction such as Richardson read Conrad differently from those whom we normally associate with his influence? One way of approaching this issue is to broaden the field of inquiry, and rather than emphasize the distinction between the writers' aims, instead to engage with the possibilities of a common ground—one that in fact arises from a "reading practice" that developed within the "contact zones" of practitioners of literary modernism. Again, to emphasize the spatial model for "influence," internal reading groups provide an important location for the borderland transmission of experiments in literary aesthetic.

Returning to include Greiffenhagen in the frame, we find that a distinctive feature of all three artists' methodology alerts us to a striking relationship between them, and offers an intriguing example of how modernist aesthetics were often disseminated through the most unlikely conjunctions, ones that collapse our traditional assumptions about the distinction between genres and disciplines, or between "high" and "popular" culture. One particular aspect of modernism provides a link among the three protagonists of this essay—the modernists' preoccupation with absences, spaces, and gaps as metaphorical signifiers undermining conventional notions of aesthetic unity. For, not only am I concerned with the intellectual spaces or borderlands in which Conrad rubbed shoulders with and influenced figures apparently peripheral to his work, I want also to consider the issue of spaces or borders encountered within the texts themselves. But before moving on to the discussion of *Typhoon*, I will first explore modernism's use of a representational "gap," placing Conrad's narrative methods in a wider artistic context.

II.

The idea of a hiatus in the text commonly occurs throughout Conrad's fiction, frequently identified as a hallmark of his skepticism, sometimes characterized as a failure of language, and often signified typographically as a series of ellipses—dots or hyphens or simply chapter breaks. Such spaces may represent in the protagonist some form of physical or psychological crisis, a dislocation of consciousness or memory, an epistemological dilemma; or in the narrator, an uncertainty about literary subjectivity or authority. For example, Marlow's narrative in *Heart of Darkness* or in *Lord Jim* frequently trails off into a series of ellipses. Jim himself registers grammatically a gap in his memory, sometimes interpreted as self-deceiving amnesia, of his jump from the *Patna*. In recounting the event to Marlow, he declares, moving swiftly from the pluperfect, distant but active past to the equivocal, intransitive present tense, "I had jumped ... It seems" (111).

But this modernist preoccupation with gaps frequently lends itself to visual as well as to literary representation. In the field of visual theory, we find some of the most interesting discussions of this issue. The late Louis Marin, for example, drew on traditional iconographies in the visual arts to show the implicit tensions residing within the issue of representation (Marin 79). He observed that *any* form of representation deals with the contesting antitheses of presence and absence and that the conflict running through the definitions for the verb "represent" are apparent from at least Furetière's late-seventeenth-century dictionary(Marin 79).[8] To represent first means to substitute something present for something absent. Yet to represent can also mean to display, to exhibit something that is present:[9]

> In other words, to represent signifies to present oneself representing something else. Every representational sign, every process of signification thus comprises two dimensions ... first reflexive—to present oneself—and second transitive—to represent something. (Marin 79)

As Marin goes on to observe, "these two dimensions are not far from what contemporary semantics and pragmatics have conceptualized as the opacity and the transparency of the representational sign" (Marin 79).

What distinguishes the modernists' attitude toward representation, however, is an extreme self consciousness about both these aspects of the definition. First, there is a skepticism about the mimetic operation between presence and absence, an operation that authorizes the present to function in the place of what is not there. And second, a further skepticism arises about the performative operation that assigns that substitution its legitimacy—the self-presentation involved in representing. Thus, we typically encounter in modernist art the deconstruction of one-point perspective and an emphasis on the two-dimensionality of the frame (as in the cubist paintings of Picasso and Braque). Equally frequently, gaps or spaces appear at unexpected points on the picture plane, drawing our attention to the way in which we conventionally read an image—disrupting the apparent logic of framing and composition that traditionally renders mimetically a form of visual realism (Cézanne, Matisse, Wyndham Lewis).

III.

Typhoon (1903) provides us with an unusual example of the confluence in both literary and visual fields of this form of skeptical thinking about representation. Indeed, one of the marks of Conrad's "modernist" development frequently appears in his narratorial refinement of authorial intervention. Dwight Purdy has, for example, shown how Conrad carefully eliminated authorial commentary on the action or the characters in revising the New York *Critic* text of *Typhoon* (Purdy 112–115). Indeed, the final version of *Typhoon* derives much of its ironic bathos from the economy with which third-person narratorial interventions are made. Gaps appear in the disposition of the plot, in its lack of logical sequencing and narratorial explanation, and the reader must complete the meaning of the tale. This is how the story reaches its climax at the end of Chapter V. As MacWhirr prepares to lead the ship straight into the typhoon we learn:

> before the renewed wrath of winds swooped on his ship, Captain MacWhirr was moved to declare, in a tone of vexation, as it were: "I wouldn't like to lose her." He was spared that annoyance.

Chapter VI begins: "On a bright sunshiny day, with the breeze chasing her smoke far ahead, the *Nan-Shan* came into Fu-Chau" (112–113).

The description of the crucial event is missing, substituted only by an ironic gesture on the part of an omniscient narrator—"He was spared that annoyance." This refusal to offer the sensational climax constitutes a gap in the text. The reader may glean the story by piecing together narratorial hints from alternative textual evidence such as letters and dramatized moments of dialogue. The lack of a consistent analysis of the action as experienced from MacWhirr's point of view draws the reader's attention away from the kind of story that privileges plot and action—and onto a form of extended moral meditation requiring the rigorous input of the reader. The plot's metaphorical resonances prevail, a focus on action replaced by the moral focus of the story, revealing the distinction between MacWhirr's and Jukes's perspectives on a moment of human crisis, and, as Paul Kirschner has put it, one that forces the modern world—in the light of nineteenth-century Darwinism—to ponder the distinction between instinctive and intellectual behavior (5–13).

What is immediately striking about Greiffenhagen's illustrations for the serialized *Typhoon* in *Pall Mall Magazine*, is how the artist complements the written text with a visual representation of discontinuity or dislocation. Greiffenhagen's images show a more radical strategy than usually accorded to magazine illustration at the turn of the twentieth century, when periodicals often conformed to conservative generic expectations or relied on syndicated images to match the text.[10] On the one hand, Greiffenhagen's presentation of the angular slant and patterning of ships' masts and the interweaving pipes and engines provides a realist evocation of the storm-tossed vessel. But it also anticipates the Vorticists' disruptive compositional style and their emphasis on technology. Above all, the arrangement of figures in the picture plane is curiously disjunctive (see Figure 11.1 and Figure 11.2). Unlike most illustrators of the period, Greiffenhagen rarely places the focus of the incident at the center of the frame, although occasionally he follows Conrad's representation of MacWhirr's imperturbable character by positioning him near the middle. Otherwise, characters always occupy peripheral spaces, and the eye is drawn to the gaps foregrounded in the picture plane, matching to some extent Conrad's narratorial experiments with textual gaps (again, see Figures 11.1 and 11.2).

Conrad clearly recognized the compatibility of Greiffenhagen's artistic vision with his own, and in a letter of May 31, 1902, to William Blackwood, cited Greiffenhagen as one of the "widely different personalities" to whom his talent appealed. (W.H. Henley, Shaw, Wells, and "a charming old lady in Winchester" were among the others [*Letters* 2: 416]). Then again in 1919, Conrad had occasion to remember Greiffenhagen. During a dispute with the editor of *Land and Water* over the illustrations for *The Rescue*, he had registered dissatisfaction with the illustrations for the earlier installments and had urged him to hire Greiffenhagen to complete the later issues. He had, on December 12, 1918, complained that Dudley Hardy's illustrations for the early chapters had depicted Lingard in a fur cap looking like a hotel waiter—"What is it—a joke?" he wrote, " . . . in a story whose action takes place in the tropics?" Whereas Greiffenhagen "had imagination enough to understand the words I had written" (qtd. in Karl *three Lives*, 821).

The illustrations for *The Rescue* demonstrate the more overtly decorative style of Greiffenhagen's later period (we can perhaps detect the influence of

"The sun, pale and without rays, poured down a leaden heat, and the Chinamen were lying prostrate about the decks" (page 100)

Fig. 11.1 Maurice Greiffenhagen illustration for *The Rescue.*

Charles Rennie Macintosh, since Greiffenhagen had been working for some years in Glasgow). Square, solid figures are arranged with greater attention to surface patterning and angular symmetry. Yet again he seems to engage closely with Conrad's text, capturing for example the operatic features of the novel, especially in his depiction of Lingard's summit meeting in the tribal enclosure (May 29, 1919). He creates a highly formalized pattern of stacked heads that hug the frame of the illustration—again leaving the uneasy space at the center of the image (see Figure 11.3). We might think of Woolf's future presentation of the artist Lily Briscoe in *To The Lighthouse* (1927) as she contemplates the resolution of a gap at the center of her painting.

In 1919, as Conrad resuscitated and extended "The Rescuer," a short story of the early years, his encounter with Greiffenhagen tells us something of his position on the borderlands of the modernist novel. As a forerunner of *Country Life, Land and Water* was a British representative of a new (largely American) market for his work.[11] We have to remember that Greiffenhagen was already an established illustrator, at ease with the context of popular publication. Yet his illustrations for Haggard's romances of imperial adventure, or indeed his other work in *Pall Mall*, equally demonstrate his boldly protomodernist style. One

Fig. 11.2 Maurice Greiffenhagen illustration for *The Rescue*.

The momentous negotiation had begun and it went on in low undertones with long pauses and in the immobility of all the attendants squatting on the ground.

DRAWN BY MAURICE GREIFFENHAGEN, A.R.A.

Fig. 11.3 Maurice Greiffenhagen illustration for *The Rescue*.

famous illustration for the serial edition of Haggard's *She* (1886), now reproduced in Patrick Brantlinger's *Rule of Darkness*, shows Greiffenhagen's sensitivity to the gothic register of Haggard's novel (Brantlinger 226). Yet his disposition of figures again confounds any conventional reading of the scene. The curiously statuesque figure of the faceless, enveiled Ayesha, arms raised in dramatic movement, hugs the periphery of the right hand frame, while one male protagonist regards her covetously from the other side, and another, lying supine on a slab that follows the line of the upper edge of the illustration, remains inert. Thus Greiffenhagen once more creates an oddly disturbing space in the foreground. And his illustration for Israel Zangwill's "The Model of Sorrow," also from *Pall Mall* in 1902, depicts a strange family grouping (displaying a solidity not dissimilar to that of a Van Gogh *Potato Eaters*), so that the figures recede into the back of the frame, while the table and lighted, empty floorboards occupy the immediate foreground—drawing the viewer's eye to the space, rather than to the human gestures and action of the scene (see Figure 11.4).

" The unloveliness of the three women who stood there."

Fig. 11.4 Maurice Greiffenhagen illustration for *The Rescue*.

Conrad must have empathized with the resolutely strained and unconventional style of Greiffenhagen's images. But he may also have seen how the visual component of the text helped him negotiate between the experimental modernist strategies associated with his own earlier work and the later, more populist contexts of publication to which he was deliberately directing his work by 1919. Conrad acknowledged the importance of his initial encounter with Greiffenhagen in his 1919 "Author's Note" to *Typhoon and Other Stories*: "Mr. Maurice Greiffenhagen knew how to combine in his illustrations the effect of his own most distinguished personal vision with an absolute fidelity to the inspiration of the writer" (Wright 182).Conrad's words undermine the received view of him as largely indifferent to the serialization of his work, or, for that matter, indifferent to the visual arts in general.

This encounter enables us to rethink certain aspects of the canonization of Conrad's work. It also allows us to rethink the modernists' debt to popular forms (conventionally acknowledged in the referential gesturing of Eliot, Joyce, or Pound to "low" culture). In Greiffenhagen's interpretation of perspective and of the foreshortened, foregrounded spaces of his compositions, we might entertain the notion that popular contexts themselves engender modernist forms more frequently than we suspect.

IV.

Yet we could also think about how "borderland" associations might affect a canonization of influence. Critics cite *Typhoon* regularly as an influential text—as part of the "modernist" Conrad—but also as a text that entered a canon of influence on high modernism. For example, Woolf firmly establishes the enduring place of *Typhoon* in an essay of 1924, published in *The Common Reader* in 1925: "It is the earlier books—*Youth, Lord Jim, Typhoon, The Nigger of the 'Narcissus'*—that we will read in their entirety," claiming that "after the middle period Conrad never again was able to bring his figures into perfect relation with their background" ("Joseph Conrad" 289–291). In spite of the acclaim accorded to Conrad by Woolf—or perhaps *because* she endorses the sea fiction of the middle years—we do not associate Conrad with issues of women's writing or, apart from Woolf herself, with women and modernism.

Woolf's reputation has largely obliterated the place of equally experimental female contemporaries, such as May Sinclair and Dorothy Richardson. Yet Richardson herself remarked, somewhat incredulously, that Ford, in his "general survey of English literature" had "cited, so folks tell me, my work as the most valuable of our time" (qtd. in Fromm, *Selected Letters* 526).[12] Richardson is now best remembered for *Pilgrimage*, and critics mainly attribute to her the influence of Proust and Joyce. In particular, her exploration of the female consciousness has been associated with that of Henry James.[13] But Richardson acknowledged the impact on her of a wide range of sources. As testament to her unexpected debt to others, a rather second-rate elegy, entitled "Disaster," appeared in September 1924 in London in John Middleton Murry's literary journal, *The Adelphi*:

> Upon the homing ship, the conqueror,
> Fell radiant sunset light revealing her,
> Her stature and her strength and all her grace
> At last before the eyes even of those
> Who never saw her as she ranged the seas.
> Who saw her as she sank.
> Sank without signal, mighty and unassailed,
> Regal and kind, and proud in modesty.
> And where she rode, heaven comfort us, a sea
> Empty and cruel assails our desolate eyes.

There is no overt reference to Joseph Conrad here, but the subject and occasion of Conrad's death would have been clear enough to an informed readership. It is perhaps surprising that the author of this rather sentimental poem was Dorothy Richardson, given her reputation for radical technique in her novels. But her references to Conrad throughout her letters express affection for the older writer, as well as an affinity in certain aspects of theme and style in the writing. A sense of enduring empathy for him emerges in Richardson's letters to John Cowper Powys, P. Beaumont Wadsworth, Ogden Heath, and Winifred Bryher. Her familiarity is characterized by her knowledge of "Conrad's old place," her casual but astute citation of texts such as the essay on the sinking of the *Titanic*, and *Typhoon*, her discussions of his death and the nature of the obituaries dedicated to him (she comments wryly but affectionately on T.W.H. Crosland's misrepresentation of the author).[14] And, in her elegy for the *Adelphi*, there are some intriguing features. The feminization of the subject throughout derives from an obvious metaphorical association of the sea and ships with the female. But the absence of *any* masculine pronoun or reference to the actual gender of the departed suggests the close identification of the author with the subject of the poem, while the anaphoric "Who never saw her as she ranged the seas,/Who saw her for a moment ere she sank" conveys Richardson's belated acknowledgment of Conrad's impact on her (intriguingly, she uses Conrad's most famous visual metaphor here). This strong identification with Conrad is borne out in a letter Richardson wrote to Winifred Bryher in August 1924: "Fifty times [a] day I take myself by the shoulders & say Conrad is dead ... And we've just got to go on without him. Its [*sic*] inconceivable ...." (Fromm, *Selected Letters* 102).

And then, in April 1932, she makes a specific allusion to *Typhoon*. Richardson is writing to Ogden Heath about James as someone so entrenched in his "occupation" that he "feared to turn aside, had the odd, human, half-conscious illusion that he must hold to it always, stand fixed in relation to it (like the man on deck in Conrad's *Typhoon,* who feared to move lest the ship founder)" (Fromm, *Selected Letters* 236).

Richardson's work has been described primarily as an exploration of a fundamentally singular, interior female consciousness—that of her protagonist, Miriam Henderson. So the reference to *Typhoon* is all the more intriguing in that the incident Richardson recalls is not incompatible with a striking moment in the first volume of *Pilgrimage,* when Miriam responds to her mother's suicide. Here the narrator alludes to Miriam's perception of her mother's restless movements on the night of her suicide as a kind of domesticized typhoon: "She woke[...] to the sound of violent language, furniture being roughly moved, a swift angry splashing of water ... something breaking out, breaking through the confinements of this furniture-filled room ..." (488).

The suicide itself is intimated, yet never articulated fully. A temporal leap backward occurs between the description of events on the night of the suicide and an earlier moment, in which the narrator instead describes the Hendersons' visit to a homeopath earlier in the day at the seaside resort where they are staying. Mrs. Henderson here alludes to her death proleptically in one brief utterance of despair: "' ... it is too late,' said Mrs. Henderson with clear, quiet bitterness, 'God has deserted me'"(489), and we then get Miriam's intuitive anticipation of tragedy: "A thought touched Miriam, touched and flashed. She grasped at it to hold and speak it, but it passed off into the world of grey houses" (489). But the narrative refuses any direct representation of the event of Mrs. Henderson's suicide. No text fills the space between Miriam's intimation of her mother's mortality earlier in the day and the events of the morning following her mother's death. Instead, a space on the page constitutes another temporal leap to the subsequent day. This is how the sequence appears in the text:

> She summoned her strength, but her body seemed outside her, empty, pacing forward in a world full of perfect unanswering silences.
> The bony old woman held Miriam clasped closely in her arms. "You must never, as long as you live, blame yourself, my gurl." She went away. Miriam had not heard her come in ... Everything was dream; the world. I will not have any life. I can never have any life; all my days. There were cold tears running into her mouth .... Her heavy hot light impalpable body was the only solid thing in the world, weighing tons; and like a lifeless feather. There was a tray of plates of fish and fruit on the table. She looked at it, heaving with sickness and looking at it. I am hungry. Sitting down near it she tried to pull the tray .... I must eat the food. Go on eating food, till the end of my life .... (489–490)

Elisabeth Bronfen has identified three types of psychological "spaces" represented in *Pilgrimage,* in which the protagonist moves steadily from "atmospheric" and "active" spaces, to "contemplative" spaces. Miriam increasingly enters the "contemplative space" as the text becomes more introspective, and as a more centered, self-reflexive "I" gains momentum throughout the novel sequence (Bronfen 61). This assessment of a shift in the presentation of interiority depends very much on an assumption that Miriam's consciousness is at all times the "moral" center of the novel in an almost Jamesian sense, and that Richardson's representation of that consciousness acts as a principle of continuity presiding over the text. Yet this moment, when representation itself appears to break down, does not altogether fit any of Bronfen's categories. In fact, it is curious that none of Richardson's critics discuss or analyze at any great length the presentation of Mrs. Henderson's suicide, passing over it in the same way that the text itself eludes it. Richardson's methodology here seems uncharacteristic or uncharacterizable.

However, if we now go back and compare this episode with the "climax" of *Typhoon* we will see that, however distinctive in theme, Richardson employs a similar narrative method in one fundamental respect. In both stories, the actual events themselves—the ship's encounter with the eye of the typhoon, or the suicide of Mrs. Henderson—are passed over. They remain gaps in the text—fugue states, or crises in the experience of the protagonists so over-whelming as to be unrepresentable—spaces to be completed only in the imag-ination of the reader. In both cases, the protagonist "holds to," "stands in a fixed relation to" the necessity of "going on" (to use a Beckettian phrase). The narrative focuses on the event's *outcome*—the protagonist's survival in each case. MacWhirr brings his battered ship into port, and Miriam's final thoughts rest on the plates of food that will ensure the continuity of her own life. In both texts, the metaphorical register predominates—the typhoon as crisis, or the psychological typhoon as crisis; the gap in the text represents the moral center of the story—a response to crisis as a kind of bodily emptiness that nevertheless prevails beyond the moment of trauma.

To return now to Marin's observations, we see that both authors doubt the transitive aspect of representation. For if all representation tries to replace ab-sence with presence, how do you replace that which is always already absent, unrepresentable?

Finally, in their attempts to elide the reflexive aspect of representation, both remain skeptical about the *legitimizing* function of the subject who pre-sents. But in their use of narrators, Richardson appears to indicate a more radical move toward the techniques of high modernism. In her seamless slip-page between third-person narrator and interior monologue, Richardson has, as it were, taken away the strings. The third-person narrator is not really omniscient but actually a limited angle of vision that effectively presents Miriam's view—we are left simply with the representation of a single perspec-tive residing in the female consciousness. In Conrad's narrative, the third-person narrator emerges momentarily to provide a clue to the completion of meaning: "He was spared that annoyance." Richardson refuses us any form of narrative guidance through the text, such as the self-reflexive gesture of an ironizing and performing narrator. Her skepticism seems more thoroughgo-ing than Conrad's. But is it? The textual patterning and ellipses of *Pilgrimage* are choreographed with such complexity that, paradoxically, it is Richardson who might lead us to suspect the more thoroughly performative nature of high modernism.

Yet Richardson confirms her "borderland" association with Conrad in her technical use of a textual gap to represent a response to human crisis, a moment in which narrative, indeed all representation, breaks down, just as the defining center of consciousness of the novel has itself momentarily refused to "perform." The evidence of her letters, her obituary of Conrad, and this episode in *Pilgrimage* suggest that, in Fuss's terminology, Richardson "inhabited a reading practice" among innovators of literary modernism where Conrad's writing may have seemed less emphatically masculinist than we often assume.

In conclusion, these examples show the ways in which modernist methodologies often develop through unrecognized and elliptical conjunctions occurring in "borderland" territories away from the mainstream trajectories of the modernist canon. Recent scholarship in popular culture and aesthetics, and particularly the study of Conrad's novels' serial texts have facilitated a deeper analysis of the composition of his work. Yet the impact of the *context* of popular periodical publication on what we now recognize as "modernist" literary works has still to be fully explored. In the case of Conrad, we rarely take into consideration the intersection of literary and visual components of the text arising from this context.

Moreover, Greiffenhagen's illustrations for *Typhoon* draw attention to, and deconstruct the way in which we have become accustomed to identify a hierarchical relationship between exponents of "high" and "low" culture.

On the other hand, we are often too ready to assume that Conrad only influenced certain well-known high modernist writers. But Richardson and Conrad often appear compatible in their responses to marketing and popularity, and to the role of an autonomous reader. In a letter to Harriet Capes written on March 22, 1902, Conrad remarked that "the reader collaborates with the author," a sentiment echoed later by Richardson (*Letters* 2:394). In an unfinished draft of her essay "Authors and Readers," Richardson observed of this relationship that "to do anything like full justice to their relationship, we need a composite word, something like the telegraphic name of a form, expressing both partnership & collaboration."[15] Certainly both writers' technical use of a hiatus in the text to express a modernist skepticism about representation testifies to their engagement with a rigorous and collaborative reader. But perhaps we could argue that it was Conrad's greater willingness to attend to market forces and the visual world of serial publication that helped him finally to secure a more extensive readership, while, regrettably, Richardson remains on the periphery of the modernist canon. A recovery of her association with Conrad might help to shift the grounds of our more conventional assumptions about the modernist project and contribute positively to the reception of both authors in the future.

Indeed, as we have seen, the development of a variety of theoretical positions, ranging from those exploring visual representation to reception, cultural, and gender theory, have enabled us to reevaluate Conrad's relevance to today's reader. By shifting our perspective to modernism's "contact zones," we might now engage with Conrad as a writer who operated with a greater degree of interdisciplinarity than we usually acknowledge, speaking to a wider audience of both genders. Further, we might also appreciate Conrad as a writer whose impact on unexpected areas of literary modernism dismantles our assumptions about canons of influence on the aesthetic practices developing in the early twentieth century.

NOTES

1. Maurice William Greiffenhagen (1862–1931) was trained at the Royal Academy Schools in 1878. During the first part of his career, he principally worked in book and periodical illustrations, but he later also turned to portrait-oils and large-scale decorative work. In 1906 he became headmaster of the life department of the Glasgow School of Art.

2. Dorothy Richardson (1873–1957) wrote essays on literature and film besides her life's work, a 13-volume series of novels, *Pilgrimage*, which she wrote between 1912 and 1954 (the first volume, *Pointed Roofs*, was published in 1915; the last, unfinished novel, *March Moonlight*, was published posthumously in 1967).

3. "That some epochal change occurred . . . as the Victorian age ended can be more or less agreed" (Bradbury 5).

4. See Sinclair, "The Novels of Dorothy Richardson" (1918), reprinted in Scott.

5. Compare Wollaeger's account of the relationship between Virginia and Leonard Woolf and Conrad in "Woolfs in the Jungle."

6. See especially Butler, *Gender Trouble*.

7. See, for example, Roberts, *Conrad and Masculinity*.

8. Marin quotes the following entry under *representation* in Furetière's *Dictionnaire universel* (1690) (translated into English here): "An image that supplies us with an idea and a memory of absent objects and that paints them as they are: 'When one goes to see the dead Rulers lying in state, one only sees a *representation*, an effigy.'"

9. "Representation: A word used in court to describe the exhibition of something. During a criminal trial, weapons seized at the time of arrest, even the body of the victim, are exhibited before the accused. To represent also signifies to appear in person and exhibit the items."

10. See Monmonier 77–84 for a discussion of the practice of syndication of newspaper illustrations from 1884.

11. Conrad experimented with serialization in popular periodicals from a much earlier moment than is sometimes recognized, although his success with *Chance* in the *New York Herald* Sunday Magazine January–June 1912 consolidated this trend. "Amy Foster" appeared in *Illustrated London News* in 1901; essays that contributed to *The Mirror of the Sea: Memories and Impressions* (1906) appeared initially in *Pall Mall Magazine*, *Harper's Weekly*, and *Daily Mail* (1904–1906); all the stories from *A Set of Six* (1908) appeared variously in *Pall Mall Magazine*, *Harper's*, *Daily Chronicle*, and *Cassell's* from 1906–1908.

12. Richardson is probably referring to Ford's *The March of Literature*, where Ford refers to Richardson as an "abominably unknown" writer (848).

13. See Fromm *Biography*; Staley; Carol Watts.

14. See, for example, the following letters in Fromm, *Selected Letters*: 4/5 September 1929 (174); 19 May 1930 (197); 10 August 1933 (247); April 1932 (236); August 1924 (102); 19 June 1942 (440).

15. Dorothy Richardson, "Authors & Readers," MS, Dorothy Richardson Collection, Beinecke Library, Yale University. Qtd. in Leong 166. I am immensely grateful to Dr. Leong for reawakening my interest in Richardson.

12
Conrad and Posthumanist Narration:Fabricating Class and Consciousness onboard the *Narcissus*

BRIAN RICHARDSON

Conrad's *The Nigger of the "Narcissus,"* the author's tribute to his fellow seamen, remains one of the most impressive portraits of proletarian lives in a period in which workmen, if they appeared at all, were usually presented in the most stereotypical and demeaning postures. It also creates an original—in fact, virtually unprecedented—narrative form for representing a collective consciousness. Partly because of its radical departure from conventional representational practice, this form still remains imperfectly understood, and its impressive lineage has gone largely unrecognized. The text is further haunted by a specter—the specter of socialism and other radical social movements that purported to represent (in both senses of the term) working-class consciousness unconfined by national boundaries. It is Conrad's complex negotiation of these three components that I explore in what follows.

Conrad has not received sufficient credit for his positive and verisimilar portrayals of working-class characters. In *The Nigger of the "Narcissus,"* he captures many neglected proletarian virtues, such as the uncalculating generosity of men who have little, as well as a fundamental egalitarian outlook, both evidenced by the impulsive generosity that provides Donkin with clothing his first day on the ship. One may also point to the self-irony and black humor of the men: their daily acts of courage, their rough geniality, modesty, alertness, general quick wittedness, and their uncommon capacity for endurance. On display also is the sensibility Marx once referred to as the Voltairean skepticism of the working class—the complete indifference to otherworldly claims by all the men except the cook, Podmore, which functions as a bracing rejection of bourgeois Victorian religious cant.

Concerning the men of Old Singleton's generation, the narrator is still more effusive and condemns the well-meaning but utterly misinformed people who "had tried to represent those men as whining over every mouthful of their food; as going about their work in fear of their lives" (25). Conrad offers the following corrective to such misinterpretation: "in truth they had been men who knew toil, privation, violence, debauchery—but knew not fear, and had no desire of spite in their hearts . . . . men enough to scorn in their hearts the sentimental voices that bewailed the hardness of their fate" (25).

Even the demeaning attribution of "the simple minds of the big children who people those dark and wandering places of the earth" (6) inspired by Singleton's laborious reading of Bulwer-Lytton is effectively refuted by the old sailor's sagacity, endurance, and self-sacrifice as demonstrated during crucial moments of the voyage—no big child or simple mind could manage the helm for thirty hours straight. When, at the end of the novella, we are back on land and are informed of the impatient clerk's disdain for seamen ("How stupid those sailors are!") just as the venerable Singleton approaches (168), readers have learned how to judge this calumny. But most important is the presentation of the gradual emergence of a collective sensibility that arises when humans must rely on others performing and even assigning themselves tasks for the success (and, at times, even the survival) of the group. It entails a suppression of self-centered actions and desires in favor of the needs of a larger collectivity and is rarely found in the daily lives of the more comfortable members of the bourgeoisie. It does appear in periods of major crisis, the ravages of war, natural disaster, and the ordinary travail of many proletarians in the more dangerous industries—circumstances whose very materiality encourage us to read Conrad's novel not simply as a nostalgic register of the shift of *Gemeinschaft* to *Gesellschaft* in industrial societies (see Watt, *Conrad in the Nineteenth*, chapter 3; Hendrickson 29–31), but as the charting of an emerging group consciousness that is much less epochal and considerably more local and common in its terms. It is the representation of this exceptional sensibility that leads, as we will see below, to Conrad's most daring innovations in narrative technique, innovations that are still imperfectly understood.

Such circumstances usually prove to be great levelers and foster a democratic sensibility that rapidly overthrows artificial social hierarchies. This is especially true of merchant ships, we are informed, "where the sense of hierarchy is weak, and where all feel themselves equal before the unconcerned immensity of the sea and the exacting appeal of the work" (16). This equality can transcend national, linguistic, and ethnic boundaries; the narrator observes how "the faces changed, passing in rotation. Youthful faces, bearded faces, dark faces: faces serene or faces moody, but all akin with the brotherhood of the sea; all with the same attentive expression of the eyes, carefully watching the compass or the sails" (30). Nationality (Irish, Norwegian, American, etc.) is eclipsed amid such an inescapable material basis for such egalitarian cooperation, as Conrad inadvertently confirms Marx's claim that the workingman has no nationality: i.e., on this ship, there is only "the brotherhood of the sea."

This sense of equality among the sailors and their knowledge of the need for collective action, of course, also constitute the social basis for labor organizing, radical workingmen's parties, and socialist programs. Conrad goes to great lengths to document and celebrate the emerging collective consciousness while simultaneously disparaging any possible left-wing recuperation of this condition and sensibility. He does this in a number of ways involving plot and characterization. The novel shows the men to have no good cause for complaint and no coherent goal once their rebellion begins, as if their usually keen sense of the ways of the world suddenly abandon them once they begin to feel restless. He also makes Donkin *both* a contemptible, lazy, selfish shirker *and* a spokesperson for socialist ideals—two types that while independently plausible, are historically unlikely as conjoined within the same person (labor organizing was, and is, a most altruistic activity), and here especially resonate as the stigmatic hybrid imagining of a conservative or reactionary. Donkin, a figure dripping with Nietzschean *ressentiment*, is no more a real socialist than Conrad was; completely self-centered, he uses radical rhetoric only if he thinks it can get him something tangible. More typical is his anti-internationalist xenophobia; his hatred of "foreigners" onboard an English ship (!) gives the lie to any larger radical or socialist agenda he might pretend to (43).

But Conrad does not cast him as a false radical so much as an exemplum of the actual agitator's true feelings and preposterous demands. Here, we can see why verisimilitude is an exceptionally interesting and central issue in the novel—precisely because in this moment a historically sensitive reader is forced to ask how Conrad's ideology, fortified by the appeal of his unique knowingness (as writer and sailor), is actually at war with his otherwise scrupulous sense of verisimilitude. A further resonant violation of probability and verisimilitude may be located in the depiction of Captain Allistoun. Though notable exceptions exist, in most of Conrad's works, authority is ultimately just, captains are usually wise, and dutiful old seamen who spent years sailing on clipper ships are invested with a particular sagacity. How ironic it is, therefore, to contrast Conrad's own experiences with authority when he was second mate on an actual ship named The *Narcissus*. As Ian Watt notes:

> When they arrived at Madras, the captain was supposedly sick; Conrad was sent ashore to fetch a doctor; he incautiously gave it as his opinion that the master was drunk; but his diagnosis was not confirmed, and as a result Conrad was forced to write a retraction .... Since the captain very soon ran his ship aground under circumstances which led to his being suspended from command for a year, it is likely in fact that he was dangerously incompetent. (*Conrad in the Nineteenth* 91)

By contrast, Conrad's insistence on the virtually infallible knowledge and judgment of the captain and the mates in his novella functions ideologically as an implausibly stark contrast to the dark confusion the men stumble into when they try to take matters into their own hands.

As a matter of narrative authority, Conrad's most impressive tribute in *The Nigger of the "Narcissus"* lies in the unprecedented form he designs to frame and partially embody the story of the men of the forecastle. Starting from the class analysis offered above, we can hope to better comprehend the otherwise critically vexed issue of the nature, identity, and merit of the narrative form of this work. Some critics, such as Ian Watt, speak of a single narrator, specifically, "a special kind of privileged narrator who functions as a collective voice" (*Conrad in the Nineteenth* 101). Others fault the narration: Jeremy Hawthorn refers to the work's "technical confusions in the manipulations of narrative perspective and distance" (*Narrative Technique*, 101), while Marvin Mudrick condemns Conrad's "gross violation of point of view" (72). Still others postulate two (or even more) narrators. Jakob Lothe identifies two main kinds of narrator, which he terms the "'narrator as character' (*I* as personal pronoun) and 'detached and reflective authorial narrator' (*they* as personal pronoun)" (97). Lothe goes on to note that these positions are repeatedly modified and blended and lists six types of narrating positions.

The problem with all of these approaches is that they presuppose an exclusively mimetic conception of the narrator; that is, they can only imagine him as one human being (or two) who writes only what an individual consciousness is likely to know or a traditional omniscient one is expected to reveal. I suggest instead that Conrad is doing something much more radical here, something that transcends the mimetic poetics that each of Conrad's critics cited above implicitly presupposes. The most helpful perspectives that incline toward this kind of stance are those offered by John Lester, who argues that Conrad's narrative technique is "more controlled and more inventive than he has generally been given credit for" (170), and Bruce Hendricksen, who states that the text "deconstructs the subject who narrates by juxtaposing a third-person narrative voice that refers to the crew as 'they' with a first person voice that says 'we'" (27). Hendricksen, however, ultimately posits that "the instabilities of the narrator's self, evident in the wavering point of view, reflect the competing voices of his world" (30). We will find Conrad's construction of voice and engagement with the social world to be much more complex than this mimetic model allows. To get to the root of Conrad's achievement in narrative technique, we must ask, "What is the narration doing now?" rather than, "Who is speaking here?" Actually no self-consistent speaking subject is in the text. By following out the varied narrative voices in this text, we find they themselves constitute a kind of narrative that complements and underscores the central events and ideas of the story.

The novella begins conventionally enough. A standard third-person narrator indicates the scene and describes the actions of the characters. The crew is mustered, the ship leaves port, and the men start to become acquainted with each other. An apparently omniscient description of the history of Captain Allistoun's shaving is quickly followed by the comment that the mate, Mr. Baker, "kept all our noses to the grindstone" (31) before returning equally rapidly to the third person. Once out at sea, several men gather in a circle and speculate on what makes a "gentleman." As they engage in seamen's speculation, their individual characters fade as a new collective identity emerges: "They disputed endlessly, obstinate and childish .... They were forgetting their toil, they were forgetting themselves" (32). Soon after, a passive construction that obscures the perceiver indicates the presence of Wait (his "head, protruding, became visible" [34]) and the next usage of a first-person plural pronoun appears: "the setting sun dipped, as though fleeing before our nigger" (34). At this point, it is not clear that the pronoun is a genuine first-person plural as opposed to an affectation (a propos of the "gentleman" conversation) in the manner of the "royal we"; the phrase also (anticipating the nominal puzzle of Nostromo, "our man") could have meant "our protagonist" and been part of an authorial discourse with the reader. After a reversion to a few more uses of "they," the term "we" becomes the privileged perspective as the narration as bond of solidarity between narrator and crew is affirmed ("We hesitated between pity and mistrust" [36]; "We spoke in low tones" [37], etc.).

"We" is a flexible pronoun; in this text it refers generally to the body of the crew, the men of the forecastle as opposed to the officers. It is also a limited group, and does not usually extend to include the malcontent Donkin, the enigmatical Wait, or Singleton, who represents an earlier generation. In the third chapter, as the storm approaches, a drama of narrative perspective and social cohesion begins to unfold. The voice of the narrator briefly returns to the third person, using "they" to refer to the men (48–50) with the sole exception of a third-person usage of "you" (that is, "you" functions as a colloquial version of the indefinite pronoun "one"): "You had to dash through a waterfall to get to your bed" (49). The "we" narration resumes for a few pages (50–53) until the storm worsens and night falls. Once the sun rises, the "we" voice briefly returns (55–56) but as the storm gathers fury it soon yields to the "they" form briefly punctuated by a few usages of "we" (57, 60). Here the narration dramatizes the men's retreat from (and brief returns to) a shared consciousness as the storm drives them back into their isolated selves: "Huddled close to one another, they fancied themselves utterly alone. They heard sustained loud noises, and again bore the pain of existence through long hours of profound silence" (82). The reversion to "we" as the sailors struggle to free Wait from his berth below deck signals a significant return to a collective consciousness (66–73); that the solidarity of the men reappears while they selflessly work to free Wait is inscribed by the first-person plural form.

The ravages of the storm continue to produce isolated selves represented by the pronoun "they" (74–99). Then Conrad transforms his narration again. A deluded "we" consciousness appears ("the conceited folly of us all" [99]) that is fueled by Donkin's rhetorical "we": "He told us we were good men—a 'bloomin' condemned lot of good men.' Who thanked us? Who took any notice of our wrongs?" (100). This period of collective false consciousness (99–103) is followed by extended third-person passages, as Conrad dramatizes the selfishness and egoism leading up to the mutiny, signaling it as a perverted kind of union. Suggestively, the mutiny itself is depicted in a depersonalized manner, as the actions are committed by unidentified agents in Conrad's representation of mob violence: "Somebody slammed the cabin door to with a kick; the darkness full of menacing mutters leaped with a short clatter over the streak of light, and the men became gesticulating shadows that growled, hissed, laughed excitedly" (121). Conrad now presents a shared disarray in the third-person plural to better underscore its contradictions: "In the shadows of the fore rigging a dark mass stamped, eddied, advanced, retreated. There were words of reproach, encouragement, unbelief, execration .... [T]hey swayed, they tramped on one spot, shouting that they would not be 'put upon'" (122). The use of the passive voice grows, further depersonalizing the action: "A lot of disputes seemed to be going on all round"; "The hurling flight of some heavy object was heard" (123). The ineffectual mutiny dissolves the men's common bond of labor and replaces it with a fragmenting discourse of labor activism and general confusion. The "they" narration continues as order is restored: "They wanted great things. And suddenly all the simple words they knew seemed to be lost .... They knew what they wanted, but they could not find anything worth saying" (134).

In the final chapter, the ship gets closer to home and the narration returns to the "we" form; it has now become archly self-reflective on its own inaccurate perceptions, and uses a metaphor of political deceit to express this relation: "We made a chorus of affirmation to his wildest assertions, as though he had been a millionaire, a politician, or a reformer—and we a crowd of ambitious lubbers" (139); this cluster of self-interested and therefore unreliable speakers ranging from the capitalist to the reformer is revealing in its inclusiveness, justifying the reformer's critique of the discourse of wealth even as it impugns the truth and character of the reformer. Donkin returns to center stage and his thoughts and private dialogue with Wait are narrated (143–155). It is not clear whether to attribute this rather extensive passage to the third-person voice or first-person plural, since when either discusses an individual, it is always in the form of the third person. Nor can we say that, since the private thoughts of Donkin and Wait are revealed, we must be in the presence of a third-person narrator, since it is just this kind of assumption that Conrad desires to contest. The "we" voice appears for the final time as the *Narcissus* comes into its port (166). Once on land, the narration employs "they" to depict the men in their last moments together in the shipping office where they are paid off ("The crew of the *Narcissus*, broken up into knots, pushed in the corners. They had new shore togs ..." [168]). In the final four pages of the novel, Conrad introduces his concluding perspectival transformation, as an "I" narration suddenly irrupts and continues the story seamlessly: "Only Charley and Belfast wandered off alone. As I came up I saw a red-faced, blowsy woman ... fall on Charley's neck" (170).

Like all first-person narrators, the first-person plural cannot be entirely objective; a "we," in fact, is almost as fallible as an "I" in its perceptions and judgments. Both first-person singular and first-person plural accounts can exhibit extremely different degrees of reliability. In Conrad, we find that a "we" perspective can veer greatly from a highly probable intersubjective sense of things to a palpably inaccurate we-narration, such as the following: "Jimmy's desire encouraged by us and aided by … Wamibo's spells delayed the ship in the open seas. Only lubberly fools couldn't see it" (142). At times the unreliability becomes self-conscious: "we … sympathised with all [Wait's] repulsions, shrinkings, evasions, delusions" (139). The "we" perspective affirms even when it knows it is mistaken. This may be a covert testament to the many selves that make up the "we" or, more radically, a gesture pointing toward the intersubjective nature of every self.

One of Conrad's distinctive and most misunderstood achievements is the radical, unapologetic juxtaposition of mutually exclusive narrative stances; in one passage, a sentence of we-narration is followed in the next line by a third-person plural account: "Our little world went on its curved and unswerving path carrying a discontented and aspiring population. They found comfort of a gloomy kind in an interminable and conscientious analysis of their unappreciated worth" (103). From the perspective of realism, the speaker either is or is not part of the group; one of the pronouns, hence, is misleading. Even more resistant to a naturalistic recuperation are the intimate entries into the consciousnesses of Singleton and Wait that jar against the generally physical and unindividuated emphases on the narrator at most moments: i.e., "Groaning, we dug our fingers in, and very much hurt, shook our hands, scattering nails and drops of blood" (68). But Conrad's point is not narratively to inscribe a person but rather to mirror, expressively, the crew's changing cohesion through the pronouns used to describe them—such that their fall out of successful solidarity into isolation, dissent, and mutiny is signaled by the transformation of the narration. There may even be an allegorical image of this preternatural narrator in the figure of the captain, who is said to be "one of those commanders who speak little, seem to hear nothing, look at no one—and know everything, hear every whisper, see every fleeting shadow of their ship's life" (125); his inexplicable omniscience is an apt analogue for the oscillating perspectives of the text's uncanny voice.

Conrad, appropriately enough, provides support for the kind of reading offered here in one of the more under-appreciated passages in his famous preface to the work. To show a passing phase of life in all its vibration, its color, its form, the artist "cannot be faithful to the temporary formulas of his craft," including those of "Realism, Romanticism, Naturalism, even the unofficial sentimentalism" (xiv–xv). It is precisely the mimetic conventions of realism that Conrad transcends in this work, as it expands on the practice of Flaubert (who briefly used a "we" narrator to begin *Madame Bovary*)[1] and looks forward to the more egregious abrogations of mimesis in late modernist and postmodern texts. The kind of mimetic framework that dominated narrative theory from Percy Lubbock to Gerard Genette and his followers simply cannot deal with the more ample practices of Conrad or many authors who would come later. Conrad modulates his mode of narration to counterpoint the changing consciousness of the men being depicted.

It will be useful now to reflect on the extent and significance of Conrad's experiment in narration. In this work, the author produces what I believe to be the first sustained example of "we-narration" in literature. He also provides a fascinating example of alternating modes of narration as he switches from "we" to "they" and finally to "I" to describe the same subject; among earlier writers, only Dickens's alternation of first- and third-person narrations in *Bleak House* comes readily to mind as a comparable technique, as John Lester has noted, while multi-personed narration is quite common among contemporary writers ranging from Julia Alvarez and Fay Weldon to Carlos Fuentes and Nurrudin Farah.[2] Finally and perhaps most radically, Conrad flouts the conventions of realism to achieve his specific effect. Such an abnegation of mimetic foundations has been approached only by the most daring modernists and prominent only among postmodernists. Conrad, like Woolf in *The Waves* or Joyce in the later chapters of *Ulysses*, creates a different discourse situation that cannot be found in ordinary human communication. It can best be described as a posthumanist narrating situation, one that is only now beginning to be theorized by narratologists like Monika Fludernik.

The afterlife of some of the issues and techniques discussed above in Conrad's later work is a mixed one. He would shy away from depictions of the multinational crew presented onboard the *Narcissus* for much more ethnically homogenous or nondescript sailors. Most revealing is the identity of the crew of the *Judea* in "Youth," published a few years after *The Nigger of the "Narcissus."* The narrative is based on Conrad's own voyage on the *Palestine*, but represents more faithfully the particulars of that voyage than the seamen themselves. As Cedric Watts notes, the crew of this ship "consisted of a black seaman from St Kitts, a Belgian, an Irishman, two men and a boy from Devon, three men from Cornwall, and a Norwegian"; the three officers were English, Irish, and Polish. On the fictional *Judea*, however, "the crew is depicted as distinctively and courageously British: 'That crew of Liverpool hard cases had in them the right stuff. It's my experience they always have'" (*Heart of Darkness and Other* xiv [citing *NIN* 115]). Conrad thus deracinates his source material as the crew becomes instead a merely national allegory devoid of the conflicts, radical ideas, and solidarity of the more international originals, as well as an unrepresentative portrait of the heavily multinational composition of the British Merchant Marine of the period.

Though he moved away from presentations of a transnational labor force at sea under a British flag, Conrad would continue to produce complex, affirmative portraits of working-class characters—notably Captain MacWhirr and Nostromo. "The Secret Sharer" can also be read as a vindication of a skeptical proletarian epistemology as opposed to the more naive stances set forth by the credulous middle-class narrator;[3] as such it implicitly dramatizes the kinds of issues and associations that are conveyed in *The Nigger of the "Narcissus"* by a shift in narrative voice. The "we" form, however, rarely appears again in Conrad; one of its few incarnations is in the curious eighth chapter of *Nostromo* that interrupts the third-person narration that pervades the rest of the book. The analysis above suggests that this is not such an oddity but a continuation of a strategy that selects a narrative voice out of functional rather than realistic motivations. Here the first-person voice complements and corroborates that of the omniscient narrator; there is no need to imagine an individual human voice (such as Captain Mitchell's) and likely method of its interpolation into the third-person text.

Looking at the history of narrative technique after Conrad, we can note that William Faulkner utilizes some of the strategies identified above: He juxtaposes first- and third- person narration in *The Sound and the Fury* and deftly utilizes we-narration in stories like "A Rose for Emily." More intriguingly, a number of postcolonial authors use the "we" form of narration to express their struggles against the imperial powers. Raja Rao's *Kanthapura* (1938) employs we-narration throughout his novel depicting the arrival of Gandhi's independence movement in a village in Southern India. The "we" here is the adult members of the Indian village, minus the large landowners and the Dalits or untouchables. The epistemological obscurities of Conrad's narrating situation are largely avoided in this text, as the speaker is identified as an old woman who conveys the communal sensibility through the constant use of the pronouns "we" and "us" but never strays into the territory of an omniscient voice. In fact, she communalizes (and subjectivizes) such knowledge by typically prefacing it with the words, "they say," which of course is not a third-person plural form at all but, like the synonymous formulations "one hears" or "it is said," an indeterminate form that exists on the border between conventional first- and third-person narration.[4] The key point is the inclusiveness and flexibility of the subjects depicted in this fashion.

Many of Ngugi wa Thiong'o's adaptations and transformations of Conrad are well known. His novel *A Grain of Wheat* (1967) reenacts scenes from *Heart of Darkness* in a story reminiscent of *Lord Jim*; it also uses temporal shifts that suggest the multiple, converging, polychronic storylines of *Nostromo*. Less discussed is Ngugi's employment of we-narration as a central node of the text: The most important political and social event, the arrival of Kenyan independence, is narrated by a brief, abrupt, and most Conradian foray into the first-person plural: "His name was on everybody's lips. We wove new legends around his name and imagined deeds. We hoped that Mugo would come out and join us" (204). This affirmation of narrative presence is emblematic of a unity among characters, implied author, and authorial audience, rather than a verisimilar depiction of a group of people who were literally there.

Ayi Kwei Armah also uses we-narration throughout his novel *Two Thousand Seasons* (1973). His "we," a term of resistance, is repeatedly opposed to the discourse of a "they," as we see from the beginning of the first chapter: "We are not a people of yesterday. Do they ask how many single seasons we have flowed from our beginnings till now? We shall point them to the proper beginning of their counting" (1). His "we" explicitly designates all black people of Africa, and thus posits a transnational collectivity. This produces some interesting features, including a collective memory that is set forth as authoritative: "Our clearest remembrances begin with a home before we came near the desert of the falling sun" (4).

The most recent example comes from South African writer and activist Zakes Mda, whose 1991 novel, *Ways of Dying*, uses the "we" form in a playfully self-conscious manner: "We know everything about everybody. We even know things that happen when we are not there .... When in our orature the storyteller begins the story, 'They say it once happened ...' we are the 'they'" (12). These and similar comments go beyond the presentation of a collective subject and evoke a communal mode of narrative dissemination and reception that fascinated Conrad throughout his career, as Michael Greaney has recently discussed (11–43). Together, these three examples show how powerful, compelling, and protean we-narration can be, as well as how easy it is to reconnect this practice to the socialist politics that Conrad strove to exclude.

Uri Margolin has suggested that "we" narratives are rare for three related reasons: because the exact scope of the "we" may remain ambiguous and may contain different members at different points in the narrative; because the question of the narrators' mental access to others' minds "remains inherently unresolved"; and because the sense of a collective subject is more easily conveyed in lyric or meditative texts (253). Conrad's example (which Margolin does not consider) suggests a different conclusion. He stands at the beginning of an extremely protean technique with a continuous history of over a century that continues to be deployed in a number of texts that emphasize the construction and maintenance of a powerful collective identity, including feminist and postcolonial works.[5] It may also be that, as the practice of Conrad and Ngugi suggests, we-narration is most effective in immediate juxtaposition to other more traditional modes of narrating. It is certainly the case that it is an excellent vehicle for expressing a collective consciousness; the relative rarity of its use heightens its ability to defamiliarize traditional formulas and foreground its difference from the isolated individual consciousness associated with the rise of the novel in England and the development of modernist techniques of representing minds.

Notes

1. Baines (180) mentions the Flaubert connection, further discussed by Lester (166).
2. For a sustained analysis of this kind of text, see my essay, "I etcetera."
3. For a skeptical, class-oriented reading of this work, see Brian Richardson, "Construing Conrad's *The Secret Sharer*."
4. See Brian Richardson "I etcetera."
5. See Margolin for titles of other recent "we" narratives.

13

"The Thing Which Was Not" and The Thing That Is Also: Conrad's Ironic Shadowing

LAURENCE DAVIES

Whoever is not with us is against us, shout the Serbs. Whoever is against us is not with us, shout the Croats.

(Ugrešić, *The Culture of Lies* 42)

Dubravka Ugrešić, who finds herself reluctantly a Croat, pointed out this un-reflective symmetry more than ten years ago. Denounced as a "witch" for show-ing up such embarrassing parallels and threatened with death by some of those public-spirited but anonymous patriots who strive to keep so many homelands pure, she found it wise to emigrate. Though in their Biblical form they are neither as exclusive nor as belligerent as they have become, the words she cites have ancient roots.[1] Despite their venerable ancestry, the current ver-sions show three qualities of adolescence—vigor, truculence, and simplicity. When spoken with conviction (and no fuss about excluded middles), or when taken up indeed in a spirit of political opportunity, they offer not a peep of irony; when put in the mouths of fictional characters or quoted polyphoni-cally, the ironies are resonant. To quote Kierkegaard, irony "reinforces vanity in its vanity and renders madness more mad" (271). What better example of madness than the urban planner from the besieging side who, after several months of shelling, assured the world, "We shall build Dubrovnik again, even lovelier, even older?" (Ugrešić 195). One might talk about such demented statements as a gift to the ironist, but saying so implies that irony is a career, or another variety of opportunism, or the kind of boulevard gossip practiced by Martin Decoud in his Parisian phase. I shall argue in this chapter on Conrad as ironist that, on the contrary, irony is a necessity, a mode that speaks from and to urgent yet lasting wants.

Notoriously, irony resists straightforward definition. Thanks to the protean nature of Conrad's writing, a broad location rather than a narrow siting is ap-propriate; and I shall use that excuse to defer more rigorous discussion of the concept. Conrad works with ironic disjunctions on every scale from the largest narrative structures down to words and phrases. One can recognize his irony in a whole cluster of stances and techniques: incongruity, humor, absurdity, understatement, overstatement, contrary statement, disparity of tenor and vehicle, disparity of intention and result, dramatic irony, romantic irony.[2] He deploys irony in a multitude of directions: in *Nostromo* and "The Warrior's Soul," he ironizes history; in "Falk," *The Secret Agent*, and "The Return," he follows an explicit agenda of treating melodramatic subjects ironically; in *Heart of Darkness*, *Lord Jim*, and "Karain," he gives imperial romance the same treatment; in the political novels, he exposes contemporary mantras and assumptions to an ironic and satirical gaze. More generally in Conrad's fictions, his characters suffer the unexpected and unwanted consequence of their desires. In his letters as well as in his fiction, he savages those abuses and slippages of language that are greased by semantic corruption. Through all his writings, some few essays aside, runs a streak of somber and sardonic humor.

Conrad's debt to Flaubert's ironic mastery echoes in the grimy absurdity of the pianola at the Silenus as it accompanies the Professor's grisly chat with Comrade Ossipon, just as the bleats and bellows of adjudicated farm animals and the bulky periods of local politicians punctuate Rodolphe's seduction of Emma. The debt, however, is not only a matter of building scenes. Like Flaubert, Conrad knew how to gut received ideas. Kayerts and Carlier are Bouvard and Pécuchet transplanted from Normandy to a more hazardous existence in the Congo.[3] It was "An Outpost of Progress" that won Conrad the friendship of Cunninghame Graham, another connoisseur of verbal outrage. Conrad admitted to Graham that "Half the words we use have no meaning whatever and of the other half each man understands each word after the fashion of his own folly and conceit" (*Letters* 2: 17), thus managing to anticipate on a winter's night in 1898 while Jessie Conrad lay in childbed virtually the whole trajectory of literary and linguistic theory in the twentieth century, from the revolt against rhetoric to the critique of logocentrism. "Words, as is well known, are the great foes of reality," says the teacher of languages (*UWE* 3). Because Conrad was so conscious of the capacity of words to bewilder, to hypnotize, to hide, we need to hear the ironic timbre in his language.

When acknowledging him as an ironist, however, the broadest critical consensus has formed around the development of character and plot, often to the neglect of verbal irony. Heyst begins by wanting solitude, but rescuing Lena makes solitude impossible. The newly fledged captain in "The Secret Sharer" wants to do his best by ship and crew yet endangers both so that Leggatt, an offender against the letter and spirit of maritime law, may escape arrest. Almayer dreams of living in a mansion with his daughter, but by the end of the story, Nina has rejected him, the "folly" is a looted, burned-out ruin, and the only mansions Almayer sees are shimmering through opium fumes. The Europeans in "Karain" yearn for home, for England, and they exorcize Karain with an imperial fetish; but when the narrator does return to

London, a bleaker place than he had remembered, he finds that he too is haunted—by nostalgia for the tropics. "Karain" belongs among the *Tales of Unrest*, but the title could as well apply to any of these narratives of desire frustrated or deformed.

Whatever the curvature of the story's arc, each of these cases approximates a familiar narrative pattern in which the outcome fails to match the expectations. The ironic versions of the pattern constitute a subset of traditional narrative and a subset of irony.[4] We might think of them as stories that dramatize the vanity of human wishes, or the outcome of an artistic process well-described by Friedrich Dürrenmatt: "A story has been thought out to its conclusion when it has taken its worst possible turn" (95); often they exemplify what D.C. Muecke calls the Principles of Economy (the highwayman is robbed) and High Contrast (highwaymen are rarely robbed) (52–54).

Alongside the grand scale, the one suiting a plain summary of story arranged in something close to chronological order, we need a middle scale, capable of marking the zigzag progress of the plot. In this way we can register dramatic irony, which features, for instance, in *The Secret Agent* where, in the middle chapters, the reader knows more than certain characters (such as Winnie Verloc) about what exactly happened in Greenwich Park. In this way, we can deal with what's left out. A distant view of *Typhoon* would tell us that, thanks to his utter lack of imagination, Captain MacWhirr takes the *Nan-Shan* safely through a dreadful storm; a closer view would note what happens at the end of Chapter V. Having raised the drama and suspense to an almost painful intensity, Conrad checks the pace abruptly.

> Captain MacWhirr was trying to do up the top button of his oilskin coat with unwonted haste. The hurricane, with its power to madden the seas, to sink ships, to uproot trees, to overturn strong walls and dash the very birds of the air to the ground, had found this taciturn man in its path, and, doing its utmost, had managed to wring out a few words. Before the renewed wrath of winds swooped on his ship, Captain MacWhirr was moved to declare, in a tone of vexation, as it were: "I wouldn't like to lose her."
>
> He was spared that annoyance. (*TOT* 90)

This is no mere moment of easing back before taking the narration into the eye of the hurricane. The very next words initiate Chapter Six: "On a bright sunshiny day, with the breeze chasing her smoke far ahead, the *Nan-Shan* came into Fu-Chau."

Here, then, is an imaginative work that pays ironic (perhaps envious) homage to literal-mindedness. At the place where we would expect to find a heart-stopping climax to the onset of the storm, the two quoted passages frame a hiatus. The noise of the storm dies away. Far from pulling out more stops, the author silences all but two muted voices, MacWhirr's and the narrator's. Instead of a titanic conflict between fate or nature and MacWhirr, the typhoon's "utmost" is "to wring out a few words." Instead of giving us the crew's immediate experience of the storm at its worst, Conrad shows its aftermath as, completely caked in salt, the battered *Nan-Shan* reaches port under the eyes of other sailors, who are curious or even jocular. Conrad baffles every expectation of physical and metaphysical clamor. Indeed, he even avoids the cosmic kind of irony, wherein puny humans wage a hopelessly one-sided battle against the universe, to produce another: MacWhirr is too prosaic to raise the necessary language. Conversely, no language could be adequate to match the hurricane's intensity.[5] In its place we have absence or understatement, as if this were a Jamesian story of unspoken secrets: "in a tone of vexation, as it were . . . . He was spared that annoyance."

Conrad was a master of avoidance. These scenes from *Typhoon* have several analogues in *Heart of Darkness*. As reading aloud will easily confirm, pacing, tone, and plot all create the impression that the scene with the Intended will culminate in a moment of frank confrontation operatic in its intensity, even a revelation of supranatural truth. Instead, we hear Marlow's halting speech, his embarrassment, his equivocations. He lies, but "The heavens do not fall for such a trifle" (*YOS* 162). Those who like their big concluding scenes to be conclusive must find this one inadequately wrapped. Yet Muecke's Principle of Economy is conserved: a lie commemorates a liar; poetic justice has been done.

So much of Conrad's irony turns on understatement, even silence. Every grandiloquence is quickly undercut: the "Eldorado Exploring Expedition" is a "devoted band" but its members talk like "sordid buccaneers" (87). In *Nostromo*, Conrad reduces a political speech to fragments:

> . . . over the swarming Plaza brooded a heavy silence, in which the mouth of the orator went on opening and shutting, and detached phrases—"The happiness of the people," "Sons of the country," "The entire world, *el mundo entiero*"— reached even the packed steps of the cathedral with a feeble clear ring, thin as the buzzing of a mosquito. (390)

Many of the crucial ironies, however, depend on reticence or implication, on the narrator's being cooler, more restrained than the situation warrants, on hinting that more might be said if one cared to be hysterical. The director is "somewhat discomposed" to discover Karlier dangling from a cross ("An Outpost," *TU* 117). The whole account of the report to the International Society for the Suppression of Savage Customs (another grandiloquent name) is a masterly show of ironic disparagement (*YOS* 117–118). Several tactics work together here: the deliberate manner with its judicious resort to parenthesis: "too high-strung, I think," "before his—let us say—nerves"; the damning with faint praise: "The peroration was magnificent, though difficult to remember"; the words can never be sufficient for the atrociousness they describe: "caused him to preside at certain dances." Yet the language does suffice to indict Kurtz because, unlike his, Marlow's language is so scrupulous, so measured. Where Kurtz is vaporous, Marlow is precise. In contrast to Marlow, Kurtz never treads on middle ground: He is either communing with "an exotic Immensity ruled by an august Benevolence" or advocating genocide. Muecke likens irony to a gyroscope (Muecke 4)—a moral accessory quite unknown to Kurtz.

Marlow speaks precisely but not without equivocation. The compass of his praise is usually narrower than it first appears. Examples include Marlow's affirmation that "Kurtz is a remarkable man" (138) and Marlow's expression of respect for the accountant, who dresses so meticulously—and is irritated when the groans of a dying man intrude upon his work (67–69). Again the gyroscope is spinning.

If plot and character development attract the largest consensus about Conrad's ironies, verbal irony attracts the least. Are passages such as these ironic? If so, to what extent? Are they ironic at all? Can one give any weight to the element of praise in them, or do the circumstances—the dying man, the heads on poles, the barbarous "postscriptum"—make any praises weightless? Although the critical history of *Heart of Darkness* might suggest otherwise, arguably the circumstances do. Keeping one's collar stiff and clean is not a corporate work of mercy. Formal dressing in the jungle may be a means of self-discipline, a strengthener of morale, a reproach to the sloppy, even a propitiatory sacrifice to the demons of prickly heat, but in the presence of one dying man and the proximity of many others in the grove of death, it is one of those minor virtues whose obsessive pursuit is less than virtuous.[6] Irony skewers disproportion: The Lilliputian courtiers want to execute Gulliver for pissing on the royal palace, even though by doing so, he put out a major fire.[7] Like Nietzsche's truth, irony is a matter of perspective. Yet it would be wrong for ironists to congratulate themselves on cornering all the best seats, for theirs are not the sight-lines of a theater or church. They have joined a debate between power and skepticism that never ends.

I.

As philosophers claim that no true philosophy is possible without doubt, so by the same token one may claim that no authentic human life is possible without irony.

Kierkegaard, *The Concept of Irony with Constant Reference to Socrates*

Traditional definitions of irony present it as a form of lying, or dissimulation, or saying the opposite of what one means. In a Socratic context, Muecke translates the Greek *eironeia* as "a smooth low-down way of taking people in"; Enright quotes the relevant entry from Johnson's *Dictonary*: "A mode of speech of which the meaning is contrary to the words" (Muecke 15; Enright 5). Thus, an ironist must utter what the Houyhnhnms, themselves exempt from lying, call "the thing which was not;" the people of Sambir, who are not exempt, use virtually the same words (Swift 242; *AF* 128). As a form of lying, however, irony belongs to a curious subset: the pretended lie, or the lie which is not. If Socrates were as ignorant as he pretends to be, we would not bother to read about him; unlike Thrasymachos, or Menon, or Agathon, who are innocent enough (or wise enough) to let themselves engage in Socratic dialogue, we must be in the know. While trying to make sense of irony as a cultural phenomenon, the challenge is to establish the connection between what is said and what is meant. How does irony become the thing that is also?

Hutcheon writes of irony as "the mode of the unsaid, the unheard, the unseen" (9). This classification deals well with irony's affect: the coolness where we need shock or indignation, the narrative detachment where we need dramatic closeness, even empathy. Heat examines what is left of Stevie: " ... the Chief Inspector went on peering at the table with a calm face and the slightly anxious attention of an indigent customer bending over what may be called the by-products of a butcher's shop with a view to an inexpensive Sunday dinner" (*SA* 88). The narrator takes his time, selects his details calmly, never raising his voice.[8] Almost the whole of Chapter 11, the episode of Verloc's murder, relies on linguistic disproportion. In the twenty-seven pages of this scene, Winnie utters thirty-five words, "for what were words to her now?" (250); her husband reaches that total on the second page, and continues to gush self-justifications and hopelessly misdirected condolences: "Do be reasonable, Winnie. What would it have been if you had lost me?" (234). As the narrator observes, rendering Verloc's emotional condition: "He had had a full day, and his nerves had been tried to their utmost" (178). In addition to the dramatic irony of this remark (the carving-knife is already on the table), it and dozens more point to the abyss separating what is thought and spoken in this scene and what, morally and emotionally, is at stake. Sometimes Conrad makes his narrative voice or his characters' dialogue too meager for the situation, as it is here; sometimes he makes them over-rich (and thus too lofty to be bothered with particulars) as in Kurtz's pamphlet and the political orations in *Nostromo*. Inadequate words, inadequate people: Ironized characters such as Verloc and Captain Mitchell lack the knowledge, understanding, attentiveness, and imagination to rise (or fall) to the occasion. Speaking in a haze of clichés and cigars, Captain Mitchell stages himself as an insider, a Man Who Knows, but about what has happened in Sulaco, he doesn't have a clue.[9]

Thus we can profitably speak the dialect of absence—the absence of history, perspective, wit, decorum, wisdom, proper words, humanity—but, as a means of understanding irony in general and Conradian irony in particular, the dialect of presence is equally rewarding. How do we act when something's missing from a text? By supplying the missing element from our existing knowledge (of the history of the Occidental Republic, for example) and our understanding (from personal and communal experience), or by seeing the need for something new. Each ironic moment is a miniature version of the void which, Alain Badiou argues, reproaches the "plenitude" of an older mode of thought.[10] This process of creating or discovering a gap and inviting the reader to fill it is well suited to fiction, with its preference for staged identities and indirection. What Friedrich Schlegel claimed two centuries ago still holds: novels are "the Socratic dialogues of our time" (qtd. in Enright 17).

The process, however, is not dialectical in a sense that Hegel or Schelling might understand; most fiction is too open-ended for that, and ironic statement isn't necessarily the antithesis of ironic implication. A pun in Kierkegaard hints at a more satisfactory model: " ... the ironic nothingness is that deathly stillness in which irony returns to 'haunt and jest' (this last word taken wholly ambiguously)." "Haunt and jest" translates the Danish word *spøger* (275, 444, n. 52), an etymological cousin of the English *spook*. We might say, then, that irony both mocks and haunts, a combination of effects perfectly illustrated in the scene with the Intended. Not all irony is uncanny, though: what could be more aggressively materialist than the motif of butchery in *The Secret Agent*? Irony is the play of mockery and shadow. The mockery may lead toward compassion or toward contempt. The shadows make us wonder—or remember—what has cast them, its hue, its shape, and its history.[11] Irony is a way of bringing to light without being dazzled by the meretricious or made despondent by the lingering darkness, a mode of seeing double. Now you grasp it, now you don't.

II.

A mercurial writer, Conrad uses a tone that shifts often and surprisingly. One moment the text will be mockingly ironic, the next, judiciously editorial. Carefully neutral in tone like a passage from the Goncourts or Maupassant, a somber description of Almayer's desolate office (*AF* 199–200) precedes a flash of Dickensian wit: "During a great flood the jetty of Lingard and Co. left the bank and floated down the river, probably in search of more cheerful surroundings" (203). As Nina tells her father of her love for Dain, her language would suit a Loti novel or an orientalist opera, while the barrel-organ scene turns opera into "tearful and endless iteration" (89). A view of Sambir through Babalatchi's eyes starts as a deeply purple passage (of the sort Beerbohm was to parody in *A Christmas Garland*) but rounds off with the inescapable smells of "decaying blossoms ... drying fish ... and ... acrid smoke" (131–132). Conrad's writing veers between the extravagantly serious and the extravagantly comic, the romantic and the naturalistic, the ironic and the operatic. Far from being a weakness, these abrupt changes of course give his work tremendous energy and tension. Short of knowing a book by heart, we never know which way he will tack. Conrad loved surprises.[12]

Then is Conrad's irony an incisive way of writing to which he frequently yet unpredictably resorts, or a comprehensive way of seeing? The distinction between irony as "momentary expression" and "irony in the eminent sense" originates with Kierkegaard (270–271). The former is a rhetorical maneuver, the latter is the standpoint for an ironic view of life. "Irony in the eminent sense directs itself not against this or that particular existence but against the whole given actuality of a certain time and situation." Even Talleyrand's "deep irony against the world," the observation that "man was given speech not in order to reveal his thoughts but to conceal them," is not enough to reach this state of eminence, for, Kierkegaard argues, diplomats must sometimes mean what they say: "There are many things" they "would seriously maintain" (271). Here "seriously" must imply a distinction not so much between gravity and frivolity as between what is frank and what is veiled. But what if "the whole given actuality of a certain time and place" is so complex and so varied that no one mode, not even irony, not even frankness, is adequate to render it? While Conrad's writings reflect a diverse experience of living in the Russian, Austrian, French, and British Empires (not to mention trading in the Dutch), and while they also echo a tumult of philosophical and political controversies, his life as *homo multiplex* converged with an experimental bent more characteristic of the next generation of authors than of his own. Conrad thought of himself as "*modern . . .* 'new'" (*Letters* 2: 418).[13] Although mortgaged to the old-fashioned practice of serial publication, Conrad wagered his livelihood over and over to try out something new.

Whoever wants to claim Conrad for some favorite stance or cause will easily find the necessary evidence. Besides Conrad the cosmopolitan and literary sophisticate, there is the author enchanted by romance and adventure, and the man whose moral sense appears in Marlow's respect for "that belief in a few simple notions you must cling to if you want to live decently and would like to die easy!" (*LJ* 43). Yet at other moments Marlow's notions are far from simple. To assign Conrad purely to one mode reduces him; he ironizes morality and moralizes irony; he lets the shadow of the ironic fall across the operatic and vice versa—as if to recognize that we do not live in a steady frame of mind. No one mode exists autonomously, no one mode cancels the others out. For all its fascination with romance, *Lord Jim* best reveals this symbiosis.

III.

"Where did you get the pluck to jump—you coward?" Conrad, *Lord Jim*

When the fugitive officers in the *Patna's* lifeboat sneer at Jim, he misses the knotted ironies in what they say. Although incapable of ever being "clear" about the reason that (177), he has abandoned ship as if in answer to their urgent pleas of "Jump! Oh, jump!" which were actually intended for the donkey-man: "Eight hundred living people, and they were yelling after the one dead man to come down and be saved" (110). Now he has joined his colleagues in the lifeboat, they accuse him of cowardice, a subject on which they speak with vehemence and considerable authority. Ignoring all other insults, he seizes on their threat to throw him overboard, and wants to pick a fight about it—wishing they had the stomach to fight back.

The strange attractor of a myriad ironies, Jim remains immune to them; he is indeed a model of resistance. Marlow's sarcasms pass unnoticed: "the perfidious shaft fell harmless at his feet ... and he did not think of picking it up" (84). Even though he misconstrues them, as in the episode of "that wretched cur" (70), straightforward insults rile him, while subtler gibes slip by. Considering himself a victim of fate, he sees his plight as "awfully unfair" (128), avoiding not only the pains of irony but its rueful comforts. He does not recognize its immediate presence in his life and cannot recognize, of course, the net of ironic commentary the narrative weaves around him. Above all, he will never recognize that his ambiguous exit from the *Patna*—a tumble or a jump, a voluntary or involuntary act—has a virtually inexhaustible power to generate more ironies.

Well before the jump, well before we first hear Marlow's voice, the weaving begins with the tale of Jim's inadequate but storybook formation. He has spent his childhood in a country rectory, a lovely, well-appointed place next to the "little church on a hill" which "had the mossy greyness of a rock"—exactly the kind of place that the heroes of R.M. Ballantine adventures must leave behind but won't forget, and thus a likely first-chapter setting in the "course of light holiday reading" that inspires Jim's fair-weather dedication to the sea. In this idyllic setting lived his father, the rector, who "possessed such certain knowledge of the Unknowable as made for the righteousness of people in cottages without disturbing the ease of mind of those whom an unerring Providence enables to live in mansions" (5): the judgment is pure Cunninghame Graham, down to the fleering at "Providence." If Conrad cherished the "ideal meaning ... of the Victorian spirit" (Winner 1), he chose a peculiar way of showing it.

As Jim begins his first voyage at the start of Chapter Two, the omniscient narrator goes into incantatory *Mirror of the Sea* mode with the third sentence, but drops it in the fourth: "He knew the magic monotony of existence between sky and water .... he had to bear ... the prosaic severity of the daily task that gives bread—but whose only reward is in the perfect love of the work. This reward eluded him" (10). Thus ironic shadows fall again across the prose. Injured by a falling spar, Jim is "secretly glad" to be able to wait out the storm below, but, the narrator hints, he suffers badly from seasickness, a sharp check on any feeling of adventure. His lameness strands him in Singapore among the "officers of country ships," who love "short passages, good deck-chairs, large native crews, and the distinction of being white" (13). This is Jim's introduction to colonial life. Expecting romance or at any rate bustle, he finds indolence and unearned privilege. One would dearly like to know what *Blackwood's* readers made of this scandalous little sentence about the "officers of country ships" who so let down the side.

Not only does the narrator keep a weather eye for irony; his gaze is covering the broader scene as Jim falls prey to cosmic forces. Sunlight falls on the

Patna like "a flame flicked at her from a heaven without pity. The nights descended on her like a benediction" (16). This vastness, however, does not worry Jim, for he is "penetrated by the great certitude of unbounded safety and peace" (17); the dramatic irony shows itself only on reacquaintance, but even a virgin reader might suspect that, under the aegis of such an ironic narrator, this certitude is sure to be confounded. When Marlow at last takes up the narrative torch, his arrival on the scene seems like a rescue operation, but soon Jim's story will be subject to another round of ironizing, more intimate and more intense. (Because he knows of this scrutiny only at a physical level, the target is Jim's story, rather than Jim himself.) Marlow refers to Jim, who never acquires a family name, as "Master Jim," (35), a title implying that he's still a boy. In the courtroom, Jim has already deteriorated from an articulate witness capable of expressive metaphor (28) and ready with the proper nautical terms (29–30) to somebody "extremely discouraged and weary," who cannot find the appropriate words to testify (31). Henceforth, he will never be as articulate as Marlow, and so his rescuer will have to interpret "the pauses between the words" (105). When Jim does manage to express himself emphatically, he disconcerts Marlow (185), but, as for instance in Chapter Sixteen, Jim's sometimes halting, sometimes merely banal language sounds in marked contrast to Marlow's nuanced and eloquent report. Marlow reserves this eloquence for his audience; face to face with Jim, Marlow is laconic, even gruff.

To Marlow, Jim is a puzzle, a burden, a responsibility he is fated to accept, a challenge, all because, in the celebrated phrase, "He was of the right sort; he was one of us" (78). As it recurs (93, 224, 325, 331, 416), it always invokes some kind of solidarity—of nationality, gender, class, profession—but with a glint of irony's edge (Hutcheon 37). Marlow insists on his affiliation with Jim even though his conduct on the *Patna* has been scandalous and dishonorable.[14] The most jarring occurrence of the formula comes when Marlow feels he is "being bullied" by Jim's questioning: "What would you have done? You are sure of yourself—aren't you?" Marlow isn't entirely sure of himself—if it weren't too theological for this character, one would say that there but for the grace of God goes Marlow—and Jim's body language adds to the force of his words: "Don't forget I had him before me, and really he was too much like one of us not to be dangerous" (106). Jim's Anglo-Saxon fists and bluntness come too close to home.

This is the most perilous moment of identity with Jim. In general, Marlow keeps his distance in the classical pairing of *eiron* and *alazon*: the one an ironist, the other deaf to irony (Muecke 37–39).[15] Consider, for instance, Marlow's gift of a revolver and ammunition when Jim is about to sail for Patusan.

> "Pray take this," I said. "It may help you to remain." No sooner were these words
> out of my mouth than I perceived what grim meaning they could bear. "May

help you to get in," I corrected myself, remorsefully. He, however, was not troubled by obscure meanings. (237–238)

Jim then rushes off, forgetting the cartridge boxes, an omission, he later claims, which has saved his life (245). Directly after the scene with the presents, as if to parody the whole theme of misprision, Marlow meets the skipper of the brigantine, who sprays him with a burst of malapropisms.

Marlow's worldliness is that of an experienced man dealing with someone younger and far more naive, but it is also that of a man who is not entirely constrained by the principles of his own kind, of his "us." The "easy morality" of the father's letter to his son seems inadequate to Marlow: the Rector has told Jim that "Virtue is one all over the world, and there is only one faith, one conceivable conduct of life, one manner of dying" (341). Such attitudes have no place in Marlow's more hospitable Book of Virtues; Marlow, indeed, is something of a moral relativist. The comments on the Rector's letter accompany a much longer letter to a "privileged man" (337), who has been one of Marlow's audiences. Now returned to London, this man believes firmly in a symmetry between morality and pigmentation, "in the truth of ideas racially our own." With a judicious "Possibly!" backed up with a subsequent "I affirm nothing" (339), Marlow diplomatically suggests that his correspondent's understanding is inadequate to make sense of happenings in Patusan. The contrast between Dain Waris and Gentleman Brown will not do much for the cause of racial solidarity, let alone supremacy.

Marlow's broader views encourage his skepticism, which is by no means the same position as nihilism. Talking of Jim, he maintains, "the less I understood the more I was bound to him in the name of the doubt which is the inseparable part of our knowledge" (221). And he further observes: "Are not our lives too short for that full utterance which through all our stammerings is of course our only and abiding intention? I have given up expecting those last words, whose ring, if they only could be pronounced, would shake both heaven and earth" (225). He is close here to the Marlow who could not bring the scene with the Intended to a resonant and satisfactory conclusion. With regard to Jim's story, he speaks of brightest light and deepest shadow (93), but also of "a burlesque meanness pervading that particular disaster at sea," and of "a fiendish and appalling joke" (121). It is both the eiron's pleasure and his pain to see the joke where others don't. Yet as the narrative expands, so does the chance of finding a like-minded audience. In the movement from filiation (loyalty by birth) to affiliation (loyalty by temperament and choice), even the ironist may find a place in the community of Marlow's "us."[16]

After his visit to Patusan, Marlow's opinions begin to mellow. "He had proved his grasp of the unfamiliar situation, his intellectual alertness in that field of thought . . . . He was not eloquent, but there was a dignity in this constitutional reticence, there was a high seriousness in his stammerings" (248). Marlow now sees Jim as having entered a new landscape of experience "three hundred miles beyond the end of telegraph cables and mail-boat lines," where the "haggard utilitarian lies of our civilisation" give way to "pure exercises of imagination." Closer to the "utilitarian lies," the proper response is irony, but out there it is "Romance" (283). Or so Marlow thinks. With its population of Sumatrans, Bugis, Arabs, and sundry wanderers, Patusan is fertile ground for ironies, and Dain Waris himself has "an ironic smile" (262)—this, too, before the arrival of Gentleman Brown. Nevertheless, the thinness or absence that many readers sense in the Patusan narratives and the "shift between two distinct cultural spaces, that of 'high' culture and that of mass culture" (Jameson 207) come in part from the slackening of Marlow's irony now that Jim has left his orbit. Yet for Marlow, the shadows don't entirely disappear (265); Brown is an elongated shadow of colonial enterprise and daring, not to mention artificial solidarity, and Jim himself "goes away from a living woman to celebrate his pitiless wedding with a shadowy ideal of conduct" (416). Although it has blurred somewhat, Marlow keeps his double vision to the last. Often taken as the epitome of Conradian romance, *Lord Jim* is also among the richest instances of Conradian irony, because the two modes coexist, each challenging the other to justify itself. Instead of the ironic assurance of, for example, *The Secret Agent*, we have an irony that keeps us guessing, capable even of compassion, certainly capable of misgivings. At its fullest, irony is a process rather than a product or a tool.

IV.

> … *he thought he had saved his life, while all its glamour had gone with the ship in the night. What more natural! It was tragic enough and funny enough in all conscience to call aloud for compassion, and in what was I better than the rest of us to refuse him my pity?* Conrad, *Lord Jim*

The bill of indictment against irony is a long and contradictory one. It is said to be snobbish and subversive, archaic and postmodern, frivolous and bleak, detached and self-indulgent, unattached and narrow. Marlow's remarks speak, unintentionally, to several of these charges. Both the "funny" and the "tragic" elicit compassion, and pity stems from honesty and humility rather than moral arrogance.[17] Because exposure to irony makes one suspect good words without good deeds, one should add that this passage describes Marlow's future conduct rather well. In his relations with Jim, he displays the qualities of "integrity, tolerance, and compassion" associated with Emilia Gould (*No* 67), a closet ironist yoked to an unironic man. In her the compassion and the tolerance are manifest, the irony hidden: The prickly Dr. Monygham is her contrary:

> What he lacked was the polished callousness of men of the world, the callousness from which springs an easy tolerance for oneself and others; the tolerance wide as poles asunder from true sympathy and human compassion. This want of callousness accounted for his sardonic turn of mind and his biting speeches. (520)

This man, be it remembered, has gone through far worse experiences than the temporary loss of a presentation chronometer. Although irony may be the resort of the flâneur, the pedant, and the boss, nothing inevitably makes it so; the worker on the factory floor, the maid, the soldier in the rank and file, the tenant farmer, even the tortured prisoner may resort to irony rather more than those with power over them. To quote a recent story by Ursula K. Le Guin: "He knew she'd understand him. Underdogs know irony like they know air and water" (173). Although too versatile to associate with any one political position (Hutcheon 10), irony does have a restorative power, a power to remember what the mighty want us to forget, to ask what's in the shadows, to redress unequal balances.

We probably regard the Marlow who returns from the Congo as someone privileged, a white man, a member of the officer class, yet he is out of alignment with his cohort, a witness who does not know just how to speak of what he's seen. Like Monygham, he treats his audiences to bursts of sarcasm, but unlike the Doctor, he wants to put across an enigmatic and provoking story. Linguistic restraint is among his most significant strategies. He admires restraint because he has seen or heard so little of it, but also because it represents a kind of stoicism, a means of hanging on to sense, and his restraint appears, precisely, in his ironic moments.[18] The group of ex-sailors in the *Nellie* is a discursive community in miniature, a microcosm of the larger world of *Blackwood's* readers, one whose shared values, those of the late-Victorian upper middle classes, would surely include restraint; the ironic shock effect comes from Marlow's associating restraint with cannibals and its absence with a depraved colonial administrator who has at least a touch of English in him.[19]

In *Lord Jim*, Marlow also faces an audience of potential skeptics—his not-inevitably like-minded peers—and again he resorts to ironic shock and ironic persuasion. Seeing the janiform faces of irony, he calls Jim's understanding of the *Patna* affair "funny" as well as "tragic." "But that's not funny," a listener might reply; "And it's not tragic, either," another might add, yet to an ironic sensibility, they remain both without completely merging.[20] Thomas Mann's essay on *The Secret Agent* positions it as a tragicomedy, the mode, he suggests, best suited to modernity (Mann 240–241). Even in *The Secret Agent*, his most blatantly ironic novel, Conrad shifts from mode to mode. Irony is an essential part of his complexity, and indeed the part most complex in itself.

Some columnists assert that irony died in the fall of 2001. But unless it means only narcissism, lack of engagement, artistic constipation, and half-embarrassed glorification of the banal, irony still lives and still is necessary. It is needed, hearkening back to Kierkegaard, above all in times of "vanity" or "madness," when irony becomes a way of comprehension and survival. Those who have proclaimed the death of irony also insist that there are ideas we must not visit, conventions we must never challenge. In his practice—though not always in his publicly expressed opinions—Conrad acted otherwise. Rather than plump for reassurance or a spurious clarity, he was willing to acknowledge shadows, scandals, contradictions. Those who read him as a complex but literal-minded moralist or political observer, as well as those who dwell upon the lushness of his style, ignore the ironic texture of his work, the weave of tone and narrative outcome. Irony is not the mode of all he wrote, but it is one that weathers sturdily. It reveals Conrad at his most daring, where he is least bound by the pieties of his time and place, pieties that still linger in our own. Contrary to editorial superstition, the world has not grown simpler in the last few years; to be willing to hold more than one set of ideas in one's mind at the same time, and, better still, stay critically alert to all of them, is not immoral, decadent or weak (as single-minded folk would have us think), but fortifying. Here are Conrad's writings when we need our shadows back.

Notes

1. "For he that is not against us is for us" (Mark 9.40); Christ is speaking for the defense, not the prosecution.
2. For reasons of space, romantic irony can be only a phantom topic here. In *Culture and Irony*, the sole book-length study of Conrad as ironist, Winner offers an ample discussion. See in particular his chapter on *Lord Jim*.
3. Wallace Watson, Lawrence Graver, and Hervouet all notice this affinity (see Hervouet 37–38, 265 nn. 29, 30).
4. Imagine a Venn diagram with two overlapping circles; one represents irony, one, traditional narrative patterns: some but not all patterns are ironic; not all ironies are narrative.
5. Instead of "delayed decoding," which puts effect before cause, we get delayed response.
6. Winner writes of "the fond but condescending irony surrounding the chief accountant" (1). Lionel Trilling nods toward ironic sensibility but then discounts it: " ... Marlow, although he does indeed treat him with hostile irony, does not find it possible to suppose that Kurtz is anything but a hero of the spirit" (20). Even Leavis, among the first to write on Conrad's irony, balks at an ironic reading of the scene with the Intended, which he calls "another bad patch" (181). I cite these judgments not in a spirit of contention, but to show how broad the hermeneutic leeway is.
7. A Lilliputian ironist would play on the absurdity of valuing the mere preservation of property, even royal property, over the sanctity of tradition, monarchy, and law.
8. Besides reinforcing the ghastliness of the dismemberment, these details evoke the Saturday-night hunt for cheap offal or cuts too stale for better customers so characteristic of London poverty, and thus recall Stevie's anger against deprivation and injustice.
9. Yet, sometimes in Conrad, the absence of imagination may make the heart grow stronger. Jim has too much imagination, MacWhirr too little, but in his unflagging attention to his ship, the latter makes up for the defect.
10. "To take a well-known example: Marx is an event for political thought because he designates, under the name 'proletariat,' the central void of early bourgeois societies" (Badiou 69).
11. Definitions have a way of being more hospitable than intended. As metaphors for irony, haunting and shadowing invite extra company: the uncanny in the former case, the elegiac in the latter. Both possibilities feature in "Karain."
12. Remembering their conversations, Ford singles out surprise as an effect they both admired (Ford *Remembrance* 189–198).
13. Scholars who associate Conrad's irony with Modernism present him as a full participant, rather than a precursor from a slightly earlier period; see, for example, J.H. Stape's article on irony in the *Oxford Companion*: "In High Modernism generally, and throughout Conrad's canon, irony is a mode of perception deriving from a realization that the human experience is quintessentially disjunctive."
14. The motif of discreditable behavior runs all the way from the officers in Singapore basking in unearned privilege to Gentleman Brown, a brutal challenge to the whole idea of racial solidarity. Though not a Victorian novel, this is a novel about Victorians. To use Ruth Benedict's terms, theirs was mainly a guilt culture, but among officers and gentry, aversion to shame was just as powerful.

15. For Theophrastus, who made this model, "both were dissimulators" (Muecke 39): the *eiron* self-deprecating, and the *alazon* boastful. Although Jim overbears occasionally, he is far from boastful, and Marlow is reserved rather than self-deprecating, but the old dynamic still obtains.

16. On filiation and affiliation, see Said, *World* 16–24.

17. Perhaps in deference to W.E. Henley's contempt for the very idea, "pity" comes in for much abuse in *The Nigger of the "Narcissus,"* but there is nothing in *Lord Jim* to match that quasi-Nietzschean stance. Paul B. Armstrong suggests that, in *The Secret Agent* above all, "the distancing, reifying effects of irony work against compassion and community" ("Reading Irony" 91). Nevertheless, "Conrad demonstrates a generous belief in the reader's capacity to develop not only an ironic sense but also an ironic awareness of the problems of irony" (99).

18. Martin Bock concludes that for Conrad himself restraint was a buttress against mental breakdown (84–117).

19. According to Hutcheon, discursive communities are what brings irony to life (89–115).

20. Just as the comic passages in Shakespearean tragedies never become just "comic relief." Both Cleopatra and the clown who banters with her know that his basket carries deadly snakes.

4
Conrad and Subjectivity

14
Writing from Within: Autobiography and Immigrant Subjectivity in *The Mirror of the Sea*

ANDREA WHITE

He was born in an occupied country and journeyed into exile with his parents when very young. The rest of his life was marked by displacements and abandonments of various sorts and the eventual embrace of a new land and language. French was his second language and English became his third. That his first was Arabic marks one of the few dissimilarities from Conrad's case, a figure Edward Said felt compelled to write about from early on. But among the many similarities between the two, a major difference also appears as one reads Said's recent memoir, *Out of Place,* which tells of the complex displacements of a colonial boyhood in land and language and identity. Said is aware of the constructedness of identity, especially under such real pressures as colonialism, and he reveals in his memoir the ways in which cultural and personal identity were bewilderingly thrust upon him, coming to understand that those who claimed him as "one of us" were outsiders themselves. *The Mirror of the Sea* could very well have told the same story as Said's, about perceived otherness and out-of-placeness; for both, identity would be an irrevocably complicated matter, and neither could ever "go home." However, while an end-of-the-century Edward Said can be very clear about his own crises of cultural identity-colonial encounters as an Arab in English-dominated Egypt, the only American in his English scout troop, the outsider to his Palestinian relatives, the Palestinian in Lebanon who spoke a wrongly inflected Arabic—as he is in *Out of Place*—Conrad, writing almost a century earlier, felt compelled to announce his allegiance to his adopted country unequivocably, and as one of us.

As many readers have noticed, Conrad's "Memories and Impressions" are more of a meta-fiction than an autobiography; the "very intimate revelation" he talks about in his "Note of 1919" strikes Said, for example, as "an evasive masterpiece of truly impersonal intimacy" (*Joseph Conrad* 58). Others have considered *The Mirror of the Sea* as concerned more with concealing than revealing, and have found the few autobiographical facts mentioned in its pages to be either unverifiable or verifiably inaccurate. But as Avrom Fleishman has argued in his defense of *Mirror* as autobiography, "the form of a life [can be found here] amid apparently desultory reminiscences" (142). In any case, my approach here, familiar to readers of Regenia Gagnier, is a pragmatic one. Rather than evaluating the truth of a statement, "pragmatics seeks to locate the purpose an autobiographical statement serves in the life and circumstances of its author and readers" (Gagnier 4). I want to argue that this first foray into autobiographical writing constitutes not just "the form of a life" but a presentation of credentials. After all, who gets to speak about English fiction? Certainly not an outsider, a "guest" as Virginia Woolf was to refer to Conrad , even as late as 1924. Thus, this early memoir cannot be simply nonfictional revelation. Rather, writing from within, constituting himself as "one of us," he works in *The Mirror of the Sea* to construct a self authorized to speak.

What can account for the fact that so many contemporary memoirs, Said's among them, can be so forthcoming about their subjects' complex madeness, their naturalization rather than their naturalness, and can openly deal with the complex routes by which identity has been shaped? Said is among those who have made identity and its constructedness discussable, and his writing benefits from such theorizations of identity as Stuart Hall's, who interests himself in how "identities are constructed within, not outside, discourse" (4). That identity is discursively constructed across difference, and is a positional not an essentialist concept that relates less to our "roots" than a coming-to-terms with our "routes" (Hall 4), was not yet on the theoretical agenda in the early 1900s. Well aware of himself as *Homo Duplex*, Conrad is an early instance of a writer for whom cultural identity was a complex issue, but although his texts are themselves "products of a historical moment in which the older notion of a stable continuous self was becoming exhausted … the decentered subject had not yet been fully theorized" (Hendricksen 9). Within the constructed fields of belongingness and homogeneity, of difference and exclusion, of inauthenticity and "the real thing," then, the writer of "Amy Foster" worked to obscure his affinity with Yanko Gooral. Fearing the very real xenophobia chronicled in that story, and not wanting to be made into an exotic himself, Conrad's "Memories" construct an English subject; the Polish past would have to wait. Not yet eager to talk about those Polish roots or the various routes his life had followed to arrive in England—"I would lose my public if I spoke of Poland," he reportedly protested (Najder, *Polish* 26)—Conrad chose to connect himself with a particularly English past and to foreground an essentially English lineage. Called upon to account for himself by his reading public, Conrad constructed his own genealogy, inserting himself into an existing tradition in order to write from within, the only tenable position available within contemporary conversations about belongingness, about outside and inside. Of course, the tradition itself had been invented discursively, produced by the innumerable works of adventure fiction and travel writing that filled the periodical literature for both juvenile and adult audiences and the shelves of bookstores, lending libraries, private clubs, and ships' messrooms for over 100 years. In *Mirror of the Sea*, Conrad grounds himself in that discourse as though it were stable, not only as a consumer but also as a producer of it, in pursuit of an appropriate English self.

With the publication of *Typhoon*, and already with some major works behind him, Conrad was an acknowledged man of letters on the English writing scene. As a result, among the book reviewers and critics of the popular press, there was a general complaint that too little was known about him. In the September 1903 issue of *The Critic*, M.H. Vorse pointed out that Conrad harmed his popularity by holding himself aloof instead of advertising himself more. Because he "has neglected to court the interviewer," his success, at least in America, Vorse maintains, is being outstripped by inferior but better advertised works. In fact, Vorse admits, "a very little originality or sincerity will put a book on every book-store counter, the author's likeness on every elevated station. In a few months he is well known, and in a few months more well-to-do." But in Conrad's case, he continues:

> we do not even know whether Mr. Conrad takes lemon or cream in his tea, or just what the circumstances were which induced him to leave his earlier profession for the trade of writing books, or any of the other interesting details which we feel entitled to know about authors—details which make an author popular. Then, too, we see no pictures in newspapers or magazines of Mr. Conrad reefing a sail in a breeze, Mr. Conrad and his dogs, Mr. Conrad putting trees in his shoes.

And he concludes that "all of his work is so unusual and of so high a standard that for the sake of the public one could wish that Mr. Conrad would advertise himself more." Perhaps Mr. Vorse hadn't seen Edward Garnett's review in the *Academy* five years before, from which at least that journal's readers learned that Mr. Conrad had left his native Ukraine early and had sailed "in English ships to the ends of the earth" (Sherry, *The Critical Heritage* 106). A year after Mr. Vorse's complaint, another *Academy* reviewer, in an article devoted to Conrad, argued the necessity of "knowing something of the man" in order to entirely understand the work. He went on to complain of Mr. Conrad's "shyness" and his "terror" of being interviewed but boasted that he once in fact did interview Conrad, and had determined that "Joseph Conrad is a Pole and a sailor" (Sherry, *The Critical Heritage* 162–163). Given such pressures, Conrad must have been at great pains to present another picture of himself; that of a British seaman learning his craft from those who had gone before would prove a more acceptable public image than "Pole," "foreigner," and, most hated, "Slav." His reported "terror" at being interviewed suggests a deep desire to conceal a felt inauthenticity, and a revelation that he was not the real thing.[1]

It was in October of 1903 that Conrad began a correspondence with a Polish historian, Kazimierz Waliszewski, who had expressed his interest in writing an article about his countryman. Conrad responded positively but with the proviso that he not be made "to appear as a kind of literary phenomenon" (*Letters* 3:70) and knowing that the article would appear in only the French and Polish presses. Within a few months the article was published in the French journal *Revue des Revues* as "Un Cas de naturalisation litteraire: Joseph Conrad." Having overcome with his compatriot his "slight repugnance where publicity is involved" (*Letters* 3: 70) must have eased his way toward the autobiographical exposure much demanded by his reading public, for within a few months, while still battling *Nostromo*, he also began work on "a series of sea sketches." To his literary agent, J.B. Pinker he described his project as chiefly a financial expedient: "Essays-impressions, descriptions, reminiscences anecdotes and typical traits of the old sailing fleet which passes away for good with the last century. Easy narrative style. Work it for all it's worth!" (*Letters* 3:114). He acknowledges here, then, through a backward, proprietary glance, an already existing field to work, already discursively constructed in a centuries-old tradition of memoirs, tales, magazine stories, and articles about the brave endeavors of Her and His Majesties' navies and the British merchant service. A few months later, after having finished several of the sketches, he wrote to Pinker of other advantages they could serve. They would make money, and doubly more money, published in England and the United States in serial publication and again in book form. In their initial serial publication they would also serve as an advertisement for *Nostromo*, acquainting potential readers with its author's name and biography: "Moreover those who want to know something of Conrad (the individual) shall find it there, and the serialisation being commenced at the right time may help the vogue of *Nostromo*. Here is Conrad talking of the events and feelings of his own life as he would talk to a friend. They have been always asking for something of the sort and here it is with as little egoism and as much sincerity as is possible in a thing of that sort" (*Letters* 3:133). Although he objected to the commercialization of literary journalism and the need to reveal himself to the public, he courted that public as well (Watts, *Joseph Conrad* 24): "I have a feeling that the book would do me no harm in my struggle to a decent popularity" (*Letters* 3:136), he wrote Pinker in May. Indeed, as Watts has argued, he was an aesthete engaged in artistic endeavor and a canny self-promoter, both at once (*Joseph Conrad* 24).

But what self could Conrad present to be advertised on the huskings, pictured in the illustrated papers, and featured in newspaper columns? Although at this time he was in fact writing freely about his Polish past to Waliszewski, and he would soon speak more fully, for the moment he resisted foregrounding his "bloody foreign[ness]," and was less eager to release this image to the British reading public; he was reticent about revealing his naturalized status and worked to suggest a more natural one. He would be writing soon of the contrast between Verloc as "a natural-born British subject" and the assistant commissioner, disguised to look like "one more of the queer foreign fish" (*SA* 151). Conrad, for whom the assistant commissioner was a projection of himself, according to Paul Kirschner (87), was keenly aware of the difference between "natural-born British" and a "queer foreign fish." In spite of his desire not to be typed as a marine writer, the merchant service offered the least objectionable originary scene and diverted interest, he must have felt, from those reports already published of his otherness. And he must have known what Garnett would later observe, that it was in the sea writing that the "English element preponderated" (*Conrad's Prefaces* 4).

If identity is constructed largely across difference, then the self Conrad asserts here is an authoritative one, authentic and knowledgeable, in contrast to those Others, the landlubbers and especially the newspapermen. Particularly in the first three sections of *The Mirror of the Sea*, "Landfalls and Departures," "Emblems of Hope," and "The Fine Art," Conrad asserts an authoritative self through its difference from those misinformed facile paragraphists. Frequently in these early sections, he complains of the "degradation of the sea language in the daily press of this country" (13). He carefully positions himself as the genuine inheritor of a great tradition, in opposition to those landlubberly journalists who need to be informed that "casting" anchors and "going to sea 'on' a ship (ough) and other blunders, [are] inexcusable in writers for the newspapers of the greatest maritime country in the world" (14–15). Unlike those "poor miserable 'cast-anchor' devils," he writes with insider knowledge of anchors and chains, landfalls and departures.

The self dramatized in these pages is a positional one, constructed across differences of them and us, and also of now and then, steam and sail. The heroic past of sail and the skill it required is now eclipsed by a fast-paced present in which the demands of speed make craft and skill impossible. The loading of ships, for example, discussed in "The Weight of the Burden," was once a matter of skill; now the cargo of steamships is not stowed, it is simply dumped, he writes disparagingly. If *A Personal Record* concerns beginnings, as Said noticed, then Conrad's first autobiographical writing records the writer's backward glance at endings, of sailing ships, of occupations, of heroes. For although such an elegiac tone is unexpected in a writer not yet ten years into his writing career, the persona thus created attempts to satisfy the public's growing interest in the writer of *Almayer's Folly, The Nigger of the "Narcissus," Youth*, and most recently *Typhoon*; and the eulogizing places the narrator of these "memories" within a glorious English past, while at the same time helping to construct that past. We see him as a seaman in the British merchant service, moving up from a third mate initiated into the knowledge of the sea's "cynical indifference ... to the merits of human suffering and courage" (141), to a "youngster ... suffering from weariness, cold, and imperfect oilskins" (78), on to a well regarded and trusted first mate, and finally to a young commander. That these moments unfold as achronologically as in any of Conrad's fiction is very much to the purpose, as Fleishman argues. Indeed they provide "no steady developmental process but a succession of ironic correlations" (Fleishman 148).

Unconventional *Bildungsroman* that it is, the mirror produced here reflects the subject's growth into an able, initiated British seaman who has come up through the ranks and the tutelage of predecessors and tradition.

Interestingly, these tropes of continuity Conrad deployed in his production of an English self are also common to the discourse of nation-building, much discussed by Benedict Anderson. Like the nation establishing its legitimacy, so Conrad imaged his merchant mariner self in ancestral terms, terms he felt he needed to appropriate, having an inappropriate genealogy himself. In both cases, the tropes of continuity and inheritance establish the seeming natural-ness of their belonging. As "the nation inherits from its predecessors the idea that it is natural" ("Narrating" 659), so Conrad depicts his younger self as standing in a long line looking back on his ancestors in the craft, and in turn receiving his inheritance from "those masters whose influence left a trace upon my character to this very day" (*MS* 33). In *A Personal Record*, this persona will be reasserted where he speaks of his examiner as "a professional ancestor, a sort of grandfather in the craft" (119). When he passed his master mariner exam, his examiner revealed an experience of his own in the year of Conrad's birth that awakened in the younger man "the sense of the continuity of that sea-life into which I had stepped from outside … I felt adopted. His experi-ence was for me, too, as though he had been an ancestor" (*PR* 118). All sailors, he writes in a later chapter of *The Mirror of the Sea*, "belong to one family . . . . All are descended from that adventurous and shaggy ancestor, who bestriding a shapeless log and paddling with a crooked branch, accomplished the first coasting trip in a sheltered bay ringing with the admiring howls of his tribe" (148–149). Here the tropes of continuity and inheritance, "adopted," "as though he had been an ancestor," and belonging "to one family," while assert-ing his belongingness also suggest a certain insecure self-consciousness in doing so. At the end of "The Heroic Age," which he placed at the stern of the *Mirror* volume and which he originally wrote for the centenary of the Battle of Trafalgar, Conrad invokes a long succession of officers in the English navy, de-picting Nelson as their successor (186) and "the heroic spirit" itself as Nelson's legacy (188). And he concludes the article and the volume: "the national spirit, which, superior in its force and continuity to good and evil fortune, can alone give us the feeling of an enduring existence and of an invincible power against the fates" (194). "[C]an alone give *us*"—he is clearly one of us; and thus he writes himself firmly into English life and literature. Here he moves to insert his image into the family album as firmly as he has claimed his place in the hierarchy of the merchant service.

But in doing so, he proves himself as much a consumer as a contributor to an already constructed conversation whose terms were in place as though they were long established truths, ones that privileged England as a great maritime power historically. At the beginning of his career, while struggling with *The Rescue* on Ile Grande, he had complained to Garnett:

> And I am frightened when I remember that I have to drag it all out of myself. Other writers have some starting point. Something to catch hold of. They start from an anecdote .... They lean on dialect—or on tradition- or on history ... they trade upon some tie or some conviction of their time—or upon the absence of these things—which they can abuse or praise. But at any rate they know something to begin with—while I don't. (*Letters* 1: 288)

Conrad's sense here of having to supply something he lacked—tradition, history, cultural knowledge—reveals his own need to compose a self while suggesting the positional and discursively constructed nature of all identity.

The Mirror of the Sea, then, was as complexly motivated as any act conceived and committed in Conrad's fiction. To make money, to respond to appeals for biography, to turn the publicity to advantage, he presented a self in *The Mirror of the Sea* that claimed the British merchant service as his cradle, his originary scene, the site of his initiation. Here he charts his coming of age during England's maritime past, claiming for himself an authority from which to watch the receding of the good old days and with which to write, a crucial move at the beginning of the decade that would see *Nostromo, The Secret Agent,* and *Under Western Eyes,* marked as it was for Conrad by issues of belonging, of foreignness, and inauthenticity. We don't get an answer to the milk or lemon riddle nor do we get the originary "once upon a time" of an English boyhood that a Galsworthy could provide or a Graves or a Colvin or a Garnett or even a Hueffer in whose remembered childhood in Fitzroy Square the presences of Carlyle, Mr. Browning, and Mr. Ruskin figured prominently (Ford, *Your Mirror* 3). But Conrad had no such infantile English moments to remember nor the serene confidence of belonging so naturally to the national past. The grand narratives of origin that informed the autobiographical accounts of other English writers were not his, so the sea and the British merchant service became his primal scene, his founding myth of selfhood.

Finally, I would like to suggest that our own struggles today with authenticity and imposture, perceived or alleged, can be articulated more readily among current discussions of identities in terms of affinity and circumstance. The old certainty that cultures, peoples, identities, and places were homologous has been recently challenged by "a varied set of forces [that] include national liberation movements ... and the waves of migration from the former colonized territories" (Lavie and Swedenburg 2), the very movements that have enabled a Said to speak so freely about his background. Conrad felt the effects of that old certainty all his life and the resultant out-of-place feelings it engendered. He was especially sensitive to his friend Garnett's confidence in the inseparability of identity and place. That Garnett insisted upon speaking of Conrad's alienness, his Slavic temperament as the key to his personality, sapped their friendship eventually. By 1922, Conrad could still complain about reviewers who, like Mencken, "harp[ed] on his Slavonism" (Zabel 752). He had hoped to be given the credit of "being just an individual somewhat out of the common, instead of [being rammed] into a category, which proceeding, anyhow, is an exploded superstition" (Zabel 753). This somewhat disingenuous complaint covers up the discursive moves he made throughout his writing life to do just that, to place himself in a category, in constructing a self authorized to speak. A few months before his death, Conrad reiterated his belief that those who explained his characteristics in terms of race rather than individual temperament were mistaken and had done him a disservice. "I have asked myself more than once whether if I had preserved the secret of my origins under the neutral pseudonym of 'Joseph Conrad' that temperamental similitude would have been put forward at all "(Jean-Aubry 2:336). But while Conrad rejected this fixity, charges of inauthenticity pursued him nonetheless. Not only was he hurt by Garnett's continued insistence on his "Slavonism" but he was devastated by Robert Lynd's charge of inauthenticity in a 1908 review: "Mr. Conrad, without either country or language may be thought to have found a new patriotism for himself in the sea. His vision of men, however, is the vision of a cosmopolitan, of a homeless person. He should have remained a Polish writer" (Sherry 212). Lynd's own complex loyalties notwithstanding—an Irish nationalist assigned to the *Daily News* to write on things English—he concluded that Conrad's work was second rate, not the real thing, and even though Lynd would come to repent of that initial opinion, the pain it caused Conrad at the time can be measured by the intensity of his response to Garnett. Lynd's charge, Conrad wrote, is "like abusing a tongue-tied man .... The statement is simple and brutal; and any answer would involve too many feelings of one's inner life, stir too much secret bitterness and complex loyalty to be even attempted with any hope of being understood" (*Letters* 4: 107–108).

The same unhomeliness Lynd charged Conrad with Said acknowledges as well, but, to more recent thinking, Homi Bhabha's and others, enabled by the complex movements of postcolonial displacements, re-representations, and de-centerings of various metropolitan privilegings, such unhomeliness is seen as an advantage; the migrant writer is better positioned to observe and is, in fact, enabled to speak, rather than being tongue-tied. But at the time there were no Stuart Halls, Zadie Smiths, or Edward Saids to frame the discussion so familiar to us today of identity and the dangers of its reification.

It has seemed strange to many then and now to regard these "sea sketches" as a response to those critics who "have always been asking for something of that [autobiographical] sort" (*Letters* 3:133), but they did serve Conrad's purpose of temporarily displacing his rumored foreignness with a solid English performance. And he must have been pleased by the immediate response to the volume from fellow artists and writers. Glowing letters of praise arrived from Wells ("delightful talk of sea and wind and ships"), Galsworthy ("magnificent"), Kipling ("splendid"), and from that other expatriate Henry James, who sang Conrad's praises for his "beautiful sea green volume" (Stape and Knowles 53–57). But perhaps the most valued praise of all came from his friend, the English painter, soon to be Sir William Rothenstein, who wrote: "I felt a sort of glow of pride all the time I was reading it, that it should be 'one of us' who has so enriched the world" (Stape and Knowles 58).

Note

1. In his October 1912 review of *'Twixt Land and Sea*, he wrote: "If anyone has any doubts of Mr. Conrad's genius he will do well to read 'The Secret Sharer,' the second story in this volume. I confess repentantly that I once had such doubts. But I had not read *Typhoon* then" (Sherry, *The Critical Heritage* 251).

15

"A Matter of Tears": Grieving in *Under Western Eyes*

JENNIFER MARGARET FRASER

I "worked" this morning, but you now know what I understand by that: mourning—mourning me, the us in me.

Jacques Derrida, *The Post Card from Socrates to Freud*

Sounding much like Derrida, but in a letter rather than a post card, Joseph Conrad also imagines his writing as the work of mourning: "It is thus, with poignant grief in my heart, that I write novels to amuse the English!" (*Letters* 2: 55). In *Under Western Eyes*, the Russian characters imagine the English individual as "[c]ollected—cool as a cucumber" (*UWE* 21–22); and Conrad employs this perspective to chart the ebb and flow of ostensibly Russian, but in fact childhood, grief. Positioning the narrator as an English teacher, Conrad explores both the shedding and suppression of tears. The English teacher discovers that what democracies take for granted, namely "liberalism of outlook," is certainly for autocratic Russia "a matter of tears" (*UWE* 318). In this novel, Conrad connects the grieving self with the childhood self and, as Keith Carabine shows, the link is personal: The author himself is "haunted" by "shadows," and these "[s]hades" are of none other than Conrad's own parents, lost when he was a child (Carabine, *Life and Art* 16). Moreover, Derrida's work offers insight into Conrad's complex study of grief, for the French philosopher also conjures the figures of specters and children as he mourns.

David Farrell Krell concludes his analysis of Derrida's thoughts on mourning and art by asking: "Will we never be finished with critique, precisely because crisis accompanies every endeavour to encapsulate, circumscribe, and frame? Is every critical endeavour tied to withdrawal, loss, and mourning?" (47). These questions presuppose the deconstructionist (anti)-position that every word is haunted by its past use in other contexts. From this perspective, every sentence a character utters records echoes lost to the critic, the one who strives to interpret according to the present instance without having his or her ideas opened to other possibilities and sundered by alternative meanings. Derrida imagines mourning as a deconstructive process that resists encapsulating, circumscribing, and framing; he intensifies this crisis by noting that the narcissistic mirror breaks apart with death and "becomes terribly sharp" as it "increases and neutralizes suffering." The work of mourning becomes an act of remembering—being haunted, hearing echoes—requiring us to confront the "possibility of stating the other or speaking *to* the other" across the gap or loss of death (Derrida, *Reader* 203).

In *Under Western Eyes*, as recorded in his journal, Razumov asks the man he betrayed, Victor Haldin, across the gap of death: "Is this the way you are going to haunt me?" He confesses to Haldin's sister, Natalia, that this experience of addressing his victim beyond death feels like it is "tearing [him] to pieces" (358). This is Razumov's breaking point, the result of mourning. For Derrida and Conrad, mourning requires articulation: one must hear *and* speak. For a long while, Razumov seems incapable of speech: He "could only make a sort of gurgling grumpy sound" (*UWE* 254). He is closed off from communion with others and thus his voice is "muffled"; he forces himself "to produce it with visible repugnance, as if speech were something disgusting or deadly" (346). The narrator describes Razumov as "full of unexpressed suffering" (342). But while the narrator usually draws our attention to the fact that he is translating and paraphrasing Razumov's journal as well as his behavior, he quotes directly from his documentary source in the novel's final section. There, we read Razumov according to his narrative "I," and may thus assume that the teacher of languages is merely translating. Having direct access to the journal is significant, for Razumov's claim to Haldin when he betrays him—"[I]t's done" (35)—differs dramatically from his written confession to Natalia: "I have done it; and as I write here, I am in the depths of anguish" (361). Razumov no longer feels he is a victim; instead, his written act expresses an acceptance of individual responsibility. Paradoxically, Razumov's assertion of the "I" allows him to address, through grief, what Derrida calls the "us in me"; hence the belated anguish for the man he betrays.

Conrad associates the shattering of the narcissistic mirror with the act of writing. The narrator initially describes Razumov's journal as a projective image: he "looked at it, I suppose, as a man looks at himself in a mirror, with wonder, perhaps with anguish, with anger or despair" (*UWE* 214). When he gazes into this mirror with grief, expressed in his confession first to Natalia and then the revolutionaries, Razumov expects to be "torn to pieces" (366). More aptly described by the narrator as "smashing himself" (370), Razumov breaks apart due to his opening up to grief. When the revolutionaries deafen Razumov, they believe they have encapsulated him, fixed him in stone, stopped him from communicating—rendering him "stone deaf" so that he "won't talk" again (371–373). But just the reverse occurs. As Sophia Antonovna explains, the revolutionaries continue visiting him because "[h]e talks well" (379). Prior to mourning, Razumov, solitary and taciturn, is defined by his unwillingness to speak. But across the gap or loss of death, through his deafness, Razumov begins to address others and thus to break apart the narcissistic mirror.

Comparably, at the novel's end, Natalia devotes her life to mourning, which she also defines as breaking up; she attends "the heartrending misery of bereaved homes" (378).

According to political theorist Michael Ignatieff, this narcissistic mirror is generally reflective of our condition as we enter the twenty-first century. As a result of his travels in the 1990s, in an attempt to understand the resurgence of nationalism on a global scale, Ignatieff wrote an internationally acclaimed book—*Blood and Belonging*—whose title resonates for Conrad's Razumov, who yearns for a blood relation, a family to love; however, Razumov's mother's death and his father's rejection lead him to create a sense of belonging from his bond with Russia. Silencing the voices speaking to him across the gap, he listens instead only to his own narcissistic rhetoric. He "fe[els] the hard ground of Russia, inanimate, cold, inert, like a sullen and tragic mother," and concludes that his maternal nation needs "a will strong and one: it wanted not the babble of many voices, but a man—strong and one!" (*UWE* 32-33). Razumov's gazing into the mirror of a strong, mono-vocal man leads to his betrayal of Haldin, a kind of political betrayal that Ignatieff traces to the narcissism of minor difference: "A Croat, thus, is someone who is not a Serb. A Serb is someone who is not a Croat. Without hatred of the other, there would be no clearly defined national self to worship and adore" (22). With the term "brother" echoing in the background, Razumov bonds with autocratic Russia by silencing the revolutionary Haldin. Refusing to hear the echoes of Haldin in himself, in outright denial of his similarity, Razumov nearly falls headlong into a pool of suppressed mourning. What saves him is Haldin's haunting, which exposes the dead youth as in fact more solid than his betrayer, a mere projection of his own narcissism. Razumov realizes: "It was the other who had attained to repose and yet continued to exist in the affection of that mourning old woman, in the thoughts of all these people posing for lovers of humanity. It was impossible to get rid of him." Here Razumov realizes that he himself has been "given up to destruction" (*UWE* 341).

In *Specters of Marx*, Derrida suggests one must open up the self to the very "babble of voices" Razumov strives to silence. Derrida considers the grieving, haunted Hamlet: "One must lend an ear and read closely, reckon with every word of the language; we are still in the cemetery, the gravediggers are working hard, digging up skulls, trying to identify them, one by one, and Hamlet recalls that this one 'had a tongue' and it used to sing" (*Specters* 114). In Shakespeare's play and Conrad's novel, the protagonist is pursued by a specter. But, whereas the ghost of Hamlet's father wants revenge, Haldin appears to Razumov in a grieving pose—"solid, distinct, real, with his inverted hands over his eyes" (*UWE* 36)—which he strikes after having "burst into tears" and "wept for a long time" (22).

Conrad evokes various forms of mourning from *Hamlet*, a play he draws on generally to express his own writing processes.[1] In *A Personal Record*, Conrad explains how he came to write *Under Western Eyes*, in which he was determined to remain "the figure behind the veil; a suspected rather than a seen presence—a movement and a voice behind the draperies of fiction" (9). In this novel, Conrad depicts the suppression of mourning as immobility and deafness and thus his own sense of writing as movement and voice acts as an emotive release. Mirroring *Hamlet*, Conrad positions himself as a grieving son behind the veil of mourning. Just as Hamlet will open the stage curtains on a scene he himself inserts and directs, Conrad imagines himself as the moving force behind the "draperies of fiction." Moreover, the veil that covers his movement and voice is specifically the mourning veil that Natalia wears to signify grief for her dead brother. Indeed, Razumov, by wrapping his journal in the sister's "black veil," marks it as a work of mourning (*UWE* 362). Razumov bonds with a force beyond the violent cycle of oppression and receives a response from nature: "The steep incline of the street ran with water, the thick fall of rain enveloped him like a luminous veil" (363). Grief, not reason, enlightens Razumov here.

Much as Razumov speaks "with difficulty" and in "strangled phrases" when he tries to express grief (*UWE* 338), Derrida sees mourning as the breakdown of language; in grieving for a friend, he anticipates that his address will "traverse speech at the very point where words fail us." Those who open up to grief speak with "tears in their voices" (*Mourning* 200). Derrida's phrase foregrounds the punning potential in Razumov's fear that they will "tear him apart": his incipient knowledge that grief, his "tears," will be what tears him. So, in his journal Razumov wonders: "What could I have known of what was tearing me to pieces" (358). In *Under Western Eyes*, breaking apart, eyes tearing, is the work of mourning.

Grief dismantles the cool, collected self; and thus Conrad's English narrator privileges taciturnity and silence. He exclaims: "I was grateful to Miss Haldin for not embarrassing me by an outward display of deep feeling." He delights in her "wonderful command over herself" (112). This self-suppression is not only an English characteristic, for the Russian Sophia Antonovna also advises: "You've got to trample down every particle of your own feelings" (245). Conrad, in contrast, celebrates emotive communication. In this novel, writing that denies the emotional self turns one to stone, while fragmented writing has fertile, life-giving qualities. The "broken sentences" of Razumov's grieving journal contain a "dormant seed" (358), while his polished, intellectual writing is "dead matter" (68). Though "a mere piece of dead furniture," Natalia's desk, as it holds Razumov's journal, also contains "something living" (375).

Before feeling grief, Razumov has "stony eyes" (222) and immobile limbs (301, 355), and looks "as if his heart were lying as heavy as a stone" (344). These qualities are attractive to Victor Haldin, who seeks out Razumov due to his "frigid English manner" (16). In response to her brother's execution and Razumov's confession, Natalia is "turned to stone" (353): "Her face went stony in a moment—her eyes—her limbs" (111)—a stoic response the English narrator praises (375). Natalia's mother also suppresses her grief: she "has not shed a tear" and her face appears "as calm as a stone" (343, 322). Conrad stresses the paralyzing and alienating effects of suppressed grief, for the mother actually turns on her daughter with an accusatory silence; she becomes "the motionless dumb figure of the mother" (324) and conveys "mute distrust of her daughter" (372). These figures—expressive of both Eastern and Western heritage—become statues as they refuse to mourn; their hearts turn to stone and they remain silent.

Natalia looks "forward to the day when all discord shall be silenced" (376). While ostensibly a noble sentiment, the novel works to expose the dangers inherent in silencing the babble of voices residing within and without. The narrator participates, for he positions himself as a "mute witness of things" (381); and while registering "the stifled cry of our great distress" (376), he believes it "hopeless to raise [his] voice" (374). Conrad links the babbling voice, the cry within the novel, to the stifled child-self who haunts mourning's work. When Natalia first meets Razumov, she is disturbed by his show of grief and ironically (for the novel) condemns herself for being childish: "An emotional, tearful girl is not a person to confide in" (176; cf. 171). Haldin confided in a young man who, like an Englishman, seemed to have his emotions firmly in check, and he was betrayed. Perhaps if Razumov were more accustomed to grieving, this betrayal would never have happened.

In Conrad's novel, being an adult seems to require severing ties with one's emotional childhood self. Thus, scolded like a child, Tekla weeps when she does not cook the eggs properly, but she confronts the crippled Razumov without shedding a tear (166, 371). This is the split or gap between childhood and the mature self that Derrida believes it is mourning's purpose precisely to bridge: i.e., one reconnects with the childhood self in feeling grief. Faced with the loss of a dear friend, Derrida seeks "words as childlike and as disarmed as [his] sorrow" (*Mourning* 200). For both Conrad and Derrida, grief and childhood are basically inarticulate, and the two inform the section of Razumov's journal the narrator chooses not to record because of its incoherence (*UWE* 357).

Conrad contrasts immobile, stone-like writing with the movement and voice conveyed in the "broken sentences" of the grieving section of Razumov's journal. Peter Ivanovitch requires Tekla to take his words from dictation, and she must "sit perfectly motionless" (*UWE* 147). Though saved by a woman's "redeeming tears" (124), Ivanovitch does not want Natalia to shed any "tears," but rather fight for the revolution (131). Forming a different kind of rebellion, Conrad has his characters repeatedly "break the silence" to the point where the phrase accrues force beyond its idiomatic meaning. Yet it's Razumov's journal that is truly written in broken language; and prior to writing *Under Western Eyes* Conrad imagines his own writing process as the breaking up of stone. In a letter to Stephen Crane, Conrad describes distrusting himself as a kind of "taint" and his remedy is to become a "stone breaker": "There's no doubt about breaking a stone," although there is "doubt, fear—a black horror, in every page one writes" (*Letters* 1: 410).[2] As noted, Razumov strives to break stone by grieving; in the diary, he expresses himself "in broken sentences," but the narrator does not quote from the "page and a half of incoherent writing" (357). Conrad has us anticipate the idea of writing on stone or breaking up stone in the discussion between Sophia Antonovna, who speaks of the tragedy of "broken lives," and Razumov, who dismisses her claim that the revolutionaries "carve" their message on the "hard rock," for he believes they write "in water" (263).

Initially, Razumov defines himself by being solid like a statue. When first haunted by Haldin, whom he is about to betray, Razumov appears coherent and consistent, a man without breaking point: "After passing he turned his head for a glance, and saw only the unbroken track of his footsteps over the place where the breast of the phantom had been lying" (28). His steps do not falter; the track is unbroken. Initially, Razumov finds this a reassuring statement about his identity. Later, having betrayed Haldin, Razumov returns to this haunting moment, but finds his discourse "growing thick in his throat" and breaking up. Choked up, he addresses Councillor Mikulin: "What is his death to me? If he were lying here on the floor I could walk over his breast . . . . The fellow is a mere phantom . . . ." The broken sentences, with gaps marked by ellipses, culminate in an image of his division: "Razumov's voice died out very much against his will" (96). In contrast, the two men who seek Haldin's torture and execution—Mikulin, who does "not allow himself the slightest movement" (96), and the general, with his "stony stare" (47)—respond with complete immobility. Though Razumov strives to model himself on such suppressed, powerful figures, something within him—almost against his will—ultimately breaks up his plan. He becomes heartbroken like his victim. When the two students exchange thoughts on the revolution, broken phrases and ellipses mark their discussion, and Conrad describes Haldin as "heartbroken," speaking "mournfully" and "sadly" (62). While Haldin can speak his grief, Razumov experiences only inarticulate emptiness: "He felt sad, as if his heart had become empty suddenly" (200).

The sons of *Under Western Eyes* echo the haunted son Hamlet, who exclaims: "But break, my heart, for I must hold my tongue" (1.2.158). All three youths suffer from overwhelming grief that cannot be expressed and all three commit terrible crimes. In a famous speech, Hamlet distinguishes between mourning, "actions that a man might play," and grief, "that within that passes show" (1.2.82–83). This line is echoed when the teacher of languages describes Razumov's journal as having "passeth [his] understanding" (*UWE* 5). According to Hamlet, mourning theatrically manifests what one feels while actual grief is beyond communication. Sophia Antonovna stresses this distinction when she confronts Razumov: "What are you flinging your very heart against? Or, perhaps, you are only playing a part" (251). In *Hamlet*, Claudius condemns his nephew's grief as "unmanly" and Hamlet's educators for having failed to teach him to suppress his grief (1.2.94–97). Thus, *Hamlet* imagines the theater as a kind of subversive education, necessary in a society suppressing grief and honoring manly power. In his soliloquy following the players' exit, Hamlet raises vital questions about grief, its suppression, and the role of art: "tears, in his eyes, distraction in his aspect, / A broken voice, and his whole function suiting / With forms to his conceit? And all for nothing! / What's Hecuba to him, or he to her, / That he should weep for her?" (2.2.549–554). Conrad quotes this final line in a letter (*Letters* 1: 247), and thus Razumov's "broken sentences" may well be read as an attempt to sound the "broken voice" suppressed by the grieving son.

Conrad is the movement and voice behind the veil in *Under Western Eyes* where he dramatizes the impact on self and community when one is deaf to haunting voices. "Let us begin by letting him speak," announces Derrida in mourning Louis Marin (*Mourning* 143). Yet Derrida also claims "[s]peaking is impossible" when he confronts Paul de Man's death. At the same time, he admits that "so too would be silence or absence or refusal to share one's sadness" (*Memoires* xvi). Hence, the editors of Derrida's essays on mourning present him laying out "not so much a middle ground as a series of aporias, aporias that, curiously, do not paralyze speech but inhabit and mobilize it" (Brault and Naas, *Mourning* 9). Conrad translates into disturbing images enactments of the way in which the suppression of grief immobilizes and paralyzes speech and thus the self. Anticipating Derrida, Conrad strives to mobilize mourning—to harness storytelling as "a way to tell the unspeakable" (Le Boulicaut 143–145).

The unspeakable is a fundamental component of Razumov and Natalia's relationship; when she finally meets him, she stands before him "speechless, swallowing her sobs" (*UWE* 172). Even more disturbing, she responds to his confession with silence and never speaks to him again. This novel circles around inabilities, coercions, and refusals to speak. When Haldin explains that he has come to Razumov because he has "confidence" in him, "This word sealed Razumov's lips as if a hand had been clapped on his mouth" (19). When Haldin learns of his mistake, Razumov watches him leave "with parted, voiceless lips" (63). The drama of whether to speak or not to speak becomes more intense as Razumov betrays Haldin to the authorities: He must not be "drawn into saying too much." He then hallucinates about being on the rack, tortured for information (87–88). His "dream-like experience of anguish" anticipates Haldin's fate, and Mikulin ruthlessly quotes the record of his torture: "Refuses to answer— refuses to answer." Razumov defines Mikulin's "art" as "getting people to talk" (92). When Razumov meets the narrator, his throat is parched and paralyzed (184). This imagery of the desiccated self, dry as stone, transforms into nature's stormy tears raining down on the night Razumov wraps his journal in the mourning veil.

Haldin's terrible error is to believe that despite Razumov's "frigid English manner," he can hear "the sound of weeping" (16). Again recalling *Hamlet*, Razumov is deafened before he can hear of grief. King Hamlet is poisoned through his ear and when his murderer, Claudius, sees Ophelia in a state of madness, he blames "the poison of deep grief" (4.5.75). The narrator imagines the grieving Natalia as trapped in "poisoned air" (*UWE* 356). Natalia worries that her mother's "mind had given way from grief" (360). Conrad provides a radically different way of assessing these figures: Grief's *suppression* brings on madness. Society silences grief, turns a deaf ear, fears that grief will infect and destabilize the coherent, and thus, powerful self. Unlike Hamlet and the other men, Claudius is unable to hear the ghost of his brother and victim.

In *Under Western Eyes*, Conrad defines his protagonist by a "haunting" (167, 172) that is mirrored by the many years that "long haunted" Conrad in writing the novel (*Letters* 4: 14). Derrida writes of such hauntings:

> If death weighs on the living brain of the living, and still more on the brains of revolutionaries, it must then have some spectral density. To weigh (*lasten*) is also to charge, tax, impose, indebt, accuse, assign, enjoin. And the more life there is, the graver the specter of the other becomes, the heavier its imposition. And the more the living have to answer for it. To answer for the dead, to respond to the dead. (109)

Under Western Eyes contends with revolutionaries and autocrats whose minds are weighted with death. Locating them in a "land of spectral ideas," the novel defines them by how they acknowledge the weight of haunting (34). To Razumov, Haldin's living body has less "substance than its own phantom" (55). Likewise, Haldin cares less for his body than for his goal to be free of "the destroyers of souls" who "shall be haunted" (58). This dismissal of the individual bodily self in favor of political positions removes the weight, the density, from these young men and allows them to commit destructive acts. Bombing people or betraying someone to torture and execution should weigh heavily on one's heart; it is when one can lightly dismiss others that such political violence becomes a chosen vehicle.

Derrida's *Specters of Marx* concerns revolution activated by the failure to integrate one's haunting double, leading to a never-ending cycle of war. He writes: "It is as if Marx and Marxism had run away, fled from themselves, and had scared themselves. In the course of the same chase, the same persecution, the same infernal pursuit" (105). Conrad conveys a comparable idea in the bronze figure "Flight of Youth" associated with both Razumov and Haldin, displayed in the prince's home, eternally fleeing (*UWE* 43). Derrida sees this cycle as "[r]evolution against the revolution as the figure of *Les Misérables* suggests. More precisely, given the number and the frequency, it is as if they had been frightened by someone within themselves" (*Specters* 105). Conrad's narrator describes the cycle as one "where virtues themselves fester into crimes in the cynicism of oppression and revolt" (*UWE* 356); for Russians, the shadow of autocracy "haunt[s] the secret of their silences" (107). Both Derrida and Conrad explore how political specters relate to the ghostly child who haunts. Both Tekla and Sophia Antonovna stress this child's defining role in their respective political identities. Tekla sees a "ragged little girl" begging (111), and Sophia— "almost a child" (193)—watches her father die according to the dictates of an oppressive system (149, 262).

Conrad constructs both Haldin and Razumov as victims who carry death's load: Haldin's bomb kills not only the political figure but also his fellow revolutionist and several innocents; Razumov knows that betraying Haldin means he will be tortured and executed. Both imprisoned in a cycle of revolutions, these two murderous men—haunted by yet refusing to integrate the other— are distinguished in that Haldin mourns the death he causes, whereas Razumov learns how to mourn as the novel unfolds. Speaking in broken sentences, Haldin tells Razumov of "scattering death" among "innocent people," and then breaks down sobbing (22). In contrast, Razumov hides his emotions— "Inwardly he wept"—and then crushes them altogether: "A strange softening emotion came over Razumov—made his knees shake a little. He repressed it with a new-born austerity. All that sentiment was pernicious nonsense" (40). Razumov can imagine saving Haldin: "to pour out a full confession in passionate words that would stir the whole being of that man to its innermost depths; that would end in embraces and tears; in an incredible fellowship of souls— such as the world had never seen" (40). However, he takes the feelings this imaginative leap evokes and channels them instead into a father who has never cared for him, who has not even claimed him as a son. In the big political play, Haldin is the phantom; but in the play within the play, the child Razumov is the haunter. Just as Mrs. Haldin refuses to give her son up, Razumov will not give up his hopes of a familial bond with an absent father. Razumov is haunted by the child within him, figuratively murdered by the loss and abandonment of his parents, and this ghostly child drives Razumov to betray Haldin to the father who has rejected him.

Derrida asks: "Is it not derisory, naïve, and downright childish to come before the dead to ask their forgiveness? Is there any meaning in this? Unless it is the origin of meaning itself?" (*Mourning* 44). Razumov needs to perform precisely this childish act: to come before the child, haunting and dead within him, and to ask its forgiveness. This childish act could be described as the origin of Razumov's meaning in the novel. However, just as he demonstrates power to himself by walking over rather than listening to Haldin's ghost exhibits his power to himself, he stamps his foot—like an angry child—on Mother Earth: "and under the soft carpet of snow [he] felt the hard ground of Russia, inanimate, cold, inert, like a sullen and tragic mother hiding her face under a winding-sheet" (32–33). This contradictory description of the mother is disturbing. Razumov's mother literally died when he was a child; here he projects her specter onto Mother Russia, who appears like a corpse and yet still conveys rejection, being "sullen" and "tragic" and hiding her face from her son. Until Razumov begins the work of mourning and grieves for the time when they were "us," he will be caught as a youth running, fleeing from his true work and thus working for the cycle of powerful, manly, stone-cold leaders.

Critics like Catherine Rising have shown that Razumov constructs his identity in compensatory relation to his illegitimate paternity and unknown mother. Yet more remains to be said about a key motivation of Razumov's betrayal of Haldin, i.e., his attempt to secure his father's love and respect. As a university student, Razumov is called to meet the royal father who financially supports him without ever seeing him: "the most amazing thing of all was to feel suddenly a distinct pressure of the white shapely hand just before it was withdrawn: a light pressure like a secret sign. The emotion of it was terrible. Razumov's heart seemed to leap into his throat" (12). Conrad's description of the son's emotion—"heart seemed to leap into his throat"—echoes the phrase commonly used to convey the effect of grief, a lump in the throat. An abandoned child who yearns for affection must surely have a double-edged reaction of joy and grief when the parent shows any kind of affection.

The abandoned son recalls Prince K–: "the man who once had pressed his hand as no other man had pressed it—a faint but lingering pressure like a secret sign, like a half-unwilling caress" (40). Heartbreakingly, the only affection Razumov has ever received from this man is a slight, unwilling pressure; yet, in response to the "secret sign," he brings the terrible secret of the hidden Haldin to Prince K–, desperate for more contact. Reverting to a child's view of the world, a son sitting on his father's lap, Razumov imagines Prince K– according to his beard; he exclaims desperately to Haldin, in an oblique attempt to articulate to himself and his victim why he has betrayed him: "[t]he most unlikely things have a secret power over one's thoughts—the grey whiskers of a particular person" (59). These words inscribe the yearning of the lonely, abandoned ghost-child who haunts Razumov's thoughts and actions; for as Sophia Antonovna states: "a man is a child always" (241). Razumov learns this too late and, hence, does not understand why his betrayal of Haldin and subsequent dependence on corrupt authorities feels like a "game of make-believe" (314).

Razumov tries to explain himself to Haldin by telling him that he does not know family, only teachers; Conrad ironically emphasizes this truth by having a teacher tell his story. Razumov's reason has been well trained, but his emotional self has been starved: "I have been brought up in an educational institute where they did not give us enough to eat. To talk of affection in such a connexion—you perceive yourself .... As to ties, the only ties I have in the world are social" (60). Razumov is unaware that he seeks nourishment from a system that simply devours him. Challenging Peter Ivanovitch, Razumov refuses to participate in paternal rhetoric and to call the Russian people "children." Instead, he prefers "brutes," and forcefully argues: "You just try to give these children the power and the stature of men and see what they will be like" (227). Conrad's irony seeps into this speech, for of course Razumov has conducted himself fully as a child seeking a father in his recent political acts, themselves nothing short of brutal.

Councillor Mikulin manipulates Razumov's hunger and thus, when he wants to use him to spy on the revolutionaries abroad, he asks the prince to display some other form of paternal care so as to nourish the affection-starved child. Notably, what Razumov discovers from the "sudden embrace of that man" is "something within his own breast"; however, rather than feel bonded to Prince K –, the illegitimate son surprisingly recognizes a common humanity shared by this well-fed, powerful, ruling-class figure and the "famine-stricken" revolutionary student. Razumov's ability to articulate his yearning for "suppressed paternal affection" catalyzes the work of mourning that's necessary after his betrayal of Haldin and the ruin of both their lives (308). Far from distinguishing between ruling power and the revolutionary power, Razumov suddenly identifies with common humanity, and thus his treatment of Haldin and the destruction brought into his own life require grieving.

Derrida would identify Razumov's behavior as a sign of what he calls "spectrology": "It is always to the father, the secret of a father that a frightened child calls for help against the specter" (*Specters* 106). Even more striking, Derrida himself seems almost to analyze Razumov's predicament of illegitimate birth and parental abandonment. For Derrida, the act of writing may be what Krell calls "the orphan-bastard in distress" (206). Derrida contends that this distressed, abandoned act of writing rolls:

> this way and that like someone who has lost his way, who doesn't know where he is going, having strayed from the correct path, the right direction, the rule of rectitude, the norm; but also like someone who has lost his rights, an outlaw, a pervert, a bad seed, a vagrant, an adventurer, a bum. Wandering in the streets, he doesn't even know who he is, what his identity—if he has one—might be, what his name is, what his father's name is. (*Dissemination* 143)

At the novel's outset, Conrad stresses that his character is a man without a name: "The word Razumov was the mere label of a solitary individuality. There were no Razumovs belonging to him anywhere" (10). One way to map Razumov's movements, as he strays from the correct path searching for a father, is by comparing his two writing acts: one is correct, right, the rule of rectitude, the norm, namely "the prize essay." The other is more in the style of someone Derrida sees wandering outside society; Razumov composes his grieving journal as one who has perverted human decency, one who has sown the "bad seed" that society imagines as poisonous and threatening, but that the narrator recognizes as a "dormant seed" as grief awakens (358). The narrator differentiates the two writing styles: "In this queer pedantism of a man who had read, thought, lived, pen in hand, there is the sincerity of the attempt to grapple by the same means with another profounder knowledge" (357). Indeed, the narrator notes the abrupt shift in Razumov's journal from the author who seeks the "silver medal" to the one who writes incoherently of his grief (357). Anthony Fothergill writes insightfully of the literary prize Razumov seeks: "the silver medal had functioned as a metonym for a successful academic life, so its proleptic loss demands a revised narrative" (41). I would add that the revised text this loss demands is a grieving one. Whether writing for the silver medal, an act of suppression, or writing his journal, an act of expressing grief, Razumov—as fully as Prince K– is defined by his whiskers to Razumov—lives, dies, and is defined by his pen. The father is physical, but the son is literary. The father is a character, the son an author.

When Razumov confronts Natalia, he makes clear that he "had never known a home"; he must choose and create one (299). He explains: "Do you know why I came to you? It is simply because there is no one anywhere in the whole great world I could go to .... No one to go to. Do you conceive of the desolation of the thought—no one—to—go—to?" (354). Much as he once sought the silver medal to secure his father's attention (14), this is perhaps the most striking comment on Razumov's continuing pathetic attempts to please his father. Razumov expresses powerful emotion, but he calls it "thought." The silent dashes, dramatizing his desperation and pain, construct a broken sentence. Conrad thus connects this sentence with the writer of the journal, the one who discovers too late that his name is Victor Haldin. Debra Romanick's etymological research deconstructs this name as it hovers between German and Slavic roots: "Haldin" conveys both heroism and wretchedness. Since Razumov is also described as a "wretch," she concludes: "Haldin's name—literally—reflects not Haldin's moral being, but Razumov's. The name is not an external referent, but an internal mirror" (49). Clearly, this is the reverse of the narcissistic mirror.

In his alternate style of writing, the one that breaks the rules and strays from the right, correct way, Razumov discovers his true identity: "In giving Victor Haldin up, it was myself, after all, whom I have betrayed most basely. You must believe what I say now, you can't refuse to believe this" (361). Derrida would concur with Conrad on this process of mourning; he writes: "The replacement of 'absence' by 'other' here no doubt indicates that the substitutive value is no longer operative in the couple 'absence/presence' but in the couple 'same/other' that introduces the dimension of mourning" (*Mourning* 150). While grieving, one looks into the mirror and sees reflected the image of one's loss. Razumov can only hope that his reader, Natalia, will grieve and understand this new kind of writing. However, she may remain a student of the old English teacher and not recognize that Razumov and her brother are doubles. Though ambiguous, Natalia's act of handing the journal to the narrator implies that she is taking the role of teacher and hoping that the narrator may learn about the translation of feelings. Yet her decision to avoid Razumov as he dies complicates her response.

Razumov and Victor are traumatized by personal and political events. They are initially doubles because they commit brutal acts of violence in response to trauma; they are ultimately doubles because they mourn. Derrida argues that "[m]ourning always follows a trauma" and that "the work of mourning is not one kind of work among others. It is work itself, work in general, the trait by means of which one ought perhaps to reconsider the very concept of production—in what links it to trauma, to mourning" (*Specters* 97). One way to deconstruct Razumov's act of betrayal is to recognize his failure to respond to trauma. He does not mourn his lack of home, family, parents; instead, he turns to his secret father, in the name of his motherland, to stamp out the specter Haldin who seeks his help to escape. What exactly is the work of mourning? Why must we reconsider our concept of production?

In *Under Western Eyes*, the work of mourning is unproductive: It will not produce a medal-winning essay, nor will it advance Razumov's studies or career, or earn him a living. But the novel's tragic force lies in revealing that without the work of mourning, all other work becomes meaningless. Grieving is done within and for oneself, yet viewed from the outside it looks unproductive. Razumov's work of mourning is in his diary. This document underlies the story of the novel—and the mourning work Conrad undertakes in composing it. For, as Carabine shows in *The Life and the Art*, this act involves the author's listening to the ghosts who haunt him.

When Conrad stopped work on *Under Western Eyes* to write "The Secret Sharer," he developed a contrast between the captain and Razumov in terms of productivity. Both the captain and Razumov realize that the murderer they hide in their room threatens their future; but whereas the captain assists the sympathetic killer whose protection and escape are placed in his hands, Razumov betrays his secret sharer to the police. The contrast highlights the captain's sympathy and compassion, thus implying that the work of mourning requires imagination. Despite his crew's sense that he is dangerously unproductive, the captain performs his work within; in contrast, Razumov strives for the outward productivity that yields the praise of the powerful.

Gail Fraser argues that what leads to the captain's fulfillment, as opposed to Razumov's destruction, is the former's emotional engagement. From the start, the captain allows for "the preeminence of feeling over the sober consideration of fact" (117–118). He accepts Leggatt as part of himself, as a shadow he casts, a ghost who haunts him. Able to imagine himself in a comparable plight, the captain marks his command by an imaginative integration of this murderous figure. Razumov, however, refuses identification with Haldin; he describes himself in disturbing terms to the man he has betrayed: "I have no domestic tradition. I have nothing to think against. My tradition is historical" (61). Attempting to blot out Haldin's haunting figure (341), Razumov fails—for though he argues that his tradition is historical, it is in fact domestic: the tradition of a wounded child. Confronted with the revolutionary Haldin and the drunken driver he's sent to find, Razumov thinks these two men are acting like children, and his response is revealing: "It was a sort of terrible childishness. But children had their masters. 'Ah! the stick, the stick, the stern hand,' thought Razumov, longing for power to hurt and destroy" (31). Razumov has just beaten the drunken man with a pitchfork. The master of Razumov's actions is the ghost-child, the autocrat and the revolutionary who tear the adult apart. Until he grieves this haunting child's trauma, he cannot respond to Haldin with sympathy and compassion. Unaware of his own profundity, the narrator states that "all ideas of political plots and conspiracies seem childish, crude inventions for the theatre or a novel" (109).

Conrad stresses in his Author's Note to *Under Western Eyes* his aim to reveal the inextricable bond between self and other; he thus articulates what Derrida has made into the philosophy of deconstruction: "These people are unable to see that all they can effect is merely a change of names. The oppressors and the oppressed are all Russians together" (x). Conrad applies this belief directly to Razumov: "Being nobody's child he feels rather more keenly than another would that he is a Russian—or he is nothing" (ix). Yet, instead of keening for the fact that he is nobody's child, the suppressed Razumov believes that he will reconnect with his father, and be something, and feel keenly, by constructing a bond built on Haldin's destruction. Rather than his usual attribute of the pen, Razumov uses his "penknife" to stab his credo of binary opposites into the wall: "History not Theory. / Patriotism not Internationalism. / Evolution not Revolution. / Direction not destruction. / Unity not disruption" (66). If one erases the "nots," by which Razumov separates self and other and replaces them with "ins," the result is a deconstructive credo whereby binary opposites are destroyed—revealed as simply name changes—opposite sides of the coin—and reconstructed as all Russian or Western together: History in Theory. Patriotism in Internationalism. Evolution in Revolution, and so on. The words would no longer be "foes of reality," to quote the old teacher of languages (3); instead, they would become reality's sharers. Notably, Razumov's "neat minute handwriting" becomes "long scrawly letters" as he returns to an "unsteady, almost childish" self (66). In this act of writing, Conrad reveals the orphan-bastard who haunts and deconstructs the philosophy student's words.

When Razumov confesses to the revolutionaries, a group of men take him outside while the terrorist Nikita hits him to render him deaf. Listen to Conrad's description of Razumov's deafness: "In this unearthly stillness his footsteps fell silent on the pavement, while a dumb wind drove him on and on, like a lost mortal in a phantom world ravaged by a soundless thunderstorm" (369–370). Razumov strives to walk over, crush, and ultimately escape his haunting phantoms. Yet he enters at the novel's end into a phantom world whose silence is deafening. His tragedy is that he learns too late the haunting gravity of secret selves: The suppression of grief makes one as heavy as a stone, striving to hear, although stone deaf. Haunting stories must be told, even with broken sentences. Derrida expresses this concisely: "Ego = ghost. Therefore 'I am' would mean 'I am haunted'" (*Specters* 133). In *Under Western Eyes,* Conrad reveals that the ghost who haunts may well be a hurt and grieving child.

Notes

1. Josiane Paccaud-Huguet foregrounds Conrad's familiarity with *Hamlet* before exploring its role in *Under Western Eyes* from a Lacanian perspective. Likening Conrad's position to those of Claudius and the Russian police, she also reads the novel as an exploration of a failure to perform the rites of mourning — albeit reaching a different conclusion (see esp. 173, 177).

2. Stephen Crane's *The Red Badge of Courage* not only details the living face to face with the dead and turning to stone (46), but it repeatedly depicts the men as children, oftentimes as grieving children (32). This includes the man at the youth's side in mid war in whose "babbling" "there was something soft and tender like the monologue of a babe" (34). Crane was well positioned to understand Conrad's desire to "break stone" with his writing.

16

Beyond Gender: Deconstructions of Masculinity and Femininity from "Karain" to *Under Western Eyes*

CAROLA M. KAPLAN

The time has come to counter the myth of Conrad's misogyny. The chronological and critical distance that has enabled us recently to reassess Conrad's attitudes toward race and colonialism can now help us to reconsider as well the long-held view of Conrad as a "masculine" author who wrote almost exclusively about a male world for a male readership. Toward this end, I will argue that a reexamination of such complex, multifaceted, and nuanced female characters as Winnie Verloc, Natalia Haldin, and Sophia Antonovna encourages us to revise the notion that Conrad knew women little and liked them less.[1] Further, by reviewing several key works by Conrad from the beginning to the middle of his career, I propose to establish that from his earliest fiction, Conrad was centrally concerned with issues of gender and sexuality and that his treatment of these issues grew more unconventional and more iconoclastic over time. Finally, I will argue that Conrad's revisionist thinking on these matters reaches its fullest and most "revolutionary" expression in his 1911 novel *Under Western Eyes*, which paved the way for his later novels centered on and addressed to women. So ahead of its time was Conrad's treatment of gender divisions and female sexuality in this novel that only now, a century later, are we able, I believe, to appreciate its originality.

Perhaps the best way for me to make my case for a position so much at variance with that of many Conrad scholars[2] is to begin at the beginning—that is, at or close to the beginning of Conrad's literary career. As early as 1897, in his short story "Karain," Conrad deals with gender and sexuality in a way that seems to confirm yet in fact diverges from a central paradigm of English fiction by male writers, as charted by Gayle Rubin and Eve Sedgwick, among others. I will note briefly the characteristics of this paradigm, so as to show Conrad's deviation from it. In many works written by Conrad's male literary contemporaries (as well as forebears), a female character serves the function of cementing an intense bond between two men. They unite in and through their hold over a woman, whose life (physical, social, or psychological) they manipulate or control. Their relationship is primary and self-justified; her relationship with them, auxiliary and instrumental to theirs. Such is the role of Adela Quested in *A Passage to India* (connecting the British Fielding and the Indian Aziz), of Gudrun Brangwen in *Women in Love* (uniting upper-class Gerald with middle-class Rupert), of Florence Ashburnham in *The Good Soldier* (joining the introverted John Dowell and the charismatic Edward Ashburnham); and of Molly Bloom in *Ulysses* (tying the common man Leopold to the artist Stephen).

Apparently, this is also the role of principal female characters in Conrad's early fiction: of the Intended who unites Marlow and Kurtz in *Heart of Darkness* (1898); of Jewel in *Lord Jim* (1900), who passes from Jim's care to Marlow's (via Stein); and of Amy Foster in her eponymous story (1901), who serves as pretext for Doctor Kennedy's fixation on Yanko Gooral. Interpreted in this way, all these female characters serve as objects of exchange within a patriarchal kinship system, as Gayle Rubin describes it in "The Traffic in Women." Such a social structure keeps women subordinate by ensuring that the only relationships are between men: They are the givers, women are the gift. As Eve Sedgwick elaborates Rubin's thesis within a literary context in *Between Men*, the triumph over the body of a woman serves to erase differences of class, power, and ideology between male rivals: "The spectacle of the ruin of a woman—apparently almost regardless of what counts as "ruin," or what counts as "woman"—is just the right lubricant for an adjustment of differentials of power between landlord and tenant, master and servant, tradesman and customer, or even king and subject" (76). Thus, victory over a woman is the means of consolidating the homosocial bonds between the principal male figures in many works of fiction. Their relationship is symbolically consummated in and through the body of the woman they subdue.

While many of Conrad's early fictions appear to feature this particular homosocial dynamic, I will argue that, upon closer scrutiny, they largely defy rather than conform to it. And increasingly, a far more complex pattern emerges in the triangular configurations of his later fiction. When the triangle consists of two men and one woman, their friendship or rivalry operates to empower rather than subordinate the female character. When, as often happens, the triangle is formed by two women and one man, the women form an alliance through which they subdue or control the man—an outcome just the reverse of that proposed by Sedgwick. By the time he comes to write *Under Western Eyes*, Conrad creates powerful and independent female characters who help to undermine traditional patriarchal constructions of gender and sexuality by effacing the boundaries between male and female and by blurring the distinctions between homosexual and heterosexual relationships.[3]

Even in his early short story "Karain," Conrad subverts while appearing to reinforce these patriarchal literary conventions. In "Karain," two men, one English, one Malay, engage in an improvised ritual of homosocial bonding. In an effort to exorcize the avenging ghost of the friend Karain betrayed, the

young Englishman Hollis devises an amulet to protect Karain. The amulet enlists, unbeknownst to them, the help of two women—Hollis's beloved and
Queen Victoria. The sacrifice of a love token from Hollis's sweetheart, her
glove, which Hollis cuts up to make a sheath for Karain's amulet, clearly fits the
male-bonding paradigm of a friendship between men secured by subduing or
exploiting a woman that Sedgwick proposes (the sexual imagery of Hollis's act
is too overt to require commentary). But the amulet itself, a Jubilee sixpence,
does not relegate Victoria to the role of sacrificial female. Rather, Victoria is
envisaged as a powerful, protective mother figure, one that corresponds to the
imposing figure of Karain's own mother, the ruler of his tribe (*TU* 13). This
casting of a female figure in the role of presiding genius, agent in securing a
friendship that connects men across racial and colonial divisions, will become
a recurrent motif in Conrad's fictions. In his newly protected position, Karain
is, in effect, situated between two women, one an implicitly submissive, conventional Victorian maiden, the other the ruler of the earth's most powerful
empire: England's queen, whom Karain reverently terms "Great, Invincible,
Pious, and Fortunate" (13). Although the amulet seals a new friendship between men, it also recalls the earlier betrayal of male friendship that constitutes the central event in Karain's life story and thus evokes the fragility of
male bonding and the tenuousness of any homosocial pact.

Similarly, in *Heart of Darkness*, Marlow, who insists that women are "out of
it," discloses, as I have argued elsewhere ("Colonizers" 326–329), that his life is
bordered and its course largely determined by powerful women—his aunt and
the Intended, perhaps even the fateful knitting women (as they continue to
haunt him along his perilous journey). And Kurtz's own life is framed and
partly determined by two women, his Intended, for whose sake he went to
Africa (to obtain sufficient means to marry her), and the African woman whose
position of leadership wins Kurtz entrée to her tribe; she is apparently the
leader of a polyandrous female warrior culture, the "tenebrous and passionate"
soul of the all-powerful female wilderness (Kaplan, "Colonizers" 329).[4]

Even Jim, who never quite overcomes the passive mind set of a man to
whom things happen—"I had jumped .... It seems" (*LJ* 111)—rather than
one who charts his own course, finds himself in his domestic life positioned
between two women, Jewel and her mother, whose ghostly presence and tragic
legacy haunt their relationship. Indeed, Jewel's mother's half-told story of
colonial victimization points up Jim's questionable position as leader of a
Malay tribe and presages his betrayal of the Bugis (and of Jewel). Further, the
novel makes clear that Jewel chooses Jim as her sexual partner (as Jim himself
acknowledges—"she was fond of me, don't you see" [181])—and, contrary to
conventional adventure narrative, rescues Jim rather than vice versa. Not only
does Jewel tell Jim she does not need him to kill Cornelius because if she were
so inclined she could kill him herself, but she acts as Jim's protector and saves
Jim's life when he is ambushed.

Yet, in his depiction of forceful women, Conrad never loses sight of the fact that even courage and determination may be insufficient in the long run to ensure a woman's success or even her independence. For Conrad is aware that the status of a woman within a patriarchal culture generally depends on her connection with a man, usually in the form of marriage, an institution that at best affords women scanty rights and little freedom and at worst exposes them to exploitation and even brutality. Seen in this light, the alliances between women are often compensatory for a lack of legitimate power. In no text does Conrad so clearly depict this awareness as in *The Secret Agent*. In this novel, which exposes the sordid underside of the marriage contract, Conrad demonstrates the need for a revised model for female existence—for an alternative to the role of self-sacrificing helpmate (or sister or daughter, for that matter).

In *The Secret Agent*, the strongest bond is between women; the ostensible protagonist, Verloc, has had the nature and terms of his marriage decided by his wife and his mother-in-law, whose tacit compact is designed, futilely as events prove, to compensate for their previous victimization and current powerlessness in a patriarchal society. Above all, they wish to protect Stevie, the brother and son who cannot protect himself and whom they cannot protect without male help. Nowhere else in Conrad's fiction is his condemnation of male impercipience and cruelty so scathing nor his sympathy for the vulnerability of women so clear. While this is Conrad's most satirical novel, he reserves his satire for its male figures, most particularly singling out Verloc, the husband of the unfortunate Winnie: "Mr. Verloc loved his wife as a wife should be loved—that is, maritally, with the regard one has for one's chief possession" (179); "He had grown older, fatter, heavier in the belief that he lacked no fascination for being loved for his own sake" (190). Winnie's sexual subservience to him which—despite the repugnance she feels for him—she considers part of her marriage "transaction"(252), indicts marriage within patriarchal culture as a form of sexual slavery.[5] As Winnie laments: "Seven years—seven years a good wife to him .... And he loved me. Oh yes. He loved me till I sometimes wished myself—Seven years—seven years a wife to him" (276).

Unlike the men, whom Conrad exposes as parasitic and predatory in their dealings with women, the female characters, in particular Winnie and her mother, evoke Conrad's admiration for their sacrifice and courage. Of the "existence created by Mrs. Verloc's genius," the narrator observes, although it is "an existence foreign to all grace and charm, without beauty and almost without decency," it is "admirable in the continuity of feeling and tenacity of purpose" (244). As he expatiates: "It was a life of single purpose and of a noble unity of inspiration, like those rare lives that have left their mark on the thoughts and feelings of mankind" (241–242). When he goes on to qualify his praise of her with the observation, "But the visions of Mrs. Verloc lacked nobility and magnificence" (242), this addendum points up the wasted life of a valiant spirit—and points to the myriad lives of other brave, obscure women that are similarly forfeited.[6]

But it is Conrad's account of the abuse inflicted by their father upon Winnie and Stevie as children that lends an almost unbearable poignancy to Winnie's story, as well as makes comprehensible her sacrifice in adulthood. Even as a child, Winnie was Stevie's protector:

> She remembered ... the consolations administered to a small and badly scared creature by another creature nearly as small but not quite so badly scared; she had the vision of the blows intercepted (often with her own head), of a door held desperately shut against a man's rage (not for very long); of a poker flung once (not very far), which stilled that particular storm into the dumb and awful silence which follows a thunder-clap. (242)

As a woman, Winnie continues in this role. But she is faced with the impossible task of protecting the weak in the face of the world's indifference or cruelty, even violence. As Conrad maintains in his "Author's Note," *The Secret Agent* is "Winnie Verloc's story" (xv), a tale of "maternal passion"(xii), played out against the background of a "monstrous town," "a cruel devourer of the world's light," with "darkness enough to bury five millions of lives" (xii).

Similarly, Winnie's mother's sacrifice of the remainder of her life in a futile effort to ensure Stevie's security is one of the most painful portions of the novel. Conrad refers to her arduous and complex efforts to obtain lodging in a home for destitute widows as "heroic proceedings" (*SA* 144). And, in a letter to Edward Garnett, Conrad reiterates this point: " I am no end proud that you've spotted my old woman. You've got a fiendishly penetrating eye for one's own most secret intentions. She *is* the heroine" (*Letters* 3: 487).

All these stratagems by both mother and daughter to achieve security fail because, as the novel demonstrates, there is no safety for women and children in a world dominated by men (Kaplan, "No Refuge" 139). At the end of the novel, Winnie is ostensibly a "free woman" but "she did not exactly know what use to make of her freedom .... *The street, silent and deserted from end to end, repelled her by taking sides with that man who was so certain of his impunity.* She was afraid to shout lest no one should come. *Obviously no one would come*" (254, italics mine). The ordinarily silent and unreflective Winnie articulates her new awareness to Ossipon: "The police were on that man's side" (279). Through Winnie's words and experiences, the novel exposes as a lie the protection of women and children that is the common justification for male ascendancy.

Having gone as far as he could go in his indictment of marriage as female imprisonment, Conrad in *Under Western Eyes* takes pains to present alternative possibilities for the course of women's lives. The novel signals this shift of direction by getting off to a false start that promises, only to reject, a conventional marriage plot proceeding from a homosocial compact. *Under Western Eyes* begins with an offer from one man to another that appears to fit the "traffic in women" paradigm proposed by Rubin and elaborated by Sedgwick. A young man, Victor Haldin, implicitly proffers his sister in marriage to a man he greatly admires, Kirylo Sidorovitch Razumov, whose friendship he seeks to secure. That his overtures of friendship contain sexual undertones is suggested by his intense idealization of Razumov, his precipitous attachment to him, and his premature trust in him. This motivation helps to explain his repeated assertion, "Men like me leave no posterity" (22). On the surface, this statement merely indicates that revolutionaries generally get themselves killed before they can produce offspring. But the statement, if only in its repetition, suggests another meaning as well. Haldin's declaration hints that he belongs to another community of men, in addition to the cadre of his revolutionary comrades—a society of men who will have no progeny because they love other men. On the basis of his feelings for Razumov, Haldin proposes that Razumov help and protect him, then transfer this commitment to his sister and so ensure vicariously Haldin's posterity. He tells Razumov, "She will marry well, I hope. She may have children—sons, perhaps" (22). Haldin's vision of Razumov's future assumes both reciprocity and continuity in love, as well as flexibility in love objects. And, as the narrative proceeds, the figure of Victor merges into the figure of Natalia, who greatly resembles her brother in appearance and ideas. Indeed, the novel confirms the necessity for the human connection that Victor demands, without regard for the gender of the principals.

But the narrative also unfolds to defeat the proposed homosocial pact, sealed by the exchange of a woman, that Haldin initially proposed. On the level of plot, Razumov breaks the contract by betraying Haldin and thereby forfeiting his claim to Natalia. More importantly, on the level of character, Natalia defies the narrow role of woman as gift. Further, she confounds conventional gender prescriptions by exhibiting traits and engaging in actions traditionally coded as male. That Natalia as sexual object is interchangeable with Victor is emphasized by her "masculine" qualities: her "deep" voice (102), her "strong vitality" (102), her "glance as direct and trustful as that of a young man" (102), "the firmness of her muscles" (111), and the "exquisite virility" (118) of her handshake. From his first meeting with her, Natalia supplants Victor as the object of Razumov's obsession: "It was she who had been haunting him now .... ever since she had suddenly appeared before him in the garden of the Villa Borel with an extended hand and the name of her brother on her lips ..." (342).

In her allure, Natalia is indistinguishable from the male protagonists of heroic fiction. She is strong, determined, and courageous. Like the brave, decisive revolutionary leader Sophia Antonovna, she refuses marriage, chooses a career, forges her own destiny. An autonomous figure who, unlike her brother, needs no one to save her, she succumbs neither to Peter Ivanovitch's injunction to enter the public arena nor to her brother's determination to ensure his posterity through her. By contrast, her admirers, the language professor and Razumov, are passive and indecisive. Similarly, Sophia's lover, her revolutionary cohort, is weak and ineffectual.

Through these female characters who choose their lives rather than allow some man, lover or brother, to choose for them, the novel demonstrates that gender is "performative," in Judith Butler's sense of the term (24–25, 134–141); that is to say, fluid, unstable, and contextual. What constitutes male or female emerges in action. Each action is discrete, particular to the subject, yet the subject too is not fixed. Thus gender emerges through repetition but can never be permanently established. Nor are the designations male and female mutually exclusive categories.[7] As gender is performative, so too is sexuality. Neither heterosexuality nor homosexuality is stable or self-contained. Each exists only in terms of the other; and each can establish itself only through a process of repetition that demonstrates the instability of the very category it inhabits. Nor, despite cultural myth, is heterosexuality originary. As Jonathan Dollimore has pointed out, civilization depends upon that which is anterior to it and is deemed incompatible with it, particularly homosexuality (9–10). As if to demonstrate that heterosexuality does not have priority, the novel begins with the homosocial relationship between Razumov and Haldin that makes possible the heterosexual relationship between Razumov and Natalia.

In short, in *Under Western Eyes*, Conrad eschews the conventional patriarchal narrative that contains women within a homosocial economy and that limits the play of desire to heterosexual performance. Through the androgynous characters Natalia and Sophia, the novel effaces the boundaries between male and female, reveals the constructedness of gender, and helps to demonstrate the polyvalence of desire and the polymorphism of sexual expression.

The question arises, to what purpose does *Under Western Eyes* focus on these issues of gender and sexuality? I propose that it does so to critique, enlarge, and to some extent counter the conventions of male-centered narrative. The beginning of *Under Western Eyes* promises a traditional *Bildungsroman*, focusing on the career of a talented young man, but Razumov's possibilities are foreclosed by the end of Part First. To the consternation of many critics, the protagonist drops out of the novel one fourth of the way through, reappears later only in an attenuated form, and never again occupies the narrative center. But what Razumov's story loses in momentum and definition, it gains in fullness and complexity. For, as Razumov's worldly ambitions are thwarted, his sentimental education begins. His progress, not onward but inward, proceeds through his acquaintance with four strong women who disrupt and enlarge his previously all-male existence and masculinist outlook. These women present a counter-narrative to the tale of male heroism, ambition, compact, and betrayal that open the novel.

More a series of ordeals than a set of experiences he seeks, his sentimental education provides Razumov (and the reader) with several key insights. Among these are a recognition of the artificiality of gender boundaries and an awareness of maleness and femaleness as an overlapping continuum. As a student in Russia, Razumov had lived in an entirely male world and so, when he declared his kinship with other Russians, he thought only of other men: "Have I not got forty million brothers?" (*UWE 35*). When he arrives in Geneva, he knows nothing of women and therefore has everything to learn about them. This point is made explicitly in a passage Conrad later deleted from the text: "The fact that these were women he was going to meet did not trouble him especially. As a matter of fact, he did not recognize women as women. There had been literally no feminine influence in his life.... It may be said that, in a manner, he had never seen a woman." (Kirschner 292).

Much the same can be said about many of the other young male protagonists of novels from the same period as *Under Western Eyes*—George Pontifex, Philip Carey, Paul Morel, Stephen Dedalus, Rickie Elliott, to name a few: However frequently they encounter women, they do not see them; or, rather, they regard women only as accessories to men's lives. Following the prevailing masculinist assumptions of their time, Razumov, Haldin, and the language teacher would like to confine women to the domestic sphere in which their sexual expression would be limited to heterosexual monogamy within marriage; their principal task, to provide progeny, so as to ensure patriarchal lineage. Indeed, Conrad initially considered but rejected a plan for the novel that would have fitted Natalia into the traditional roles of wife and mother. Conrad's original plot had Razumov marry Natalia and, after a while, confess to her "the part he played in the arrest and death of her brother" (*Letters* 4: 9). In this original version, it was Razumov who had all the agency in his relationship with Natalia. But this construction of events denies the power, autonomy, and clear-sightedness that characterize Natalia. Indeed, it is her moral authority, along with that of her mother, Sophia, and Tekla, that undermines Razumov's plan to deceive and betray her. By her independent actions and moral choices, she refutes the language teacher's masculinist view that Victor Haldin's death severed Natalia's only "link with the wider world" and that "the very groundwork of active existence for Nathalie Haldin is gone with him" (135).[8]

The view that women cannot act without men is refuted not only by Natalia's choices but by Sophia's and Tekla's as well. As becomes clear, these women hold revolutionary ideas not only about politics but also about sexuality. Each reserves to herself the right to make her own sexual choices, without regard for social convention. Accordingly, Sophia lives with but does not marry a fellow revolutionary, and channels her maternal impulses into her protection of (and flirtation with) younger men, including Razumov. Tekla acts as both mother and lover to the male victims she adopts. Julius Laspara's daughter leaves home and, without explanation, returns with a child.

Thus, the book reveals that the traditional patriarchal prescription for women of heterosexuality within marriage fails to reckon with the breadth of female sexuality. Through the sexually emancipated Sophia Antonovna, the book makes clear the connection between political and sexual passion. Sophia points out that women's social activism is fueled by desire. As she tells Razumov:

You men can love here and hate there and desire something or other—and you make a great to-do about it, and you call it passion! Yes! While it lasts. But we women are in love with love, and with hate, with these very things, I tell you, and with desire itself. That's why we can't be bribed off so easily as you men. In life, you see, there is not much choice. You have either to rot or to burn. And there is not one of us, painted or unpainted, that would not rather burn than rot. (177)

Thus Sophia proclaims the existence of a natural alliance between women, not in the form of a pact or explicit contract (which men often undertake only to violate) but in the form of a community of outlook and purpose.

In contradistinction to her praise for women's passion, Sophia deplores the faintheartedness of men. She upbraids Razumov—and, through him, all men—for prudery with regard to women's sexual behavior:

Oh, you squeamish, masculine creature …. There's no looking into the secrets of the heart …. It is not for us to judge an inspired person. That's where you men have an advantage … when you *are* inspired, when you manage to throw off your masculine cowardice and prudishness you are not to be equalled by us. Only, how seldom ….Whereas the silliest woman can always be made of use. And why? Because we have passion, unappeasable passion. (249)

In refusing and exceeding the stereotypic sexual roles that men would assign them, the women in the novel point out the connections between the public and private spheres that are often eclipsed in male heroic narratives. From a negative perspective, the novel, in Susan Jones's words, "exposes the vulnerability of the domestic sphere" (*Women* 65). In this respect, it is reminiscent of *The Secret Agent*. Mrs. Haldin, in particular, manifests the toll on human lives exacted of its subjects by an autocratic state and also registers the suffering inflicted upon their families by idealistic, impractical—and egotistical—revolutionaries.

On the positive side, the novel points out that women are able to integrate thought and feeling and so are more capable than men of understanding other human beings and of making accurate judgments about them. As Mrs. Haldin, Natalia, Tekla, and Sophia demonstrate, women connect what men compartmentalize. In becoming activists, women do not leave their feelings behind. In fact, the book makes clear that women's activism is initially impelled by pity and compassion for injustices they have witnessed. Unlike Victor Haldin, who acts only upon emotion, or Razumov who, as a student, attempted to act only through reason, women synthesize and act upon both what they think and what they feel.

At the beginning of the novel, after his first encounter with Victor, Razumov desires so overwhelmingly to be understood that he by turns considers confessing to Haldin, Mikulin, and General T. But it is only at the end of his story that he acts upon this impulse because he has found a worthy confidante in Natalia, whose character, as Michael Andrew Roberts points out, "prompts disclosure" (146). Although in Conrad's earlier fictions the general pattern is for knowledge to be shared by men but withheld from women, in *Under Western Eyes*, as Roberts notes, "what is exchanged between men ... is less knowledge ... than ignorance and misunderstanding" (147). On the other hand, it is the women Razumov encounters who show independence of mind, keen intelligence, and compassion for the downtrodden. Sophia Antonovna, ostensibly Razumov's greatest adversary, comes very near to understanding him in his resentful and self-revealing outbursts. He himself acknowledges to her, "You seem to understand one's feelings" (184).

So too, despite Razumov's attempt to deceive her, Mrs. Haldin appears to discern his darker side, as none of his fellow students had been able to do, including her son. Razumov does not inspire confidence in Mrs. Haldin, as he does in other men: "The man, trusted impulsively by the ill-fated Victor Haldin, had failed to gain the confidence of Victor Haldin's mother .... She had not believed him" (261).

Conversely and paradoxically, from his relationships with women Razumov also learns about the one aspect of human life that exceeds judgment, that is, about love—romantic, maternal, familial, communal. So, too, he learns from them how to love himself, not in the way of the narcissism he exhibited in his isolated student days but in the form of the recognition of his essential humanity. As he affirms to Natalia: "In giving Victor Haldin up, it was myself, after all, whom I have betrayed most basely .... It is through you that I came to feel this so deeply" (253–254). Finally, he confides to her that he has concluded his emotional journey:

> You were appointed to undo the evil by making me betray myself back into truth and peace. You! And you have done it in the same way, too, in which he [Victor] ruined me: by forcing upon me your confidence. Only what I detested him for, in you ended by appearing noble and exalted .... You ... have freed me from the blindness of anger and hate—the truth shining in you drew the truth out of me. (252–253)

Thus, his contact with women, particularly with Natalia, has humanized him, and his sentimental education is complete.

What, we may ask, has Razumov learned in his education by women? What is the nature of the truth he claims to have found? And what greater overall significance does the novel assign to Razumov's enlarged understanding? I will suggest that Razumov's learning has consisted of a vast unlearning. For Razumov, all previously established categories, all the divisions he had insisted upon, have broken down, however desperately he tried to preserve them—in his words, "History not Theory," "Patriotism not Internationalism," "Evolution not Revolution," "Direction not Destruction," "Unity not Disruption." As the novel unfolds, these distinctions collapse: Russia's history has been infiltrated and will necessarily be shaped by the theory of revolutionaries (such as Haldin, Natalia, and Sophia); revolutionary activity has become an intrinsic part of Russia's evolution; its direction has been largely determined by destruction, as exemplified by the assassination of M. de P——, the execution of Haldin, the maiming of Razumov; the disunity that separated Razumov from Haldin characterizes as well the relationships among Russians in general, as shown in the schisms among the revolutionaries; and Razumov is forced to express his "patriotism" internationally in his role of spy.

Resonant with Razumov's expanded awareness of multiplicity, ambiguity, and contradiction, the larger text refuses clear divisions and fixed categories. The novel's events demonstrate, for example, that there is no distinction between public and private life, no separation between the political and the personal. As Razumov's involvement with the Haldin family discloses to him, public acts have private consequences. Further, political action stems from personal motives, from "unappeasable passion," and indignation at "the great social iniquity of the system resting on unrequited toil and unpitied sufferings" (186). Nor is this indignation based on abstractions: rather it stems from hardships endured in one's personal life, from childhood on, as Sophia's and Tekla's stories make clear. And political action consists less in heroic acts (which, even when possible, often prove destructive) than in prosaic daily tasks. As Sophia declares: "You men are so impressionable and self-conscious. One day is like another, hard, hard and there's an end of it, till the great day comes" (170). Again:

> You men are ridiculously pitiful in your aptitude to cherish childish illusions down to the very grave. There are a lot of us who have been at work for fifteen years—I mean constantly—trying one way after another, underground and above ground, looking neither to the right nor to the left! I can talk about it. I have been one of those that never rested. (174–175)

Finally—and most importantly for my argument—the lives and words of the novel's female characters demonstrate that in no aspect of life is the blurring of boundaries more pronounced than in the sphere of gender. Throughout, the novel suggests that there are no clear gender divisions. Rather, what the language of the narrative creates, through the androgynous description of its characters, is a kind of gender blending. The novel's admirable female characters have attributes generally ascribed to males: courage, conviction, honesty, independence, even "virility." And its male figures, Razumov in particular, are encouraged to assume or explore in themselves characteristics usually associated with women. This is in part the meaning of Sophia Antonovna's reproach to Razumov: "Remember, Razumov, that women, children, and revolutionists hate irony, which is the negation of all saving instincts, of all faith, of all devotion, of all action" (197). In this criticism, Sophia is urging Razumov to adopt the commitment, faith, and earnestness that characterize the lives of women. She also implies that revolutionaries, like children, have no divisions along preordained gender lines.

This composite identity for men and women has been made possible, the novel suggests, by their movement from the entirely masculine world of Russia, composed exclusively of men who cannot understand or trust each other, to the new terrain of Geneva, where men turn to women not only for comfort and understanding, but also for leadership. This movement from Russia to Geneva proceeds in part from Conrad's general rejection of the world of Tolstoy and Dostoevsky, which I have discussed elsewhere ("Narrative Occupation" 97–105)—and in part from his specific rejection of the limited roles women play in their fiction. Never autonomous, female characters in Russian fiction are either auxiliary or dependent on men. In this regard, women in Russian fiction differ markedly from women in Polish romantic fiction, which features many heroic and independent female characters, as Susan Jones has pointed out in her groundbreaking *Conrad and Women*.[9] And it was Polish romantic literature, as Jones has convincingly argued, that largely shaped Conrad's work—and in particular his treatment of women.

Within the discrete self-contained island called "Little Russia," cut off from the larger conservative nominally democratic Western world of Geneva, Conrad creates a distinct space or, rather, a nonspace for the consideration of revolutionary ideas, which he purports not to endorse but which the reader must at least consider. These ideas include a radical revision of gender definitions which, if unacceptable to his readers, can be attributed, after all, to misguided if individually sympathetic revolutionaries.

In this way, the novel admits into its proceedings the voice or voices of the Other—of women in particular—and forces the reader, like Razumov, to consider what women have to teach. Often the views his female characters express do not accord with Conrad's. Frequently they seem to get out of hand, exceeding the confines of the text (Kaplan, "Narrative Occupation" 108–112). More often than not, these female characters disagree. For, what women share, as Sophia Antonovna puts it, is "passion," not a program. Some, like Natalia and Sophia have clear, if divergent, political agendas. Others, like Tekla, do not. While women often express sympathy for each other, as Natalia does for Tekla, they do not generally enter into formal compacts, as do men. Accordingly, they are less prone to betray each other.

Contrasting with the novel's attention to the individuality of its female characters is Peter Ivanovitch's programmatic, reductive, and self-serving "feminism." His role as roguish buffoon points not to Conrad's lack of support for women but rather to his opposition to fixed political positions of all kinds, for they lead, like Peter Ivanovitch's, to blindness and despotism, as in his mistreatment of Tekla. (Peter Ivanovitch's dogmatism is echoed, albeit less dismissively, in Sophia Antonovna's sweeping criticisms of men and in Victor Haldin's obliviousness to the innocent victims of his fanaticism.) Arguably, as well, Peter Ivanovitch's unreliability constitutes a kind of containment of Conrad's anxieties about the power of women and its potential long-term effects.[10]

In contrast to fixed positions of all kinds, the novel argues for openness and indeterminacy. Indeed, *Under Western Eyes* is exploratory and nonprescriptive in its treatment of masculinity and femininity. Just as its structure is open-ended, so too is its treatment of masculinity and femininity fluid and overlapping. In fact, in its approach to gender, Conrad creates in this small pocket of Geneva a kind of utopian space, a space in which men and women share attributes and aspirations, in which women speak and men listen, in which men can be dependent and women autonomous. By creating a fictional terrain in which to present a variety of relationships between men and women, all of them alternative to although not necessarily superior to marriage, Conrad acknowledges that the future of relations between men and women, like the land of Russia, is as yet a "blank page awaiting the record of an inconceivable history" (25). All that Conrad can do—and what he has done in this novel—is to prepare some notes for a future that is yet to be written.

Notes

1. I could cite, among Conrad's characters, many other complex and powerful women, including Emilia Gould in *Nostromo*, Lena in *Victory*, and Flora de Barral in *Chance.*

2. For critics who consider Conrad a misogynist, see among others: Straus; Hyland; Mongia, "Ghosts"; Johanna M. Smith; Erdinast-Vulcan, *The Strange Short Fiction* (153–184).

3. For considerations of homosociality, homoeroticism, and homosexuality in Conrad, see Casarino; Ruppel; Lane; Kaplan "Women's Caring."

4. This wilderness—and by implication his African lover—by embracing Kurtz, undoes him: "The wilderness had patted him on the head, and, behold, it was like a ball—an ivory ball; it had caressed him, and—lo!—he had withered; it had taken him, loved him, embraced him, got into his veins, consumed his flesh, and sealed his soul to its own by the inconceivable ceremonies of some devilish initiation. He was its spoiled and pampered favourite" (64).

5. This theme emerges in some of Conrad's other fictions, including the short stories "The Return" and "The Idiots."

6. Tellingly, after she has killed her husband, Winnie feels her kinship with Mrs. Neale, the washerwoman, whose downtrodden existence embodies the extremity of female abjection.

7. As Judith Butler points out: "The bisexuality that is said to be 'outside' the Symbolic and that serves as the locus of subversion is, in fact, a construction within the terms of that constitutive discourse, the construction of an 'outside' that is nevertheless fully 'inside,' not a possibility beyond culture" (77).

8. As Keith Carabine acutely demonstrates, Conrad carefully pared down his depiction of Natalia for fear she would run away with his story (see "From *Razumov*") Yet I propose that Conrad did not entirely succeed in containing Natalia: while he did streamline his depiction of her, he did not significantly diminish her agency or her moral stature.

9. From childhood, as Jones discloses, Conrad was intimately familiar with Polish romantic literature "that often ironises as well as idealises the notion of self-sacrifice in women" (55). Further, she notes that "while the presentation of female self-sacrifice may often be ambivalent, the mother figures of Polish romanticism usually represent integrity, and are rarely tainted by a sceptical treatment" (58). In addition, Jones points out "analogies between the presentation of the mother-figure of the Polish tradition and Conrad's personal tribute to his mother's memory in his fiction" (59).

10. As Marianne DeKoven avers, male modernist writers reacted with ambivalence to the "empowered maternal," as evidenced in the rise of the New Woman and the Women's Suffrage movement. While Conrad personally supported female suffrage, he presents a much more complex response in his fiction to the prospect of a politically empowered female populace (85–138, 139–178).

5
Traveling with Conrad

17
An Interview with Edward Said

The following is an abridged version of a three-hour interview conducted between Edward W. Said and Peter Mallios on Friday, February 28, 2003, at Columbia University. It is, to our knowledge, the last formal interview Said gave.

PM: You write in your 2002 collection *Reflections on Exile*: "Over the years I have found myself writing about Conrad like a *cantus firmus*, a steady ground bass to much that I have experienced." This is a provocative testament to an author who has clearly captured your imagination from your first book, *Joseph Conrad and the Fiction of Autobiography*, through crucial chapters in *Beginnings* and *The World, the Text, and the Critic*, up through *Culture and Imperialism* and your most contemporary writings. How did you originally become interested in Conrad, and what would you say the key terms of your interest in him have been over the years?

ES: I think the first time I was ever aware of Conrad was when I read "Youth" as a schoolboy. And it made absolutely no impression on me. I remember exactly where I read it. I was about 14 in Victoria College, and it was the same year that we read in that class, as part of the set curriculum for the Oxford and Cambridge school system, other books like C.S. Forester's *The Commodore*. There seemed to be a nautical theme running through the course, and we read a couple of other texts in that vein, and the Shakespeare play that we did was *Twelfth Night*, which I've never really liked. "Youth" made no impression on me because the context was completely missing: I had no idea who this person was, though the story seemed peculiar. The master who taught us the text didn't have much to say about it either—except that it was an adventure story, rather in the same league as C.S. Forester. But then, to jump ahead three years later to when I was a freshman at Princeton, we read there for a course on Victorian literature *Heart of Darkness*. It was then I began to see connections between *Heart of Darkness* and "Youth," which I still remembered. And I was completely wiped out. I mean, I remember staying up nights trying to figure out what it all meant. What of course got me, at least initially, was the atmosphere of mystery and even solemnity, and the whole jungle episode, with the mysterious evocations of a primitive time, of ivory trade, of scenes frankly that reminded me of something that captivated my youth, which is the Tarzan movies—it was very much like that but much more vast and pensive. And at that stage I still didn't know who Conrad was.

The professor who gave the big lecture course was a man named Dudley Johnson—quite a famous figure who wrote a book called *The Alien Vision of Victorian Poetry*: one of the first books to deal with Tennyson and Hopkins and Browning as not just simple celebrants of British life but as tortured, anguished souls—straight out of Auden. But he was a mesmerizing lecturer. So we read *Heart of Darkness* and *A Passage to India* and *Mrs. Dalloway* and Carlyle and Ruskin. At Princeton the lectures were like the French style. There were very formal lectures in a big theater; they met twice a week; and then you had what was called a precept, a preceptorial, of five or six people. The preceptor, who was usually a younger member of the faculty, was in this case a man I have never heard of since called Jesse Reese, who was I think a medievalist at Princeton, and he was astonishing. He had this extraordinary style of picking on the most enigmatic and difficult passages in the book, and really not saying anything about them. He would just read and raise his eyebrows like this, getting us all .... And he did this perfectly with Conrad! So with sonorous, eloquent lectures with dramatic pauses and such by Dudley Johnson, who had quite a theatrical flair about him, followed by the preceptorial, I literally could not sleep. I was so entranced, so captivated, by this world.

PM: This "world" that you speak of: Was this the world of Princeton, of a certain style of education and culture that Conrad was facilitating, or was your relationship to Conrad more individual, even a kind of resistance?

ES: Totally individual. Princeton was a pretty alienating place for me. There were no black students, no women; they were all basically upper-middle-class, white, Northeastern and Southern types who populated the place. It was very anti-intellectual, although the education itself was quite rigorous. I think it was one of the best things that happened to me; I had a fantastic education. I remember—thinking of Conrad—that I always wished to have heard Blackmur lecture on Conrad, but he never did. I used to go to his lectures, and I know he read my dissertation, which was on Gide and Graham Greene—God only knows why I put those two together—but of course Greene was very influenced by Conrad, and I caught echoes of Conrad; and then I began to read more Conrad on my own. But my captivation was entirely individual, and I still knew very little about Conrad's life. Don't forget: At the time, there was only Jean-Aubry,[1] a two-volume work that an undergraduate is unlikely to read. Then I recall when Jocelyn Baines's book came out I found out more about him; and then I read Morf[2]—and by that point

I was simply hooked. When I went on to graduate school—there still weren't many books written on Conrad at this time—I read Guerard and Moser, [3] both of whom I found myself informed by but also resisting. Guerard had written about Gide and Hardy and Conrad at the last—but Moser's book was written about the decline of Conrad, a hypothesis I didn't agree with—because I thought *Victory* was a splendid book. *Victory*, by the way, was another text we read in a novel course I took with Lawrance Thompson in my junior year. I still think it is a splendid book. Do you like it?

PM: I just edited it.

ES: Really! So you don't think it's a decline?

PM: I think it's the beginning of a poetics of democracy in Conrad's work. But what do you find so compelling about *Victory*—and perhaps Conrad's other late work as well?

ES: I treat *Victory* in a book I'm doing on late style—*Spätstil*: it's a German term, one of Adorno's—and late work generally. Adorno bases his distinction about late style on the third period of Beethoven, where his style is very difficult, and it's as if Beethoven is writing for himself; that he's lost his audience as he's lost his hearing. Adorno argues that the style of the late work—the *Hammerklavier* sonata, the last sonata, the bagatelles, the *Missa Solemnis*, etc.—introduces a shift in interest from the revolutionary work of the middle period—like the Eroica Symphony and *Fidelio*: works that really address an audience, try to stir people up, are full of development—into this later, more difficult, meta-poetic work, work that turns on questions of the medium itself. In this work, there are striking juxtapositions of banality and extreme difficulty, because in this late phase, Beethoven starts writing these incredibly complicated fugues à la Bach, which nevertheless combine unison, songful passages of extreme simplicity. And there's no transition between them; the style is very episodic. Given this late style, I draw the distinction between late works that are about reconciliation, about the final work, what Wilson Knight called "the crown of life,"[4] where the artist has this vision of wholeness, of putting everything together, of reconciling conflict—you know, the reconciliation of Prospero with all the young people at the end of *The Tempest*—versus another late style, which is the one I'm interested in, which is the opposite, where everything gets torn apart and instead of reconciliation there's a kind of nihilism and a kind of tension that is quite unique. I think *Victory* is very much of that style—I've alluded to it in some passage, I don't quite remember where.

PM: What, to use one of your terms, would the "worldly" stakes of this late-style argument be? In your first Conrad book, you are one of the very first to make a serious case for the importance of Conrad's "late" fiction. There you do so with reference to questions of international tension and new world order unfolding after World War I, questions that strike a haunting chord with the world conditions of today.

ES: When I wrote that book, I felt that, on the one hand, much of what I'd read about Conrad was very much part of the New Criticism. For critics like Guerard, Conrad was a kind of high modernist, and he was about the aesthetics—or rather, the aestheticization—of experience in a way that interested me also. But on the other hand, everything about Conrad that you found was full of the most untidy sentiments about the world he lived in, about his family, about his own self. And I realized how much he was connected to the world in which he lived— I mean the essential world. I felt one should be able to connect this worldly untidiness—the strange, even ultra-strange, circumstances of his life as a sailor, as a Pole, as an exile, as a sort of unhoused and extraterritorial being wandering all over the place—with the fiction. And I still feel that's what the process is about. I'm sorry—did I answer your question properly?

PM: Yes, indeed. But one of the undercurrents of my question would be: How would one teach *Victory* today, given the similar circumstances of the post-Great War world and today, and working through in this respect the kind of project of late style that you see? Is *Victory* predicated on turning Beethoven's deaf ear to the world? A critique of this? How might it be useful to think through the novel's late style now?

ES: Well, I think *Victory*'s manifest story, on the level of what happens, is typical of the late style: it is, indeed, about withdrawal—from the world, and also the failure of that whole project. I think Conrad in this way is very much like, and even influenced by, Flaubert. I once gave a seminar on Flaubert in which I compared *Victory* with *Bouvard et Pécuchet*—which is also about withdrawal from the world into an aesthetic project as, you know, these two scribes plunge themselves into learning to produce in the end only nonsense, which Flaubert pursues in a very comic and sardonic way. Conrad doesn't have that side, but he does have an additional element: a constant sense of being invaded by outside forces. A second element—and this is also very typical of the late style—is that *Victory* is a novel full of reminiscences. In other words, it's full of self-quotation. The island, for instance, is obviously a re-creation of "Lord" Jim on Patusan or one of the Malay islands of the early books, and all the sea going details are clearly a re-articulation of the earlier Conrad as well. But it's all become much more essentialized now; it's become—I wouldn't say a parody of itself—but rather quite clearly *recollection*. There's a third element too. When you think of Conrad in his late phase—you know, as an older man, who's gone through a lot, and was slightly more famous and successful than he was, say, when he wrote *Lord Jim* or even *Nostromo*—there's still this haunting sense that he's somehow not pulling it off; it comes out to be just as dark as his other work. Now, however, it is full of a new kind of mannerism which is also an aspect of the late style. In the late Beethoven, for example, there are a lot of trills that have no particular structural function; and in *Victory*, to draw a parallel, the whole business about Schomberg, who has this jarring music buzzing about his place, is puzzlingly gratuitous as well. It's not clear what he's doing there, why so much attention is lavished upon him—except as a backdrop to Lena and the all-girl band, which is extremely parodic in an unsettling way, which seems to get back to what Schomberg is all about.

Now you say: Why read *Victory* today? Well, I think that just as today's world is extremely unsettled, so too is Conrad's, as symbolized by the apparition of the novel's infernal trio, coming to the island, bringing with them the vestiges, in the case of Mr. Jones, of a kind of European underground, almost Wildean in its misogyny, strange kicks, gambling, fear of women, and the like. There's also Ricardo, the kind of figure you see explored further in works like *The Secret Agent*: you know, *that* world, the lower-middle-class and working-class world of the prisoner. And finally there's Pedro—a reversion to *Heart of Darkness*, the world of savage ferocity and so on. So in that respect *Victory* presents a very interesting re-invasion of his past by Conrad, whom one would have thought, by that time, had settled himself, as it were. It's one of the most unsettling and disturbing novels I've ever read. I read it recently, about a year or two ago, and I found it very disturbing for that reason. I couldn't understand what it was about the novel that Tom Moser didn't like—except that, well, Conrad was never good at describing intimacy and passionate intensity between men and women. But where does that ever happen?

PM: Well, in the Conrad book I think you make a good case for "The Return" depicting domestic intensity with excruciating clarity; but let's change the subject to the novella you just brought up, *Heart of Darkness*. This text seems to be of special importance to you, for you discuss it not only throughout your literary criticism but also repeatedly in your more immediately political writings as well. I suppose the first question I would ask you is this: In assembling this volume, we, the co-editors, were very surprised to discover that *Heart of Darkness*, despite what might seem its over-saturation by critical discussion over the years, is still, if submissions to this volume are any indicator, the single Conrad text that commands by far the most plentiful, the most varied, and the most urgent interest among contemporary readers. I wonder whether that surprises you too...

ES: No. It's obviously a great work.

PM: ... and why you think it is that *Heart of Darkness* is of such vital interest *now*, in the present moment—and from so many different points of view?

ES: Yes, from so many different points of view. First, I think *Heart of Darkness* is the most uncompromised, unafraid confrontation with the irrational and the unknown—in every sense of the world: political, psychological, geographical, cultural—that has ever been done. I think it is so radical from that point of view; it is really a voyage into the unknown. Second, and at the same time, it registers more subtly, and with the most carefully rendered inflections, all the states of consciousness that are possible on such a voyage, on all kinds of levels. There's the political—we know now, for instance, how perceptive Conrad was to the Congo that one finds described in books written by Adam Hochschild[5] and others nearly a hundred years after Conrad's. But Conrad saw it all, understood it, impressionistically but in a sense more profoundly, as part of some conjunction between nature, the human mind, and more abstract forces like "will" and the "unconscious"—and he put those in conjunction with the historical world. I don't think anybody's ever done anything quite like it—so economically, so intensely. The intensity and the power of what Conrad jams together is really unparalleled, I think, in the world of literature. And then third, to me what's especially tremendous about the novella is that it has obviously compelled many, many other writers to write in its wake. It provides perhaps the most influential portrait of a continent ever done—in history. Nobody has written about an entire place the way Conrad has written about Africa, for better or for worse.

PM: What is the secret to its influence, its longevity, over time?

ES: I think perhaps the style: There isn't a dead moment in it. Every work has certain moments of lull and letdown, but *Heart of Darkness* is intense from the very beginning. And second, the images are so, in a sense, primordial. There's something almost Jungian in their authority and influence: the river, the boat, the jungle, the different kinds of human beings he has—the trader, the harlequin, the black, the cannibals, the woman, the Intended, Marlow himself. It's just a miraculous thing. You might say that it's Conrad's fortunate fall, more so than anything that comes before and anything that comes after. I was going to add one last thing too. The influential quality of it is such that you can find novelists like Achebe—who hated it, right?—but he can't stop talking about it, and he can't stop writing about it.[6] Some of his early work, like *Things Fall Apart*, is unintelligible without *Heart of Darkness*. Then you have Naipaul, who is the opposite, yet he is also—how shall I put it?—spellbound by the thing. There's further Tayeb Salih—who's a great novelist, not known so much in the U.S.—and Ngugi and

Carpentier and Graham Greene and on and on and on.[7] There's a whole series of these people. And it's not even simply a matter of literary artists who engage in the act of rewriting Conrad; there's also a huge secondary literature that uses the book as a touchstone and resource—like *Exterminate the Brutes*, by the Swedish writer Sven Lindqvist, or *In the Footsteps of Mr. Kurtz*, by Michaela Wrong, who's a correspondent for the *Guardian* and wrote this extraordinary book about the Congo. There's also the Lumumba story—I don't know whether you saw the film *Lumumba: The Death of a Prophet*, directed by Raoul Peck?—which is straight out of Conrad too. So there's nothing like it really. The only thing one can think of that is similar to it is, of course, its opposite: *Moby-Dick*! The whiteness, you know—but that's so much more insistent, there's almost something hectoring about it, so that it's not quite the same subtlety as Conrad, and not quite as profound.

PM: Can I ask you a question about your own personal perspective on *Heart of Darkness*, for I think the case could be made that you're part of this trajectory of the novella's rewriters as well?

ES: Absolutely.

PM: It's interesting that your discussions of *Heart of Darkness* occur not just in literary-critical texts—like *Culture and Imperialism*, where it provides the epigraph and seems to hold a special place in your analysis—but in your large body of political writings on the subject of Palestine as well. One consequently gets the feeling that this text, as well as Conrad in general, has been instrumental in helping you to think through questions of Palestinian importance—that it has played some significant role in your grapplings with and struggles on behalf of the Palestinian people. Is this true?

ES: Unquestionably. You know, there are two great presences in my life intellectually: one of them literary, which is Conrad, the other one musical, which is Bach. And there's something about the organization of both—it's there in the passage you read me about the *cantus firmus*—that's really, well, polyphonic. Consequently, they both infiltrate my thinking on many different levels. In Conrad, of course, it's the whole: I don't know a better, more encyclopedic description of the world from which I come than is provided by Conrad's novels. That is to say: the world of empire, the world of British empire, the aftermath of empire, the struggle with and against empire. Where, in *Culture and Imperialism*, I talk about "two visions" of *Heart of Darkness*, one of them is, of course, a potentially limited vision with respect to blacks, but the other is a kind of relentlessly open-ended, aggressively critical inquiry into the mechanisms and presuppositions and situatedness and abuses of imperialism. Conrad, in these respects, is a constant challenge in one way and another. But part of his radicality—not political radicality, but metaphysical radicalism, which is so powerful precisely because of his tremendous skepticism: you know, of all schemes of betterment and progress, or industry in *Nostromo*, for example, or political ideology in *Under Western Eyes* and *The Secret Agent*—all this is predicated on a profound urge to get to the bottom of things. And yet—and this is the other part of it now—I have a feeling that Conrad and I would never, could never be friends!

PM: Why?

ES: Well, I think he's really the opposite of me in many ways. I mean, he's a man who believes in no political action. I think he thought it was all vain, and that's, of course, what's going on in his discussions with Cunninghame Graham,[8] who is the opposite. That is to say: I am the Cunninghame Graham figure in this model, rather than Conrad. But you need a Conrad, I think, to have a Cunninghame Graham—that's the whole point. I've often felt that Conrad would have deeply disapproved of everything I did—i.e., as idealistic and pointless and so on. But—I don't know whether you've ever read the couple of essays I wrote as the Tanner lectures on Lost Causes?

PM: Yes. It's in *Reflections on Exile*, yes?

ES: Right. So you know I've been attracted to lost causes most of my life—and Conrad is the great illuminator of that particular. But he does it from an ironic and disengaged and quite skeptical view, whereas mine's productive. It is engaged, but I'll get up and do it again.

PM: Two questions to follow up on this. First as to Conrad's general world-view: Is it nevertheless possible, to use a term that's been applied to you, to think of Conrad as a "pessoptimist?" Because it does seem to me, perhaps with all the emphasis on holding on to dreams *usque ad finem* in *Lord Jim*, and perhaps with reference to the "Henry James" essay that Faulkner draws on in his Nobel speech, that one could conceive Conrad in this doomed but indomitable way.[9]

ES: I agree that you could, yes, you could—but inadvertently. I think he really was genuinely a pessimist—you know, he really had a very dark vision. But he was a pessimist in the way that Nietzsche is a pessimist—don't forget I wrote about Conrad and Nietzsche[10]—and I think this quality is what they both have in common. It helps to explain their mutual veneration for Schopenhauer: I don't think that it's entirely an accident that they share that particular forebear. There are different ways, of course, of being pessimistic. I think what I remember from Borys's[11] description of his father was his saying—he didn't use the word "unapproachable," but there was something to suggest that there was something unwelcoming about his father's manner when he was in one of his moods. Another thing—if you'll forgive a digression—I remember about Borys was his saying that Jessie hated Ford Madox Ford. He said: "My mother's opinion of him is unprintable"—and she resented him profoundly. "But, of course," Borys went on to add, "my father knew that, and he kept bringing him back anyway." So you could tell that this was not a very . . . harmonious set-up!

PM: Second question—which will push us toward *Nostromo*, the "other" Conrad text that seems to have a special hold on your imagination over time. What are we to think of the politics of Conrad's stylistic experimentalism? There are, of course, a number of very different aesthetic styles and experiments Conrad wages across his fiction. But if we were to consider *Nostromo*, for instance, which Conrad seems to have thought of as his most daring canvas: Are we to interpret that text's complexities—formal or thematic—as an obfuscation and hence preservation of the material injustices of the world, or are they rather more an invitation to read the world more closely, critically, carefully, and to become a resister of the status quo?

ES: I think very much the latter. To me, *Nostromo* is the great novel of empire and imperial arrogance—whether the kind associated with Holroyd, or rather the more quiet, more unobtrusive but in the end more sinister kind associated with Charles Gould, and even to a lesser degree with Emilia Gould. This is what I meant when I referred to the world I grew up in. I was surrounded by British and Americans who were basically missionaries: people who had ideas of betterment planned for the natives. What was concealed, of course, which Conrad brings out with ruthless tenacity, was that these schemes were also for the benefit of the people creating the schemes. They weren't just out to develop "Costaguana"; they were also about getting rich and getting powerful. Conrad wanted that to be registered as carefully as he did the other more familiar ameliorative ideas—about the fact that the natives were poor and didn't have a stable economy and hadn't even begun to have a history, etc., etc. I think that's what he's talking about. But I think that what Conrad does is show, in a very unforgiving way, that the ends of all action are really doomed to failure of one thing or another. I draw a different conclusion from that. In other words, this may be Conrad's view, but I think one can take from it the very different lesson that you can't expect the kinds of rewards entailed by your actions: that the action itself has to be one of continual re-investigation, a ploughing and reploughing of the sea, as it were,[12] with respect to basic propositions like "the Americas are ungovernable," which is what we have in *Nostromo*, and other political propositions as well. I believe, in other words, that there *is* something in trying to plough the sea. For me, the answer lies in the vocation of the intellectual, who is never attached to power, never attached to keeping an uncritical judgment, never a sort of lobbyist in Washington or member of one of these think-tanks. Oh, I have great contempt for such policy-intellectuals. I learned that all from Conrad. That if you get involved in the machine, as he calls it in that famous letter,[13] or, say, in something like the mine in Costaguana, there's no escape. What you must try to do is to maintain division: of corruption; of power, leading to all sorts of dark places ; and from becoming part of it oneself. And also to be able to do what Conrad did aesthetically, which is to stand outside and to say: Well, yes, those things are happening, but there are always alternatives. But the big difference between Conrad and me in the end—and this is true of *Nostromo* as well as *Heart of Darkness*—is that politically for Conrad there are no real alternatives. And I disagree with that: there's always an alternative.

PM: A paradox informs your thinking about *Nostromo* over time. On the one hand, in *Culture and Imperialism* you make it quite clear that even though you see the novel as uncompromising in its critique of imperialism, you also see it as completely incapable of seeing *beyond* the machinery of imperialism, of acknowledging, apropos of the comments you've just made, the autonomy, the alternative possibilities, and the voices of non-Western peoples. Yet on the other hand, your involved discussion of the discrepancy between "action" and "record" in *Nostromo* in *Beginnings* has led other critics to believe that the novel is profoundly attentive to voices and processes of opposition and history that get lost in the process of "Western" recording, as, indeed, even an invitation to unearth such "native" articulations from the discursive or political unconscious. Both views are ultimately traceable to your work. Where, at the end of the day, do you stand on the postcolonial politics of *Nostromo*?

ES: I think it's important to remember that the thing about Conrad that is so masterful is that he is very severe. The discrepancy that I point out in *Culture and Imperialism*, and which I still believe to be the case, is absolutely healthy. What you have is a record that endures. Not all of the actions come out; there is much you could perceive as having escaped its view. Indeed, I think the novel quite carefully shuts all the doors as it goes on and maintains its own sense of discrepancy right through. And I don't think that in itself provides any hope. I think Conrad is just incapable of that kind of constitutive hope, and I would even call it frivolous to ascribe it to him. Because I think what he's really interested in is doing exactly the opposite.

PM: Why?

ES: Because I think Conrad is utterly convinced—and I think *Nostromo*, really less magically and attractively than *Heart of Darkness*, is a kind of positivist novel; it doesn't leave anything to poetic suggestion or symbolist evocation—*Nostromo* is utterly convinced of itself as a hard-nosed practical book about the failures of political action. What Conrad wants us to be left with is just that: the way the natives as well as the white men and the half-castes are all part of the same futile procession. Now, if you say you can read that and react against it, that's something else. But to say that it's in the book itself—that there's something "in" there about the people of Costaguana—I think it's just the opposite. I don't think there's anything about the "people" in there at all. They're all subjugated and destroyed and in a sense denatured—in a very rigorous way by Conrad. I think this is why *Nostromo* is in many ways Conrad's most pessimistic book.

PM: One case that often gets made for *Nostromo*'s special relevance at the present moment—Nadine Gordimer, for instance, makes this case in her new introduction to *Almayer's Folly*—is that the novel uncannily forecasts the course of much of Latin American political history in and beyond the twentieth century, with respect to its string of United Fruit Companies, its regime instabilities, the interventions by the United States, proto-globalization, and the like. I wonder, however, whether this predictive approach is the only way, or even the best way, to assess the novel's contemporary interest. Are there ways besides the oracular of articulating *Nostromo*'s particular interest and gravity at the present moment?

ES: Well, there are two things. First, I do think that one does not want to dismiss the achievement of what Conrad has envisioned of Latin America today—as you could, for instance, articulate the world from the perspective of dependence theorists and so on. So it is contemporary in that way. But the other fact about the book, which I think is more interesting, is an aesthetic fact that stands against contemporary history in an Adornian way. This is to say that what Conrad is attempting in *Nostromo* is a structure of such monumental solidity that it has an integrity of its own quite without reference to the outside world. Though this is only a speculation, I think that halfway through the book it's as if Conrad loses interest in the real world of human beings and becomes fascinated with the workings of his own method and his own writing. *It* has an integrity quite of its own—the way, for example, Bach might construct a fugue around a very uninteresting subject, and by the middle of the piece you are so involved in keeping the five, or four, voices going, and understanding the relationships between them, that this becomes the most interesting thing about it. I think there is a similar impulse at work in *Nostromo*.

PM: Indeed! H.L. Mencken, a critic whom one might not expect to mention in the same sentence with you, makes precisely this comparison—and in very much the same terms: of fugue-like evolutions from a simple underlying pattern—between his favorite novelist, Conrad, and his favorite musician, Bach![14]

ES: No! Are you serious?

PM: Yes; it's really remarkable. How might we take this insight, which the two of you arrive at independently, and think about the aesthetic phenomenon in Conrad that both of you are so powerfully responding to?

ES: Well, I think it's the notion of what I would call elaboration. I mean, what's really interesting about the world we live in—and this is obviously what the great artist develops obsessively—is the fact that there is a kind of labor in all human activity which is similar to the labor you can see in a tapestry or a piece of music. This is a labor that's elaborated, worked over, what the French call *travaillé*. And that's what interests me about the world we live in: It's one of the ways of rendering human effort, and you can see it in its most unadorned way in Bach. But it's also in *Nostromo*, where Conrad's attempting a canvas of nothing less than an entire civilization—let's say an entire culture, or country—and longing to see all of the possible workings of this from its fantasies to its sordid, everyday, practical worldly realities. And you know it's a fantastic achievement; not many people could do it.

PM: Perhaps even more than *Nostromo*, *The Secret Agent* is arguably the most "contemporary" of Conrad's novels. I say this with respect to issues of "terrorism," and with respect to the attempt to blow up the Greenwich Observatory featured in the book as it might relate to the events of September 11, 2001; and, indeed, a few weeks after September 11, an article entitled "Novelists Gaze into Terror's Dark Soul" appeared in the *New York Times* making precisely this comparison, and citing you for the proposition that the character of the Professor in *The Secret Agent* is a portrait of "the archetypal terrorist." I suppose the first thing I should ask you is whether or where you remember writing this—for I haven't been able to find it, and it doesn't sound like the sort of thing you would say.

ES: I must confess, as I was reading over your list of questions, I kept asking myself: Did I really say all these things? But as to this one in particular, no, I don't recall it, and I don't think the idea of an "archetypal terrorist" is very helpful in any event. But I do think the notion of an archetype does get to certain aesthetic and political limitations of *The Secret Agent* itself.

PM: How so?

ES: Let me be honest with you. Despite certain parallels, you know, between the World Trade Center and the events depicted in the book, *The Secret Agent* is a novel that has never really captivated my interest. I remember, for example, being struck by how highly Thomas Mann thought of the book. It strikes me as a kind of thin book, because it's exactly the archetypal that comprises what the book is looking for, and

Conrad is no good at this kind of archetype—or at least I'm not especially interested in that. It's a sort of essentializing and abstraction, and it's really a "psychological" move—in the bad sense of that word. And therefore, it never really struck me as a fantastic contemporary book. On the contrary, I think—precisely pursuant to this archetypal emphasis—it expresses Conrad's abhorrence and misunderstanding of politics: his caricaturing of the life of political struggle, and his cynical undermining of all things that he saw emanating from Russia, as that case gets elaborated even further in *Under Western Eyes*. It even goes back to the essay "Autocracy and War": Russia and Germany; *The Secret Agent* extends Conrad's case against them.

PM: Let's shift from talking about Conrad as an object of critical inquiry to considering him more as a fellow writer—as a kind of "secret sharer," as it were, who may have influenced you or whom you may have found meaningfully dovetailing with the development of your own voice and writing processes. For me, for instance, it's impossible to read your very moving essay "Return to Palestine" without thinking of Conrad's 1914 essay "Poland Revisited"—in which just like you, and uncannily so far as the thoughts and structure of the essay go, Conrad describes his own return to an erased and colonized homeland after an exilic period of many years.

ES: Really! Well, I must say I've read everything by Conrad, but this particular one I don't recall very well. It must have sunk in at some very deep level and stayed with me. Conrad is very interesting in this way. What is the phrase from *Heart of Darkness*: "the hint of half-remembered thoughts"? Because one of the characteristics of his style which I am deeply taken with is its reverberative quality: as if everything is an echo or quotation of something else. This echoic quality is why he haunts one—it's at least why he haunts me—and taking Conrad in at an early age, from the time I was in my late teens and twenties, must have inflected and informed my vision beyond my conscious recognition. But I must say I have no recollection of this essay at all!

PM: Have there been important moments when you have consciously, even self-consciously, recognized yourself writing in the mold of Conrad? It strikes me, for instance, that both of you write two full-length autobiographies, the first of which, in each case, has an unusually "public," extra-personal quality to it. It also seems to me that your first Conrad book is "about" autobiography, and that in many ways the phenomenological and existential issues you trace out there with respect to Conrad become materially elaborated in your own autobiographical *After the Last Sky*. And finally, I have to ask you about *Beginnings*, which might seem to many to be very distant from the kind of literary criticism you practice today, but which seems to me arguably your most "Conradian" book, not merely in its spiraling and spectacular experimental form, but also in a certain quality of reticence and distance with which, for all its magic, it refuses to disclose the personality and "ground" of the author. Is there any truth to any of this?

ES: Certainly *Beginnings*, very much so. *Beginnings* comes out of a very dark period in my life. I remember it very well. It was in the late '60s, just after the '67 War. I was going through the travail of an unhappy marriage at the time, and I was in a very unhappy place—namely, the University of Illinois, Urbana-Champaign, where I spent the year. And I started writing something called "A Meditation on Beginnings," which was first published as an essay in *Salmagundi*, which had just started at the time. I was invigorated to do this, as it were—or rather not invigorated but what was it—inspired—or pushed to do this by that sentence in *Heart of Darkness* which reads: "Traveling up that river was like traveling back to the beginnings of time." That's what was in my mind, and I said, I wonder if it's possible to do that in another way; I mean, one can't repeat Conrad, but one can go back to the very idea of beginning in some way that had been unexcavated before. Later, as I continued to work on this, and narrative and Freud and other things like that came up, the two things that remained on my mind were Conrad and Vico, who is the other great figure in my intellectual development. If I were to write a second volume after *Out of Place*, that's what I would start with: Vico and Conrad. Vico's *New Science* is exactly an exploration of the beginning, and beginnings are for him, like Conrad, a fabulous place of the gigantic and poetic. *The New Science* is an extraordinary book, and the coincidence between it and Conrad's description of Africa in *Heart of Darkness* is quite extraordinary as well—though Vico's book is written 200 years before, and he doesn't talk about Africa but rather a kind of post-diluvian conception of Europe. Anyway, this is what I was concentrating on at the time. Also, I had just reviewed and had been made very intransigent by Frank Kermode's book *The Sense of an Ending*. To me it was all wrong. Sure, some people are interested in how everything's going to end, but I wasn't really interested in endings. I was interested in why people do things at this radical and beginning level—at this primitive level, which is where I found myself in thinking about my own life, and the world that I had come from, which had just been obliterated in the war of '67. So, yes: That's probably the most Conradian moment I've ever known.

PM: I'd like to ask you in this vein about a connection that you've never, to my knowledge, articulated explicitly. You've written often of the attachment of the Palestinian people to the land, and how to be landless, to be deprived of one's land, especially for a people so grounded in its traditions, is to put a social polity like the Palestinians in grave jeopardy. I'm wondering whether such concerns might relate to your interest in Conrad's sea stories, which generally present embattled communities of one form or another struggling to survive upon the literally groundless terrain of the sea—or a book like *Nostromo*, whose nationalizing efforts, as you suggested earlier, are predicated on the desperate analogy of "ploughing the sea."

ES: Very much so, very much so. I think that Conrad, especially in books like *Typhoon* or *The Nigger of the "Narcissus,"* sets out via the trope and terrain of the sea to express a sense of enormous struggle against unbelievable odds—and how one must keep going. And you know, back in the 1960s and '70s I really took, and I still take, such matters very seriously. People may dismiss such things as Conrad being simple-minded for the public, but I think he's not only dead serious but absolutely right. I think one can extend it into political principles, political in the sense of having to do with principles and certain values that really don't, in my view, get changed or compromised by different cultures—which really are not relativized at all. And I don't think they were for Conrad either. There is, of course, also the special difficulty of conducting a personal struggle in an element in which there is no foothold, where the foothold itself is challenged. Don't forget that I began my political writings about Palestine at much the same moment that I began writing *Beginnings*. And there, at the Stanford International House where I worked, I gave a talk that I will never forget as long as I live. The talk was entitled "Palestine," and outside there were people demonstrating with placards saying: "There is no Palestine." That is what I had to overcome. I felt that's what I was doing—against all odds. I was like MacWhirr in *Typhoon*.

PM: I'm very struck by what you're saying right now, because it points to the key question of authorial voice that I think anyone who reads both you and Conrad in extensive relation would want to ask. First, two things: one, on the first page of your Conrad book, you talk about the image of Almayer covering his daughter's footsteps at the end of *Almayer's Folly* as a moment of masking, of hiding, of covering over what's going on inside the author; and two, a bit later in your book, you reference the famous letter in which Conrad describes himself as "*homo duplex* in more ways than one"—again, speaking to the discrepancy between the text of what gets written and the person and values and political commitments and, say, Polish origins of the writer. Always a division, then, so that we have to wait for Conrad's viewpoints on Poland in his essays rather than his fictions; and such that even in his "autobiographies"—and this is where I was going earlier—there is a strange sense of defensive distance, covered tracks, public impersonality—always conveniently anglophied or anglophilic, at least on the surface. This seems to me the same kind of division you are talking about in the discrepancy between *Beginnings* and the political writings you were doing on Palestine at the time—but it seems that you have somehow, over the years, managed to reconcile this problem of "duplexity" in a way that Conrad was never. . .

ES: No, I haven't: I would say I haven't. I'm sorry to interrupt you, but I feel very strongly about that. I really haven't. I've tried in different ways to do that, but I think—and this is something I think about in the context of what I was calling earlier "late style"—there is a problem of irreconcilability. In other words, there are certain things that can't be reconciled. The truth is, try as I can I've never been able to reconcile my two lives with each other: the fact that I am a professor here and that I do other things, you know, wherever it is. And I think: Why should I? I remember once asking [Noam] Chomsky that—he's a friend of mine—and I said to him: How do you connect your intellectual life as a linguist and your life as a political activist? And he said: I don't. I try to keep them as far apart as possible. That was an important hint: Why should you reconcile? Why should you try to assume wholeness when, as Adorno says, "the whole is the false?"

PM: Fascinating. Nevertheless, there are pieces you have written recently—one of them just appeared in *PMLA*—which have to do with the weakness of the institutionalized humanities when it comes to intervening meaningfully in world affairs. This is a crucial subject—especially given the date of this interview, when it seems all but inevitable that the United States, with or without world support, will soon be commencing deeply questionable military activities in the Middle East.

ES: Immoral, in my word.

PM: I agree. Given this situation, and given all that you've written concerning the problems afflicting the institutionalized humanities—the slashing of resources, the entrenchment of disciplines, the commodification of the educational product, the cooptation of potentially subversive political energies, etc., etc.—how would you advise literature professors to address this situation as best we can, and to maximize the impact we can have under these circumstances?

ES: I've just written a book on this subject drawn from a series of lectures I gave at Cambridge on humanism. I think a reinvigorated attitude toward the humanities and toward the practice of humanism is the key. Its major component is re-appropriating agency—from globalization, from the military-industrial complex, from institutions, from everything that threatens the university, which I consider a kind of utopian place. I believe in the importance of rethinking the relationship between these forces and the university as one not of complementarity but rather antagonism, and of taking the fight out there—in an unreconciled way.

There are deep, irreconcilable oppositions which it is our duty to maintain. Between the obscenity of the imperial world view and that of the Christian fundamentalists which Bush represents, and his inexperienced, in my opinion, abstract, and in the end [**XXX**][15] advisors like Wolfowitz and Perle weighing in on a part of the world I know something about—I think it is our moral duty to oppose these people and to expose them precisely for the impractical, the abstract, the mechanical, the inexperienced, the ideological villains that they really are. And that's what we do, I think: we oppose it through all the means at our disposal. Not instrumentally, of course. I don't mean that you take a work of literature and say: Well, this is against the war. Rather I mean to emphasize the practice of humanistic activity, which encompasses reading and understanding and critically comprehending. My third lecture is called "The Return to Philology," and in emphasizing philology, a deep understanding of the word, it shows how words are misused and traduced by manipulators of power. It culminates and comes out of all my work on intellectuals and political activity and so on, and I think the only answer to the situation that we are in is an expanded idea of what humanism is. It isn't about the worship of the great works: i.e., on the model of the traditional humanities course, where one reads Dante and Shakespeare and Plato and talks about how wonderful they are. No, it's not that. It's not a possession but an activity. And the activity I have in mind is basically oppositional. It's—to use a word I used before—*severe* in its holding-on to particular human ideas, to human *secular* agency: secular—key word. Auerbach uses it in the book on Dante;[16] he uses the word *irdische*, which in German means "earthly." In this view, what Dante does is give us the earthly—almost a secular— reading of the universal and the timeless. All those things strike me as absolutely key to what we do, and any sign, in my opinion, of defeatism or dandyism or aestheticism à la Harold Bloom with his pathetic imitation of Oscar Wilde is exactly the opposite of that—and is to be resisted.

PM: You've emphasized the importance of vigorous oppositional thinking, and in doing so you've repeated a phrase which recurs throughout your literary-critical and political writings too, i.e., "irreconcilable antagonisms." Do you use that phrase in self-conscious reference to Conrad?

ES: Oh yes, absolutely. Because he uses it a lot too! It's one of his phrases, no?

PM: Indeed, but somewhat obscurely so,[17] and I've often wondered whether your use of it, which comes across less as a quotation than as an organic element of your own vocabulary, was self-consciously anchored in Conrad. But speaking of "irreconcilable antagonisms," I have a hard question to put to you that directly implicates the teaching of

Conrad. Is there not an irreconcilable tension at work between teaching canonical texts—like, say, Conrad's—in however worldly or political or secular a fashion, and nevertheless implicitly re-inscribing their *a priori* canonicity through the very act of making them the primary object of humanistic scrutiny in the first place?

ES: Well, I think there potentially is such a tension. One of the criticisms I have of this Memorial course called "The Humanities" that they've taught here for years and years is the fact that it's taken out of historical context. I think what one has to do with any work one reads is to re-inscribe it in the world from which it came. That's the main principle of philological reading, that you read a text from the point of view of the maker. This is a point of view you can't have by an act of inspiration but which rather requires complete historical understanding of the situation— socio-political, spiritual, etc.—on the part of the person who is doing it. So in that respect, the engagement with the canon has to be historical engagement, and it has to be one where—this is a second, no less crucial element—there's an appreciation of the aesthetical element, which can't be reduced simply to an ideological or superstructural phenomenon, but which has its own integrity. And this integrity to me is an important one: That is to say, it cannot be reconciled with the world from which it came. In other words, you can't explain Dante simply by talking about quarrels between the Guelphs and the Ghibellines, the human elements of the *Divine Comedy*. There has to be a way of dealing with a work that in a certain sense escapes its historical determinism.

PM: I'd like finally to return us to the subject of the Middle-Eastern implications and resonances of Conrad's fiction. During the past thirty years, you have devoted a tremendous amount of energy, theoretical and practical, not only to addressing tensions between Arab Palestinians and Israeli Jews, but also to encouraging reciprocity, recognition, and coexistence between the two groups. You write, for instance, in a 1980 essay entitled "Peace and Palestinian Rights": "Israelis and Palestinians are two communities that will never go away or leave each other alone. What better way of beginning to come to terms with each other than to open one community up to the other's history, actuality, and aspirations?"[18] Now Conrad's fiction consistently turns on many of these same issues: opening oneself up to alterity; the problems of witnessing and writing history; indomitable aspirations built on irreconcilable antagonisms. And, indeed: Conrad, whose fiction, as you've already explained, is so readily legible from a Palestinian point of view, was actually in his own time mistaken by many readers to be Jewish— prompting Conrad, in fact, to have a letter published in *The New Republic* in 1917 denying that this was the case. Question, then: In what ways might Conrad be useful in thinking through and opening up, of searching for terms of understanding and reciprocity with respect to, the Palestinian–Israeli situation of today?

ES: Very simple. Conrad's fiction is a search for—and an opportunity for us to learn to search for—ways of living in an impossible situation. That's to me what he's all about. That is to say, if you think of all of his work, and the extremism, the extremity, of all that work—for it is always about extremism of one form or another: extremes of difficulty, extremes of experience, extremes of political viewpoint, and so forth—what you get in Conrad is a style of maintaining a dream, of maintaining certain principles or codes of conduct amid a compound of impossible elements. You have to learn, as Stein says in *Lord Jim*, how to survive in "the destructive element." I can't tell you how profound I think that is.

PM: So what would that mean in this context and in the context of the contemporary world generally: immersing and surviving in the destructive element, where "the deep, deep sea keeps you up"?

ES: This is to say, in my reading, that we live in a world where there are so many opposing positions and irreconcilable frames of experience, of truth, of reality, that they can never be transcended. Take, for example, in my opinion, the irreconcilability of the Palestinian and Israeli claims. There's just no way I've thought about which you could tell me that you have a state which is based on the ruins of another state, and that's why there's so much conflict, supplemented by other reasons. But the basic fact—just like *Lord Jim* with its basic "naked fact"—is there, and it will not go away. And *that* is the destructive element, that clash of oppositions. Yet they are sustained by history and reality—as opposites. So the genius of the situation is that there might be some mode of sustainment—not in a state of extremism and impossibly aggressive opposition, but rather in some state, however irreconcilable the elements, of maintained coexistence, without minimizing the extremes and antagonisms involved. And this is what I think is so important. It points to musical metaphors of one sort or another—the contrapuntal, for example—rather than a grand Hegelian solution of synthesis. There's something wordless about it—and music may be the element Conrad is thinking of when he thinks of the "deep, deep sea" as grounded in oppositions but which nevertheless keep disparate parts afloat and alive.

PM: "It is certain my conviction gains infinitely the moment another soul believes in it," reads the epigraph to *Lord Jim*. One gets the sense from your political writings over the past 30 years that some such feeling of *recognition*—of acknowledgment that a foundational wrong has been done—lies at the core of what's been missing, from the Palestinian perspective, at every stage of the various peace processes over the years.

ES: I think that's the core sticking thing for me—not for everyone. But I've often said, and in fact was just giving a series of talks last week on this note, that what the Palestinians want is something that they have never gotten from any responsible party: that is, an acknowledgment of the injustice that was done to them. That would be like hope. But the failure often was that there was no admission that there was even an occupation—nothing. The most, for instance, that Barak said was that we recognize you as sovereign. But it's not that; it's that you recognized that you caused the suffering. Now I'm not saying that you've caused it all, but I am talking about the recognition that you played a major role in it. That's the important thing. The essence of the situation is this non-recognition, and so many claims and grievances and possibilities turn upon it, especially on the Palestinian side.

PM: Professor Said, I and the readers of this volume, I am sure, deeply appreciate your taking the time to speak so generously and thoughtfully about Conrad. Would you share one last thought about what Conrad means to you at this particular moment in your life?

ES: Let me answer that question indirectly. I was very sick last year—from about May to a good while after—and the one person I was reading was Auerbach. I just finished writing a long introduction to *Mimesis*, and it set me thinking about a good number of things. Nobody could be more different than me in a way: he was German, Jewish, Prussian. But in spite of all that, and what he represents, what interests me is this attempt to go beyond: to go into the realm of the alien and different, and to try to comprehend it in an aesthetic way. I think that this is one of the great things Conrad does too: He gets into situations that in and of themselves don't remove the difficulties. There's no flattening it all out, no saying, "We're all going to play in the same park together"—there's none of that at all in Conrad. It all remains quite rigorously there. But the kind of identity you get—a frightening identity like the one at the end of *Heart of Darkness*, where the characters sit along the river looking out into the heart of an immense darkness—that's really unique. In Conrad, peculiarity is always preserved right to the last moment. When he talks, for instance, in his letters about Dostoevsky grimacing endlessly into the night, he's talking about himself. And his characters are exactly the same. They're all haunted, they're all tormented, every one of them, every last figure he created from Almayer and James Wait right down to Heyst in *Victory* and Lingard in *The Rescue*.

PM: *Usque ad finem.*

ES: *Usque ad finem.*

Notes

1. Gerard Jean-Aubry, *Joseph Conrad: Life and Letters* (1927).
2. Jocelyn Baines, *Joseph Conrad: A Critical Biography* (1959); Gustav Morf, *The Polish Heritage of Joseph Conrad* (1930).
3. Albert Guerard wrote two books on Conrad: *Joseph Conrad* (*New Directions*, 1947) and *Conrad the Novelist* (1958). Thomas C. Moser Sr.'s *Joseph Conrad: Achievement and Decline* (1957) advances a hypothesis concerning a period of achievement in Conrad's fiction followed by decline that has proven one of the most influential, and controversial, in Conrad criticism.
4. See G. Wilson Knight's *Crown of Life* (1958).
5. Adam Hochschild, *King Leopold's Ghost* (1998).
6. Chinua Achebe first delivered "An Image of Africa: Racism in Conrad's Heart of Darkness," which accuses Conrad of racism, as the second Chancellor's Lecture at the University of Massachusetts, Amherst on February 18, 1975. This lecture was published in essay form in 1977, and was then amended in, and variously republished since 1987. In a compelling essay in *The Guardian* (London) on February 22, 2003, British/Caribbean novelist Caryl Phillips presents the results of the latest interview with Achebe on the same article and subject.
7. See V.S. Naipaul's *A Bend in the River* (1979), Tayeb Salih's *Season of Migration to the North* (1970), Ngugi wa Thiong'o's *A Grain of Wheat* (1967), Alejo Carpentier's *The Lost Steps* (1953), and Graham Greene's *The Heart of the Matter* (1948)—all rewritings of *Heart of Darkness*, in one way or another.
8. See Cedric Watts, *Letters to Cunnighame Graham.*
9. See Imil Habibi, *The Secret Life of Saeed: The Pessoptimist* (1974; 1st Am. trans. 2001); Conrad, "Henry James: An Appreciation" (1904) (NLL 11–19).
10. See "Conrad and Nietzsche," *Reflections on Exile* 70–82.
11. Borys Conrad: the eldest of the two sons of Joseph and Jessie Conrad. As Said explains in a longer version of this interview, he met Borys in Poland at an international Conrad conference sponsored by the Polish Academy of Sciences in 1972.
12. In *Nostromo*, Decoud quotes the historical Simon Bolívar, who "said in the bitterness of his spirit, 'America is ungovernable. Those who worked for her independence have ploughed the sea'" (No 119).
13. *Letters* 1: 424–426.
14. See Nolte 239–243, 41–42.
15. This adjective cannot be made out from the recording.
16. Erich Auerbach, *Dante, Poet of the Secular World* (1929; *Dante als Dichter der irdischen Welt*).
17. See *Letters* 2: 348–349.
18. See *Politics of Dispossession* 43–52, 49.

Bibliography

Abrams, Meyer. *Natural Supernaturalism*. New York: Norton, 1971.

"Academy Praises 'Conrad's heir.'" *Ottawa Citizen*. October 12, 2001: D3.

Achebe, Chinua. "An Image of Africa." *Massachusetts Review* 18 (1977): 782–94. Rpt. in Kimbrough 251–262.

Adorno, Theodor. *Philosophie der neuen Musik*. Frankfurt am Main: Suhrkamp, 1978.

——. "On the Fetish-Character in Music and the Regression of Listening (1938). *Essays on Music*. Trans. Susan Gillespie. Berkeley: University of California Press, 2002. 288–317.

Agamben, Giorgio. *The Man Without Content*. Trans. Georgia Albert. Meridian Series. Stanford: Stanford UP, 1999.

Allen, Walter. *The English Novel: A Short Critical History*. London: Phoenix, 1954.

Anderson, Benedict. *Language and Power: Exploring Political Cultures in Indonesia*. Ithaca: Cornell UP, 1990.

Anderson, Benedict. *Imagined Communities*. London: Verso, 1983.

——. "Narrating the Nation." *Times Literary Supplement*. June 13, 1986: 659.

Apter, Emily. "Global *Translatio*: The 'Invention' of Comparative Literature, Istanbul, 1933." *Critical Inquiry* 29 (Winter 2003): 253–81.

——. "The Human in the Humanities." *October* 96 (Spring 2001): 71–85.

Arac, Jonathan. "Romanticism, the Self, and the City: *The Secret Agent* in Literary History." *Boundary 2* 9.1 Supp. on Irony (Autumn 1980): 75–90.

Armah, Ayi Kwei. *Two Thousand Seasons*. London: Heinemann, 1973.

Armstrong, Paul B. "The Politics of Reading Irony in Conrad." *Conradiana* 26 (1994): 85–101.

——. "Conrad's Contradictory Politics: The Ontology of Society in *Nostromo*." *Twentieth Century Literature* 31 (1981): 1–21.

Ashcroft, Bill, Gareth Griffiths, and Helen Tiffin. *The Empire Writes Back: Theory and Practice in Post-Colonial Literatures*. London: Routledge, 1989.

Badiou, Alain. *Ethics: An Essay on the Understanding of Evil*. Trans. Peter Hallward. London: Verso, 2001.

Baines, Jocelyn. *Joseph Conrad: A Critical Biography*. London: Weidenfeld, 1960.

Baker, Keith Michael. "A Foucauldian French Revolution?" *Foucault and the Writing of History*. Ed. J. Goldstein. Oxford: Blackwell, 1994. 187–205.

Baudrillard, Jean. *The Gulf War Did Not Take Place*. Trans. Paul Patton. Bloomington: Indiana UP, 1995.

——. *Simulacra and Simulation*. Trans. Sheila Faria Glaser. Ann Arbor: Michigan UP, 1994.

Becker, A.L. "Text-Building, Epistemology, and Aesthetics in Javanese Shadow Theatre." *The Imagination of Reality*. Eds. Becker and Aram A. Yengoyan. Norwood, NJ: Albex, 1979.

Benjamin, Walter. "Critique of Violence." In *Reflections* 277–300.

——. "Karl Kraus." In *Reflections* 239–76.

Benjamin, Walter. *Illuminations*. Ed. Hannah Arendt. New York: Schocken, 1968.

——. *Reflections*. Trans. Edmund Jephcott. New York: Schocken, 1978.

——. "The Paris of the Second Empire in Baudelaire." *Walter Benjamin: Selected Writings. Volume 4 1938-1940*. Ed. Michael W. Jennings. Cambridge, MA: Harvard UP, 2003. 3–92.

Berthoud, Jacques. "The Modernization of Sulaco." In Moore, *Conrad's Cities* 139–157.

——. "*The Secret Agent*." In Stape, *Cambridge Companion* 100–121.

Bhabha, Homi K. *The Location of Culture*. New York: Routledge, 1994.

——. "DissemiNation: Time, Narrative, and the Margins of the Modern Nation." *Nation and Narration*. Ed. Homi Bhabha. New York: Routledge, 1990. 291–322.

Black, Jeremy. *Maps and Politics*. London: Reaktion, 1997.

Bleasdale, Marcus. *One Hundred Years of Darkness : A Photographic Journey to the Heart of the Congo*. London : Art Books Intl., 2002.

Bloch, Ernst et al. *Aesthetics and Politics*. London: New Left Books, 1977.

Blunt, Alison and Gillian Rose. *Writing Women and Space: Colonial and Postcolonial Geographies*. New York and London: Guilford, 1994.

Bock, Martin. *Joseph Conrad and Psychological Medicine*. Lubbock: Texas Tech UP, 2002.

Boorstin, Daniel. *The Image*. New York: Harper, 1961.

Bongie, Chris. *Exotic Memories: Literature, Colonialism, and the Fin de Siècle*. Stanford: Stanford UP, 1991.

Bonney, William. "Conrad's Romanticism Reconsidered." *Conradiana* 27 (1995): 189–221.

Borradori, Giovanni, Ed. *Philosophy in a Time of Terror: Dialogues with Jürgen Habermas and Jacques Derrida.* Chicago: Chicago UP, 2003.

Bourdieu, Pierre. *Acts of Resistance: Against the New Myths of Our Time.* Trans. Richard Nice. London: Polity, 1998.

Boyce, George. "The Fourth Estate: the Reappraisal of a Concept." In Boyce, Curran 19–40.

Boyce, George, James Curran, and Pauline Wingate, Eds. *Newspaper History from the Seventeenth Century to the Present Day.* London: Constable, 1978.

Bradbury, Malcolm. *The Modern British Novel.* London: Secker, 1993.

Brantlinger, Patrick. *Rule of Darkness: British Literature and Imperialism, 1830-1914.* Ithaca: Cornell UP, 1988.

Breunig, Charles. *The Age of Revolution and Reaction, 1789-1850.* New York: Norton, 1970.

Bristow, Joseph, ed. *Sexual Sameness: Textual Differences in Lesbian and Gay Writing.* London: Routledge, 1992.

Brittain, Victoria. "Colonialism and the Predatory State in the Congo." *New Left Review* 236 (1999): 133–44.

Bronfen, Elisabeth. *Dorothy Richardson's Art of Memory: Space, Identity, Text.* Trans. Victoria Appelbe. Manchester: Manchester UP, 1999.

Brotton, Jeremy. "'This Tunis, Sir, Was Carthage': Contesting Colonialism in *The Tempest*." Eds. Ania Loomba and Martin Orkin. *Postcolonial Shakespeares.* London: Routledge, 1998. 23-42.

Bruntz, George G. *Allied Propaganda and the Collapse of the German Empire in 1918.* Stanford: Stanford UP, 1938.

Buchan, John. *The Battle of the Somme.* New York: Doran, 1917.

Budden, Julian. *The Operas of Verdi.* Vol. 2. New York: Oxford University Press, 1979.

Buitenhuis, Peter. *The Great War of Words: British, American, and Canadian Propaganda and Fiction, 1914–1933.* Vancouver: U British Columbia P, 1987.

Butler, Judith. *Bodies that Matter: On the Discursive Limits of 'Sex.'* New York: Routledge, 1993.

———. *Gender Trouble: Feminism and the Subversion of Identity.* New York: Routledge, 1990.

Carabine, Keith. "'Gestures' and 'The Moral Satirical Idea' in Conrad's 'The Informer.'" *Conradiana* 31 (1999): 26–41.

———. *The Life and the Art: A Study of Conrad's* Under Western Eyes. Amsterdam: Rodopi, 1996.

———. "From *Razumov* to *Under Western Eyes*: The Dwindling of Natalia Haldin's Possibilities." In Carabine, *Life and the Art.* Chapter Four.

———. *Joseph Conrad: Critical Assessments.* 4 vols. Sussex: Helm Information, 1992.

———, Ed. *Nostromo.* By Joseph Conrad. World's Classics Ed. Oxford: Oxford UP, 1984.

Carlyle, Thomas. *The French Revolution.* New York: Random House, n.d.

Carpentier, Alejo. *The Lost Steps* (1953). Trans. Harriet de Onis. London: Gollancz,1956.

Cartwright, Justin. "Unspeakable Fear." *The Guardian.* August 20 1998: 14.

Casarino, Cesare. "The Sublime of the Closet; or, Joseph Conrad's Secret Sharing." *Boundary 2* 24.2 (Summer 1997): 199–243.

Castlereagh, (Lord) Robert Stewart. *Hansard.* xci (1819): col. 1177.

Cecil, Lord Robert. "British Propaganda in Allied and Neutral Countries." Kew, England: Public Record Office, INF 4/1B.

Chafetz, Josh. "Body Count: Inside the Voodoo Science of Calculating Civilian Casualties." *Daily Standard.* April 16, 2003. November 5, 2003 http://www.weeklystandard.com/ Content/ Public/Articles/000/000/002/554awdqo.asp

Chakrabarty, Dipesh. "Postcoloniality and the Artifice of History: Who Speaks for 'Indian' Pasts?" In Ranajit Guha, Ed. *A Subaltern Studies Reader.* Minneapolis: University of Minnesota Press 1997. 263–93.

Chrisman, Laura. *Postcolonial Contraventions: Cultural Readings of Race, Imperialism and Transnationalism.* Manchester: Palgrave MacMillan, 2003.

Clemens, Samuel. *A Connecticut Yankee in King Arthur's Court.* New York: Random House, 1949.

Clifford, James. "On Ethnographic Self-fashioning: Conrad and Malinowski." *Reconstructing Individualism.* Eds. T.C. Heller et al. Stanford: Stanford UP, 1986. 140–62.

Conboy, Katie, et al. Eds. *Writing on the Body: Female Embodiment and Feminist Theory.* New York: Columbia UP, 1997.

Conrad, Joseph. *Congo Diary and Other Unpublished Pieces.* Ed. Zdzisław Najder. New York: Doubleday, 1978.

———. *Letters to R.B. Cunninghame Graham.* Ed. Cedric Watts. Cambridge: Cambridge UP, 1969.

Corner, James. "The Agency of Mapping: Speculation, Critique and Invention." In move *Mappings*. Ed. Denis Cosgrove. London: Reaktion, 1999.

Coroneos, Con. *Space, Conrad, and Modernity*. Oxford: Oxford University Press, 2002.

Cox, C. B., Ed. *A Casebook on* Heart of Darkness, Nostromo *and* Under Western Eyes. London: Macmillan, 1981.

Crane, Stephen. *The Red Badge of Courage* (1895). New York: Bantam, 1983.

Curran, James. "The Press As an Agency of Social Control: An Historical Perspective." In Boyce, Curran 51–78.

Daly, Nicholas. *Modernism, Romance and the Fin de Siècle*. Cambridge: Cambridge UP, 1999.

Daly, Herman. "The Perils of Free Trade." *Scientific American* 269 (1993): 50–57.

de Certeau, Michel. *The Practice of Everyday Life*. Berkeley: U California P, 1984.

DeKoven, Marianne. *Rich and Strange: Gender, History, Modernism*. Princeton: Princeton UP, 1991.

de Man, Paul. "The Concept of Irony." *Aesthetic Ideology*. Ed. Andrzej Warminski. Minneapolis: U Minnesota P, 1996.

Derrida, Jacques. *A Derrida Reader: Between the Blinds*. Ed. Peggy Kamuf. New York: Columbia UP, 2003.

——. *The Work of Mourning*. Eds. Pascale-Anne Brault and Michael Naas. Chicago: Chicago UP, 2001.

——. *Specters of Marx: The State of the Debt, the Work of Mourning, and the New International*. Trans. Peggy Kamuf. New York: Routledge, 1994.

——. *Memoires for Paul de Man*. Rev. Ed. Trans. Cecile Lindsay, Jonathan Culler, Eduardo Cadava, and Peggy Kamuf. New York: Columbia UP, 1989.

——. *Dissemination*. Trans. Barbara Johnson. Chicago: Chicago UP, 1981.

DeWitte, Ludo. *The Assassination of Lumumba*. Trans. Ann Wright and Renee Femby. London: Verso, 2001.

Dhareshwar, Vivek. "Toward a Narrative Epistemology of the Postcolonial Predicament." *Inscriptions* 5 (1989): 135–57.

Dollimore, Jonathan. "The Cultural Politics of Perversion." In *Sexual Sameness: Textual Differences in Gay and Lesbian Writing*. Ed. Joseph Bristow. London: Routledge, 1992. 9–25.

Duncan, Ian. *Modern Romance and the Transformations of the Novel*. Cambridge: Cambridge UP, 1992.

Durant, Will and Ariel Durant. *The Age of Napoleon: A History of European Civilization from 1789 to 1815*. New York: Simon, 1975.

Dürrenmatt, Friedrich. *The Physicists*. Trans. James Kirkup. New York: Grove, 1964.

Edney, Matthew. *Mapping an Empire: The Geographical Construction of British India 1765–1843*. Chicago: Chicago UP, 1997.

Eliot, T.S. "'Ulysses,' Order, and Myth." *Selected Prose of T.S. Eliot*. Ed. Frank Kermode. New York: Harcourt, 1975.

Ellul, Jacques. *Propaganda*. Trans. Konrad Kellen and Jean Lerner. New York: Vintage, 1973.

——. *The Technological Society*. Trans. John Wilkinson. New York: Vintage, 1964.

——. "Information and Propaganda." *Diogenes* 18 (Summer 1957): 61–77.

Enright, D.J. *The Alluring Problem: An Essay on Irony*. Oxford: Oxford UP, 1986.

Erdinast-Vulcan, Daphna. "*Heart of Darkness* and the Ends of Man." *The Conradian* 28.1 (Spring 2003): 17–33.

——. *The Strange Short Fiction of Joseph Conrad*. Oxford: Oxford UP, 1999.

Fanon, Frantz. *The Wretched of the Earth*. Trans. Constance Farrington. New York: Grove, 1963.

Felman, Shoshana and Laub, Dori. *Testimony: Crises of Witnessing in Literature, Psychoanalysis, and History*. New York: Routledge, 1992.

Felman, Shoshana. *Jacques Lacan and the Adventure of Insight: Psychoanalysis in Contemporary Culture*. Cambridge, MA: Harvard UP, 1987.

Fernback, D., Ed. *Surveys from Exile: Political Writings*. By Karl Marx. Vol. 2. New York: Random House, 1974.

Firchow, Peter Edgerly. *Envisioning Africa: Racism and Imperialism in Conrad's* Heart of Darkness. Lexington: Kentucky UP, 2000.

Flaubert, Gustave. *Madame Bovary*. Trans. Alan Russell. Harmondsworth: Penguin, 1950.

Fleishman, Avrom. "The Mirror of the Sea: Fragments of a Great Confession." *L'Epoque Conradienne* (May 1979): 136–51.

Florida, Nancy. *Writing the Past, Inscribing the Future: History as Prophecy in Colonial Java*. Durham: Duke University Press, 1995.

Fludernik, Monika. "Old Wine in New Bottles? Voice, Focalization, and New Writing." *NLH* 32 (2001): 619–638.

Fogel, Aaron. *Coercion to Speak: Conrad's Poetics of Dialogue*. Cambridge, MA: Harvard UP, 1985.

Forbes, Jack. *Atlas of Native History*. Davis, CA.: D-Q UP, 1981.

Ford, Ford Madox. *The March of Literature*. London: Allen, 1939.

——. *Joseph Conrad: A Personal Remembrance*. London: Duckworth, 1924.

——. *The Critical Attitude*. London: Duckworth, 1911.

Fornäs, Johan. *Cultural Theory and Late Modernity*. London: Sage, 1995.

Forster, Michael. "Hegel's Dialectical Method." In *The Cambridge Companion to Hegel*. Ed. F. Beiser. New York: Cambridge UP, 1993. 130–170.

Fothergill, Anthony. "Signs, Interpolations, Meanings: Conrad and the Politics of Utterance." In *Conrad and Theory*. Eds. Andrew Gibson and Robert Hampson. Amsterdam: Rodopi, 1998. 39–57.

Foucault, Michel. *Foucault Live: Interviews 1966-1984*. Ed. S. Lotringer. Trans. J. Johnston. New York: Columbia UP, 1989.

——. "Of Other Spaces." *Diacritics* 16.1 (Spring 1986): 22–27.

——. *Power/Knowledge: Selected Interviews and Other Writings 1972–1977*. Eds. and trans. C. Gordon, et al. New York: Pantheon, 1980.

——. *Discipline and Punish: The Birth of the Prison*. Trans. A. Sheridan. New York: Pantheon, 1977.

Fraser, Gail. *Interweaving Patterns in the Works of Joseph Conrad*. Ann Arbor and London: UMI Research Press, 1988.

Freud, Sigmund. *Moses and Monotheism* (I, 1937; III, 1939). Trans. Katherine Jones. New York: Vintage, 1955.

——. "Beyond the Pleasure Principle" (1920). *Complete Works*. XVIII: 3–66.

——. "The Uncanny" (1919). *Complete Works*. XVII: 219–252.

Fromm, Gloria. *Dorothy Richardson: A Biography*. Urbana: U Illinois P, 1977.

——. *Totem and Taboo* (1912–1913). Trans. A.A. Brill. Harmonsworth, Middlesex: Penguin, 1942.

——, ed. *Windows on Modernism: Selected Letters of Dorothy Richardson*. Athens: U Georgia P, 1995.

Fukuyama, Francis, *The End of History and the Last Man*. Harmondsworth: Penguin, 1992.

Fuss, Diana. *Essentially Speaking*. London: Routledge, 1989.

Gagnier, Regenia. *Subjectivities: A History of Self-Representation in Britain, 1832–1920*. New York: Oxford UP, 1991.

Garnett, Edward. *Conrad's Prefaces to His Works*. New York: Books for Libraries, 1937.

Garnett, Edward. *Letters from Conrad 1895–1924*. London: The Nonesuch Press, 1928.

Gathorne-Hardy, R., Ed. *Memoirs: A Study in Friendship 1873–1915*. New York: Alfred A. Knopf, 1964.

Geertz, Clifford. *The Religion of Java*. Glencoe, IL: Free Press, 1960.

Ghosh, Amitav. *The Shadow Lines*. New York: Penguin, 1990.

——. "The March of the Novel through History: The Testimony of My Grandfather's Bookcase." In *The Imam and the Indian*. New Delhi: Ravi Dayal and Permanent Black, 2002.

GoGwilt, Chris. "Pramoedya's Fiction and History." *Yale Journal of Criticism*. 9.1 (1996): 147–64.

GoGwilt, Christopher. *The Invention of the West: Joseph Conrad and the Double-Mapping of Europe and Empire*. Stanford: Stanford UP, 1995.

Gordimer, Nadine. "Introduction." In *Almayer's Folly*. By Joseph Conrad. New York: Modern Library, 2002. ix–xv.

Gordon, Colin. "Governmental Rationality: An Introduction." In *The Foucault Effect: Studies in Governmentality*. Eds. G. Burchell, et al. Chicago: Chicago UP. 1991. 1–51.

Gray, John. *Al Qaeda and What It Means To Be Modern*. London: Faber, 2003.

——. "The NS Essay—A Target for Destructive Ferocity." *New Statesman*. April 29, 2002.

Greaney, Michael. *Conrad, Language, and Narrative*. Cambridge: Cambridge UP, 2002.

Green, Martin. *Dreams of Adventure, Deeds of Empire*. New York: Basic, 1979.

Greene, Graham. *The Heart of the Matter*. New York: Viking, 1948.

Guerard, Albert. *Conrad the Novelist*. Cambridge, MA: Harvard UP, 1958.

——. *Joseph Conrad*. New York: New Directions, 1947.

Habibi, Imil Habibi. *The Secret Life of Saeed: The Ill-Fated Pessoptimist*. 1974. Trans. Salma Khadra Jayyusi and Trevor Le Gassick. New York: Vantage, 1982.

Hall, Stuart, Ed. *Questions of Cultural Identity*. London: Sage, 1996.

Hallin, Daniel. *We Keep American on Top of the World: Television Journalism and the Popular Sphere*. New York: Routledge, 1994.

Hammond, Dorothy and Alta Jablow. *The Myth of Africa.* New York: Library of Social Science, 1977.

——. *The Africa That Never Was: Four Centuries of British Writing about Africa.* New York: Twayne, 1970.

Hamner, Robert. *Joseph Conrad: Third World Perspectives.* Washington: Three Continents, 1990.

——. "Colony, Nationhood and Beyond: Third World Writers and Critics Contend with Joseph Conrad." In Carabine, *Critical Assessments* 2: 419–427.

Hampson, Robert. "'A Passion for Maps': Conrad, Africa, Australia and South-East Asia." *The Conradian* 28.1 (Spring 2003): 34–56.

——. *Cross-Cultural Encounters in Joseph Conrad's Malay Fiction.* Basingstoke: Macmillan, 2000.

——. "Conrad and the Formation of Legends." In *Conrad's Literary Career.* Eds. Keith Carabine, Owen Knowles, Wiesław Krajka. Boulder: East European Monographs, 1992. 167–86.

Harpham, Geoffrey Galt. *Language Alone: The Critical Fetish of Modernity.* New York: Routledge, 2002.

Harpham, Geoffrey Galt. "Conrad's Global Homeland." *Raritan* XXI.1 (Summer 2001): 20–33.

——. "Abroad Only by a Fiction: Creation, Irony, and Necessity in Conrad's *The Secret Agent.*" *Representations* 37 (Winter 1992): 78–103.

Harris, Roy. *The Language Machine.* London: Duckworth, 1987.

Harrison, Nicholas. *Postcolonial Criticism: History, Theory and the Work of Fiction.* Oxford: Polity, 2003.

Harth, Phillip. *Contexts for Dryden's Thought.* Chicago: Chicago UP, 1968.

Hawkins, Hunt and Brian Shaffer. *Approaches to Teaching Conrad's* Heart of Darkness *and "The Secret Sharer."* New York: MLA, 2002.

Hawkins, Hunt. "Conrad's Critique of Imperialism in *Heart of Darkness.*" *PMLA* 94 (1979): 286–99.

Hawthorn, Jeremy. "Introduction." In *The Shadow-Line.* Oxford: Oxford University Press, 2003.

——. *Joseph Conrad: Narrative Technique and Ideological Commitment.* London: Arnold, 1990.

Hay, Eloise Knapp. *The Political Novels of Joseph Conrad.* Chicago: Chicago UP, 1963.

Hegel, G.W.F. *Aesthetics: Lectures on Fine Art.* Vol. II. Trans. T.M. Knox. Oxford: Clarendon Press, 1998.

Hegel, G.W.F. *Lectures on the Philosophy of World History.* Trans. H.B. Nisbet. New York: Cambridge UP, 1981.

——. *Phenomenology of Spirit.* Trans. A.V. Miller. Oxford: Oxford UP, 1977.

Hendricksen, Bruce. *Nomadic Voices: Conrad and the Subject of Narrative.* Urbana: U Illinois P, 1992.

Hervouet, Yves. *The French Face of Joseph Conrad.* Cambridge: Cambridge UP, 1990.

Hitler, Adolf. *Mein Kampf.* Eds. John Chamberlain, et al. New York: Reyna, 1939.

Hobson, J.A. *Imperialism: A Study* (1902). London: Unwin Hyman, 1988.

——. *The Psychology of Jingoism.* London: Grant Richards, 1901.

Hochschild, Adam. *King Leopold's Ghost: A Story of Greed, Terror, and Heroism in Colonial Africa.* Boston: Houghton, 1999.

Hoffman, Frederick J. and Olga W. Vichery, Eds. *Three Decades of Faulkner Criticism.* (New York: Harcourt Brace, 1963.

Hollis, Patricia. *The Pauper Press: A Study in Working-Class Radicalism of the 1830's.* Oxford: Oxford UP, 1970.

Hood, Mantle. "The Enduring Tradition: Music and Theater in Java and Bali." *Indonesia.* Ed. Ruth T. McVey. New Haven, CT: HRAF, 1963.

Hopkin, Deian. "The Socialist Press in Britain, 1890–1910." In Boyce, Curran 294–306.

Hopkins, Gerard Manley. *Poems.* 4th ed. Ed. W.H. Gardner and N.H. MacKenzie. London: Oxford UP, 1970.

Houen, Alex. *Terrorism and Modern Literature, from Joseph Conrad to Ciaran Carson.* Oxford: Oxford University Press, 2002.

Huggan, Graham. "Anxieties of Influence: Conrad in the Caribbean." In Carabine, *Critical Assessments* 2: 447–459.

Hulme, Peter. *Colonial Encounters: Europe and the Native Caribbean 1492–1797.* Routledge, 1992.

Hutcheon, Linda. *Irony's Edge: The Theory and Politics of Irony.* London: Routledge, 1994.

Hyam, Roger. "Empire and Sexual Opportunity." *Journal of Imperial and Commonwealth History* 14.2 (1986): 34–89.

Hyland, Peter. "The Little Woman in the *Heart of Darkness.*" *Conradiana* 20.1 (1988): 3–11.

Ignatieff, Michael. *Blood and Belonging: Journeys into the New Nationalism.* New York: Penguin, 1993.

Iraq Body Count (viewed August 26, 2003). <http://www.iraqbodycount.net/>

Israel, Nico. *Outlandish: Writing Between Exile and Diaspora*. Stanford: Stanford UP, 2000.

James, Henry. "The New Novel" (1913). In *Literary Criticism: Essays on Literature; American Writers, English Writers*. New York: Library of America, 1984. 124–59.

Jameson, Fredric. "Cognitive Mapping." In Cary Nelson and Lawrence Grossberg, Eds. *Marxism and the Interpretation of Culture*. Urbana: University of Illinois Press, 1988. 347–57.

——"Afterword." *Aesethetics and Politics*. By Ernst Bloch et al. London: New Left Books, 1979.

Jameson, Fredric. *Modernism and Empire*. Derry: Field Day, 1988.

——. *The Political Unconscious: Narrative as a Socially Symbolic Act*. Ithaca: Cornell UP, 1981.

Jauss, Hans Robert. "Literary History as a Challenge to Literary Theory." *New Literary History* II (Autumn 1970): 7–37.

Jean-Aubry, Gerard. *Joseph Conrad: Life and Letters*. 2 vols. Garden City, NY: Doubleday, 1927.

Johnson, Paul. *The Birth of the Modern: World Society 1815–1830*. New York: Harper, 1991.

Johnstone, Alex. *The Life and Letters of Sir Harry Johnston*. London: Jonathan Cape, 1929.

Joll, James. *The Anarchists*. Cambridge, MA: Harvard UP, 1980.

Jones, Susan. *Conrad and Women*. Oxford: Oxford UP, 1999.

Kaplan, Carola M. "Colonizers, Cannibals, and the Horror of Good Intentions in Joseph Conrad's *Heart of Darkness*." *Studies in Short Fiction*. 34.2 (Summer 1997): 323–334.

——. "Joseph Conrad's Narrative Occupation of/by Russia in *Under Western Eyes*." *Conradiana* 27.2 (1995): 97–114.

——. "No Refuge: The Duplicity of Domestic Safety in Conrad's Fiction." *The Conradian*. 22.1–2 (Spring/Winter 1997): 138–146.

——. "Women's Caring and Men's Secret Sharing: Gender and Sexuality in Conrad's 'The Secret Sharer' and *Heart of Darkness*." In Hawkins and Shaffer.

Karl, Frederick R. *Joseph Conrad: The Three Lives*. London: Faber, 1979.

——. "Introduction to the *Danse Macabre*: Conrad's *Heart of Darkness*." *Modern Fiction Studies* 14 (1968): 143–156.

Kaul, Suvir. "Separation Anxiety: Growing Up Inter/National in Amitav Ghosh's *The Shadow Lines*." *Oxford Literary Review* 16.1–2 (1994): 125–145.

Keay, John. *The Honourable Company*. London: Harper, 1993.

Kennedy, Pagan. *Black Livingstone: A True Tale of Adventure in the Nineteenth Century Congo*. New York: Penguin, 2003.

Keppel, Henry. *The Expedition to Borneo of H.M.S. Dido for the Suppression of Piracy*. London: Chapman, 1846.

Kermani, Navid. "A Dynamite of the Spirit." *Times Literary Supplement*. March 29, 2002: 13–15.

Kerr, Douglas. "Conrad's Magic Circles." *Essays in Criticism* LIII.4 (October 2003): 345–365.

Kierkegaard, Søren. *The Concept of Irony with Constant Reference to Socrates*. Trans. and Ed. Lee M. Capel. New York: Harper, 1966.

Kimbrough, Robert, Ed. *Heart of Darkness*. By Joseph Conrad. New York: W.W. Norton, 1988.

Kirschner, Paul, ed. "Introduction." *Under Western Eyes*. By Joseph Conrad. London and New York: Penguin, 1996.xvii–lxxii.

——, ed. *Typhoon and Other Stories*. By Joseph Conrad. Harmondsworth: Penguin, 1990.

——. *Conrad: The Psychologist as Artist*. Edinburgh: Oliver, 1968.

Kittler, Frederich. *Gramophone, Film, Typewriter*. Trans. Geoffrey Winthrop-Young and Michael Wutz. Stanford: Stanford UP, 1999.

Knight, G. Wilson. *Crown of Life*. London: Methuen, 1958.

Knightley, Phillip. *The First Casualty: The War Correspondent as Hero, Propagandist, and Myth Maker from Crimea to Vietnam*. New York: Harcourt, Brace, 1975.

Koss, Stephen. *The Rise and Fall of the Political Press in Britain*. 2 vols. Chapel Hill: U North Carolina P, 1981.

Kreilkamp, Ivan. "A Voice without a Body: the Phonographic Logic of *Heart of Darkness*." *Victorian Studies* 40.2 (Winter 1997): 211–243.

Krell, David Farrell. *The Purest of Bastards: Works of Mourning, Art, and Affirmation in the Thought of Jacques Derrida*. University Park, PA: Pennsylvania State UP, 2000.

Lacan, Jacques. *The Ethics of Psychoanalysis:1959–1960: The Seminar of Jacques Lacan*. Trans. D. Porter. London: Routledge, 1992.

——. *Feminine Sexuality*. Ed. and trans. J. Mitchell and J. Rose. London: Norton, 1985.

——. *The Four Fundamental Concepts of Psycho-Analysis*. Trans. A. Sheridan. Harmondsworth: Penguin, 1977.

——. *Ecrits: A Selection* (1966). Trans. Alan Sheridan. London: Tavistock, 1977.

Lane, Christopher. "Fostering Subjection: Masculine Identification and Homosexual Allegory in Conrad's *Victory.*" *The Ruling Passion: British Colonial Allegory and the Paradox of Homosexual Desire.* Durham: Duke UP, 1995.

Lasswell, Harold D. *Propaganda Technique in the World War.* New York: Knopf, 1927.

Lavie, Smadar and Ted Swedenburg, Eds. *Displacement, Diaspora, and Geographies of Identity.* Durham: Duke UP, 1996.

Leavis, F.R. *The Great Tradition: George Eliot, Henry James, Joseph Conrad.* London: Chatto, 1948.

Le Boulicaut, Yannick. "Is There Therapy in Speech in Conrad's Works?" *Conradiana* 34.1–2 (2002): 137-146.

Le Guin, Ursula K. *The Birthday of the World and Other Stories.* New York: Harper, 2002.

Lester, John. "Conrad's Narrators in *The Nigger of the 'Narcissus'.*" *Conradiana* 12 (1980): 163–172.

Lewis, Paula Gilbert. *The Aesthetics of Stéphane Mallarmé in Relation to his Public.* Cranbury, NJ: AP, 1976.

Lindquist, Sven. *Exterminate All the Brutes.* London: *Granta*, 1997.

London, Jack. *The Iron Heel.* Hertfordshire: Wadsworth, 1996.

Lothe, Jakob. *Conrad's Narrative Method.* Oxford: Clarendon, 1989.

Lowth, Karl. *From Hegel to Nietzsche: The Revolution in Nineteenth-Century Thought.* Trans. D. E. Green. New York: Doubleday, 1967.

Luxemburg, Rosa. *The Accumulation of Capital* (1913). Trans. Agnes Schwarzchild. London: Routledge, 1951.

Lyotard, Jean-François. *The Differend: Phrases in Dispute.* Trans. Georges Van Den Abbele. Minneapolis: University of Minnesota Press, 1988.

MacArthur, John R. *Second Front: Censorship and Propaganda in the Gulf War.* New York: Hill, 1992.

MacKenzie, John M. *Propaganda and Empire.* Manchester: Manchester UP, 1984.

"Making of America." May 7, 2003. U Michigan. January 10, 2004. http://www.hti.umich.edu/m/moagrp/

Mallios, Peter Lancelot, Ed. "Afterword: The Desert of Conrad." *The Secret Agent.* By Joseph Conrad. New York: Modern Library, 2004.

——, Ed. "Introduction." *Victory.* By Joseph Conrad. New York: Modern Library, 2003.

——. "Undiscovering the Country: Conrad, Fitzgerald and Meta-National Form." *Modern Fiction Studies* 47.2 (Summer 2001): 356–390.

Mann, Thomas. *Past Masters and Other Papers.* Trans. H.T. Lowe-Porter. New York: Knopf, 1933.

Manusama, A. T. *Komedie Stamboel of de Oost-Indische Opera.* Weltevreden: V. Electrische Drukkerij 'Favoriet', 1922.

Marcuse, Herbert. *The Aesthetic Dimension: Toward a Critique of Marxist Aesthetic.* London & Basingstoke: Macmillan, 1979.

Margaronis, Maria. "Greenwashed." *The Nation.* October 19, 1998: 10.

Margolin, Uri. "Collective Perspective, Individual Perspective, and the Speaker in Between: On 'We' Literary Narratives." In *New Perspectives on Narrative Perspective.* Eds. Willie van Peer and Seymour Chatman. Albany: SUNY Press, 2001. 243–255.

Marin, Louis. "The Frame of Representation and Some of its Figures." In *Rhetoric of the Image.* Ed. Paul Duro. Cambridge: Cambridge UP, 1996.

Marx, Karl. *Surveys from Exile: Political Writings.* Vol. 2. Ed. D. Fernbach. New York: Random House, 1974.

Masterman, C.F.G. *Report of the Work of the Bureau established for the purpose of laying before Neutral Nations and the Dominions the case of Great Britain and her Allies.* Kew, England Public Record Office June 7, 1915; INF 4/5.

——. *Second Report on the Work Conducted for the Government at Wellington House.* Kew, England: Public Record Office February 1, 1916; INF 4/5.

McAleer, Joseph. *Popular Reading and Publishing in Britain, 1914–1950.* Oxford: Clarendon, 1992.

McClure, John. "Late Imperial Romance." *Raritan* 10.4 (1991): 111–130.

McDonald, Peter D. *British Literary Culture and Publishing Practice, 1880–1914.* Cambridge: Cambridge UP, 1997.

Mda, Zakes. *Ways of Dying.* New York: Picador USA, 1995.

Messinger, Gary S. *British Propaganda and the State in the First World War.* Manchester, Eng.: Manchester UP, 1992.

Meyer, Bernard C. *Joseph Conrad: A Psychoanalytic Biography.* Princeton: Princeton UP, 1967.

Meynell, Wilfrid (pseud. John Oldcastle). *Journals and Journalism, with a Guide for Literary Beginners.* London: Field, 1880.

"Military Press Control: A History of the Work of MI.7, 1914–1919." Kew, England: Public Record Office, INF 4/1B.

Miller, Christopher. *Blank Darkness: Africanist Discourse in French.* Chicago: U Chicago P, 1985.

Miller, D. A. *The Novel and the Police.* Berkeley: U California P, 1988.

Mongia, Padmini. "Empire, Narrative, and the Feminine in Conrad's *Lord Jim* and *Heart of Darkness.*" In *Contexts for Conrad.* Eds. Keith Carabine, Owen Knowles, and Wieslaw Krajka. East European Monographs. Boulder: U Colorado P, 1993. 135–150.

———. "'Ghosts of the Gothic': Spectral Women and Colonized Spaces in *Lord Jim.*" In *Conrad and Gender.* Ed. Michael Andrew Roberts. Amsterdam: Rodopi, 1993. 1–16.

Monmonier, Mark. *Maps With the News.* Chicago: U Chicago P, 1989.

Moore, Gene M. "In Defense of *Suspense.*" *Conradiana* 25 (1993): 99–114.

———, Ed. *Conrad's Cities: Essays for Hans van Marle.* Amsterdam: Rodopi, 1992.

Morf, Gustav. *The Polish Heritage of Joseph Conrad.* London: Sampson, 1930.

Morrell, Lady Ottoline. *Memoirs: A Study in Friendship 1873–1915.* Ed. R. Gathorne-Hardy. New York: Knopf, 1964.

Moser, Thomas C., Sr. *Joseph Conrad: Achievement and Decline.* Cambridge, MA: Harvard UP, 1957.

Mrazek, Rudolph. *Engineers of Happy Land: Technology and Nationalism in a Colony.* Princeton: Princeton University Press, 2002.

Mudrick, Marvin. "The Artist's Conscience and *The Nigger of the 'Narcissus'.*" In *Twentieth Century Interpretations of* The Nigger of the "Narcissus." Ed. John A. Palmer. Englewood Cliffs: Prentice Hall, 1969.

Muecke, D. C. *Irony and the Ironic.* London and New York: Methuen, 1970.

Mukherjee Meenakshi, *The Twice-Born Fiction.* London: Heinemann, 1971.

Murfin, Ross C., ed. *Heart of Darkness: A Case Study in Contemporary Criticism.* 2nd ed. New York: St. Martin's, 1989.

Mursia, Ugo. "Notes on Conrad's Italian Novel: *Suspense.*" In Moore, *Conrad's Cities* 269–281.

Naipaul, V. S. *The Return of Eva Peron.* London: Deutsch, 1980.

———. *A Bend in the River.* New York: Knopf, 1979.

———. "Conrad's Darkness" (1974). In Carabine, *Critical Assessments* 2: 380–392.

Najder, Zdzisław. *Conrad's Polish Background: Letters to and from Polish Friends.* Ed. and trans. Halina Carroll. London: Oxford UP, 1964.

———. *Joseph Conrad: A Chronicle.* Cambridge: Cambridge UP, 1983.

Nakai, Asako. *The English Book and Its Marginalia.* Amsterdam: Rodopi, 2000.

Nazareth, Peter. "Conrad's Descendants." *Conradiana* 22.2 (1990): 101–109.

———. "Out of Darkness: Conrad and Other Third World Writers." *Conradiana* 14.3 (1982): 173–187.

Nicholson, Ivor. "An Aspect of British Official Wartime Propaganda." *Cornhill Magazine* Series 3, 70.419 (May 1931).

Nieuwenhuys, Rob. *Komen en Blijven: Tempo Doeloe—Een Verzonken Wereld.* Amsterdam: Querido, 1998.

Nohrnberg, Peter. "'I Wish He'd Never Been to School': Stevie, Newspapers, and the Reader in *The Secret Agent.*" *Conradiana.* 35.1–2 (Spring/Summer 2003): 49–62.

North, Michael. *The Dialect of Modernism.* Oxford: Oxford University Press, 1994.

Nzongola-Ntalja, Georges. *The Congo: From Leopold to Kabila: A People's History.* London: Zed, 2002.

Orr, David W. "What Is Education For?" *Earth Ethics* 3 (1992): 1–5.

Paccaud-Huguet, Josiane. "*Under Western Eyes* and *Hamlet*: Where Angels Fear to Tread." *Conradiana* 26.2–3 (1994): 169–186.

Parry, Benita. "*Tono-Bungay*: Modernisation, Modernity, Modernism and Imperialism; or, The Failed Electrification of the Empire of Light." *New Formations* 34 (Summer 1998): 91–108.

———. *Conrad and Imperialism: Ideological Boundaries and Visionary Frontiers.* London: Macmillan, 1983.

Pease, Donald and Robyn Wiegman, Eds. *The Futures of American Studies.* Durham: Duke UP, 2002.

Peckham, Morse. *The Birth of Romanticism, 1790–1815.* Greenwood, FL: Penkevill, 1986.

Pemberton, John. *On the Subject of "Java".* Ithaca: Cornell University Press, 1994.

"Pentagon Scraps Plan for Betting on Terror Strike." *Daily Telegraph* (London). July 30, 2003: 12.

Perris, Earnest. Report on the News Section to Mr. Donald. Kew, England: Public Record Office, July 11, 1917; INF 4/10.

Perrot, Michelle, and A. Martin-Fugier. "The Family Triumphant." In *A History of Private Life.* 5 vols. Ed. M. Perrot. Trans. A. Goldhammer. Cambridge, MA: Harvard UP, 1990. Vol. 4: 99–166.

Phillips, Caryl. "Out of Africa." *The Guardian*. February 22, 2003: 4–6. http://books.guardian. co.uk/review/story/0.1284,900102,00.html.

Phipps, William E. *William Sheppard: Congo's African-American Livingstone*. Louisville, KY: Geneva Press, 2002.

Poovey, Mary, Ed. *The Financial System in Nineteenth-Century Britain*. New York: Oxford UP, 2003.

——. *A History of the Modern Fact*. Chicago: U Chicago P, 1998.

Pramoedya Ananta Toer. *The Mute's Soliloquy: A Memoir*. Trans. Willem Samuels. New York: Hyperion, 1999.

——. *This Earth of Mankind*. Trans. Max Lane. New York: Penguin, 1996.

——. *Nyanyi Sunyi Seorang Bisu [I]: Catatan-catatan Dari P. Buru*. Jakarta: Lentera, 1995.

——. *House of Glass* (1988). New York: Penguin, 1992.

——. *Footsteps* (1985). New York: Penguin, 1990.

——. *Sang Pemula*. Jakarta: Hasta Mitra, 1985.

——. *Tempoe Doeloe: Antologi Sastra Pra-Indonesia*. Jakarta: Hasta Mitra, 1982.

——. *Bumi Manusia: sebuah roman*. Jakarta: Hasta Mitra, 1981.

——. *Child of All Nations* (1980). New York: Penguin, 1996.

Pratt, Mary Louise. *Imperial Eyes: Travel Writing and Transculturation*. London: Routledge, 1992.

Pulc, I. P. "The Imprint of Polish on Conrad's Style." In *Joseph Conrad: Theory and World Fiction*. Eds. Zyla T. Wolodymyr and Wendell M. Aycock. Lubbock: Texas Tech UP, 1974. 117–139.

Purdy, Dwight H. "Conrad at Work: The Two Serial Texts of *Typhoon*." *Conradiana* 19 (1987): 112–115.

Quail, John. *The Slow Burning Fuse: The Lost History of the British Anarchists*. London: Paladin, 1978.

Rado, Lisa. "Walking Through Phantoms: Irony, Skepticism, and Razumov's Self-Delusion in *Under Western Eyes*." *Conradiana* 24.2 (1992): 83–99.

Rao, Raja. *Kanthapura*. New York: New Directions, 1963.

Reed, John. *Victorian Conventions*. Athens: Ohio UP, 1975.

Richardson, Brian. "I etcetera: On the Poetics and Ideology of Multipersoned Narratives." *Style* 28 (1994): 312–328.

——. "Construing Conrad's *The Secret Sharer*: Suppressed Narratives, Subaltern Reception, and the Act of Narration." *Studies in the Novel* 33 (2001): 306–321.

Richardson, Dorothy. *Honeycomb. Pilgrimage Vol. 1*. New York: Knopf, 1967.

Rifkin, Jeremy. *Biosphere Politics*. New York: Crown, 1991.

Rising, Catherine. "Raskolnikov and Razumov: From Passive to Active Subjectivity in *Under Western Eyes*." *Conradiana* 33.1 (2001): 24–39.

Ritter, Scott and William Rivers Pitt. *War on Iraq: What Team Bush Doesn't Want You To Know*. London: Profile, 2002.

Roberts, Michael Andrew. *Conrad and Masculinity*. Basingstoke: Macmillan, 2000.

Romanick, Debra. "Victorious Wretch?: The Puzzle of Haldin's Name in *Under Western Eyes*." *Conradiana* 30.1 (1998): 44–52.

Roy, Arundhati. *The God of Small Things*. New York: Random, 1997.

Rubin, Gayle. "The Traffic in Women: Notes on the 'Political Economy' of Sex." In *Toward an Anthropology of Women*. Ed. Rayna R. Reiter. New York: Monthly Review P. 157–210.

Ruppel, Richard. "Joseph Conrad and the Ghost of Oscar Wilde." *The Conradian* 23.1 (Spring 1998): 19–36.

Rushdie, Salman. *Midnight's Children*. London: Cape, 1981.

Ruskin, John. *Modern Painters*. 5 vols. Boston: Dana Estes. n.d.

——. *The Crown of Wild Olive*. New York: Burt, n.d.

Said, Edward. "Presidential Address 1999: Humanism and Heroism." *PMLA* 115.3 (2000): 285–91.

Said, Edward W. *Reflections on Exile*. Cambridge, Mass: Harvard UP 2002.

——. *Out of Place: A Memoir*. New York: Vintage, 1999.

——. *Culture and Imperialism*. London: Chatto, 1993.

——. "Introduction." Rudyard Kipling. In *Kim*. New York: Penguin. 1987. 7–46.

——. "Intellectuals and the Postcolonial World." *Salmagundi*. 70.1 (1986): 44–80.

——. *The World, The Text, and the Critic*. Cambridge, MA: Harvard UP, 1983.

——. *Orientalism*. New York: Pantheon, 1978.

——. *The Politics of Dispossession: The Struggle for Palestinian Self-Determination 1969–1994*. New York: Random House, 1975.

——. *Joseph Conrad and the Fiction of Autobiography*. Cambridge, MA: Harvard UP, 1966.

Salih, Tayeb. *Season of Migration to the North*. Trans. Denys Johnson-Davis. London: Heinemann Educational, 1969.

Sanders, M.L. and Philip M. Taylor. *British Propaganda during the First World War, 1914–1918.* London: Macmillan, 1982.

Saussure, Ferdinand de. *Course in General Linguistics.* Eds. Charles Bally and Albert Sechehaye. New York: Philosophical Library, 1966.

Schama, Simon. *Citizens: A Chronicle of the French Revolution.* New York: Knopf, 1989.

Schirato, Tony and Jen Webb. *Understanding Globalization.* London: Sage, 2003.

Schudson, Michael. *Discovering the News: A Social History of American Newspapers.* New York: HarperCollins, 1978.

Scott, Bonnie Kime, Ed. *The Gender of Modernism.* Bloomington: Indiana UP, 1990.

Sedgwick, Eve Kosofsky. *Between Men: English Literature and Male Homosocial Desire.* New York: Columbia UP, 1985.

Seymour-Ure, Colin. *The Press, Politics and the Public.* London: Methuen, 1968.

Shakespeare, William. *Hamlet.* Ed. Harold Jenkins. London: Methuen, 1982.

Sherry, Norman. *Conrad: The Critical Heritage.* London: Routledge, 1973.

Sherry, Norman. *Conrad's Eastern World.* Cambridge: Cambridge University Press, 1966.

Shetty, Sandhya. "*Heart of Darkness*: Out of Africa Some New Thing Rarely Comes." *Journal of Modern Literature* 15.4 (1989): 461–474.

Shiva, Vandana. *Biopiracy.* Boston: South End, 1997.

Shivelbusch, Wolfgang. *Disenchanted Light: The Industrialization of Light in the Nineteenth Century.* Berkeley: U California P, 1988.

Shulevitz, Judith. "Chasing After Conrad's *Secret Agent.*" *Slate Magazine.* Microsoft Corporation. September 27, 2001. Culturebox.

Simmel, Georg. "The Metropolis and Mental Life." *Modernism.* Eds. Vassiliki Kolocotroni, Jane Goldman, and Olga Taxidou. Chicago: Chicago UP, 1998.

Smith, Anthony. *The Newspaper: An International History.* London: Thames, 1979.

Sonn, Richard D. *Anarchism.* New York: Twayne, 1992.

Spitzer, Leo. *Classical and Christian Ideas of World Harmony: Prolegonmena to an Interpretation of the World "Stimmung".* Baltimore: Johns Hopkins University Press, 1963

Spivak, Gayatri. *In Other Worlds: Essays in Cultural Politics.* New York: Methuen, 1987.

Squires, J. D. *British Propaganda at Home and in The United States, from 1914 to 1917.* London: Humphrey Milford [Oxford UP], 1935.

Staley, Thomas F. *Dorothy Richardson.* Boston: Twayne, 1976.

Stape, J.H. "Irony." *Oxford Reader's Companion to Conrad.* Eds. Owen Knowles and Gene M. Moore. Oxford: Oxford UP, 2000.

Stape, J.H. and Owen Knowles. *A Portrait in Letters: Correspondence to and about Conrad.* Amsterdam: Rodopi, 1996.

Stape, J.H. and Hans van Marle, Eds. *An Outcast of the Islands.* Oxford: Oxford University Press, 1992.

——, Ed. *The Cambridge Companion to Joseph Conrad.* Cambridge: Cambridge UP, 1996.

Stephens, Mitchell. *A History of the News: From the Drum to the Satellite.* New York: Viking, 1988.

Sterne, Lawrence. *Tristram Shandy.* New York: Norton. 1980.

Straus, Nina Pelikan. "The Exclusion of the Intended from Secret Sharing in *Heart of Darkness.*" *Novel* 20 (1987): 123–137.

"*Suspiria de Profundis.*" *Blackwood's Edinburgh Magazine.* 57 (April 1845): 489–502. http://www.bodley.ox.ac.uk/ilej.

Sutherland, J. G. *At Sea with Joseph Conrad.* London: Grant Richards, 1922.

Swanberg, W. A. *Citizen Hearst, A Biography of William Randolph Hearst.* New York: Scribner, 1961.

Swift, Jonathan. *Gulliver's Travels.* Ed. Paul Turner. Oxford: Oxford UP, 1986.

Tan Sooi Beng. *Bangsawan: A Social and Stylistic History of Popular Malay Opera.* Singapore: Oxford University Press, 1993.

Tarling, Nicholas. *Sulu and Sabah: A Study of British Policy Towards the Philippines and North Borneo from the Late Eighteenth Century.* Kuala Lumpur: Oxford UP, 1978.

Thieme, John. "Passages to England." In *Liminal Postmodernisms: The Postmodern, the (Post-) Colonial, and the (Post-) Feminist.* Amsterdam: Rodopi, 1994. 55–78.

Thiong'o, Ngugi wa. *A Grain of Wheat.* London: Heinemann, 1967.

Trilling, Lionel. "On the Teaching of Modern Literature." In *Beyond Culture: Essays on Literature and Learning.* New York: Viking, 1965. 3–30.

Ugrešić, Dubravka. *The Culture of Lies: Antipolitical Essays.* Trans. Celia Hawkesworth. University Park: Pennsylvania State UP, 1998.

van Marle, Hans and Gene M. Moore. "The Sources of Conrad's *Suspense.*" *Conrad: Intertexts and Appropriations: Essays in Memory of Yves Hervouet.* Ed. Gene Moore. Amsterdam: Rodopi, 1997. 141–156.

Virillio, Paul. *Ground Zero.* London: Verso 2003.

Vorse, M. H. [A review article of *Youth.*] *The Critic* (September, 1903): 280.

Watt, Ian. *Essays on Conrad.* Cambridge: Cambridge UP, 2000.

——. "Introduction." Joseph Conrad. In *Almayer's Folly.* Eds. Floyd Eugene Eddleman and David Leon Higdon. Cambridge: Cambridge UP, 1994. xxi–xxxii.

——. *Conrad in the Nineteenth Century.* Berkeley: U California P, 1979.

Watts, Carol. *Dorothy Richardson.* Plymouth: Northcote House, 1995.

Watts, Cedric. *Joseph Conrad: A Literary Life.* New York: St. Martin's, 1989.

——, Ed. *Nostromo.* By Joseph Conrad. London: Everyman, 1995.

——, Ed. *Nostromo.* By Joseph Conrad. Harmondsworth: Penguin, 1990.

——, Ed. "Introduction." In *Heart of Darkness and Other Tales.* By Joseph Conrad. Oxford: Oxford UP, 1990. vii–xxiii.

——, Ed. *Joseph Conrad's Letters to R.B. Cunninghame-Graham.* London: Cambridge UP, 1969.

Watts, Cedric. *The Deceptive Text: An Introduction to Covert Plots.* Sussex: Harvester, NJ: Barnes & Noble, 1984.

White, Lynn, Jr. "The Historical Roots of Our Ecological Crisis." *Science* (March 10, 1967): 1203–1207.

Williams, Raymond. "Communications Technologies and Social Institutions." In *Contact: Human Communication and its History.* London: Thames and Hudson, 1981.

——. "The Press and Popular Culture: An Historical Perspective." In Boyce, Curran 41–50.

Wilson, Donald S. "The Beast in the Congo: How Victorian Homophobia Inflects Marlow's *Heart of Darkness.*" *Conradiana* 32.2 (2000): 96–118.

Wilson, Edmund. *Axel's Castle* (1931). New York: Norton, 1984.

Winner, Anthony. *Culture and Irony: Studies in Joseph Conrad's Major Novels.* Charlottesville: U of Virginia P, 1988.

Wollaeger, Mark. "The Woolfs in the Jungle: Intertextuality, Sexuality, and the Emergence of Female Modernism in *The Voyage Out, The Village in the Jungle,* and *Heart of Darkness.*" *Modern Language Quarterly* 64.1 (2003): 33–69.

——. "Posters, Modernism, Cosmopolitanism: *Ulysses* and World War One Recruiting Posters in Ireland." *Yale Journal of Criticism* 6.2 (1993): 87–131.

——. *Joseph Conrad and the Fictions of Skepticism.* Stanford: Stanford UP, 1990.

Woodcock, George, ed. *An Anarchist Reader.* London: Fontana, 1970.

Woolf, Virginia. "Joseph Conrad." In *The Common Reader.* London: Hogarth, 1948.

Wordsworth, William. *The Poetical Works of William Wordsworth.* Ed. E. de Selincourt. Oxford: Oxford UP, 1959.

Wright, Walter F., Ed. *Joseph Conrad on Fiction.* Lincoln: U Nebraska P, 1964.

Wrong, Michaela. *In the Footsteps of Mr. Kurtz.* London: Fourth Estate, 2001.

Yeow, Agnes. "Envisioning the 'Malay World': A study of Conrad's Eastern Tales." Unpublished Ph.D. Thesis. National University of Singapore, 2003.

Youngs, Tim. *Travellers in Africa: British Travelogues, 1850–1900.* Manchester: Manchester UP, 1994.

Zabel, Morton Dauwen, Ed. *The Portable Conrad* (1947). Revised Frederick R. Karl. New York: Penguin, 1976.

Ziolkowski, Theodore. *German Romanticism and Its Institutions.* Princeton: Princeton UP, 1990.

Notes on Contributors

William W. Bonney, author of *Thorns and Arabesques: Contexts for Conrad's Fiction* (Johns Hopkins 1986), teaches English at Mississippi State University. His foremost commitment is to direct-action eco-defense.

Laurence Davies, who teaches English and Comparative Literature at Dartmouth College, has co-edited seven volumes of Conrad's collected letters and, with Cedric Watts, co-authored a critical biography of R.B. Cunninghame Graham.

Daphna Erdinast-Vulcan has authored *Graham Greene's Childless Fathers* (Macmillan 1988), *Joseph Conrad and the Modern Temper* (Oxford 1991), and *The Strange Short Fiction of Joseph Conrad* (Oxford 1999). She teaches at Haifa University, Israel, and is active in peace organizations.

Anthony Fothergill, who teaches at University of Exeter, has published numerous articles on Conrad and edited the Everyman editions of Conrad's *Tales of Unrest* (2003), and *Oscar Wilde: Plays, Prose Writings, and Poems* (1996).

Jennifer Fraser, author of *Rites of Passage in the Narratives of Dante and Joyce* (Florida 2002), is currently completing a book entitled: *Be a Good Soldier: Suppressing Grief and Making Warriors in Modern British Fiction*.

Christopher GoGwilt, chair and professor of English at Fordham University, has published *The Invention of the West: Joseph Conrad and the Double-Mapping of Europe and Empire* (Stanford 1995) and *The Fiction of Geopolitics: AfterImages of Culture from Wilkie Collins to Alfred Hitchcock* (Stanford 2000)

Robert Hampson, chair of English Department at Royal Holloway College, University of London, has authored *Cross-Cultural Encounters in Conrad's Malay Fiction* (Palgrave 2000) and *Joseph Conrad: Betrayal and Identity* (Palgrave 1992); and has edited *Conrad and Theory* (Rodopi 1998) and the Penguin editions of *Lord Jim*, *Victory*, and *Heart of Darkness*.

Geoffrey Galt Harpham is president and director of the National Humanities Center, and Research Professor at Duke University and the University of North Carolina at Chapel Hill. Among his recent books are *One of Us: The Mastery of Joseph Conrad* (U Chicago P 1996), and *Language Alone: The Critical Fetish of Modernity* (Routledge 2002).

Susan Jones, fellow and university lecturer in English at St. Hilda's College, Oxford, published *Conrad and Women* (Oxford 1999) and is currently co-editing the Cambridge Edition of Conrad's *Chance* and writing a book on literary narrative and dance.

Carola M. Kaplan, president of the Joseph Conrad Society of America, co-edited *Seeing Double: Revisioning Edwardian and Modernist Literature* (Palgrave 1996). Author of articles on Conrad, E.M. Forster, T.E. Lawrence, and Christopher Isherwood, she is completing a book on emigration in British modernist literature.

Peter Lancelot Mallios, teaches English and American Studies at the University of Maryland. He has edited the Modern Library editions of *The Secret Agent* (2004), *Victory* (2003), and *Almayer's Folly* (2002), and is currently completing a book entitled *Our Conrad: The American Invention of Joseph Conrad, 1914–1925*.

J. Hillis Miller, having taught at Johns Hopkins and Yale universities, is currently UCI Distinguished Research Professor at University of California, Irvine. Author of many works on nineteenth- and twentieth-century literatures and on literary theory, his most recent books are *Others* (Princeton 2001), *Speech Acts in Literature* (Stanford 2002), and *On Literature* (Routledge 2002). He is writing a book on speech acts in the fiction of Henry James.

Padmini Mongia, professor of English at Franklin and Marshall College, has published numerous essays on Conrad as well as edited *Contemporary Postcolonial Theory: A Reader* (Edward Arnold 1996).

Benita Parry is author of *Delusions and Discoveries: India in the British Imagination 1880–1930* (1972), republished 1998; *Conrad and Imperialism: Ideological Boundaries and Visionary Frontiers* (1984); and *Postcolonial Studies: A Materialist Critique* (Routledge 2004). She is an honorary professor of English and Comparative Literary Studies, University of Warwick.

Brian Richardson, professor of English, University of Maryland, has published *Narrative Dynamics: Essays on Time, Plot, Closure, and Frames* (Ohio State 2002) and *Unlikely Stories: Causality and the Nature of Modern Narration* (Delaware 1997), and is the guest editor of a recent special issue of *Conradiana* on "Conrad and the Reader."

Edward W. Said was University Professor of English and Comparative Literature, Columbia University. Author of over twenty books, including *Orientalism, The Question of Palestine, Culture and Imperialism, Out of Place,* and *Reflections on Exile,* he was one of the most distinguished literary, political, and intellectual figures of our time.

Andrea White, who teaches English at California State University, Dominguez Hills, has published many articles on Conrad. She is author of *Joseph Conrad and the Adventure Tradition: Constructing and Deconstructing the Imperial Subject* (Cambridge 1993).

Mark A. Wollaeger teaches English at Vanderbilt University. He is author of *Joseph Conrad and the Fictions of Skepticism* (Stanford 1990), editor of James Joyce's *A Portrait of the Artist as a Young Man: A Casebook* (Oxford 2003), and co-editor of *Joyce and the Subject of History* (Michigan 1996).

Index